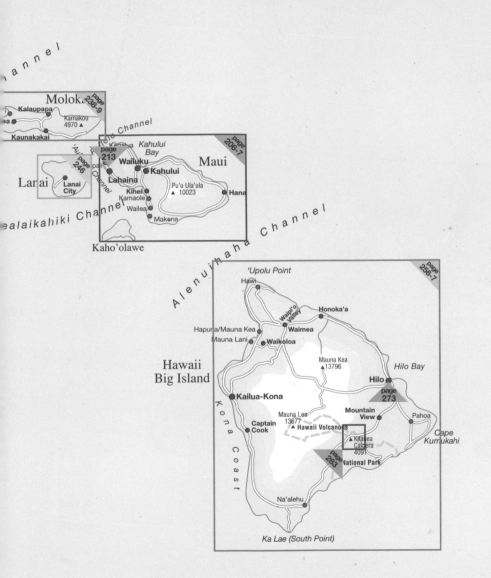

PACIFIC OCEAN

Hawaiian Archipelago

0   30 miles

0   30 km

P9-DFJ-920

Molokai

Kalaupapa

Kamakou
4970 ▲

Kaunakakai

page 238-9

Kahului
Bay

Kahului

Kapalua

page 213

Wailuku

Lahaina

Maui

page 206-7

Lanai

Lanai
City

page 246

Kihei
Kamaole

Wailea

Makena

Pu'u Ula'ula
▲ 10023

Hana

Kaho'olawe

Alenuihaha Channel

'Upolu Point

Hawi

page 256-7

Waipi'o Valley

Honoka'a

Hapuna/Mauna Kea

Waimea

Mauna Lani

Waikoloa

Hawaii
Big Island

Mauna Kea
▲13796

Hilo Bay

Kailua-Kona

Hilo

page 273

Captain
Cook

Mauna Lea
13677
▲ Hawaii Volcanoes

Mountain
View

Pahoa

Kona Coast

▲ Kilauea
Caldera
409

National Park

page 283

Cape
Kumukahi

Na'alehu

Ka Lae (South Point)

INSIGHT GUIDES

HAWAII

Discovery CHANNEL

APA PUBLICATIONS L

Part of the Langenscheidt Publishing Group

INSIGHT GUIDE
HAWAII

Editorial
Project Editor
Scott Rutherford
Editorial Director
Brian Bell

Distribution
UK & Ireland
GeoCenter International Ltd
Meridian House, Churchill Way West
Basingstoke, Hampshire RG21 6YR
Fax: (44) 1256 817988

United States
Langenscheidt Publishers, Inc.
36–36 33rd Street 4th Floor
Long Island City, NY 11106
Fax: 1 (718) 784 0640

Australia
Universal Publishers
1 Waterloo Road
Macquarie Park, NSW 2113
Fax: (61) 2 9888 9074

New Zealand
Hema Maps New Zealand Ltd (HNZ)
Unit D, 24 Ra ORA Drive
East Tamaki, Auckland
Fax: (64) 9 273 6479

Worldwide
Apa Publications GmbH & Co.
Verlag KG (Singapore branch)
38 Joo Koon Road, Singapore 628990
Tel: (65) 6865 1600. Fax: (65) 6861 6438

Printing
Insight Print Services (Pte) Ltd
38 Joo Koon Road, Singapore 628990
Tel: (65) 6865 1600. Fax: (65) 6861 6438

©2008 Apa Publications GmbH & Co.
Verlag KG (Singapore branch)
All Rights Reserved

First Edition 1980
Twelfth Edition 2000
Reprinted 2007, Updated 2008

CONTACTING THE EDITORS
We would appreciate it if readers
would alert us to errors or out-
dated information by writing to:
Insight Guides, P.O. Box 7910,
London SE1 1WE, England.
Fax: (44) 20 7403 0290.
insight@apaguide.co.uk

www.insightguides.com

ABOUT THIS BOOK

The first Insight Guide pioneered the use of creative full-color photography in travel guides in 1970. Since then, we have expanded our range to cater for our readers' need not only for reliable information about their chosen destination but also for a real understanding of the culture and workings of that destination. Now, when the internet can supply inexhaustible (but not always reliable) facts, our books marry text and pictures to provide those much more elusive qualities: knowledge and discernment. To achieve this, they rely heavily on the authority of locally based writers and photographers.

How to use this book
Insight Guide: Hawaii is carefully structured to convey an incisive understanding of the Hawaiian islands and their cultures and to guide readers through the wide range of sights and activities on offer to visitors there:

◆ To understand Hawaii, it is important to know something of its past. The **Features** section, which is indicated by a yellow bar at the top of each page, covers the islands' convoluted history and culture in a series of lively, authoritative and evocative essays.

◆ The main **Places** section, marked by a blue bar at the top of each page, provides a full run-down of all the many attractions and destinations that are worth seeing in Hawaii. Places of major interest on all of the islands are coordinated by number with full-color maps.

♦ The **Travel Tips** listings section, headed by an orange bar, provides a convenient point of reference for up-to-date practical information on travel, hotels, restaurants, shops, and festivals.

The contributors

This edition was supervised by **Scott Rutherford**, who lived in Hawaii for many years. It builds on the original 1980 edition and on the ten subsequent editions. Supervising a team of Hawaii-based updaters was **Cheryl Chee Tsutsumi**, who has worked in travel journalism since the 1970s. Maui updater **Paul Wood** calls the island's Upcountry region home. Editing the Oahu chapter was **Lance Tominaga**, editor of *Aloha* magazine. Kauai and the

Big Island were updated by **Betty Fullard-Leo**, while Oahu-based **Joyce Akamine** overhauled the Travel Tips. Also contributing were **Susan Essoyan** and **Beverly Fujita**.

Important contributors to previous editions include **Martha Ellen Zenfell**, **Kekuni Blaisdell**, **Susan Scott**, **Marty Wentzel**, **Jerry Hopkins**, **Joan Conrow**, **Alberta de Jetley**, **Ronn Ronck**, **Larry Lindsey Kimura**, and **Leonard Lueras**.

This entire book was thoroughly updated by **Greg Ward**, who also wrote the South Maui chapter. Thanks also to **Pam Barrett** and **Roger Williams**. **Paula Soper** edited the book in the London office.

It's nearly impossible to take a dismal photograph in Hawaii. This fact, it should be made clear, docsn't diminish the efforts of photographers who illustrated this Insight Guide, including **Catherine Karnow**, **Ron Dahlquist**, **Galen Rowell**, **Frank Salmoiraghi**, **Scott Rutherford**, **Tim Thomson** and **Ray Jerome Baker**.

Once an independent kingdom ruled by a monarchy, Hawaii is now an American state – the 50th and most recent – but still sometimes feels a little out of synchronism with the mainland. On the same latitude as Mexico City, the state's ambiance is Asian and Pacific Islander, peppered with only a little North American quirkiness. This combination is, and has long been, an enticing one, sparking such descriptions of Hawaii as that by the writer Mark Twain as "the loveliest fleet of islands anchored in any ocean," and inspiring many visitors to come to its exotic shores.

Map Legend

▪	National Park
✈	Airport
🚌	Bus Station
P	Parking
❶	Tourist Information
✉	Post Office
✝ ⚥	Church/Ruins
∴	Archeological Site
∩	Cave
★	Place of Interest

The main places of interest in the Places section are coordinated by number with a full-color map (e.g. ❶), and a symbol at the top of every right-hand page tells you where to find the map.

INSIGHT GUIDE
HAWAII

CONTENTS

Maps

Hanalei Bay, Kauai.

THE BEST OF HAWAII

Stunning landscapes straight from your dreams of a South Seas paradise, ravishing golden beaches, fascinating historical sites, dynamic resorts and charming 19th-century towns...here, at a glance, are our top picks for a fabulous visit

MAJOR HIGHLIGHTS

- **Na Pali Coast, Kauai** Familiar from many a Hollywood movie, the pleated, towering cliffs of Kauai's North Shore are mythic in scale. *See page 304.*
- **Kalaupapa Peninsula, Molokai** This spectacular, extraordinarily isolated shelf of land was where Father Damien ministered to his flock of "lepers," and ultimately succumbed to the disease himself. *See page 240.*
- **Haleakala, Maui** The crumbling, multi-colored sands in the summit caldera of Maui's highest volcano serve as a treasure trove for rare species. *See page 218.*
- **Kilauea, Big Island** Watch new land burst into life, literally at your feet, as the world's most active volcano makes the Big Island even bigger, day by day. *See page 281.*

BEST SURFING SITES

- **Honolua Bay, Maui** Beautifully located bay at the top of verdant West Maui, blessed with dependably towering waves. *See page 215.*
- **Honoli'i Bay, Big Island** A lovely spot on the Windward side of the Big Island, where Hilo's best surfers battle with fierce surf. *See page 274.*
- **Hanalei Bay, Kauai** This huge curving bay, in view of the Na Pali cliffs, is the spiritual home to Kauai's surfing community. *See page 303.*
- **Sunset Beach, Oahu** The regular site for several major world championships, Oahu's North Shore attracts the world's premier surfers every winter.
Novices beware. *See page 184.*
- **Waimea Bay, Oahu** Probably the world's most famous surfing venue, with the biggest, rideable waves you will ever see anywhere in the world. Extremely dangerous in winter. *See page 184.*

ABOVE: surfers ride the towering waves in Waimea Bay.
LEFT: the magnificent Na Pali coast, Kauai.

BEST WALKS

- **Kalalau Trail, Kauai** This legendary hike along Kauai's Na Pali cliffs offers Hawaii's most breathtaking scenery. *See page 304.*
- **Sliding Sands Trail, Maui** An unforgettable hike through the extraordinary moonscape at the summit of Maui's mighty Haleakala volcano. *See page 222.*
- **Alaka'i Swamp Trail, Kauai** The only way to explore the eerie rainforest swamplands with stupendous ocean views along the way. *See page 297.*
- **Kilauea Iki Trail, Big Island** Centering on the active Kilauea volcano, Hawaii Volcanoes National Park offers several exciting hikes. *See page 281.*

BEST BEACHES

- **Kailua Beach, Oahu** Tempting turquoise waters lap Oahu's Windward Shore. Ideal for kayaking. *See page 179.*
- **Papohaku Beach, Molokai** The perfect spot for swimming and beachcombing. *See page 245.*
- **Ka'anapali Beach, Maui** Hawaii's best family beach is great for relaxing with the kids. *See page 214.*
- **Waikiki Beach, Oahu** Warm waters and gentle waves make this Hawaii's most famous beach. *See page 149.*

BEST MUSEUMS AND GALLERIES

- **Bishop Museum, Honolulu, Oahu** For anyone interested in Hawaii and its Polynesian heritage, the Bishop Museum is the best place to start. *See page 163.*
- **'Imiloa Astronomy Center, Hilo, Big Island** A fascinating, hands-on new museum that explores the links between modern astronomers and ancient Hawaiian beliefs. *See page 272.*
- **Honolulu Academy of Arts, Honolulu, Oahu** This sophisticated gallery houses a globe-spanning collection of artistic treasures. *See page 138.*
- **Hale Ho'ike'ike, Wailuku, Maui** Previously known as the Bailey House, this atmospheric museum celebrates its first occupants, Maui's earliest missionaries. *See page 209.*
- **Whaling Center, Ka'anapali, Maui** An entertaining introduction to the part Hawaii played in the whaling industry. *See page 214.*

ABOVE: the start of the Kalalau Trail.
LEFT: chilling out on Waikiki Beach.
RIGHT: the Bishop Museum, Honolulu.

BEST HISTORIC SITES

● **Pearl Harbor, Oahu**
A sombre memorial to
the "date which will
live in infamy",
Hawaii's finest harbor
hauntingly evokes the
surprise Japanese
attack of 1941. *See
page 190.*

● **Pu'uhonua 'O
Honaunau, South
Kona, Big Island** A
beautiful spot in its
own right, this so-
called "place of
refuge" was once a
royal precinct, and is
still adorned with

fearsome carved
images. *See page 268.*

● **Kealakekua Bay,
South Kona, Big
Island** A stark white
obelisk marks the
precise location
where Captain Cook
lost his life in 1779.
See page 268.

● **Pi'lanihale Heiau,
Hana, Maui** The
largest ancient temple
in all Polynesia, a
multi-tiered
oceanfront pyramid
on Maui's ravishing
Hana coast. *See page
229.*

● **Pu'ukohola Heiau,
South Kohala, Big
Island** The "war
temple" where
Kamehameha the
Great performed
human sacrifices
before he conquered
all the islands, still
dominates the Kohala
shoreline. *See page
264.*

● **'Iolani Palace,
Honolulu, Oahu**
Built in 1882, this
imposing palace in
the heart of Honolulu
served as a prison for
Hawaii's last queen,
after her kingdom was
overthrown. *See page
131.*

BEST OCEAN ACTIVITIES

● **Windsurfing at
Ho'okipa, Maui**
Crowds of spectators
gather on the hillsides
to watch the amazing
feats at the planet's
premier destination
for top-class
windsurfers. *See page
219.*

● **Snorkeling at
Hanauma Bay, Oahu**
Shoals of iridescent
fish congregate in this
gorgeous nature
preserve, a volcanic
crater that's a short
ride out from Waikiki.
See page 172.

● **Diving at Molokini**
The crystal-clear
waters, a few miles off
South Maui, attract
boat-loads of divers
daily. *See page 217.*

● **Whale-watching off
Maui** Every winter,
the shallow waters
that separate Maui
from Lanai and
Molokai are teeming

with migratory
humpback whales.

● **Kayaking in Kailua
Bay, Oahu** There's
no better place to
paddle a rented kayak
than in the beautiful
shallow waters off
Oahu's finest beach.
See page 179.

LEFT: sacred carved
images at Pu'uhonua 'O
Honaunau.
ABOVE LEFT: 'Iolani Palace.
ABOVE RIGHT: a Spotted
Porcupinefish gets ready
for its
close-up.

BEST SMALL TOWNS

● **Hanapepe, Kauai** Loop off Kauai's circle-island highway to while away an hour or two in this delightful little village, with its fading antique stores and swinging rope-bridge. *See page 307.*

● **Hawi, Big Island** Hidden at the quiet northernmost tip of the Big Island, Hawi makes a great half-way stopping point on a tour of the lovely North Kohala district. *See page 266.*

● **Lanai City, Lanai** Once the pineapple capital of the world, this former plantation town, with its pretty gardens and simple cafes, is unlike any city you've ever seen. *See page 247.*

● **Hale'iwa, Oahu** The only town on Oahu's North Shore is a laidback hangout for surfers and back-packers, with quirky stores, galleries and wholefood restaurants on all sides. *See page 186.*

● **Makawao, Maui** This one-horse town still evokes the days when Maui's verdant Upcountry was home to the Hispanic cowboys known as *paniolos. See page 219.*

● **Kaunakakai, Molokai** Molokai's sleepy little capital is the perfect place to hang out for a lazy afternoon of simply "talking story". *See page 237.*

ABOVE LEFT: Hale'iwa is a meeting place for surfers.
ABOVE RIGHT: the Garden of the Gods.

HAWAII'S NATURAL WONDERS

● **'Akaka Falls, Big Island** This towering majestic waterfall is reached by a short hike deep into the rainforest of the Big Island's Hamakua coast. *See page 274.*

● **Nu'uanu Pali Lookout, Oahu** Travelers crossing the Ko'olau Mountains are suddenly con-fronted by the vast sweeping cliffs that line the Windward coast. *See page 167.*

● **'Iao Needle, Maui** An abrupt, velvet-coated pinnacle buried deep in the West Maui Mountains. *See page 210.*

● **Waimea Canyon, Kauai** This deep chasm is slowly splitting Kauai in two, and glows green, gold and red as the sun crosses the sky. *See page 309.*

● **Garden of the Gods, Lanai** These eerie red badlands are more like something you'd find in the Wild West than in lush Hawaii. *See page 249.*

● **Halawa Valley, Molokai** This magnificent valley was home to some of Hawaii's earliest Polynesian settlers. *See page 244.*

MONEY-SAVING TIPS

Inter-island Travel Hawaii's various airlines are constantly in fare-cutting competition to attract inter-island passengers. Check their websites for current rates, rather than booking your flights between the islands as part of your trans-Pacific itinerary. The new Superferry makes it possible to take your rental car from island to island.

Getting Around On Oahu's excellent public bus network, TheBus, fares are much cheaper, and the range of routes served is much wider, than on the various overpriced "trolley" services that operate in Waikiki. You can even travel around the entire island for just $2.

Cheap Eating Visitors staying on Oahu can save enormously on Waikiki's inflated prices by dining in Chinatown's fascinating markets, or in the food courts at Honolulu's major shopping centers. "Local" restaurants operated by Hawaii's various immigrant groups offer more varied cuisine at bargain prices.

Adventuring on land and sea Access to all beaches in Hawaii, and thus to the ocean as well, is always free and unrestricted. Bring your own surfing or snorkeling equipment, or rent it cheaply on the islands. Similarly, most of Hawaii's very best hiking trails, such as on the volcanoes of Maui and the Big Island, are clearly marked routes in national and state parks; there's no need to join a commercial tour.

ALOHA

Few travelers arrive in Hawaii without preconceptions.
Inevitably, expectations pale next to Hawaii's diversity

Say the word "Hawaii" and seductive images come to mind: secluded beaches, fragrant rainforests, mountains that soar above the mists, fiery sunsets silhouetting majestic waving palm trees, waterfalls shimmering like silvery ribbons in valleys unmarred by human footsteps. Of all the destinations on Earth, Hawaii ranks among the most alluring, its magic rooted far more deeply than preconceived images or even its undeniable physical beauty.

The islands of Hawaii are home to an amazingly diverse gathering of peoples: Native Hawaiians, Chinese, Japanese, Vietnamese, Koreans, Filipinos, Samoans and other Pacific islanders, and Caucasians. Over the decades, intermarriage has diluted bloodlines, so that today a *kama'aina* (local-born or long-time resident) is more likely than not a beautiful blend of races. And as with the mixing of ethnic and cultural groups, so too with the islands' cuisines, religions, languages, fashions, music, dances, and arts. Every ethnic group that came to Hawaii has added something special, creating a cultural climate unlike elsewhere in the United States or indeed the world.

Even Americans on the US mainland tend to forget that Hawaii is fully part of the United States. More than one resident, when making a business call to the mainland, has been asked if American money or postage is valid in the islands, or if Hawaii has a separate country code. (Yes to money and postage, no to a different country code.) Of course, Hawaii is administratively as much a part of the United States as Vermont. Hawaii's residents celebrate Easter, Independence Day, Thanksgiving and Christmas. But they also enthusiastically observe holidays such as the Lunar New Year, Kamehameha Day, Samoan Flag Day, and the Japanese Obon season. Along with hamburgers and cotton candy, food booths at school carnivals peddle Japanese teriyaki, Chinese noodles, Portuguese *malasadas* (donuts), Korean *kalbi* (barbecue) ribs, and Hawaiian *kalua* pig and *poi*. Houses of worship on the islands range from synagogues to cathedrals to Buddhist temples, and for some Native Hawaiians, ancient *heiau*, or sacred temples.

Hawaii's economy is driven in large part by tourism, followed by the military and agriculture. Over 7 million people visit the islands annually, pumping more than $12 billion into the state. Hawaii adopted its nickname, the Aloha State, in 1959 when it became a state. Since then, Hawaii has also chosen an official state bird, the endangered *nene* goose; a state fish, *humuhumunukunukuapua'a*; a state mammal, the humpback whale; a state tree, *kukui*, or candlenut; a state gem, black coral; and a state flower, the yellow hibiscus. Its

PRECEDING PAGES: surf's up; Ha'ena Point, Kauai.
LEFT: hula performer with a winning smile.

official anthem, "Hawaii Pono'i", is a haunting and moving melody composed in 1874 by Henry Berger, the long-time leader of the Royal Hawaiian Band who originally titled it "The Hymn of King Kamehameha I." The song's lyrics were written by King David Kalakaua.

Each of the major Hawaiian islands has its own official flower: Oahu, *'ilima*; Maui, *loke lani*; the Big Island, *red lehua*; Kauai, *mokihana*; Molokai, white *kukui* blossom; Lanai, *kauna'oa*; and Ni'ihau, white *pupu* shell. Even the uninhabited island of Kaho'olawe has an official flower, the *hinahina*.

Oahu, the main island, is perhaps the biggest surprise. Located here is Honolulu, the state capital and home to over 800,000 people. The largest city between Asia and the Americas, Honolulu offers a mix of sophistication and easy living, a blend that is at once American, Asian and Polynesian. World renowned hotels and attractions like Pearl Harbor, Waikiki and Diamond Head are just part of what makes Oahu a special place.

But just half an hour's drive from Honolulu is the Hawaii of old: majestic mountain ranges, verdant meadows, pristine beaches, and breezes scented with plumeria and *'awapuhi* (wild ginger). *Keiki* (children) fish with nylon lines tied to bamboo poles, snacking on guavas, *liliko'i* (passionfruit) and bananas plucked from roadside trees.

That precisely is the wonder of Hawaii. Two visitors arriving on the islands at the very same time may wind up having two very different experiences. There is the Hawaii of today, with its luxurious resorts, magnificent golf courses (many of which were laid atop ancient lava fields), fine dining and shopping. And there's the Hawaii of yesteryear – simple, laid-back, unspoiled, and historical.

No matter where you go, no matter what you do, you will be touched by Hawaii's *aloha*. Translated, the word *aloha* breaks down as *alo*, to face, and *ha*, the breath of life. It is the spiritual glue that binds the islands' cosmopolitan population, whatever the ethnic or cultural background

About the spelling of place names

Two symbols can be added to Hawaiian words to assist pronunciation: a glottal stop ('), called the *'okina*, and a macron, which is a horizontal line over a vowel, indicating that the sound is drawn out longer than is normal. *Insight Guide: Hawaii* uses the *'okina*, but not the macron. The glottal stop, which gives a "hard edge" to a vowel or separates two adjoining vowels with distinct sounds, is necessary for basic pronunciation in normal conversation, while the macron offers a more subtle, precise pronunciation.

All place names in this guide that need them use a glottal stop, with three exceptions: Hawaii, Oahu and Kauai, which should strictly be written as Hawai'i, O'ahu and Kaua'i. But the non-glottal spellings are so common and ubiquitous that most cartographers delete the glottal stop. In this guide, we use glottal stops for the two islands that require them for proper pronunciation: Ni'ihau (*nee-ee-how*) and Kaho'olawe (*kah-ho-o-lah-vay*). ❏

RIGHT: the day's end, Waikiki.

Decisive Dates

150,000 BC Diamond Head forms through a crack in the emerged reef of Oahu.

AD 200–500 First settlers arrive in Hawaii, probably from the Marquesas Islands.

800–1200 Next Polynesian pioneers arrive, this time from Tahiti.

circa **1750** Kamehameha (the Great) is born on the Big Island's northernmost point.

1778 In January, Captain James Cook encounters the Hawaiian islands, and anchors in Waimea Bay, off the island of Kauai. He names the islands the Sandwich

Islands, after his patron, the Earl of Sandwich. In November, he returns to Hawaii from the Arctic after a fruitless search for the Northwest Passage. He anchors at Kealakekua Bay, on the Big Island.

1779 Cook is killed in a skirmish with Hawaiians. His body is dismembered and divided among chiefs. The portion returned to the British is buried at Kealakekua Bay.

1790–1 Kamehameha I begins unification of the Hawaiian Islands by conquering Maui and Lanai, later completing his conquest of the Big Island.

1795 On Oahu, Kamehameha's forces drive the army of Kalanikupule over Nu'uanu Pali. The great warrior king now rules all the major islands except Kauai.

1810 Kauai's chief, Kaumuali'i, finally surrenders to Kamehameha without a battle.

1812 Sandalwood trade booms.

1819 Kamehameha I dies in Kailua-Kona, on the Big Island. His son, Liholiho, becomes Kamehameha II, and Kamehameha's favorite wife (he had 16–20 in his lifetime), Ka'ahumanu, becomes *kuhina nui*, sharing power as regent. They pave the way for the introduction of Christianity in the islands by abolishing the ancient *kapu* system.

WESTERN INFLUENCES

1820 The first contingent of Protestant missionaries arrives in Hawaii. The kingdom's capital and royal court are moved to Lahaina, on Maui.

1823/4 Liholiho and his favorite wife, Kamamalu, sail to England to meet King George III and are stricken with the measles and die in London.

1825 Liholiho's brother, Kauikeaouli, becomes Kamehameha III. Whaling industry begins a 40-year boom.

1831 Lahainaluna Seminary (now the oldest school west of the Rocky Mountains) welcomes its first students from both the mainland and Hawaii.

1835 First Hawaiian sugar plantation is established at Koloa, Kauai. It fails but introduces the idea of plantation agriculture to the islands.

1842 Kawaiaha'o Church dedicated in Honolulu.

1845 Hawaii's capital is moved back to Honolulu from Lahaina. First legislature in Hawaii convenes. The king announces plans for a constitutional government.

1848 Kamehameha III enacts the Great Mahele, dividing land among the crown, chiefs and commoners.

1852 The king unveils a new liberal constitution. About 300 Chinese immigrants arrive to work in the cane fields.

1854/5 Kamehameha III dies. His nephew, Alexander Liholiho, becomes Kamehameha IV.

1863 Kamehameha IV dies, and Lot Kamehameha takes the throne as Kamehameha V.

1869 "Big Five" company Alexander & Baldwin founded.

1872 Kamehameha V dies, abruptly ending the Kamehameha dynasty. He leaves no heir.

1873 Lunalilo is elected king.

1874 Lunalilo dies on 3 February. Kalakaua is elected king. The new monarch visits Washington, DC, to push for a reciprocity treaty with the US. The first such treaty is ratified, allowing Hawaiian goods, particularly rice and unrefined sugar, entry into the US tax-free.

1878 Thousands of immigrant plantation workers arrive, primarily from Portugal and Asia.

1881 Kalakaua embarks on a round-the-world trip, the first by a ruling monarch.

1883 Nine years after his ascension to the throne, Kalakaua holds an elaborate coronation ceremony at 'Iolani Palace, no doubt inspired by the lavish lifestyle he encountered on his global tour.

1885 Japanese sugar laborers arrive.

1887 Hawaiian League is formed by powerful *haole* businessmen. Kalakaua signs the Bayonet Constitution, which greatly limits his power.

1889 Robert Wilcox leads an unsuccessful revolt against opponents of the king.

1890 Kalakaua heads for California, hoping rest will improve his deteriorating health.

1891 Kalakaua dies in San Francisco. His sister, Lili'uokalani, is named queen.

END OF THE MONARCHY

1893 Anti-royalists launch successful coup. A self-proclaimed provisional government is established, led by Sanford B. Dole. President Grover Cleveland's representative recommends restoration of monarchy.

1894 The provisional government declares itself to be the Republic of Hawaii, with Dole as president.

1895 Supporters of the queen stage a counter coup, but are defeated. Lili'uokalani is arrested, found guilty of treason and imprisoned for nine months.

1898 The US Congress passes a resolution to annex Hawaii as a territory, and President William McKinley signs the legislation to annex Hawaii.

1900 Hawaii becomes a territory of the United States, with Sanford Dole as its governor. Construction of a naval base at Pearl Harbor begins.

1902 First transpacific telegraphic cable linking Hawaii and California is laid.

1903 Prince Jonah Kuhio Kalaniana'ole begins a term as Hawaii's delegate to Congress that lasts until his death in 1922.

1906 Immigrants from the Philippines arrive to work on the sugar plantations.

1912 Hawaii's premier surfer, Duke Kahanamoku wins Olympic gold medal in swimming.

1917 Queen Lili'uokalani dies.

1919 Dredging of the channel and construction of facilities at Pearl Harbor are completed.

1922 James Dole's Hawaiian Pineapple Company buys the island of Lanai.

1929 Inter-Island Airways (now Hawaiian Airlines) starts passenger service between the islands.

1935 Congress passes an act allowing workers to organize into unions and engage in collective bargaining. Over the next 30 years, unions in Hawaii grow.

1936 Pan American Airways launches transpacific passenger service to Hawaii.

1941 Japanese fighter planes bomb Pearl Harbor, propelling the United States into World War II.

LEFT: the Earl of Sandwich. **RIGHT:** an *ali'i* feather cape, early 1900s.

1942 Americans of Japanese ancestry form the 442nd Regimental Combat Team, the most highly decorated American military unit during World War II.

STATEHOOD

1959 Hawaii becomes the 50th state in the union.

1974 George Ariyoshi becomes the first Japanese-American governor in the US.

1978 Last scheduled passenger ship flying an American flag between mainland and Hawaii arrives.

1986 Hawaii's first ethnic Hawaiian governor, John Waihe'e, takes office.

1989 The start of Japan's bubble economy reaches Hawaii with the purchase of $17 billion in real estate.

1993 100th anniversary of the monarchy's overthrow. President Clinton and Congress apologize for this.

2000 Sugar plantations close on most islands. Only a few plantations remain: pineapple on Maui and Oahu, sugar on Kauai and Maui.

2001–2 The September 11 terrorist attacks in New York cause a downturn in Hawaii's tourist trade, reducing the number of travelers from Japan in particular.

2002 Former Maui mayor Linda Lingle, a Republican, becomes Hawaii's first female governor. She is re-elected in 2006.

2006 Del Monte ceases operating in Hawaii, leaving Dole as the island's only pineapple producer.

2007 Opening of Beachwalk development heralds new upgrading of Waikiki as upscale resort. ❏

Webber del.

CA

KARAKAKOOA, in OWYHEE.

ILES SANDWICH. UN OFFICIER DU ROI EN GRAND COSTUME.

S. Leroy d'après J. Arago.   Gravé par Lerouge.

BEGINNINGS: ANCIENT HAWAII

Thousands of centuries passed after the islands' creation before the first life took root. People, however, arrived just 15 or so centuries ago

Each year the speckled plover wends its way southward from its summer grounds in Siberia and Alaska, flying southwest as far as the Marquesas Islands, Tahiti, and New Zealand. For thousands of miles, save for a stop in Hawaii and other more obscure landing spots, the plover's wings beat rhythmically through Pacific winds until the bird finds a perch in the central or south Pacific. Once there, it spends between nine and 10 months fattening up on crustaceans, snails, and insects, before returning to Alaska and Siberia, when they are at their warmest.

Ancient seafaring Polynesians from the islands around Tahiti no doubt observed the movements of this bird and realized it had to be going somewhere, coming from somewhere. This curiosity may have led to the discovery of Hawaii, over 2,000 miles (3,200 km) north of Tahiti.

In seaworthy, double-hulled canoes embellished with *'aumakua* – carved images of their family gods – these Polynesian islanders set out on epic ocean journeys, perhaps motivated by the plover heading north. The reasons for setting off into the unknown were probably many: seeking refuge from persecution and conquering enemies, escaping the pressures of overpopulation, or simply wanderlust, intrigued about what lay beyond the horizon.

The first European to find the Marquesas Islands, Portuguese explorer Pedro Fernandez de Quirios, believed that there was no possibility of Polynesians traveling eastward very far against the prevailing trade winds. Such a journey, however long or short, would have "required instruments of navigation and vessels of burden, two things of which these people are destitute."

These "destitute" Marquesans, however, were but the last chapter of an island-hopping migration of peoples that had begun thousands of years earlier, probably in Southeast Asia. By AD 400, Marquesan canoes had sailed as far east as Easter Island, 2,500 miles (4,000 km) away. In time they also reached New Zealand and Hawaii; recently archeologists have even found proof that they reached the Americas, albeit too late to have any significant cultural input. The British explorer and navigator Captain James Cook, who first sailed to the South Pacific in 1768 to observe the transit of Venus, watched with a seaman's respect as Tahitians took visual bearings on stars, using no instruments, to plow ahead into uncertain seas.

The first Polynesians to reach Hawaii, located in latitudes high above the familiar stars, had not just ventured into the unknown, but had, in the words of contemporary American author and ecologist Kenneth Brower, literally "left their universe." They had none of Cook's navigational instruments and charts, relying instead upon an inner sense, an internal navigation system programmed by intuition, knowledge, and experience. The European explorers, too, ventured into an unknown, but it was a reasonably comfortable one referenced on a round planet consisting of magnetic poles and invisible lines of longitude and latitude. Wherever he was, however mysterious and far from home, the European navigator had a piece of paper with directions for guidance.

The Polynesian navigator's view of the world was more limited. Rather than latitude and longitude, he used an eclectic mix of information and clues to chart a steady course, studying the behavior of birds, dolphins, and the color of the ocean and the clouds.

Most obvious, of course, were the stars. The early Polynesians did not use just one star, or even a dozen stars. They used hundreds of stars that were woven into a memorized tapestry of mnemonic chants that detailed hundreds of known course settings throughout the Pacific.

KAPU AND TABOO

Hawaiian life was regulated under systematic laws known as *kapu*. The English word "taboo" comes from the Tongan word "tabu."

LEFT: a helmeted warrior in a feather cape, drawn by a French artist in 1819. The helmet offered little head protection, however. Note the extensive tattoos.

Based on observational and astronomical data accumulated over the years, it seems that Polynesians made the incredible 2,000-mile (3,200-km) journey to Hawaii by fixing on two key stars – Sirius and Arcturus. Astronomers at the Bishop Museum in Honolulu note that "Sirius, the brightest star in the sky, passed almost directly over Tahiti and Raiatea (also called Hawa'iti). The present position of Sirius with respect to the equator has changed very little from that of the days of Polynesian voyaging. Arcturus, called Hokule'a by the Hawaiians and noted for its bright redness off the Big Dipper's handle, presently passes over the northern end

Hawaii has been confirmed by carbon dating, and by comparison of fishhooks and adzes found in Hawaiian and Marquesan sites dating from around the same period. These new Hawaiians lived in isolation for several centuries, but sometime between 800 and 1200, other Polynesians arrived from Tahiti. Some researchers believe there were only a few voyages between Tahiti and Hawaii. Others argue there were numerous voyages over a period of two centuries to islands referred to as Hawaiia, or Burning Hawaii, believed to be a reference to Hawaii's volcanoes.

Scholars have speculated that this second wave of Polynesians subjugated the earlier Mar-

of the island of Hawaii. At the time of the great voyaging it passed over the island of Kauai."

Some of the most skilled Polynesian navigators did not use the stars at all. Perhaps because their boats were considerably smaller than the large European sailing ships, the Polynesians "felt" the ocean more, sensing its subtle moods and messages. They felt the ocean, literally, in the direction of swells and the subtle interference of waves reflected off distant islands.

Discovery of Hawaii

The first discoverers and settlers of Hawaii are believed to have arrived sometime between AD 200 and 500. Evidence of Marquesan landfalls in

quesans as slaves, or perhaps drove them farther north in the Hawaiian chain until they were completely eliminated. When the Tahitian migration ended, the newcomers lived in isolation for several centuries, developing into the Hawaiian culture that would later greet Captain Cook.

Conquered Marquesans may have been the *manahune*, or *menehune*, mentioned in early Hawaiian and Tahitian chants. The term *manahune* was used derisively in the Tahitian homeland to refer to slaves or plebeian castes, but its meaning changed through the centuries to mean, probably sarcastically, the mysterious gnomes supposed in Hawaiian folklore to inhabit remote corners of the islands.

Offspring of Tahiti

The Marquesans and Tahitians brought with them a similar language, as well as foods, myths, traditions, and gods. It was the Tahitian, however, who is credited with bequeathing the name "Hawaii," which was first given to the largest of the islands, now commonly called the Big Island, and later to the complete chain of islands. As the Polynesian bard Kamahualele chanted centuries ago, "Behold Hawaii, an island, a people/The people of Hawaii are the offspring of Tahiti."

Sir Peter Buck, the eminent half-Maori ethnologist who once served as the Bishop Museum's director, explained the origin of the

is exemplified by the ancient name of a channel located south of Maui, between the islands of Lanai and Kaho'olawe. The channel's Hawaiian name is Kealaikahiki. By substituting the letter *k* in the word with *t*, the word *te-ala-i-tahiti* is formed, which translates as "the pathway to Tahiti," or "the pathway to foreign lands."

Early life

When the first Polynesian canoes landed on Hawaiian shores, probably on or near the southernmost point of the Big Island, the islands were almost an unspoiled paradise. Although much of the land was barren and dry, some 2,200

VOYAGES OF THE *HOKULE'A*

In the constellation Boötes, the star Arcturus is a zenith star for Hawaii, meaning that it passes directly overhead daily. In Hawaiian, the star is called *Hokule'a* – star of gladness.

In the 1970s, a Polynesian-style voyaging canoe was built to recreate the journeys of ancient Polynesians to Hawaii. It was named *Hokule'a*. Navigation by Mau Piailug and Nainoa Thompson, his student, used only the stars and ocean swells. Since then, *Hokule'a* has made several successful voyages between Hawaii and southern Polynesia. *Hokule'a* was joined in the 1990s on expeditions by a sister canoe, *Hawai'iloa*. Unlike *Hokule'a*, made from modern materials, such as fiberglass, *Hawai'iloa* was constructed of materials closer to those used by early Polynesians. When not out exploring, *Hokule'a* is berthed at Honolulu's Hawaii Maritime Center.

word Hawaii in his book, *Vikings of the Pacific*, published in 1938. He noted that in ancient times "the headquarters of the Polynesian main body was established in the largest island of the leeward group of Tahiti, named Havai'i after an ancient homeland."

As Tahiti-based fleets set out to settle the Society Islands, Samoa, Tonga, Fiji, Hawaii, and New Zealand, they established colonies often named after their home island. Dialectal differences resulted in today's place name variations. An even more persuasive Hawaii-Tahiti relationship

kinds of plants unique to the Hawaiian Islands managed to thrive. The islands' undisturbed shoreline of reefs, wetlands and lagoons, fern forests, alluvial plains, and well-watered valleys and highlands were rich with indigenous flora and fauna. Many of the plants prominent in modern Hawaii – coconuts, orchids, sugar-cane, pineapples – were introduced to Hawaii from elsewhere.

When the Marquesans arrived, they found nearly 70 varieties of indigenous Hawaiian birds, at least two dozen of which are now extinct. But neither amphibia (frogs, newts, and the like), nor reptiles, nor mosquitoes, lice, fleas, flies, or gnats were to be found. And for nearly 1,000

LEFT: masked canoe rowers, sketched in 1779 by an artist with Captain Cook. **ABOVE:** a gourd mask.

years, until mariners began arriving from the East and West, most fatal or even debilitating diseases were also absent.

The Polynesians found only two mammals local to the islands: the hoary bat, which had somehow migrated from either North or South America, and the monk seal, a relative of the seals usually found in the Caribbean and the Mediterranean.

The hoary bat, known as the *'ope'ape'a* to Hawaiians, still haunts the nights of Big Island's Kilauea Crater area. The monk seal, still an

POETIC RAPTURE

Where is Kumukahi?
He is at Hauʻula.
He has settled down,
enraptured by a statue.
– *The Legend of Halemano*

Then came plants like the *wauke*, or paper mulberry, which was beaten and sun-bleached to make *kapa* (bark cloth), and the *ti*, a relative of the lily whose roots and leaves are still used as wrapping and matting, for hula skirts, and a liquor called *'okolehao* (lit. iron bottom).

Most of what we know of ancient Hawaiian life is from poetic oral traditions, known as *mele*. In these *mele*, the Hawaiians' *kupuna*, or ancestors, passed on to their descendants all they knew of their history. Various aspects of life,

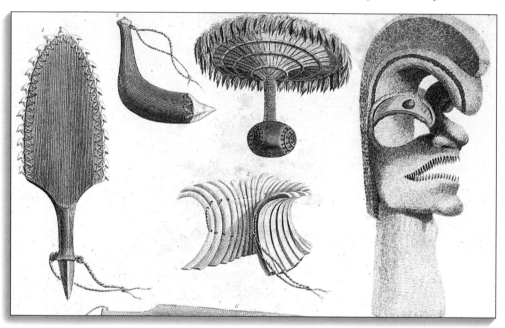

endangered species, was nearly slaughtered into extinction for its valuable skin and oil during the 1800s. The 1500 that remain are found in the isolated Northwestern Hawaiian Islands beyond Kauai, although in recent years, they have begun to come ashore on the main islands.

Introduced plants and animals

The arriving Polynesians disturbed Hawaii's ecological balance with dogs, pigs, chickens and stowaway rats. These first Hawaiians also introduced taro, a starchy, nutritious tuber from which grey, pasty *poi* is made. They also brought coconuts, bananas, yams, *kukui* (candlenuts), wild ginger, breadfruit, and sugar-cane.

from the trivial to the momentous, were reported in this unwritten literature, which consisted of family genealogies, myths, and day-to-day accounts of human experiences.

Other insights about early Hawaii come from the initial observations made by foreign explorers such as James Cook, George Vancouver, and Otto von Kotzebue. Additionally, there are the important memoirs of early Hawaiian scholars, notably John Papa Ii (1800–70), Samuel Kamakau (1815–76), Kepelino Keauokalani (1830–78), and David Malo (1793–1853).

Another source has been the antiquities and folklore collected by Abraham Fornander (1812–87), a surveyor, editor, and judge. Fornander, who was married to a Hawaiian woman, spoke and wrote the Hawaiian language fluently. He wrote a history of the islands entitled *An Account of the Polynesian Race: Its Origins and Migrations*. He also collected and translated many Hawaiian chants into English. According to these chroniclers, the people of Hawaii developed one of the most complex non-technological cultures ever encountered by early Europeans.

Kapu life

Hawaiian life was simple and straightforward, regulated under systematic laws known as *kapu*, the Hawaiian version of the Tahitian word *tapu*,

labor and working class, *maka'ainana* or commoners, worked the land. At the very bottom were the social outcasts, the slaves or *kauwa maoli*. Sometimes the unfortunate *kauwa* were marked by tattoos on their foreheads, and they were summarily conscripted as sacrificial victims by the priestly *kahuna*.

Under this hierarchy, the tightly circumscribed *kapu* and bloodlines could not be crossed. A typical penalty for a *kapu* violation was execution by stoning, clubbing, or strangulation; violators might also be buried or burned alive. Sometimes a *kapu*-breaker was singled out as a convenient sacrificial victim for a god, but

from which the word "taboo" originates. At the time of the first contact with Europeans, Hawaiian society was feudal and defined mostly by territory, with two or three *mo'i*, or kings, contending for control of each island. Ranking below the kings were hereditary groups of *ali'i*, or nobles. The *ali'i* were supported by *kahuna*, a prestigious group including priests, healers, and astrologers. Lower down was a class of craftsmen and artists, *kanaka wale*, who made the canoes, calabashes and *lei* (garlands). This class also included fishermen and hula dancers. The

LEFT: articles of ceremony from early Hawaii.
ABOVE: an 1873 engraving of female surfers.

usually he was sacrificed as a lesson to others. The Hawaiian historian David Malo wrote that a person could be put to death for allowing his shadow to fall upon the house of a chief, or for passing through that chief's stockade or doorway, or for entering the house before changing his *malo* (loincloth). He could also be executed because he appeared before the chief with his head smeared by mud. Other common *kapu* declared that women could not eat pork, coconuts, bananas, and shark meat, nor could they eat with men.

Certain seasons were established for the gathering or catching of scarce plants or animals for food, probably as conservation measures.

Sometimes sporting chiefs declared certain surfing-spots *kapu* for their own exclusive use. Some *kapu* were implemented by Machiavellian chiefs, priests or influential court retainers under the guise of religion, or to tyrannically oppress a person or group of people. Many of the laws, however, were simply to protect resources and assure social stability.

Kapu violators had a place where they could seek sanctuary, whatever their crime. These places of refuge, called *pu'uhonua*, had to be reached by the transgressor before he was caught. The odds, of course, were against the transgressor. A good example of a *pu'uhonua* is located

on a lava promontory at Pu'uhonua O Honaunau National Historical Park, on the Big Island's Kona coast. This *kapu* system affected every aspect of Hawaiian life, from birth to death, until it was abolished in 1819 by King Kamehameha II, his mother Keopuolani, and the queen regent, Ka'ahumanu. But until its abolition, *kapu* protected the powers of Hawaiian kings.

Worship

Hawaiians generally worshiped privately and at small shrines they built in their homes or outdoors, but the focal points of most major religious observances were large open-air temples known as *heiau*. Ruins of these *heiau* can be

seen throughout Hawaii. In most cases, what remains today are rudimentary platforms, terraces and walls made of large river-rounded lava stones. In ancient times, they housed *kapa*-covered oracle towers, sacrificial platform-altars, carved stone and wooden sculptures, images of gods made of thatch and feathers, sacred stones, rough-hewn monoliths, groupings of wood and stone sub-temple structures, and often a disposal pit for decayed human, animal, or plant offerings.

The most complex temples were those built by Hawaiian chiefs to initiate a war. These *heiau waikaua* (war temples), also called *luakini*, were kept spiritually "alive" by periodic human sacrifices. Only *ali'i* were allowed access to the *heiau*. Once it had been decided to wage war, and appropriate sacrifices had been made to Ku, the war god, the high chief would call for his *kilo lani* (astrologer) to determine the most auspicious day to do battle. Exceptional power might be elicited from the gods by sacrificing an enemy chief at the *luakini*.

War and arts

Given the generally clannish and feudalistic structure of ancient Hawaiian society, wars were frequent. Periodic and courtly sham battles were held between friendly chiefs to keep young warriors prepped and alert. This system of forearming and forewarning was reminiscent of European days of chivalry.

The ritual aspects of Hawaiian wars quickly gave way to brutality. There might be some opening decorum, gladiator-style, in which two renowned warriors would fight to the death in front of opposing armies. But more often than not, the two armies would meet on an impromptu or chosen battleground, usually during daylight hours and following an exchange of verbal taunts and insults, and commence battle.

Common Hawaiian weapons included spears up to 18 ft (5 meters) in length, shorter javelins, assorted daggers (some lined with shark teeth), stone-headed clubs, serrated shark-tooth clubs, a variety of sennit-and-stone tripping weapons, slingshots, strangling cords, and any and all objects (rocks, boulders, branches) that could be spontaneously introduced into the fray by resourceful warriors.

But life in ancient times was not an endless cycle of war-making, oppression, and workaday drudgery. Hawaiians developed unique forms of recreation, including such diversions as kite-flying, puppet theater and staged dances, numerous games of skill and chance, archery, tobogganing on *holua* sleds that were raced down specially prepared hillside runways; and surfing, known as *he'e nalu* or "wave sliding."

The Hawaiians also created the most exquisite variety of fine artwork and personal adornments found anywhere in Polynesia. Wood and stone sculpture was graphic and bold, while Hawaii's delicate featherwork is still considered to be the finest example of this art to be

FEATHERY PATIENCE

A chief's feather cloak could require some 450,000 feathers plucked from an estimated 80,000 birds.

royal feather-pluckers who stalked and snared their preferred prey with nets and long sticky wands. Most of the birds were released after the desired feathers had been removed.

Hawaiian *kapa*, the soft barkcloth fashioned from paper mulberry, also represents a major artistic achievement. Strips of bark were soaked, then beaten until smooth and paper thin. The cloth was then decorated by bamboo stamps with intricate designs carved on them, inked by dyes made from the leaves, bark, fruit, and roots of various native plants.

found. James Cook, in describing Hawaiian featherwork, observed that "the surface might be compared to the thickest and richest velvet." His lieutenant, James King, suggested that the "feathered cloak and helmet... in point of beauty and magnificence, is perhaps nearly equal to that of any nation in the world."

It would be impossible today to duplicate one of these cloaks, because most of the birds whose feathers were plucked for use have since become extinct. In old Hawaii, the king commissioned specially selected groups of

LEFT: wooden image of *Kakailimoku,* the war god.
ABOVE: admiring a temple's carved deities.

Perhaps the most diverse art practiced was in the form of necklaces, headbands, and anklets made of flowers, nuts, seeds, shells, ivory, teeth, turtle shells, and human hair. Tattooing, too, was popular, often as an expression of mourning. Both men and women tattooed their bodies with a variety of bright designs: some were of a topical nature, but there were also repetitious, geometric motifs. These tattoos were created with small sharp needles made of fish and bird bones, or shells.

Tattooing was condemned by the missionaries and had largely disappeared until the late 1980s, when it was revived as an art form and as a way of asserting native Hawaiian identity. ❑

ARRIVAL OF CAPTAIN COOK

Captain James Cook was noted for his sensitivity to the cultures he encountered

during his global explorations. Still, after his arrival, Hawaii changed immensely

Hawaii's modern era began in 1778, amid excitement and terror, when Hawaiians on the island of Oahu saw two strange, white-winged objects moving at sea. These floating islands, as the Hawaiians were to describe them, were the British ships HMS *Resolution* and HMS *Discovery*, commanded by Captain James Cook.

En route from the South Pacific to the north – and, it was hoped, an elusive Northwest Passage – Cook and his crew, which included an astronomer and artist assigned to the expedition by the British Admiralty, had accidentally become the first known non-Polynesians to land on the Hawaiian islands. It was a formidable find, the last significant land on Earth to be found by Europeans. In his ship's log, Cook later suggested that finding Hawaii was "in many respects the most important discovery made by Europeans throughout the extent of the Pacific Ocean." Cook marveled at the existence of the Polynesian settlements: "How shall we account for this nation spreading itself so far over this vast ocean…?" Cook named these isles the Sandwich Islands, in honor of Cook's patron, the Earl of Sandwich, First Lord of the Admiralty.

Oahu was the first island to be sighted, but Cook passed by and continued on to the northeast, making landfall on 21 January 1778 at Waimea, on Kauai's west coast, after a long search for safe anchorage. After five days of replenishment and sightseeing, strong winds at night blew his ships away from Kauai toward the smaller island of Ni'ihau. There, Cook's men received salt and yams from the islanders in exchange for goats, pigs, and the seeds of melons, pumpkins, and onions. Western flora and fauna were thus introduced.

Also introduced, against Cook's explicitly posted orders, were syphilis, gonorrhea, and other European diseases. All too aware of the effects of introduced diseases on indigenous peoples, Cook had told his men clearly that no Hawaiian women were to be allowed on board the ships, nor any person "having or suspected of having the venereal disease or any symptoms thereof, shall lie with any woman" under threat of severe lashing at the ship's masthead.

Thomas Edgar, master of the *Discovery*, said his men employed every devious scheme possible to get women on board the ships, even "dressing them up as men." But he noted also that the Hawaiian women "used all arts to entice them into their houses and even went so far as to endeavour to draw them in by force."

In February, Cook left Hawaii to continue his search for the Northwest Passage, taking his two ships far above the Arctic Circle. As winter again approached, Cook returned to Hawaii, sighting Maui in November. For two months, the *Discovery* and *Resolution* charted the islands, first Maui then the Big Island. Coming around the Big Island's southern tip from the east, Cook anchored along the Kona coast in a bay called Kealakekua, the "pathway of the god." It was exactly one year since his first landfall in Kàuai.

LEFT: the British navigator James Cook. **RIGHT:** Cook receives a special offering at his Kealakekua welcome.

If Cook was impressed a year earlier by the way Hawaiians on Kauai had prostrated themselves in his presence, he must have been even more impressed by his reception at Kealakekua Bay; Cook's second coming was monumental. He arrived at a propitious time: the *makahiki* celebration, an annual tribute to the god Lonoikamakahiki – and Cook's auspicious arrival was identified by the Hawaiians as Lono's return. Consequently, Cook was afforded the greatest welcome ever accorded a mortal in Hawaii.

One of Cook's lieutenants estimated that 10,000 Hawaiians turned out in canoes, on surfboards, swimming in the bay, and waiting on shore to greet the return of Lono. Cook wrote, "I have nowhere in this sea seen such a number of people assembled in one place; besides those in the canoes, all the shore of the bay was covered with people, and hundreds were swimming about the ship like shoals of fish." John Ledyard, an American adventurer who had signed on board the *Resolution* as corporal of the marines, reported later that two officers counted from 2,500 to 3,500 canoes afloat in Kealakekua's waters. Ledyard and others also described unusual white *kapa* (bark cloth) banners held aloft on crossbars – an ancient symbol of Lono – which resembled the ships' masts and sails. Ledyard

An OFFERING before CAP.ᵗ COOK, in the SANDWICH ISLANDS.

THE *HAOLE* ARRIVE

"The ship was first sighted from Waialua and Wai'anae (on Oahu) sailing for the north. It anchored at night at Waimea, on the island of Kauai, that particular place being nearest at hand. A man named Moapu and his companions who were fishing with heavy lines saw this strange thing move by and saw the lights... they hurried ashore and hastened to tell Ka'eo and the other chiefs of Kauai about this strange apparition.

"The next morning the ship lay outside Ka'ahe at Waimea. Chiefs and commoners saw the wonderful sight and marveled at it. Some were terrified and shrieked with fear. The valley of Waimea rang with the shouts of the excited people as they saw the boat with its masts and sails shaped like a gigantic stingray. One asked another, 'What are those branching things?' and the other answered, 'They are trees moving on the sea.' A certain *kahuna* named Kuohu declared, 'That can be nothing else than the *heiau* of Lono, the tower of Keolewa, and the place of sacrifice at the altar.' The excitement became more intense..."

– Samuel M. Kamakau
19th-century Hawaiian author and historian

wrote that when Cook went onshore, the masses of Hawaiians "all bowed and covered their faces with their hands until he was passed."

There were extravagant ceremonies held in Cook's honor, including one at a sacred temple, or *heiau*. Cook and his men tried their best to please the Hawaiians with tours of their ships, a flute and violin concert, and a fireworks display. All the while, Cook readied his ships for a voyage to Asia, and after two weeks, they set sail. But three days later, just off the Big Island's north shore, a fierce winter storm damaged the *Resolution*'s foremast. Cook returned to Kealakekua to make essential repairs.

Death of Cook

Cook now found that the *makahiki* festival at Kealakekua was finished, and because of a *kapu* put on Kealakekua Bay by King Kalaniopu'u, the area was nearly deserted. Those Hawaiians who remained were not as generous in their tribute, and in fact were surprised that a god's property could be badly damaged within his own domain.

The Hawaiians grew increasingly bold, taking objects from the ships that pleased their fancy, particularly items made of metal. When they seized the *Discovery*'s cutter, Cook went ashore with nine marines to take Kalaniopu'u hostage in exchange for return of the boat, a

strategy that had worked before on other Pacific islands. A violent scuffle broke out, and a large party of more than 200 Hawaiian warriors attacked Cook's landing party. Five of the marines escaped, but four others, as well as Cook himself, died. The British ships fired on the Hawaiians, who retreated.

Two delegations of concerned Hawaiians later returned parts of Cook's body "cut to pieces and all burnt," wrote James King, Cook's second lieutenant. One bundle of Cook's bones, wrapped in fine *kapa* and a cloak made of black and white feathers, included "the captain's hands (which were well known from a remark-

WERE THE SPANISH FIRST?

Spanish ships may have landed in Hawaii up to two centuries before Cook. Historians point to unexplained artifacts, including a map taken by the British in 1742 from a captured Spanish galleon. The map was "a chart of the northern Pacific which marked the track of the round trip between the Philippines and Acapulco." It showed islands in approximately the same latitude as Hawaii. Additionally:

• The galleon trade between Mexico and Manila began in 1556, and lasted 200 years. Odds that a galleon would happen onto Hawaii, at the same latitude as Mexico City, are good.

• Early Western visitors reported island residents with distinctly Caucasian features.

• Hawaiian feather cloaks and helmets – not found elsewhere in Polynesia – with a Spanish look and usually of red and yellow, the royal colors of Spain, were found in Hawaii.

able cut), the scalp, the skull, wanting the lower jaw, thigh bones and arm bone; the hands only had flesh on them, and were cut in holes, and salt crammed in; the leg bones, lower jaw and feet, which were all that remained and had escaped the fire, he said were dispersed among other chiefs."

What remained of Cook was buried at Kealakekua Bay, and in late February of 1779, the *Discovery* and *Resolution* set sail, passing Maui, Molokai and Oahu before anchoring again briefly at Waimea, on Kauai. ❏

LEFT: the warrior's helmet appears Spanish in style.
RIGHT: this Spanish map may show Hawaii as Los Mojas.

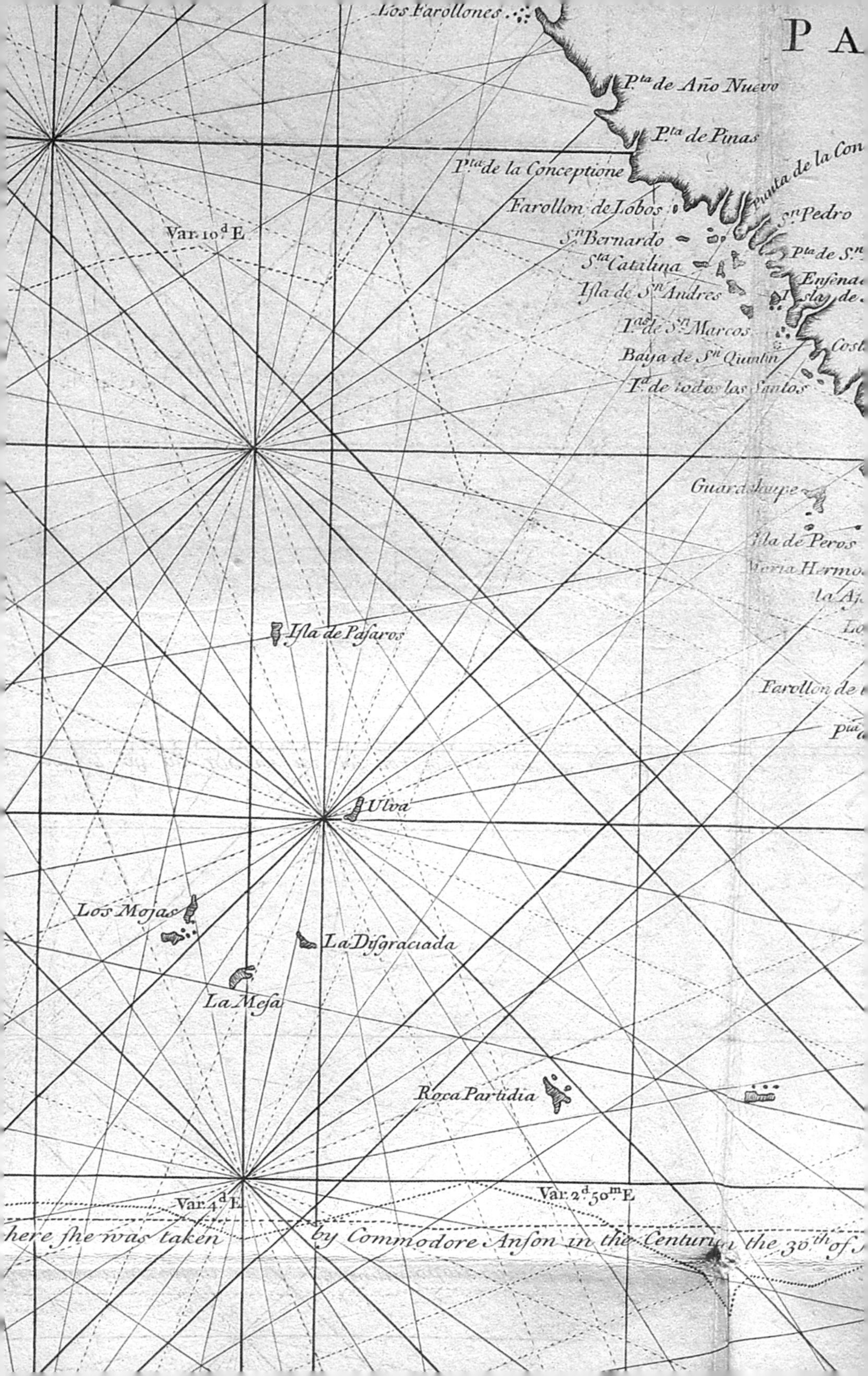

Los Farollones

PA

P.ta de Año Nuevo

P.ta de Pinas

P.ta de la Conceptione

Punta de la Con

Farollon de Lobos

Sn Pedro

Sn Bernardo

Pta de Sn.

Sta Catalina

Enfenad

Isla de Sn Andres

Isla de.

Var. 10d E

Ias de Sn Marcos

Costa

Baya de Sn Quintin

Ta de todos los Santos

Guadaloupe

Isla de Peros

Maria Hermo

la Aj

Lo

Isla de Pajaros

Farollon de

Piu

Ulva

Los Mojas

La Disgraciada

La Mesa

Roca Partida

Var. 4d E

Var. 2d 50m E

here she was taken

by Commodore Anson in the Centurion the 30th of

Louvergne del

SCÈNE DE DANSE

SOUVENIR.

ALOHA OE

(My love to you.)

MARCH.

The Queen Kapiolani.

The Princess Liliuokalani.

Composed and arranged by

J. THOMAS BALDWIN.

Incorporating the popular Song "Aloha Oe"

BY THE

Princess Liliuokalani

And performed by

BALDWIN'S BOSTON CADET BAND

AT THE

Grand Reception given by the City of Boston to

Queen Kapiolani and Princess Liliuokalani

May 12th 1887.

THE HAWAIIAN MONARCHY

The monarchy of Hawaii began with Kamehameha the Great, who united the Hawaiian islands. It ended with the overthrow of Queen Lili'uokalani

It would be over five years after Cook's death before other Europeans visited Hawaii. In 1785, a China-bound trading ship stopped for supplies, and in the following year, four ships from England and France visited the islands. They were followed by Russian, Spanish and American ships. Soon frigates, sloops and schooners laden with American furs began dropping anchor in Hawaii. Most were bound for Macau, Shanghai, and Guangzhou (Canton), where the furs would be traded for silks and tea.

Kamehameha I (1795–1819)

Often mentioned in the logs and diaries of visiting ships' captains and merchants was Kamehameha, which means "the lonely one." A distinguished warrior and one of King Kalaniopu'u's nephews and subordinate chiefs, Kamehameha (pron. *ka may-ha may-ha*) had impressed Cook at Kealakekua Bay. Cook's lieutenant, James King, wrote that Kamehameha's hair "was now plaisted over with a brown dirty sort of paste or powder, and which added to as savage a looking face as I ever saw, it however by no means seemed an emblem of his disposition, which was good natured and humorous, although his manner showed somewhat of an overbearing spirit, and he seemed to be the principal director in this interview."

Kamehameha was a careful observer of the *haole* (Caucasians). He had been wounded by a gun on the beach when Cook was killed, and it was evident to Kamehameha that one man with a small brass cannon could have a great advantage over several warriors with clubs and spears. By 1789, Kamehameha's own large double canoe was carrying a swivel gun mounted on a platform strapped across the hulls.

A 10-year civil war involving Kamehameha and others erupted on the Big Island in 1782. When the timing seemed astrologically and mil-

itarily propitious, Kamehameha conquered Maui and Lanai in 1790. He then returned to the Big Island to deal with the continuing civil war there, only to lose Maui almost immediately. Maui's own chief then invaded Kamehameha's Big Island domain in turn, with a fleet of war canoes. Kamehameha repelled the Maui

invaders, assisted by the swivel guns and military expertise of Englishmen John Young and Isaac Davis, who had been taken in by Kamehameha as advisers and later made high chiefs. Keoua, Kamehameha's chief Big Island rival, however, was not yielding easily.

Kamehameha took no chances. He built the immense Pu'u Kohala *heiau* (temple) to his war god near Kawaihae in Kohala – it still stands – and invited Keoua to meet him there. When he arrived, Kamehameha had him killed. Kamehameha was now king of the entire Big Island. He recaptured Maui, then Molokai. In the meantime, civil war had erupted on Oahu, and Kamehameha took advantage of the disorder to land

PRECEDING PAGES: French seamen enjoy an Oahu hula. **LEFT:** Princess Lili'uokalani, Hawaii's last queen, was a celebrated composer. **RIGHT:** Kamehameha the Great, looking uncomfortably dressed.

his fleet there, at the foot of Diamond Head in 1795. In a display of military strength, his warriors drove Oahu's defenders into Nu'uanu Valley and over the edge of Nu'uanu Pali, a precipitous cliff. With Oahu's conquest, and the ritual sacrifice of its king, Kalanikupule, to Kamehameha's war god, Kamehameha became monarch of all of Hawaii, except Kauai and Ni'ihau, more than 70 miles (110 km) west of Oahu.

In both 1796 and 1809, Kamehameha assembled invasion fleets destined for Kauai and Ni'ihau, the most distant of the main islands. The channel from Oahu to Kauai is treacherous, and the invasion attempts were foiled by the weather

Honu – the Eye of the Turtle – in what is now Kailua-Kona town on the Big Island. He was about 63 years old. So that nobody could defile them or use their powerful *mana* (spirit), Kamehameha's bones were hidden in a still-secret location somewhere on the Kona coast.

Kamehameha II (1819–24)

Kamehameha's son and successor, Liholiho, was not a strong and commanding ruler like his father. But Ka'ahumanu, the favorite of Kamehameha the Great's many wives, was intelligent, fearless, and powerful. Upon Kamehameha's death, she made it clear to Liholiho that it was

and disease. In 1810, however, Kauai's king peacefully yielded to Kamehameha. The islands thus finally became united under a single ruler, Kamehameha the Great.

Although Kamehameha retained the traditional ways, he also learned from the Europeans whose ships he supplied with provisions. Hawaii's sandalwood proved a lucrative trade for Kamehameha, and he directed commoners by the thousands to harvest it for shipment to Asia. Exports continued until there were no more sandalwood trees in the islands. In the meantime, agriculture suffered from neglect.

Kamehameha the Great died after a long illness in 1819, at his royal compound Kamaka

CIVILIZED MISSIONARIES

Rev. Hiram Bingham, unofficial leader of the first group of Christian missionaries to Hawaii, wrote of his followers' impressions: "The appearance of destitution, degradation, and barbarism among the chattering, and almost naked savages, whose heads and feet, and much of their sunburnt skins were bare, was appalling. Some of our number, with gushing tears, turned away from the spectacle. Others, with firmer nerve, continued their gaze, but were ready to exclaim, 'Can these be human beings? Can such things be civilized?'"

his father's wish that she be the *kuhina nui*, the joint ruler or queen regent of Hawaii.

One of Ka'ahumanu's first actions was to abolish the ancient *kapu* system. Urged on by Ka'ahumanu, Liholiho sat down with his mother, Keopuolani, and Ka'ahumanu at a feast, violating the *kapu* that prohibited men and women from eating together. Ka'ahumanu and Liholiho then ordered that all the *heiau* and carved wooden idols be destroyed. The social and cultural shock to Hawaiians was enormous, leaving an overwhelming spiritual vacuum.

The vacuum didn't last long. The first party of 14 New England missionaries arrived in 1820 aboard the American brig *Thaddeus*, ready to fill the religious void. Had the timing of the *kapu* collapse and the arrival of Christian missionaries not been so coincidental, the history of Hawaii could have been very different.

Although Ka'ahumanu and Liholiho had reservations about these overdressed *haole*, they let the American missionaries preach at Kailua-Kona and Honolulu for a one-year trial. The missionaries never left, and their descendants garnered land and power.

The English had retained an interest in Hawaii since Cook's first contact, and in 1822 Liholiho received a gift from King George IV: a small schooner named the *Prince Regent*. Delighted, Liholiho left Hawaii the next year on a British whaling ship to visit King George and negotiate a treaty. Liholiho and his entourage were royally feted in London, but before he could meet with King George, he and his queen, Kamamalu, caught the measles and died. Liholiho designated his younger brother Kauikeaouli as his logical successor.

Kamehameha III (1825–54)

The early years of Kauikeaouli – Kamehameha III – would better be called the reign of Ka'ahumanu. Kauikeaouli was only 10 years old when his brother Liholiho died. As *kuhina nui*, Ka'ahumanu exerted a strong influence on both the boy king and the Hawaiian people, most of whom were still disoriented and adrift after the demise of the *kapu* system.

Half a year after Liholiho left on his ill-fated trip to England, Ka'ahumanu had announced a system of civil laws obviously based on the

LEFT: Queen Ka'ahumanu in an 1816 sketch.
RIGHT: Hawaii's first royal coat-of-arms.

Congregationalist missionaries' teachings. In fact, the Congregationalists had cultivated considerable spiritual and political influence over Ka'ahumanu, eventually converting her to Christianity. Ka'ahumanu became one of the Congregationalists' most enthusiastic converts. Another convert to Christianity was an *ali'i* peer, the Big Island high chiefess Kapi'olani.

In 1824, Kapi'olani (not to be confused with her niece and namesake, the future Queen Kapi'olani) hiked to the mouth of Halema'uma'u in the Kilauea caldera on the Big Island. There, at the edge of the fire goddess Pele's domain, Kapi'olani defiantly renounced her. She lived to

PRECURSOR OF HAWAII'S COAT OF ARMS
Prepared in London in 1843–44 at the order of Timothy Haalilio and the Reverend William Richards

tell the tale, and at the Hilo Congregationalist mission, 90 impressed Hawaiians instantly became new converts.

Encouraged by the royal support, missionaries built churches and schools throughout the islands. Even more, as "messengers of Jehovah," the missionaries used their court influence to veil Hawaiians with everything Puritan. Bare skin on women in any degree – much less nudity – was condemned, and women were draped in dresses mostly ill-suited to the tropics. The ancient and sacred *hula*, which combined dance and poetry, was outlawed as lewd and lascivious.

Equally high on the agenda was putting the Hawaiian language into romanized script. The missionaries' intent in doing so was evangelical, no doubt, but teaching Hawaiians to read and write gave them a new tool with which to communicate their own histories and thought. This was especially important as the missionaries had suppressed traditional storytelling methods like the *hula*.

When Ka'ahumanu died in 1832, Kamehameha III took full control of the government in a reign noted for a couple of frivolous early years of horseracing, gambling, drinking, and dancing. His half-sister, Kina'u, the *kuhina nui* successor to Ka'ahumanu, managed state matters during his bouts with the bottle. The

missionaries continued to consolidate power, accepting government appointments.

In the mid 1820s, just as the sandalwood trees had all but disappeared in the islands, whaling became Hawaii's major source of revenue, with Honolulu and Lahaina among the Pacific's most important ports. Whaling kept Hawaii's economy above water for over 30 years. At its peak in 1846, 429 ships were anchored in Maui's Lahaina Harbor.

The missionaries, of course, protested the extracurricular activities of sailors on liberty. One visiting preacher in the early 1840s complained that Lahaina had become "one of the breathing holes of hell... a sight to make a mis-

sionary weep." Attempts by the missionaries to quench liquor and prostitution were not well received, and the homes of several preachers in Lahaina were bombarded with cannon by angry sailors from aboard the safety of anchored ships.

Perhaps Kamehameha III's most significant act was an edict issued in 1848, which became known as the Great Mahele. Under subtle pressure from missionary advisers and businessmen, the king divided Hawaii's land ownership – previously the pleasure of the royalty – among the monarchy, government, and common people, thus allowing ordinary Hawaiians to own property for the first time.

Two years later, foreigners also were permitted land ownership. Within a few years, the *haole* had accumulated large estates; by 1886, about two-thirds of all government lands sold had been bought by resident *haole*. Hawaiians, unfamiliar with land ownership, had done little to thwart the foreigners' acquisitions.

By the late 1850s, whales had been hunted nearly to extinction, petroleum and coal were replacing whale oil, and the United States was sinking into a civil war. The boom days of the Hawaiian Islands were over.

Hawaii's business and political interests turned from whaling to a new commodity, sugar. During California's gold rush in 1849, a handful of small sugar planters in Hawaii had made great profits when Kaleponi – California – turned to Hawaii for its sugar supply. Sugar's potential looked sweet, especially for those with the land under the cane. Whereas whaling had been mostly a merchants' boom, sugar would be a land barons' boom. But sugar plantations are labor intensive, and the local pool of laborers was almost nil, as the population had been devastated by disease. More pragmatically, Hawaiians saw little appeal in the low-paying, backbreaking work of harvesting sugar-cane, especially as the islands offered plenty of traditional foods.

For sugar to become a major industry, thousands of laborers needed to be imported. The first group of 293 Chinese arrived in 1852, followed over the decades by Japanese, Portuguese, Filipinos, Norwegians, Germans, Koreans, Puerto Ricans, Spaniards, and Russians. A significant percentage of Hawaii's ethnic mix today descends from those early immigrant laborers.

The 30-year reign of Kamehameha III, the longest of any Hawaiian monarch, was one of considerable change and adjustment, and often stability and growth; foreign ways were also adopted. The king established a supreme court, an upper house of royalty and a lower house of elected representatives. Kamehameha III had no children and named a nephew, Alexander Liholiho, as his successor.

Kamehameha IV (1855–63)

Alexander Liholiho – the grandson of Kamehameha the Great – had a certain dislike for America, and during his short reign, he was to shift Hawaii closer to the

AMERICAN MEMORY

A train conductor in New York mistook the future Kamehameha IV for a servant and ordered him out of the railway car. That memory of America lingered long.

suffering from introduced European diseases.

In 1863, after the death of his son, Kamehameha IV died aged 29 during an asthma attack. Some Hawaiians said that he drank himself to death, while others claimed that he died of a broken heart.

Kamehameha V (1863–72)

A believer in the strong, autocratic style of Kamehameha the Great, Lot Kamehameha, an elder brother of Kamehameha IV, refused to take an oath to

British Empire both in spirit and in policy. Educated by Americans at an elite royal school, Kamehameha IV and a brother had visited Europe and America in 1849 and 1850. Their experiences in Europe, especially England, were enjoyable and enriching, but not so in America.

Alexander Liholiho was not a mover and shaker, but he is remembered for his concern for Hawaiians. One surviving legacy is the Queen's Medical Center, established by him and his wife, Queen Emma, in 1859 to care for sick and destitute Hawaiians, many of whom were still

---

LEFT: a view of old Lahaina, on Maui, around 1870.
ABOVE: Kamehameha IV and Kamehameha V.

uphold the liberal constitution of 1852. He believed that it weakened the powers of the Hawaiian monarchy, making it vulnerable to overthrow by non-royalists, a forethought that later turned out to be true.

In 1864, Lot Kamehameha declared a special convention to revise the constitution. This convention accomplished nothing, so the king then offered a new constitution that abolished the matriarchal office of *kuhina nui*, set up a one-chamber legislature for nobles and elected representatives, and decreed that persons born after 1840 be required to pass literacy tests and meet certain property qualifications before being allowed to vote or serve in the legislature. His act was in effect a bloodless but effective coup d'état. This strengthening of the monarchy led to increasing resentment among non-royalists – mostly foreign businessmen – and added fuel to the fire that would later bring down the monarchy.

Mark Twain wrote of Kamehameha V: "There was no trivial royal nonsense about him. He dressed plainly, poked about Honolulu, night or day, on his old horse, unattended; he was popular, greatly respected, even beloved."

A bachelor, Lot left no heir and named no

successor. When he died at the age of 42, the 77-year-long dynasty of Kamehameha the Great at last ended.

William Lunalilo (1873–74)

Under the constitution of 1864, the legislative assembly unanimously elected Prince Lunalilo as king in 1873. It was a popular decision with the Hawaiians, who had already voted for him a week before. As popular as Lunalilo – or Prince Bill – was with the people, he was an alcoholic and ineffective in leadership. Thirteen months later he died without an heir. The kingdom's legislative assembly once again went about the sticky business of electing a new sovereign.

> **ROYAL RUMBLE**
>
> Queen Emma's backers protested at Kalakaua's selection, and a free-for-all fight took place inside and outside the courthouse.

Kalakaua (1874–91)

There were two contenders for the throne: David Kalakaua, who had lost to Lunalilo in the previous election, and Queen Emma, widow of Kamehameha IV. After a spirited campaign, the assembly handily elected Kalakaua as king of Hawaii in 1874. Kalakaua's ancestors had been high chiefs on the Big Island.

Ruling with a flourish and style that earned him the nickname "the Merrie Monarch," Kalakaua ignored the calls for annexation by the US and devoted his energy to fashioning his kingship in the courtly tradition of European monarchs. He built himself the magnificent 'Iolani Palace; became the first monarch to circumnavigate the globe; and presented gala horse races, grand balls, and old-style Hawaiian feasts. During his reign, Kalakaua openly clashed with educators and Christians about restoring Hawaii's rapidly disappearing cultural traditions.

In 1874, the same year he ascended the throne, Kalakaua traveled to Washington, DC, hoping to negotiate a reciprocity treaty with the US. He and his entourage were grandly received by President Ulysses S. Grant and a joint session of Congress. Newspaper reporters described the state banquets arranged for Kalakaua as the most lavish ever seen in the nation's capital. Kalakaua subsequently received strong personal support from Grant.

By the following year, the US Senate approved a treaty giving Hawaii "favored nation" duty concessions and thus eliminating tariffs on sugar. While the treaty was a triumph for the new king, it also gave America a lock on the islands, presaging its future interest in Pearl Harbor as a military base, and preventing Kalakaua from using Hawaii's location to gain concessions from Britain or France.

Perhaps most importantly for Hawaii's immediate future, the treaty gave the sugar-growers increased economic confidence and security. And, as would later become clear, the agreement gave the growers disproportionate political and social leverage, eventually weakening the Hawaiian monarchy's power.

A string of scandals began to taint Kalakaua's reign, much to the self-righteous delight of the foreign business community. In 1887, an armed insurrection led by a *haole* political group called the Hawaiian League forced Kalakaua to accept a new so-called "Bayonet Constitution" that seriously constrained his powers. This new constitution required that voters own at least $3,000-worth of property or have an income of at least $600 a year, requirements that effectively eliminated most Hawaiians from the political franchise. Power conclusively shifted to Hawaii's land-owning and predominantly white minority.

Two years later, a fiery part-Hawaiian revolutionary named Robert Wilcox staged a counter coup against the businessmen. He and about 150 armed followers loyal to the kingdom swash-

they didn't agree with his dubious money-raising schemes, usually concocted by Spreckels.

In 1891, while visiting California in an effort to restore his failing health, Kalakaua died in a San Francisco hotel suite. Before leaving Hawaii, Kalakaua had appointed his sister, Princess Lydia Kamakaeha Lili'uokalani, heir to the throne, as regent during his absence. She became Hawaii's first and only reigning queen.

Lili'uokalani (1891–93)

Lili'uokalani was a staunch royalist. Right from the start, she made it clear that she planned to restore monarchical power and the rights of

buckled their way past the King's Guards and occupied 'Iolani Palace. But Wilcox's coup d'état failed miserably. Within hours, he and the other revolutionaries were flushed out with rifle fire and crude dynamite bombs laced with twenty-penny metal spikes. Seven of his men were dead and another 12 wounded.

For the remainder of his reign, Kalakaua was, for the most part, a figurehead monarch. Often at the service of the sugar baron and poker partner Claus Spreckels, who had arrived in Hawaii in 1876, Kalakaua dismissed cabinets when

LEFT: King Kalakaua, 'the Merrie Monarch,' and Hawaii's last king. ABOVE: US Marines from the *Boston*.

native Hawaiian people. Weary of the plodding cabinet government created by the Bayonet Constitution of 1887, she announced in 1893 that she would issue a new constitution placing power firmly back in the hands of the monarchy.

Pro-annexation, anti-royalist forces planned to overthrow the monarchy, to be followed by annexation negotiations with the United States. In January 1893, they launched their revolt after first enlisting John B. Stevens, the US minister in Hawaii. An ardent supporter of the pro-annexation movement, Stevens ordered the landing of Marines from the visiting gunship USS *Boston*, ostensibly to protect American lives and property – but without authorization from

Washington. That afternoon, some 160 armed Marines positioned artillery pieces and Gatling guns at strategic points in Honolulu, and by the next day, "without the drawing of a sword or the firing of a shot," a self-proclaimed government led by Sanford Dole was in power. Lili'uokalani had no choice but to abdicate her throne.

She believed that the American government, learning of the coup, would reinstate the monarchy. "I yield to the superior force of the United States of America," she protested to Sanford Dole, "to avoid any collision of armed forces and perhaps the loss of life. I do this under protest, and impelled by said force, yield my authority

until such time as the Government of the United States shall, upon the facts being presented to it, undo the action of its representatives and reinstate me in the authority which I claim as the constitutional sovereign of the Hawaiian Islands."

Unlike his predecessor, newly elected President Grover Cleveland did not support the coup, and he dispatched a special investigator to Honolulu to investigate. The investigator arrived in Hawaii to find American flags flying above Hawaii's public buildings. He ordered the flags taken down and the Marines withdrawn. He reported to Cleveland that "a great wrong has been done to the Hawaiians." Cleveland sent a message to Congress stating that the unauthorized use of American troops in Hawaii was "an act of war against a peaceful nation." Congress, lobbied by the sugar interests, ignored Cleveland.

In 1894, the provisional government established itself as the Republic of Hawaii. Sanford Dole was named president. President Cleveland sent a representative to Hawaii seeking the reinstatement of Queen Lili'uokalani, but Dole and his cabinet refused to step down. Lili'uokalani and her supporters planned a counter-coup, to be led by the indefatigable Robert Wilcox. The government arrested the royalists, including Queen Lili'uokalani, for treason. The queen denied guilt, but bombs and arms were found in her Washington Place garden.

Lili'uokalani was placed under house arrest and a week later she gave up the throne. She was found guilty of misprision of treason and sentenced to five years of hard labor and fined $5,000. The penalties were never enforced, but she remained imprisoned at 'Iolani Palace until later that year.

Fully assimilated

In November 1897, Cleveland lost the US presidential election to William McKinley, and in 1898 McKinley signed annexation papers. Two years later, Hawaii was an American territory. Sanford Dole was its first territorial governor. Lili'uokalani and Dole publicly reconciled in 1911 at the opening of the Pearl Harbor naval base. In 1917, during World War I, Hawaii's last monarch raised the American flag over Washington Place for the very first time. Seven months later, she died at the age of 79. ❑

HISTORICAL HINDSIGHT

Hawaii is ours. As I look back upon… this miserable business and as I contemplate the means used to complete the outrage, I am ashamed of the whole affair.
President Grover Cleveland, in his memoirs

Overawed by the power of the United States… the people of the Islands have no voice in determining their future, but are virtually relegated to the condition of the aboriginals of the American continent.
Queen Lili'uokalani, in her memoirs

LEFT: Queen Lili'uokalani, 1893. **RIGHT:** an 1897 German cartoon satirizes Hawaii's marriage to Uncle Sam.

What Fools these Mortals be!

PUCK BUILDING, Ecke Houston & Mulberry St.
Entered at N. Y. P. O. as Second-class Mail Matter.

Wieder eine Zwangsheirath, durch die keine der beiden Parteien besondere Freude erleben dürfte.

HAWAII
BY CLIPPER
PAN AMERICAN WORLD AIRWAYS
The System of the Flying Clippers

MODERN HAWAII

First it was sugar that defined Hawaii's economy. Pineapples came along and helped out, as did the military. Now, tourism is the state's financial anchor

At the start of the 20th century, it looked as though the schemes of the business and land barons had finally come to pass. Sugar was soon joined by a new commodity, pineapples, when James Dole (a relative of Sanford Dole) began marketing Hawaii-grown pineapples successfully on the US mainland. Hawaii would soon become the world's major supplier of the fruit.

The tenacious effort of anti-royalists, businessmen, landowners, and sugar barons to bring Hawaii under the umbrella of the United States was finally consummated two years after annexation, when President William McKinley made Hawaii an American territory in 1900.

Territorial status certainly sealed the future of the monarchy. There would be no return. The territory's governor and judges were now appointed by the American president. The governor, in turn, appointed local administrators.

The rise of sugar

With Sanford Dole leading the territorial government, just about all of the new territory's banking, commerce, and transportation remained under the continuing control of five large *haole* corporations built largely on sugar: Castle and Cooke, Alexander and Baldwin, C. Brewer, Theo. H. Davies, and American Factors (now called Amfac). By intention and default, the so-called "Big Five" controlled Hawaii's politics and government.

Sugar's future remained of paramount importance. Because it was now part of the US, Hawaii was classified a domestic producer and thus no longer subject to import tariffs. Greater profits could be anticipated, and the plantations could grow. But expansion of the sugar plantations required yet more labor. Since Hawaii had no large pool of ready local labor workers had to be imported.

PRECEDING PAGES: city view from Punchbowl Crater. **LEFT:** fly to Hawaii, a vintage travel poster from the 1940s. **RIGHT:** a US representative accepts the territory of Hawaii from President Sanford Dole.

Before, as an independent kingdom and republic, there had been no restrictions on immigration to Hawaii, and so the sugar barons had brought in tens of thousands of workers from Asia, first from China and then from Japan. Later, workers came from Portugal, Puerto Rico, Korea, and the Philippines. But now, as an American territory,

immigration quotas were determined in Washington. Immigration from Asia was curtailed. With their traditional labor sources evaporating, Hawaii's sugar plantations were nevertheless in luck with a new source: the Philippines, under the American flag since 1898.

At this time, Hawaii was very much a Republican territory, governed by an entrenched oligarchy of businessmen intent on preserving their power. Hawaii was a place of well-defined social hierarchies. White men owned the plantations and held supervisory positions, while immigrant laborers ranked low. The first generation of immigrant laborers, indentured and mostly from Asia, buttressed this rigid plantation hierarchy.

The new Americans

As Hawaii swaggered into the 20th century, something happened that had not been anticipated at all. Those first-generation Chinese, Japanese, and Filipinos who had worked hard and quietly on the plantations decided to stay in Hawaii after their labor contracts ended. They had children, and these plantation babies were by birth American citizens. Unlike their parents, they were not foreigners, nor were they newcomers, nor strangers in a strange land. Hawaii was their home.

As this second generation of Asian immigrants grew up, the power of the Big Five corporations, aircraft. Five years later, the new airline began regular inter-island mail routes. The first flight between Hawaii and another destination beyond the chain had almost been completed four years earlier when a US Navy seaplane coming from California ran out of fuel 300 miles (480 km) from Hawaii. Just two years later, the first civilian flight to reach the islands similarly ran out of fuel, and crashed into a mesquite tree on Molokai.

A more reliable air connection with the US mainland was established on an April morning in 1935, when a 19-ton Pan Am Clipper landed at the fleet air base in Pearl Harbor, completing

Hawaiian Pineapples. District of Wahiawa, Island of Oahu.

Republican politicians, and missionary landowners was challenged, their footing further undermined by an economic depression that boosted the confidence of labor movements. By pushing Hawaii to become a territory, and by admitting thousands of immigrants, the ruling powers had been hoisted with their own petard.

In 1935, 10 years after a violent strike by cane laborers in Hanapepe, Kauai, left many Filipino workers dead, legislation passed by the US Congress made it legal for workers to organize into unions and engage in collective bargaining.

Air transport between islands arrived in 1929, when Inter-Island Airways, now Hawaiian Airlines, connected the islands with amphibious an "exploratory" flight from San Francisco that took 19 hours and 48 minutes.

Seven months later, a second Pan Am aircraft touched down with a cargo of mail, then continued an island-hopping route to Manila, creating the first Pacific air connection between North America and Asia. Less than a year later, the *Hawaii Clipper* skimmed across Pearl Harbor's waters with a cargo of seven paying passengers – a new kind of tourist with money to spend.

World War II

Early on Sunday morning, December 7, 1941, two waves of Japanese aircraft – 360 planes in all – dropped below cloud cover and attacked every major military installation on Oahu. The surprise attack devastated the US Pacific fleet: 2,323 Americans were killed while Japanese casualties numbered fewer than 100. Most of the ships in the harbor were severely damaged if not sunk. Some 68 Oahu residents were killed or injured. Japanese submarines sank cargo and passenger vessels in local waters. They also surfaced to shell Hilo, Nawiliwili, and Kahului harbors.

JAPAN EXPANDS

Japan had been expanding its control in Asia. Now the Pacific was next, including Pearl Harbor, home of the US Pacific fleet since 1908.

The same day as the attack on Oahu, President Franklin Roosevelt declared war on Japan. Later

national security. (Americans of German and Italian ancestry were, in contrast, left alone.)

In Hawaii, the *nisei* were far too prominent to be confined, not only because they were a majority percentage of Hawaii's population, but also because they were a major thread in Hawaii's social and cultural fabric.

Eventually, AJAS of military age were permitted to enlist in the army. A volunteer group from Hawaii was assembled into a single unit called the 100th Infantry Battalion, later expanded into the

in the morning, Hawaii was placed under martial law. The state remained under martial law until 1944, during which time military courts completely replaced all civilian jurisdiction in Hawaii. The US Supreme Court ruled after the war that this was an unconstitutional move.

At the beginning of the war, the largest ethnic group in Hawaii were the *nisei*, of Japanese ancestry. On the mainland, Americans of Japanese ancestry (AJA) were confined in desert internment camps, a policy that was entirely racial and not substantiated by claims of

---

LEFT: pineapples and plantation workers, 1910.
ABOVE: an American destroyer explodes, Pearl Harbor.

442nd Regimental Combat Team with over 1,000 volunteers. Not trusted to fight soldiers of their ancestral homeland (Americans of German or Italian descent faced no such restrictions), the Japanese-American soldiers were shipped to Europe. Suspicions about loyalty vanished when the 442nd became the most decorated American unit in World War II. Returning home to Hawaii, many AJAS used veterans' benefits to pay for college, turning later to law and politics and becoming the core of another shift in Hawaii's structure.

After the war, a succession of workers' strikes established unions among Hawaii's major political and economic forces. They solidified their power in 1952 with a six-month work freeze on Hawaii's docks that nearly devastated the territory's economy, which was almost completely dependent on shipping. Hawaii's business and political *ancien régime*, however, were sore and sour losers, accusing the unions of being part of the Marxist plague. However, the Republican Party, which had been entrenched since well before anyone alive could remember, was knocked out of power in 1954 by a decidedly different incoming group of territorial legislators – half of

PARANOID PINEAPPLES

In the 1950s, Hawaii's activist unions were accused of being revolutionary tools of an unproven Communist conspiracy.

Statehood would be necessary to sustain Hawaii as a leading sugar producer. The Big Five and other interests pushed for statehood and eventually overcame Congressional reluctance. It has been suggested that southern congressmen were against admitting Hawaii as a state dominated by – for heaven's sake – non-Caucasians.

A deal was finally struck linking Hawaii and Alaska for statehood, and in 1959 Hawaii became the 50th American state. Statehood was ratified by Hawaii's voters by 17

whom were AJAS – and who were supported by the now-powerful labor unions.

Statehood push

Between 1903 and 1957, 22 bills addressing statehood for Hawaii failed Congressional votes in Washington. Unlike mainland areas annexed as territories, there had been no provisions in Hawaii's territorial legislation for eventual statehood. And in any case, territorial status had suited the sugar interests just fine.

But in 1934, Congress had given Hawaii's sugar barons a kick in the *'okole* (buttocks) by grouping Hawaii along with foreign producers of sugar. Exports to the mainland plummeted.

to 1. Only the precinct of Ni'ihau, the privately owned island off Kauai, peopled by native Hawaiians, voted against it. In most elections, Ni'ihau's people voted against the Democratic Party leanings of the rest of the state.

Until this time, Hawaii had rarely been thought about by mainland America. It was, after all, a long, expensive boat journey away. Statehood was one of those historical pivots, like Cook's visit and the overthrow of Lili-'uokalani, that irrevocably changed Hawaii's destiny and direction.

At the time of statehood, the tallest building in Hawaii was the 10-story-high Aloha Tower, and Waikiki was peppered here and there with just a few hotels. Defense and agriculture, primarily sugar and pineapples, were Hawaii's two main sources of revenue.

That same year, a regular commercial jet service was inaugurated by Qantas between Australia, Hawaii, and San Francisco, cutting travel time to California from nine propeller hours to less than five hours by jet. A few months later Pan Am connected Honolulu with the Pacific Coast and Tokyo, Japan.

The commercial jet's ability to maintain a constant turnover of visitors made mass tourism a very promising enterprise. The jets brought an increasing numbers of visitors, and the once-

landers and businesses arrived. Some peripheral neighborhoods expanded in population by up to 600 percent. And in the areas where it couldn't spread out, Honolulu shot up in wall to wall office buildings and high-rise condos. Small, quiet rural towns – Kailua, Kane'ohe, Mililani, Hawaii Kai, Makakilo – turned into bedroom communities for Honolulu-bound commuters.

In the early 1980s, tourism overtook government and military spending in economic importance. Agriculture slipped to a distant third. Some of the lost agricultural revenues were replaced by the exponential growth of *pakalolo*, or marijuana, cultivation, which illegally flour-

stately, low-rise Waikiki hotels soon found themselves surrounded, and dwarfed, by bigger and taller hotels.

In the neighboring islands, too, agricultural land was converted into resort developments, especially on Maui and Kauai. On the Big Island, vacation resorts were built on barren lava. Former sugar-plantation workers became hotel employees.

Hawaii's urban center since the end of whaling, Honolulu simply exploded as new main-

LEFT: a Honolulu newspaper announces statehood.
ABOVE: a trip to Kong Mountain which plays a starring role in Hollywood blockbuster, *Raiders of the Lost Ark.*

ished in Hawaii's forests, sugar-cane fields and backyards. Since then, an aggressive eradication effort, involving aerial herbicide spraying, has cut production substantially.

Yen for money

In the 1980s, Hawaii's tourism entered a period of unparalleled expansion, fueled in part by the triumph of plastic money over cash. Additionally, an influx of Asian capital, mostly from the over-heating Japanese economy, prompted a building boom that extended beyond Waikiki to the Neighbor Islands. Huge "fantasy resorts," developed to suit upscale tastes, became the new paradigm. Designed to keep visitors and therefore money on the property, the resorts themselves, not Hawaii, became the destination.

By the late 1980s, Japanese investors had injected $15 billion into Hawaii's economy. The Japanese bought heavily into hotels and resorts, acquiring 30 percent of all hotel rooms in Hawaii, and 70 percent of those that cost over $100 a day. There was some backlash against such a concentration of foreign ownership. But the Japanese kept the hotels under American management – thus successfully deflecting the worries of labor unions and local residents – and spent tens of millions of dollars to upgrade tired hotel properties. Throughout the islands, hotel standards increased.

Japan's stock markets and real estate markets crashed. The subsequent downturn in Hawaii saw property values plummet, thereby aggravating economic instability.

Land issues

The one common denominator of human history in Hawaii is the acquisition of land. The Tahitians took the land from the Marquesans. The Hawaiian kings took it from one another until only one had it all, although more in an administrative sense than as owned property. Land was a communal asset distributed by a hierarchy of chiefs, with taxes paid largely in

While immense profits were made in the 1980s by some Hawaii residents with upscale property to sell, many others were pushed out of their homes and neighborhoods where families had lived for generations. When low-income retired people started being evicted from apartments they had rented for years, Hawaii's welcome of the yen wavered.

Frank Fasi, then mayor of Honolulu, even journeyed to Tokyo to reprimand the Japanese, declaring "I don't want Honolulu to become a suburb of Tokyo."

The infusion of yen into Hawaii finally skidded to a halt in the early 1990s, when the over-leveraged Japanese investors lost their shirts as

produce. It was only after the Great Mahele introduced the concept of private property in 1848 that this changed. The missionaries and sugar barons then took it from the Hawaiians, and now everybody wants to take it from everyone else – or at least own some of it.

About half of Hawaii is owned by the state, county, and federal governments. Of the remaining land, three quarters is owned by a collection of less than 40 owners, mainly descended from the early Protestant missionary families with names like Bishop, Campbell, and Wilcox. These private landowners collectively own 60 percent of Molokai, and 40 to 50 percent of Oahu, Maui, the Big Island, and Kauai.

Nearly all of Lanai and Ni'ihau are privately owned by single families. Land ownership in Hawaii involves both "fee simple" purchase, whereby the land is included in a real-estate transaction, and leasehold, in which the land is held for a set period of time, generally ranging from 20 to 50 years. Many of Hawaii's larger hotels have been built on leased land, particularly those in Waikiki.

NO *KAPU* ON BEACHES

All of Hawaii's shoreline up to the high-tide mark is public property and must be accessible to the public.

Through the 1970s many private homes and condominiums were also built on leased land, although since that time, the land beneath most

Hawaiian sovereignty

In 1993, the land issue came to the forefront during a four-day centennial remembrance of Queen Lili'uokalani's overthrow. With 'Iolani Palace covered in black bunting, it was certainly not a time of celebration and festivities. Then Governor John Waihe'e, the state's very first governor of Hawaiian ancestry, issued executive orders that only the Hawaiian flag, not the American one, should fly over state office buildings during the four days of remembrance.

of these homes and apartment buildings has been sold to homeowners and converted to fee simple ownership.

The heady swirl of money and resort development during the 1980s rekindled concerns about the land, and about Hawaii's priorities. The state's over-heated real-estate market peaked in the early 1990s and then stagnated, along with the state's economy. The question of land, unfortunately but perhaps inevitably, has the potential to polarize and divide ethnic interests in the islands.

LEFT: students display the Hawaiian flag in solidarity.
ABOVE: agricultural land is diminishing in the islands.

There is no dispute that the overthrow of Queen Lili'uokalani was illegal under international law. In fact, the sovereignty of the islands had earlier been recognized by both the United States and the European powers. The immediate events of the overthrow were orchestrated by local businessmen and a representative of the United States whose actions, which included the dispatch of American troops from a visiting ship to sustain the coup, were taken without the authorization of the American president. This was sustained by congressional inaction.

On the centennial of the overthrow of the Hawaiian monarchy in November 1993, the then President Bill Clinton formally apologized on behalf of the US government for its role in the 1893 coup in Hawaii. The joint Congressional resolution that he signed also acknowledged the illegitimacy of the 1898 annexation.

The centennial of the overthrow offered a platform for the numerous Hawaiian sovereignty groups who were seeking a redress of the islands' annexation. Some of the groups wanted control over certain Hawaiian lands. Others advocated complete secession from the United States.

Sponsored by Senator Daniel Akaka (of Native Hawaiian blood) a bill before the US

Congress would provide "tribal status" to Native Hawaiians in their dealings with the US. It drew a mixed reaction in the Native Hawaiian community. Some fear it jeopardizes future efforts at autonomy, while others consider it a crucial step forward. At stake is the right to administer benefits from vast land holdings and trust funds set up to benefit the Native Hawaiian community by both State and Federal governments. With billions of dollars in assets, the Hawaiian community offers widely differing perspectives and ideologies as to what would best suit their needs and protect their rights.

For the moment, progress towards any form of Hawaiian sovereignty seems to be faltering.

Everyone agrees that the future of the 'aina, or land, is the crucial issue, but few of the many different factions can find much common ground, while, just as it did a century ago, the Republican federal government has shown far less sympathy to the cause than did its Democratic predecessors.

The resurgence of tourism

In 2002, former Maui mayor Linda Lingle was elected as Hawaii's first Republican governor for 40 years, as well as the first-ever woman governor. Although Democrats continue to have overwhelming majorities in both chambers of the state legislature, Lingle was re-elected as governor in 2006 by the largest margin in Hawaiian history.

Lingle earned much of her reputation as a champion of tourism on Maui, helping to spearhead the apparent recovery of Hawaii's tourist industry from its 1990s downturn. However, visitor numbers were dealt a further body blow by the terrorist attacks of September 2001. For a nerve-wracking couple of years, American travelers in particular seemed reluctant to brave the long flight from the mainland. More recently, however, the figures have first matched and then exceeded previous record levels, and Hawaii for the moment seems to be booming once more. True, no new mega-resort hotels are being built on the Neighbor Islands these days, but those that already exist have consistently upgraded their facilities to remain at the very highest international standard.

Waikiki developments

Perhaps the most significant changes have been on Oahu, where Waikiki, which had fallen rather behind the times and become a little seedy, has determinedly set about re-branding itself as a classy, upscale destination. Modern tower-blocks are replacing the small-scale, family-run places that were the last remaining vestiges of the 1950s and 1960s, with the extravagant Trump International Hotel, at the heart of the Waikiki Beachwalk development, typifying the new era with its emphasis on luxury individually-owned condos. All its 464 units sold on the very first day they were made available, for a record-breaking $700 million. ❑

LEFT: members of Ka Lahui Hawaii are outspoken.
RIGHT: a jugglers' commune on the Big Island.

NATURAL HISTORY

Today, Hawaii appears to be the proverbial paradise with its diverse and lush flora and fauna. Ironically, most of what one sees has been recently introduced by humans

Many millions of years ago, lava from the fiery interior of the earth rumbled and surged, blasting through a jagged vent 15,000 ft (4,600 meters) below the ocean's surface. A fraction of an inch at a time – 2 to 3 inches (5 to 8 cm) a year – the Pacific Plate of the earth's crust crept northwest, rafting the volcano that had formed away from the hot spot and allowing a new sea mount to build under the water. A number of islands broke the ocean's surface, grew, then eroded away into atolls, while at the same time newer islands formed. Eons later, a line of subterranean mountains, some rising to 15,000 ft (4,600 meters) above sea level, stretched majestically in a row across 1,600 miles (2,500 km) of the Pacific Ocean, from the Big Island of Hawaii to Kure Atoll.

Over the centuries, floating seeds, fish, and marine larvae drifted to the islands on ocean currents. Winds carried fern spores, tiny seeds, and insects. Birds, sometimes full of fertile eggs or viable seeds, landed here, often propelled by storm winds. These isolated colonists adapted to suit their environment, making them unique, or endemic, to Hawaii. The process, scientists theorize, began more than 50 million years ago on what are now the atolls of the northwest islands of the Hawaiian archipelago.

Hawaii's shield volcanoes

Some 30 miles (50 km) southeast of the Big Island's southernmost point, far beneath the surface of the ocean, a new island – Lo'ihi – is forming over the hot spot in the earth's crust. Such eruptions, which begin on the ocean bottom, are the first stage in building Hawaii's broad shield volcanoes; the name derives from their supposed resemblance to the shields of ancient warriors, lying on the ground. Each volcano slowly grows as a thin layer of lava covers earlier layers. Underwater, lava hardens into pumice

---

PRECEDING PAGES: Haleakala volcano, Maui.
LEFT: waves probably carried the first forms of life to the Hawaiian islands.
RIGHT: a new fern leaf begins to unfold.

– light rocks full of gas bubbles – and pillow lava, or rock hummocks with rounded, smoother shapes.

Lo'ihi is predicted to jut from the ocean as a new sheer-sided, cliff-rimmed island some tens of thousands of years from now. Depending on the forces of nature – or on the whim of the

volcano goddess Pele – it may eventually connect with Hawaii above sea level, making the Big Island even bigger.

When seamounts break the ocean's surface, the lava erupts in fiery fountains, flowing from craters and rifts in the mountain's sides. Five such seamount volcanoes formed the island of Hawaii: Kilauea, Mauna Loa, Hualalai (all have been active within the past 200 years), Mauna Kea, and Kohala, the oldest volcano on the Big Island. Basaltic lava from ancient and more recent eruptions is the most common rock in the Hawaiian chain. A drive around the Volcano area and Ka'u reveals two types of hardened lava: *paho'eho'e* and *'a'a*. Both have the same chemical composition. *Paho'eho'e*, because it retains more gas, is hotter when it erupts, producing a fluid flow that hardens to smooth, ropy lava. *'A'a*, on the other hand, hardens to rough, chunky and sharp lava.

Eventually, the tops of the volcanoes collapse, creating wide depressions known as calderas. On the Big Island, Kilauea (which is currently erupting) and Mauna Loa both have calderas. When lava from these active volcanoes reaches the sea, you can witness the awesome process of island-making.

FOURTH IN AMERICA

Consisting of 132 islands, atolls, reefs, and shoals, Hawaii ranks fourth in the United States in coastline.

rocks break down and gradually turn into soil. Plants arrive, then animals. Eventually, humans take over. What was once just a hot spot on the ocean floor is now fertile, life-supporting land.

Like the creatures that populate them, islands become middle-aged, grow old, and die. This aging process is visible in the Hawaiian Island chain. After new islands form, coral reefs start growing at the edges, circling the island like underwater *lei* (garlands). As an island erodes and sinks towards the northwest with the shifting tectonic plate, the coral

Hot lava pouring into the ocean turns shore waters into churning cauldrons, giving rise to towers of steam and cloud build-up. Sulfur dioxide released by active calderas, combines with rain from these clouds, falling as dilute sulfuric acid. Chlorine gas freed from boiling sea water mixes with the sulfur, giving the area a chemical odor. It's a primordial scene not to be missed, but it can be dangerous.

The life cycle of an island

Once the volcano-building stops, other forces take over. Wind and sun eat away at the land, surf carves the coastlines, and rain cuts valleys and ridges into the new mountains. Volcanic

grows upward, searching for the sunshine so it can survive. Reefs growing on middle-aged islands like Maui, Molokai, Lanai, Oahu and Kauai are called fringing reefs. Hawaii's fringing reef is only now just beginning.

As the Pacific Plate continues to sink, lagoons tend to form between the reef and its island. These barrier reefs can be seen in some of the older Hawaiian islands of the northwest chain. Eventually, the island in the center vanishes underwater, creating an atoll – a coral reef enclosing a lagoon. The coral reef rises above the ocean unevenly, forming numerous low islands in a circular shape. Kure, at the northwest end of the Hawaiian chain, is such an atoll.

Forces of erosion have turned gentle slopes similar to those found on Mauna Loa into breathtaking ridges like those of Kauai's Na Pali coast. The towering north shore cliffs of Molokai are the tallest ocean cliffs in the world, rising nearly 2,000 ft (600 meters) above the sea. Sandy beaches, rocky shores, and crater-shaped bays line other coastal areas throughout the state.

Climate

Ecosystems in Hawaii are many and varied, depending not only on the location of the islands on the earth's surface, but also on the topography of the land and the amount of wind, rain and sunshine in each area.

Because Hawaii is in the sub-tropics, seasonal differences are slight. Temperatures are relatively stable, varying from an average of 80°F (25°C) around the coastal areas in winter months to 88°F (31°C) in the summer. At higher elevations, the difference increases. On the same latitude as Mexico City, Hong Kong, and Cairo, Hawaii's longest day is 13 hours and 20 minutes compared to Seattle's 16 hours; the shortest day in Honolulu is 10 hours and 50 minutes, while Seattle's is 8 hours and 20 minutes.

Rainfall in the islands is most sparse in leeward areas – central mountains drain the northeasterly trade winds – and atop the highest mountains of the Big Island. The average annual rainfall ranges from less than 10 inches (25 cm) to more than 430 inches (10 meters).

Weather develops as the tradewinds carrying clouds across the ocean ascend the mountains and the air is cooled. Condensation causes rainfall on the windward side of the mountain ranges, leaving little moisture to fall as the depleted winds pass over the leeward side of each island. The climates of the islands mimic climates of much larger continents, with tropical rainforests, grasslands, deserts, and even areas of tundra represented on a smaller scale.

Ecosystems of Hawaii

Narrow bands around each island where land and ocean meet are called coastal vegetation zones. Here, hundreds of plant and animal species live, each having adapted in its own way to this unique environment. There has been human settlement in coastal zones for so long

LEFT: lava fountain, Kilauea, Big Island. **RIGHT:** tourism has affected the ecology of Hanauma Bay.

that it is difficult to find a place that hasn't been altered by human activity.

However, even with so much human influence, researchers recognize 150 different plant communities in Hawaii, which are named according to elevation, moisture, and vegetation. Within each of these, the plants and animals interact with one another and their environment to form ecosystems. In some areas, preserves – rainforests or shifting sand dunes that might hide traces of former lives, the bones of extinct birds, or ancient Hawaiian burial grounds – have been set aside. In these ecosystems, native species are protected.

A wetland is one kind of ecosystem. The term wetland refers to areas where water dominates the environment and its plants and animals. Wetlands can contain salty, brackish (salt and fresh), or fresh water, and can be up to 6 ft (2 meters) deep. Anything deeper is a lake. Hawaii's bogs, estuaries, swamps, and streams contain and nurture unique scenery, plant life and bird life that's well worth checking out. Luckily, much of what remains undeveloped is preserved as parkland, as are Hawaii's remaining wetlands and mountainous interior. Land use issues are a hot item in today's Hawaii.

Forests contain dozens of ecosystems. Hawaii's forests are divided into dryland, medium-wet, and rainforests. Before humans came to Hawaii, dryland forests covered the leeward side of the larger islands and nearly all of Lanai and Kaho'olawe.

Ancient Hawaiians cleared much of this land for agriculture; later settlers finished the job. Today, dryland forests are rare. Researchers believe that in the past, the islands were wetter, with extensive dryland forests producing and holding moisture.

Medium-wet forests, growing between 2,000–9,000 ft (600–2,700 meters), have the largest number of native tree species of all ecosystems in Hawaii, even the rainforests, which grow in the

Plants and animals

The Hawaiian Islands began as barren lava rock, thousands of miles from the nearest land. Today the islands are lush with plants and teem with animal life; some of these are native, but most have been introduced by people.

Hawaii's native species are the plants and animals that managed to establish themselves without human interference. This colonizing of the islands was a slow process. If today's Hawaiian islands are between 1 million (Big Island) and 7 million years old (Kauai), then only one plant needed to establish itself every 15,000 years to account for today's mix of

elevation zone just above the medium-wet forests. Hawaii's rainforests receive at least 100 inches (254 cm) of rain per year. During the winter, clouds often engulf these forests, producing thick, cool mists. The two native trees seen most often in both types of forests are *koa* and *'ohi'a-lehua*, which support Hawaii's famous forest birds, the honeycreepers and their relatives.

Above the forests are alpine zones where few plants grow. Some desert-type plants like Hawaii's famous silverswords thrive in these high, dry, alpine areas, along with some insects. In some of these alpine areas, on the Big Island's Mauna Loa and Maui's Haleakala, for example, snow falls in winter.

native plants. The best places to see these plants and animals are in Hawaii's national parks, wildlife refuges, and the state's marine conservation districts, where all reef-life is protected from fishing.

Most marine life encountered is native, or endemic, except for several species of snappers, imported by the state from Tahiti in the 1950s as game fish. All sea turtles in Hawaii are native, and are endangered and protected by law. It is illegal to ride or chase these harmless creatures.

Hawaii's only native land mammal is the Hawaiian bat. Because of their night-time habits and secretive natures, bats are extremely difficult to find, even for researchers.

Native marine mammals include whales, dolphins, and monk seals. These are also protected by federal laws. With only about 1,250 of them left, Hawaiian monk seals are in extreme danger of extinction. If you see one resting on a beach, which is normal behavior for them, back off quietly and consider it a lucky day.

Only a few of the flowers and trees along Hawaii's highways are native. Seven kinds of hibiscus are native, but with 200 species of hibiscus in the world and more than 5,000 hybrids, the ones you see are often not Hawaii originals.

> ### NATIVE THEY'RE NOT
> Common plants like coconut palms, bananas, sugar-cane and breadfruit were actually early imports.

alive through such voyages was a tricky business, the immigrants managed to shuttle at least 27 kinds of plants and several kinds of animals – some wanted, some not – to Hawaii.

Even though this happened centuries ago, these species are considered alien because humans had a hand in their introduction. As a result, a few plants and animals that many might think of as native to Hawaii are actually aliens, introduced by those early settlers. Some common plants on this list are coconut palms, bananas, bamboo, ti, ginger,

Pandanus, also called screwpine or *hala*, are roadside native trees. *Koa* (popular for furniture) and *'ohi'a lehua* are native trees common to parks and preserves. Since many of their seeds float, beach plants are often native, including beach morning glories and beach *naupaka*, or thick green bushes with white flowers.

Introduced species

By AD 500, Polynesians had brought with them the plants and animals they needed to live in their new home. Although keeping these species

LEFT: the humpback whale winters in Hawaiian waters.
ABOVE: the extinct *'o'o*, and the once-endangered *nene*.

breadfruit, taro, sweet potatoes, yams, sugarcane, mountain apples, and bottle gourds.

Candlenut trees, called *kukui* in Hawaiian, were also introduced, but this is still Hawaii's official state tree, partially due to the fact that the nut had so many uses in early Hawaii. The meat could be burned for light or ground up for seasoning food. The nut itself was used for body adornment. *Kukui* products are still common: the oil from the nuts is used in cosmetics, and the nuts themselves are polished to make necklaces and bracelets. It's easy to spot the abundant *kukui* trees in a forest: their leaves, which look as if they've been dusted with flour, are very pale next to others.

Sugar-cane is another introduced Polynesian plant. Ancient Hawaiians used it as a sweetener, for food during famines, and as medicine. The leaves were used for hats and thatching. For decades, sugar-cane was Hawaii's leading crop. It is still grown today, although high labor costs and steady competition from other sweeteners have caused a dramatic and continuing decline in the industry. One acre (½ hectare) of land yields more than 11 tons (9,900 kg) of cane, giving Hawaii the highest yield per acre in the agricultural world. However, it is thought that by about 2010 sugar will no longer be grown here, hopefully replaced by alternative crops.

Ancient Hawaiians brought animals such as pigs, dogs, and chickens to the islands as food stock. Left to run loose in the forests, pigs and dogs wrought havoc on native species, and continue to do so today. Pigs eat native plants, and wild dogs kill ground-nesting native birds.

The post-contact onslaught

Hawaii's landscape changed forever when the first Polynesian explorers landed with their plants and animals, but that was only the beginning. Since Cook's arrival, plants and animals have streamed into the islands from all over the world. Today, many of these are more common than native or Polynesian-introduced species.

As these aliens often out-compete or eat native species, the flood of introductions is causing the extinction of many endemic plants and animals. Hawaii has the dubious distinction of having more endangered plant and animal species than any other American state. This can be attributed partly to its isolation, as a lack of natural enemies allowed more species to adapt and survive here than elsewhere.

Obviously, introduced species aren't all bad. Exotic plants provide Hawaii with stunning flower *lei*, sweet-smelling gardens, and highways lined with color, which comes from bougainvilleas and plumerias, native to tropical America. Other common aliens are ironwood and silk oaks from Australia, banyan trees from Asia, and Cook's pines from the South Pacific Cook Islands. Orchid growers, especially on the Big Island, have made Hawaii world-famous for orchid hybrids. Hawaii has just three native orchids, a minute number compared to the 30,000 species that make up the entire family.

Many food plants associated with Hawaii are foreign, including coffee (Africa), pineapples (Brazil), mangos (India), papaya (tropical America), and lychee (China).

Many alien animals, however, are not welcome: goats, sheep, and wild cats have all caused environmental disasters. Mongooses, for example, were imported by sugar growers to eat rats, but preferred native birds and their eggs. It was realized too late that mongooses hunt during the day, while rats are active at night. Only Kauai remains mongoose-free, and it therefore holds the largest population of birds.

Some non-native creatures, such as mynah birds and red-crested cardinals, are welcome, but state officials guard against pests such as snakes, particularly the brown tree snake from Guam, which has virtually extinguished avian life there. (The snakes hitchhike in the wheel wells of commercial and military aircraft flying to Hawaii from Guam.) Strict laws have been largely successful: outside the zoo, only a few illegal snakes have been found. However, there is growing concern about the brown tree snake.

Quarantine laws have kept Hawaii rabies free, and the once-endangered *nene*, the Hawaiian goose, is now often seen in the wild at Volcano on the Big Island and Haleakala on Maui. ❑

LEFT: Norfolk pines were introduced as windbreaks.
RIGHT: the heliconia flower, also introduced by humans.

HAWAII'S DISAPPEARING FLORA AND FAUNA

No doubt both the Polynesians and Europeans had good intentions, but both groups introduced plants and animals that have decimated Hawaii's own

The Hawaiian monk seal *(left)* is a shy creature, largely keeping to itself in the uninhabited islands and atolls of northwestern Hawaii. You may encounter one on the less frequented beaches of the major islands; if you do, it is illegal to approach or touch it. It is one of only two indigenous mammals in Hawaii; the other is the hoary bat. The Polynesian rat, first introduced by ancient Polynesians, is considered by some to have evolved enough to count as a Hawaiian species.

AVIAN DISAPPEARANCE

Many species of Hawaii's native birds, evolving through the centuries with few natural predators, have all but disappeared. The mongoose, introduced to combat rats brought centuries earlier on Polynesian canoes, prefers eggs and has decimated native birds. Other introduced species threaten Hawaii's birds everywhere except Kauai. The mynah, introduced by Europeans, is a pushy creature, and it has forced many other bird species from their habitat. Snakes are not found in the wild in Hawaii. Yet. But a serious threat to both indigenous and introduced bird species is the brown snake from Guam, a potential arrival as a stowaway on commercial and military aircraft.

FLORA

Prior to the arrival of people, the level of endemic plant species was higher in Hawaii than anywhere else on the planet. Today, the flora we associate with Hawaii – plumeria, hibiscus, pineapples, bananas, guavas – are all introduced species. Hawaii's indigenous plants are fighting for survival, and many are already extinct.

▷ NOT ENOUGH TO CROW ABOUT
Hawaiian crows probably won't survive, despite conservationists' efforts. Fewer than two dozen birds remain, not enough for a strong gene pool.

△ SILVERSWORD
The silversword is adapted to high-altitude life. You're most likely to see it in Maui's Haleakala Crater; walking too close to it will crush its roots.

▽ TOO MANY PIGS
Pigs, introduced by Polynesians, and goats and cattle, introduced by Europeans, have destroyed Hawaii's native plant species

HAWAII'S BENIGN EVOLUTION

Statistically, a new species became established on Hawaii every 15,000 years. Hawaii's extreme remoteness gave those animal and plant species that arrived a unique environment in which to grow and evolve. By the time the first humans arrived 1,500 years ago, nearly 9,000 kinds of flora and fauna unique to the islands had evolved, including the silversword *(above)*.

In the absence of mammals, plants did not develop defenses such as thorns and toxins, nor did birds develop behavior that protected them from predators. When people introduced numerous animal species – from birds to grazing cattle – Hawaii's indigenous species were poorly equipped for survival.

Indigenous plants and birds today are found largely in inaccessible places such as the cliffs of Molokai's north shore, the boggy highlands of Kauai, and the restricted and fenced-in Kipahulu Valley of eastern Maui.

△ RAT REJECTION
Another introduced mammal, the mongoose, has decimated many of Hawaii's indigenous birds. Brought by Europeans to control rats, it preferred birds – it is a day mammal and rats prefer the night.

◁ *NENE*, HAWAIIAN GOOSE
The *nene*, or Hawaiian goose, is found on the Big Island, Maui, and Kauai, usually at higher elevations. Unlike other goose species, the *nene* lacks webbed feet; it has claws that are more useful on the volcanic slopes.

▷ HAWAIIAN STILT
Like most of Hawaii's native birds, the Hawaiian stilt lacks the necessary defensive behavior against introduced predators. Found only in a few inland wildlife sanctuaries, such as on Maui's central isthmus, the stilt is a delightful sighting for the birdwatcher.

▷ PROTECTED BY SHYNESS
The reclusiveness of the Hawaiian monk seal (hence, the "monk") has probably assured its species survival. Rare is the sighting of a grown monk seal, much less a pup seal *(right)*. Wisely, they prefer uninhabited islands.

SPIRIT OF THE ISLANDS

Although Hawaiian culture long ago yielded to outsiders, underlying all modern
society in Hawaii is a foundation of revived ancient values

In Hawaiian tradition, the land, or *'aina*, is mother. *'Aina* literally means "that which feeds." The land doesn't belong to people; Native Hawaiians, or *kanaka maoli*, as they call themselves, belong to it and are part of it. If separated from the land, Hawaiians and their culture tend to drift and lose meaning. The sheltering home, the trees outside, the earth beneath – all are alive and aware. The shapes of the clouds, the cries of birds at night, the sounds of waves on the reef – all have messages for the Hawaiian people. Hawaiian tradition involved constant communication with other living beings, with the land, rocks, clouds, sea, and spirits of ancestors.

Changing fortunes

The careful attention to detail and procedure of the native Hawaiians led to a pursuit of excellence stretching beyond what was necessary just to survive, resulting in creations that were extraordinary by the standards of any society.

For the *kanaka maoli*, *wa'a* (sailing canoes) were until very recently the swiftest sailing craft on the ocean. Dazzling feather capes and *lei* (garlands) were admired by jaded Europeans of the time. *Kanaka maoli* agriculturists developed more than 300 varieties of taro, many of them for dyes and medicines as well as food.

Walled *loko i'a* (fish ponds) extended from the shores and efficiently raised fish that fed on algae. Stone-faced terraced and irrigated pond-fields *(lo'i)* filled the valleys, growing shrimp and fish as well as prodigious amounts of taro and other crops. Hawaiians were master agriculturists, botanists, herbalists, and craftsmen, fulfilling all needs and creative efforts and expressions entirely from plant materials.

Today on these islands that were an independent nation over a century ago, *kanaka maoli* have the shortest life expectancy of all ethnic

---

PRECEDING PAGES: ancient petroglyph cave on the Big Island. **LEFT:** the taro plant is one of the god Kane's many forms. **RIGHT:** often found at traditionally sacred sites are offerings of lava wrapped in *ti* leaves.

groups. They have the highest mortality rates for heart disease, stroke, cancer and diabetes, the highest infant mortality, and the highest rates of suicide, accidents, and substance abuse.

Hawaiians have the highest drop-out rates in the school system, the lowest family median incomes, and the highest rates of homelessness.

Hawaiians are at the bottom of the heap in their own homeland, displaced by the fracturing of their intense connection with land and tradition.

He Kumulipo: The creation

'O ke au i kahuli wela ka honua. 'O ke au i kahuli lole ka lani. The opening lines of "He Kumulipo," the chant describing the origins of the cosmos, literally mean "at the time of the hot earth, turning against the changing sky." But the *kaona*, the hidden meaning of the words, is of the mating between the sky-father, Wakea, with the earth-mother, Papa, out of which came everything in the cosmos. According to "He Kumulipo," the *kalo*, or the taro plant, was one

of the early children of the earth-mother and the sky-father. But this *kalo*-child was born deformed, and died. From its burial place sprouted the taro plant, which became a staple food of Hawaiian life. Clustered around the central plant – the *makua*, or parent – are *'oha* (offshoots), and around them, little *keiki* (children). Collectively, this complete plant is called *'ohana*, also the Hawaiian word for family.

The next child born was Haloa, the first human ancestor and was perfect in form. But since the taro plant is the *hiapo*, or the eldest sibling of humans, it is the superior. It is also another form *(kinolau)* of Kane, one of the highest gods.

several valleys, forested uplands, a length of shoreline, and the adjoining ocean. In short, it was self-sustaining. The fisherman worked not only for himself, but for everyone; likewise the farmer and the woodsman. Of necessity, good interpersonal relationships, with sharing and exchange, were paramount.

'Ohana, the extended family

Practically all the inhabitants of an *ahupua'a* were blood relatives, an extended *'ohana*. Because there was no private ownership and no property to inherit, there was no need for households with a father, a mother, and their children. In the

Therefore, when eating taro, one is eating the god Kane, taking in his godly *mana*, or power.

'Aina, the land

Before Westerners arrived, Hawaiians had no ownership of land. They had access to all of the natural resources except those few areas that were *kapu*, or taboo – certain fishing grounds during certain seasons, for example. The chiefs or king held the land as proxy for the gods, administering it on earth. Islands were usually divided into *ahupua'a*, wedges of land extending from the mountain peaks to the coastline and into the water beyond. An *ahupua'a* typically contained ridges on both sides of one or

OF HAWAII'S PEOPLE

It is the meeting place of East and West, the very new rubs shoulders with the immeasurably old... you have come upon something singularly intriguing. All these strange people live close to each other, with different languages and different thoughts; they believe in different gods and they have different values; two passions alone they share, love and hunger. And somehow as you watch them, you have an impression of extraordinary vitality.

William Somerset Maugham
The Trembling of a Leaf, 1921

'ohana, all the men and women in the middle generation were *makua* (parents) and one mated with whomever one desired. All youngsters were *kamali'i* (children); all elders were *kupuna* (grandparents). There was no difference between parents, aunts, and uncles, and there was no word for cousin. Members of the same generation were all siblings. In the *'ohana* of ordinary farmers and fishermen, couples certainly existed, but this was not the rule and there were no separate dwellings for them. Everyone slept in the big sleeping house, or *hale noa*. Because of the communal arrangements, *kanaka maoli* children learned early about sex and childbirth.

the fontanel, the opening between the bones of a baby's skull that closes as the child matures – is the *piko po'o* (head center). Through this *piko*, the personal spirit connects with the spiritual world of the ancestors back to the beginning of time, to the natural world about us as *'aumakua*, the ancestral and guardian spirits, and into the future, where the personal spirit will continue to live in different forms forever. The third *piko* is the *piko ma'i*. *Ma'i* are the genitalia, the organs of procreation. This *piko* connects us with our children and their descendants into the limitless future. In the here and now, *kanaka maoli* are in human form, but they have existed

Children were taught about the three *piko*, or centers and were secure knowing that through the three *piko* they were firmly attached to this present life, to the earliest ancestors, and to the lives of unborn generations.

The *piko waena* is the navel, the memory of the link between mother and child in the womb. More, it is a connection with everything in this physical world. It also covers and is related to the *na'au* (the intestines), the organs of knowledge, wisdom, and feeling. The second *piko* –

LEFT: a Hawaiian *lu'au*. ABOVE LEFT: outrigger at dusk. ABOVE RIGHT: Penis of Nanahoa (Ka Ule o Nanahoa), phallic stone on Molokai.

in many previous forms and will exist in many more in the future. Time in this human form is short; after death, *kanaka maoli* join ancestors, assume spiritual form, and come back to families as *'aumakua*. Sometimes they return in the form of a bird, a fish, or a turtle, shark, tree, rock, breeze, cloud, or even a new child born into the family. The *'aumakua* protects loved ones by warning, guiding and informing them.

Traditionally, *kanaka maoli* see sex everywhere in nature, and the link between creation and procreation is direct and obvious. In the morning, the wind blows the *pali* mists in a shimmering curtain of rain down island valleys – the rain is the semen of Wakea, the sky-father,

Hawaiian Gods

From their South Pacific homelands, early Polynesian seafarers brought north with them the foods that had sustained them back home. By doing so, they also brought to Hawaii the great gods of Polynesia: Kane, Ku, Lono, and Kanaloa. As the Polynesians knew well, the gods were essential for human achievement in the new homeland.

Polynesian gods were never distant and abstract. Rather, they moved through the waters and on the earth, and they could take on many forms, including plants. Thus, the Polynesians knew that by bringing

taro, one of the god Kane's forms, to Hawaii, they carried with them Kane himself. With *'uala*, the sweet potato, they brought Lono. *'Ulu*, breadfruit, and *niu*, the coconut, bore Ku, and with *mai'a*, the banana, came Kanaloa.

Kane, the supreme god, was the procreator, the ancestor of all chiefs and commoners, the male *(kane)* power who dwells in eternity – the god of sunlight, fresh water and forests. Kane was not fond of human sacrifices. An owl was one of his assumed forms.

Hawaiians prayed to **Ku** for rain and growth, and for successful fishing and sorcery, but he was best known as a patron god of war. Resplendent images of Ku, whose combative title was "The Island Snatcher," were carried on the war canoes of Kame-

hameha the Great. According to oral traditions, these fearsome images – wrought of red *i'iwi* feathers embellished with mother-of-pearl eyes and mouths of jagged dog teeth – would utter dreadful cries during battle.

Lono was a god of thunder (*lono* means "resounding"), clouds, winds, the sea, agriculture, and fertility, but his personage could assume dozens of forms, including a fish or a man-dog being. Hawaiians never appealed to benevolent Lono with human sacrifices. Most notably, he was honored during the annual *makahiki* harvest festivals of November, December, and January, when his image was carried by chiefly retainers on their tribute-and-tax-collecting tours of the islands.

It was during *makahiki* that Captain James Cook's arrival on the Big Island was greeted joyously by Hawaiians gathered at Kealakekua Bay. Some theorize the Hawaiians mistook his visit for the prophesied return of Lono.

Kanaloa, lord of the ocean and the ocean winds, was often embodied in the octopus and squid, but also in other natural things, such as the banana. He was a companion of Kane, and according to some, the two traveled together, "moving about the land and opening spring and water holes for the benefit of men."

Coming to Polynesia from distant, unknown places, these four gods had been created before all other gods. They created the universe from the earth, symbolized as a calabash. By tossing the calabash's cover skyward, the sky, sun, and moon were formed. Seeds in the calabash became stars. The pantheon of Hawaiian deities is extensive, including the lesser specialized gods, such as Pele, the volcano goddess, and Laka, goddess of hula.

For the contemporary traveler to Hawaii, Pele is the best known of the lesser gods. As the fire goddess, she is responsible for the current eruptions of Kilauea. A common misconception is that Pele created the Hawaiian islands. The islands had already surfaced when Pele, driven by wanderlust, arrived from Tahiti in a great canoe provided by the god of sharks. From Ni'ihau, she traveled down the island chain looking for a suitable home, which was within active volcanoes.

On the Big Island, she sought out the reigning fire god, Aila'au, hoping to settle in with him. But he had heard of her awesome power and the blazing firepits she dug. As she approached Kilauea, he ran away, leaving her to build a soaring palace of fire that endures in legend and in periodic eruptions on the Big Island to this day. ❑

impregnating Papa, the earth-mother.' This is a common belief and image in many of the world's cosmologies. The opening lines of Queen Lili'uokalani's haunting song "Aloha 'Oe" speak of the proud rain on the cliff creeping into the forest, seeking the bud of the *lehua* – the male seeking the female. There are songs about *maile* (rainforest vine) wrapped around a flower *lei*, male entwined with female. Most *kanaka maoli* songs and chants celebrate the same thing: the joining of male with female. The cosmos was

PERSONAL POWER

Mana (special spiritual or personal power) derives from two sources: rank at birth and skilled training.

Talking story

One way of maintaining balance is by *mo'olelo*, or "talking story," which builds trust and emphasizes things in common. This is not to suggest that the traditional *kanaka maoli* world was without violence. Oral history holds that the high *kahuna* Pa'ao brought a strict new religion from Tahiti in about the 13th century, increasing the power of the *ali'i*, or royal elite, meting out harsh punishments for the breaking of new *kapu*, and introducing new rituals, including human sacrifice.

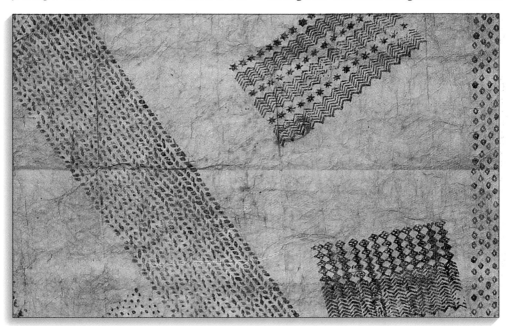

created, and continues to be created, by the mating of Papa and Wakea, "the hot earth turning against the changing heaven." Hawaiians see sexuality as a central fact of nature: from mating comes new life.

When a relationship goes out of balance, the ideal is *ho'opono pono*, a process of guided reconciliation that seeks to achieve both understanding and forgiveness. However, complex psychological issues are often at work here, and the *kanaka* may instead opt for a less harmonious solution of rage and violence.

LEFT: image of Kamehameha's war god, Kukailimoku.
ABOVE: 19th-century *kapa*, or bark cloth.

Rivalry increased between chiefs for political control. But the traditional culture of the *maka'ainana* (lit. the eyes of the land, or commoners) continued much as it had before the arrival of Pa'ao. *Maka'ainana* probably didn't pay much attention to the new hierarchy or the religious rituals, being absorbed rather with work, *'ohana* and *'aumakua*.

Why was there warfare in a society dedicated to harmony and proper relationships? One could say wars were fought to restore balance, *pono*, particularly as a growing population forced people into closer proximity with one another. In earlier times, warfare had important elements of ritual, as the warrior classes tested their strength against each other but rarely disrupted commoners. When James Cook arrived in 1778, there were bloody conflicts between Kamehameha and other high chiefs. Commoners were conscripted into their armies. But the first Westerners may have exaggerated warfare's importance in Hawaiian society, misunderstanding its role. The arrival of Westerners intensified the bloodshed; gunpowder tipped the balance of power. Introduced values about the acquisition of material goods – the sandalwood trade, for example – became goals of war. The natural world was now one of "natural resources" and no longer an extension of *'ohana*, of family.

Spiritual power

Mana (special spiritual or personal power) derives from two main sources. One source is rank at birth. *Ali'i* (royalty) are born with more *mana* than commoners. Higher-born *ali'i* have more *mana* than lesser-born. The other source is training: a skilled carver, fisherman, chanter, navigator, physician, or dancer gradually acquires this kind of *mana*, as ability is refined. These skills require long apprenticeship, and one's specialized knowledge shouldn't be too readily shared with others lest its power be diminished.

Huna – certain confidential, secret aspects of the skill – requires the understanding of how

numerous forces interact, the maintenance of certain kinds of protocol, and the observance of strict forms of behavior.

At all levels of society, *kanaka maoli* believe in balance and protocol. Preparing and consuming a meal has to be done in a certain way. Preparations for the treatment of someone who is ill, such as the gathering of *la'au lapa'au* (medicinal plants), must be completed at a certain time of day with certain rules, prayers, and thoughts. Chants, dances, and rituals have to be conducted impeccably. There is a right way to do everything, and even the smallest daily activity is enmeshed in a web of belief and practice.

The chants used in ritual, prayer, and *hula*, if the words and songs are uttered properly, carry with them considerable power. Hawaiians don't merely petition the gods and hope they'll act; Hawaiians participate by their way of asking. The belief, the ritual, and the result all become one process. And prayers are two-way communications between humans and gods. Responses are received and interpreted in whatever form they may come: patterns in the fire, images in a dream, a sudden gust of wind, a grumble of thunder, a thought that seems to come from nowhere. But of course, nothing comes from nowhere; everything has causes and exists for a reason.

To be or not to be

The *kanaka maoli* sense of balance requires being in the natural environment. The depletion of fishing grounds and the loss of lands destroyed traditional sources of livelihood, which had imparted meaning to the world.

Contemporary Hawaii is promoted as one of the world's most ethnically diverse and harmonious societies. Should the *kanaka maoli* attempt to fit in as just another ethnic group? Some advocates of Hawaiian sovereignty believe it's almost impossible to be both *kanaka maoli* and part of modern America. When immigrants come to Hawaii from, say, China and Portugal, and their children forget their ancestors' culture, the Chinese and Portuguese cultures still exist in their homelands. For *kanaka maoli*, the Hawaiian islands are the only homeland. If *kanaka maoli* language and culture die here, they're gone from the earth, and *kanaka maoli* vanish as a people. ❏

LEFT: offering to the gods at a sacred birth place, Oahu.
RIGHT: traditional beads for sale.

LIFE IN THE ISLANDS AND SYMBOLS OF THE LAND

While the Westernization of the Hawaiian islands has been thorough, it is still possible to intimately explore and experience ancient ways and textures

After the arrival of Europeans in Hawaii, a process that sociologists call "dualism" occurred, in which two distinct cultures and economies exist simultaneously. Eventually, however, Western processes and values supplanted those of traditional Hawaii. Nonetheless, one may witness the ways and places of old Hawaii even today. Archeologists, anthropologists and sociologists have undertaken exacting reconstructions and preservation of sacred temples and villages. Travelers can immerse themselves in ancient ambiance at Pu'u Kohola, Lapakahi, and Pu'uhonua 'O Honanunau, all on the Big Island; Kane'aki and Pu'u 'O Mahuka *heiau*s (temples) on Oahu; Pi'ilanihale *heiau* on Maui; and 'Ili'ili'opae *heiau* on Moloka'i.

ANCIENT WAYS

In ancient Hawaii, the *'aina*, or land, was considered the property of the gods, held in trust by a chief or king. He in turn allocated land to support the *ali'i* (royalty), who allowed *maka'ainana* (commoners) to cultivate it. The commoners, protected by the *ali'i*, turned over much of the food grown to the *ali'i*. Although living in a feudal society, commoners were not indentured to the *ali'i*, and could leave if they wanted.

The land itself was divided into wedge-shaped parcels called *ahupua'a*, which usually extended from the coast up into a mountain valley; ideally, they were self-sustaining in seafood, water, produce, and forest resources.

Life was satisfactory, but it wasn't especially idyllic. Warfare was common, and commoners had to be careful not to violate *kapu* – the taboos that were law. Surfing the chiefs' waves or trespassing through sacred temples could result in death. But whether a violator of *kapu* or a warrior escaping an enemy, a person could find safety in a *pu'uhonua*, a place of refuge. Here, absolution by a *kahuna*, or priest, cleansed transgressions or assured sanctuary.

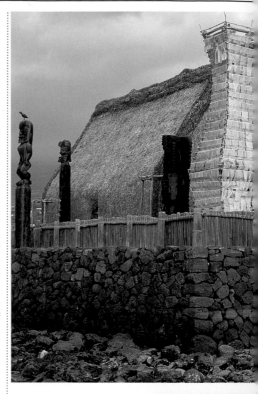

△ **AHU'ENA** *HEIAU*
This reconstructed *heiau*, or temple, is right on the harbor waterfront in Kailua-Kona. Originally a place of human sacrifices, it was restored by Kamehameha the Great as his personal *heiau*.

△ **MODERN CARVINGS**
Craftsmen still carve the fearsome sacred images called *ki'i akua*. You can see woodcarving demonstrations at the Polynesian Cultural Center, Oahu.

◁ **WEATHERED IMAGE**
The wood of carved *ki'i akua* is untreated, and so takes on a timeless cast in the tropical weather. This one is from Pu'uhonau 'O Honanuau National Historical Park, on the Big Island.

OF ROYAL STONES AND PETROGLYPHS

In central Oahu are the birth stones of Kukaniloko *(above)*. Now a clearing in a pineapple field this spot was sacred to Hawaiians as far back as the 1100s.

The wives of high-ranking chiefs gave birth on the stones' gently curved surfaces. Attendant chiefs, high priests, and physicians would gather in a ceremony marked by chants and offerings. The *ali'i* child would be named and the umbilical cord – *piko* – would be cut.

Hawaiians would place the severed *piko* in a hole carved into the rock, essentially a simple petroglyph, or *kaha ki'i*. This *piko* hole could be just a couple of inches in diameter and an inch or so deep, or it could be quite elaborate. The *piko* hole for a male child might have circles carved around it; that of a female infant would be adorned with a semicircle.

Piko were put where *mana*, or spirit, was strong, such as at Kukaniloko. It was hoped that the child might be influenced by the *mana*, and maybe even absorb some of it. Sometimes a representation of the family's *'aumakua* (family or personal god) would be carved into the rock adjacent to the *piko* hole.

On the Big Island, the Kona and Kohala districts offer several easily accessible petroglyph sites, such as at Puako. As most of them are at ground level, take extreme care and don't walk on top of them.

△ **REFUGE GUARDIANS**
Fearsome *ki'i akua*, god images or idols, were used to protect and impress. These are at Pu'u 'O Honaunau, a reconstructed place of refuge on the Big Island and a National Historical Park.

▽ **POUNDED CLOTH**
Tapa, or cloth made from bark, was used for clothes.

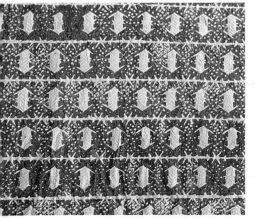

△ **NAUTICAL PROTECTION**
Kiha Wahine, the Lizard Woman, protected the voyaging canoe *Hokule'a* during its voyages to the South Pacific in the late 1990s. Kamehameha the Great carried an image of Ku, the war god, on his war canoes – for protection, good luck, and to instill fear in his enemies. It worked.

HAWAII'S PEOPLE

Hawaii has an extraordinary ethnic and cultural mix; its people originate from as far afield as Asia, Europe, North America and the South Pacific

O ver the decades, Hawaii has received waves of immigrants from various cultures. Except for the Native Hawaiians, who were here first, and the Caucasians, who came to convert or build business empires, or in later years to settle in "paradise," most of Hawaii's ethnic groups came to work on sugarcane or pineapple plantations and stayed to raise families. According to the 2000 census statistics, which used "self-defining" categories, Caucasians make up about 33 percent of the state's 1.2 million people. Japanese follow with 17 percent, then the Filipinos at 14 percent. The rest comprise Chinese, Koreans, African-Americans, Samoans, Vietnamese and a mix of Pacific islanders and other Asian races.

The Hawaiians

Indigenous Hawaiians are now among the most inconspicuous people walking the streets of Hawaii. In the century following first contact with Europeans, most of Hawaii's native people died from epidemics of introduced diseases: cholera, influenza, mumps, measles, whooping cough, and smallpox. Gonorrhea caused sterility; syphilis resulted in stillbirths.

The statistics astound. Hawaii's aboriginal population had shrunk from an estimated 300,000 at the time of Captain Cook's 1778 visit to about 40,000 in 1893, when the Hawaiian monarchy was overthrown. And many of those 40,000 were *hapa*-Hawaiian, or part-Hawaiian. By the mid-19th century, a hauntingly intangible but real disease killed many more thousands of Hawaiians: sheer psychological depression. *Na kanaka ku'u wale aku no i ka 'uhane* – The people freely gave up their souls and died.

Given the degree of inter-racial mixing over the past two centuries, it's difficult to know how many full Hawaiians remain. According to state health department estimates, there are approximately 9,100 Hawaiians of unmixed ancestry,

fewer than one percent of Hawaii's total population, including military. Those of partial Hawaiian ancestry number roughly 200,000. The most Hawaiian of islands is Ni'ihau, a privately owned island off Kauai's west coast with a population of 200 – all Hawaiian. Molokai has the next largest percentage of part Hawaiians –

about 45 percent of its population. Lanai, another mostly privately owned island, is next with just under 10 percent.

The Hawaiians have made a comeback, it might be argued, by marrying into other racial groups and thus sustaining some of the blood lines. Equally if not more important is the revival of the Hawaiian culture, nearly extinguished by Protestant missionaries in the 19th century.

A *malihini*, or newcomer, might point out that part-Hawaiians are also part something else, but part-Hawaiians, whatever their other ancestry, almost unanimously think of themselves as Hawaiian first. It's a point of pride, if not of status, to be a *keiki o ka 'aina*, a child of the soil.

LEFT: signs of friendship, the "shaka" means everything's OK.
RIGHT: wreathed for celebration.

Many Hawaiians are effectively aliens in their own land, and alienation spawns difficult problems. Hawaiians and part-Hawaiians make up the largest number of inmates in county jails and the state prison. They account for the greatest percentage of welfare recipients, the majority of school dropouts and juvenile delinquents, and have the highest rate of illegitimate children.

But Hawaiians are taking strong political and social positions in support of Hawaiian rights and self-government. Their claims for autonomy and sovereignty have substantive and irrefutable historical standing, but pragmatically, the state of Hawaii will not be turned back *in toto* to the

Hawaiians. Some critics of the sovereignty movement even charge that the more reactionary factions could lead to an ethnocentric, if not anti-*haole* (Caucasian), racism.

The Chinese

"The ball at the Court House on Thursday night last, given to their majesties the King and Queen by the Chinese merchants of Honolulu and Lahaina, was the most splendid affair of its kind ever held in Honolulu... We have heard but one opinion expressed by those present (which includes all Honolulu and his wife), and that was that the Celestials have outshone the 'outside barbarians' in fete-making for the throne."

According to this newspaper report, the party hosted by Chinese business leaders in 1856 to honor the marriage of King Kamehameha IV and Queen Emma took Honolulu by storm.

At the time of the ball, Hawaii's Chinese community numbered maybe 600 persons. It marked the entry of local Chinese into the highest circles of society. The king was so pleased that one of the Chinese sponsors married the foster sister of the future King Kalakaua, later becoming the first and only full-blooded Chinese to be appointed to the Hawaiian royal court.

Hawaii's Chinese didn't always have it so good. In the 1890s, jealous American business-

THE REAL CHARLIE CHAN

During the 1910s and 1920s, downtown Honolulu was the turf of Chang Apana, a Hawaiian-Chinese police detective. Known to the local Chinese as Kana Pung, Apana retired in 1932 after 34 years of distinguished service as a police officer and detective. At his impressive funeral the following year, the Royal Hawaiian Band marched in his cortege.

Apana was the inspiration for Charlie Chan, a fictional character of the American writer Earl Derr Biggers. In 1925, with the publication of Biggers' novel *House Without a Key*, the whimsical Inspector Chan assumed a place in fictional history. "Ah so," Chan would say in non-Chinese Japanese. Biggers wrote many installments of *The Adventures of Charlie Chan* and dozens of specials, such as *Charlie Chan in Shanghai*. Projecting dubious ethnic stereotypes, Chan was nevertheless of Hawaii.

men, in an attempt to restrict the inroads that enterprising Chinese were making into local commerce, initiated legislation that restricted the freedom of Chinese immigrant laborers. Nevertheless, over the decades the Chinese have become one of Hawaii's most prominent, influential, generous, and financially successful ethnic groups.

From the sandalwood trade of the early 1800s, the Chinese were well-acquainted with Hawaii, known to them as Tan Heung Shan, or the Country of the Fragrant Tree. The first Chinese laborers arrived here in 1852, 195 workers from Guangdong and Fujian provinces in southeastern China. Before they left China, they had signed five-year contracts promising them $36 a year, sea passage, food, clothing, and housing.

Many of those first Chinese were intent on finishing their contracts and returning to China with money. Others married local women and, with their savings, set up shops in Honolulu and Lahaina, the boom towns of the mid 1800s. The Chinese often found a niche in retail, especially as they were not welcome in the sugar industry except as laborers.

Most Chinese who used to live in Honolulu's so-called Chinatown (near the harbor) left Downtown long ago, taking their new-found affluence to other, ritzier sectors of the community, espe-

China Group) was crucial to the future success of China's revolutionary movement against foreign powers. Because Chinese patrons in the islands contributed generous support to Dr Sun's cause, Hawaii became known in some Chinese circles as the cradle of the Chinese republic.

The Japanese

When Hirohito, the late Emperor of Japan, arrived in Hawaii in 1975, his aircraft landed at Honolulu International Airport from a southeasterly approach, rather than the standard northwesterly. The reason: the emperor's pilots wanted to avoid flying over Pearl Harbor and

cially after World War II. But a few persistent old-timers stayed behind, where they still mind Hong Kong-style acupuncture clinics, market food stalls, noodle factories, and restaurants.

It was in Chinatown where Honolulu schoolmates Ho Fon and Dr Sun Yatsen met to plan a Chinese revolution. Dr Sun Yatsen, considered the father of modern China by both Communist and Nationalist Chinese, founded his original revolutionary group in Honolulu in 1895. That secret society, first known by the Chinese-Hawaiian name Hsing Chung Hui (Revive

LEFT: an early Chinese shop.
ABOVE: colorful cafe.

subjecting him to reminders of the war fought in his name 35 years earlier. Meeting him at the airport was an *aloha* delegation that included three US congressmen of Japanese descent, the recently elected Japanese-American governor of Hawaii, and an American of Japanese ancestry, then president of the University of Hawaii.

Along the highway from the airport to Downtown and Waikiki, Hirohito and his entourage rolled past dozens of businesses with Japanese names, fleets of fishing sampans wriggling with fresh tuna for Hawaii's sashimi-crazy households, and opulent Buddhist and Shinto temples and shrines. To say that the Japanese have succeeded in Hawaii is an understatement. From

World War II until the present day, their political and social power has been considerable.

This Japanese rise to prominence began with humble origins. It wasn't until 1868, during the first year of Japan's reformist Meiji Era, that an "official" group of immigrants from Japan put into Hawaii. These *gannenmono*, or first-year men, arrived at Honolulu on board the British sailing ship *Scioto*. Carrying three-year laborer contracts, all were quickly assimilated into local plantations, earning about 12 cents a day or, according to one account, about twice what they could make in Japan. By 1885 that income quadrupled to about 50 cents a day.

Strict emigration laws in Japan, however, made it difficult for more Japanese to come to Tenjiku, or the Heavenly Place, as Hawaii was called. A little diplomacy was called for on this matter. So in 1881, King Kalakaua visited Japan on the first leg of a tour around the world. He initiated treaty discussions with the Japanese and actively pursued the Japanese immigration issue until it was given sanction. In 1885, a group of 943 immigrants – 676 men, 159 women and 108 children – arrived in Honolulu.

Life was often miserable in the plantation camps, but Japanese continued to arrive in ever-increasing numbers. By 1900, there were 61,000 Japanese workers and dependents in the islands, or more than twice the number of Hawaiians, Caucasians, or Chinese in Hawaii. Until the mid-1970s, the Japanese remained Hawaii's largest ethnic group.

The Japanese, like nearly all of Hawaii's non-*haole* laborers, suffered from racial and economic prejudices under Hawaii's plantation elite. And when Japan attacked Pearl Harbor, a small number of local Japanese-Americans were forced into internment camps on the mainland.

In Hawaii, where AJAS (Americans of Japanese ancestry) made up 40 percent of the population in the early 1940s, internment of all AJAS was out of the question. But under martial law,

GOING FOR BROKE

Although the Japanese-Americans of Hawaii were not interned *en masse* as on the US mainland, nearly 1,500 were still forcibly sent to mainland internment camps. Still, second-generation *(nisei)* Japanese-Americans volunteered by the hundreds for the army.

After stalling, the government finally created an all-*nisei* unit in 1942, the 100th Battalion. A year later, so many *nisei* had volunteered that a larger unit was formed, the 442nd Infantry Regiment. Both units were sent to Italy in 1944, where they fought together as the 442nd Infantry Regiment, nicknamed "Go For Broke."

Fighting in Italy and France, the *nisei* units won seven presidential unit citations and 6,000 individual awards, the most highly decorated unit in the American military during World War II. Their casualty rate was over three times the military's average.

Japanese language schools and radio stations were shut down; Buddhist, Shinto and Zen temples were closed; and Japanese newspapers were strictly censored. Still, not a single case of Japanese-American disloyalty or sabotage occurred during the war.

Japanese *nisei* (second-generation Japanese-Americans) by the hundreds volunteered for military duty, but were turned away initially. Eventually and reluctantly, the War Department relented and in 1942, an all-*nisei* battalion of national guardsmen and draftees was created.

Regardless of ethnic background, nearly everyone in Hawaii lives a little bit of the Japanese lifestyle, knowingly or not. Few are the homes where shoes aren't removed before entering, and many are the *kama'aina* (long-time residents) who order sushi or sashimi without thinking twice. All residents of Hawaii are very much at home with things Japanese. The thump of *mochi* pounding or of drums for the Buddhist *bon odori* that honors souls of the dead are common sounds in Hawaii's diverse neighborhoods.

The Filipinos

The first Filipinos to call Hawaii home were acrobats and musicians who swept into Honolulu after a performing tour of China and Japan. In true Filipino spirit, they set to work entertaining Oahu's residents for two weeks in 1888 while waiting for their ship to San Francisco.

"The Filipino troupers pleased their Hawaiian audiences, and the spell of Hawaii upon the performers was even more potent: so much so that when sailing time came and their manager refused to pay their salaries until arrival in San Francisco, they returned to their lodgings and took up their abode in Hawaii. Four of the 12 young men found immediate employment in the Royal Hawaiian Band of King Kalakaua."

It is the sugar industry more than anything that gets the credit for making Hawaii the largest Filipino community in the world outside the Philippine archipelago. Immigration of Filipinos as laborers began in 1906 with the arrival of 15 Filipino laborers to work on a sugar plantation. For the next 40 years, Filipinos poured into Hawaii at a pace exceeded only by Japanese.

More than 125,000 Filipinos were recruited by the labor-hungry sugar companies, mostly in northern Ilocos. Of them, however, only 10,000 were women, and another 7,000 children. Not keen on being bachelors, about half of the men returned home to find wives and begin lives anew with money earned in the fields. Most who remained in Hawaii either married women from other ethnic groups or endured an extended if not eternal bachelorhood.

Tired of the plantation hierarchy and inequalities, the Filipinos organized into labor unions. The Filipino Federation and Labor Union, for example, was well-organized and actively agitating for employee benefits as early as 1919. And although some of their early labor-management confrontations ended in violence, death,

and defeat, *bum-by* (by-and-by), to use a favorite Filipino expression, their tenacity and eventual successes nurtured a collective dignity. Eventually, unions attained legal status and protection.

Filipino celebrations follow Roman Catholic observances, including an exotic candlelight festival held every spring on the Feast Day of Santa Cruz. The biggest annual event is the June Fiesta Filipina, which takes place at various locations throughout the islands. You'll find people in traditional garb enjoying Filipino music and food.

Filipino cuisine hasn't captivated island palates as have the cuisines of Korea, China,

Thailand, Vietnam and Japan. But for complete menus à la Manila or Zamboanga, stroll into one of several eateries around town and wish the proprietor a sincere *mabuhay* (hello).

The Koreans

"In Hawaii you rarely ever see a group of Koreans, but you see a Korean in every group." This comment by a Honolulu-born Korean businessman is a contemporary comment on Hawaii's highly mobile and adaptable Korean community. Unlike the more clannish Japanese and Chinese, Hawaii's 20,000-plus Koreans have rapidly fanned out into society. Their "out-marriage" rate, for example, has been as high as

---

LEFT: Aunty Edith Kanakaole, a Hawaiian personality.
RIGHT: Filipina immigrant in gown, early 1910s.

80 percent for both men and women, an inter-racial marriage statistic second only to part-Hawaiians. In the United States, Honolulu is second only to Los Angeles in the number of native-born Korean residents. Both long-established and recently immigrated Koreans have capitalized on their verve, ambition, and versatility to achieve business and social successes in Hawaii. Their overall education and income levels, for example, are the highest per capita of any ethnic group in Hawaii. Although they make up less than three percent of the population, Koreans have introduced considerable spice and fire to the islands. "It's the *kim chee*,"

jokes a man who recently married a Korean woman, and became enamored of her country's pickled vegetables. Whether in the land of Morning Calm or in Hawaii, Koreans are a down-to-earth lot, without the communicative vagueness of their Asian neighbors. Koreans speak their minds and, since Korea was opened to the West, they have been dubbed the Irish of Asia: being highly sociable people, they enjoy a drink or two.

They've adapted well to Hawaii, but many of their traditions elude the younger generation. *Halmoni* (grandmothers) who first came to Hawaii as "picture brides" still try to arrange marital matches in the traditional Korean way, but second- and third-generation children

usually have other ideas. The *haraboji* (grand-fathers) still gather at community centers to spend long hours deep into clacking rounds of an ancient Korean board game, *changgi*, or Korean chess.

In the islands, probably the most popular nickname for Koreans is *yobo*. Literally, *yobo* means "my dear" and is a way of addressing one's husband or wife. It is also the informal equivalent of "hello" or "hey there," when used to catch one's attention. Early Korean immigrants would address one another as *yobo-seyo*, . or simply *yobo*, which is not quite as polite. This term stuck as an island nickname.

Koreans first arrived as laborers in 1903. Over the next two years, more than 7,000 Koreans, most of them young men (10 for every Korean woman), signed up to work in Hawaii. But in 1905, Korea's emperor cut off all labor emigration after hearing that Korean laborers had been mistreated on hemp plantations in Mexico. Not until the Japanese annexed Korea in 1910 and allowed a thousand Korean "picture brides" to join their "picture grooms" did Korean immigration to Hawaii resume.

After Japan invaded Korea, Hawaii became a source of pro-Korean revolutionary support. In fact, most Korean social societies still in Hawaii began as anti-Japanese and restore-the-homeland groups, and some of them are highly secretive. Dr Syngman Rhee, an American-educated diplomat, turned to Koreans in Hawaii for revolutionary support against the Japanese occupation. After Japan's defeat in World War II, Dr Rhee returned to Korea triumphant as the first president of the Republic of Korea. Following a Korean military coup d'état that deposed him in 1960 at the start of his fourth term, he fled to Hawaii, dying in exile in 1965.

The Samoans

Samoans were later arrivals to the Islands, coming from the six isles that make up the territory of American Samoa, an 80 sq-mile (200 sq-km) group located about 2,600 miles (4,200 km) due southwest of Honolulu.

American Samoa's ruling chieftains officially ceded their islands to the United States in 1899 and for the first half of the 20th century, American Samoa was managed by the US Navy. After World War II, it was put under the jurisdiction of the US Department of the Interior, which appoints its governor and lieutenant governor, and oversees the election of a bicameral legislature and Congressional delegate.

Some 500 Samoans had trickled into Hawaii after World War I, the majority of them to join a Mormon community based in La'ie, on Oahu's windward shore. In 1952, after Samoan immigration to America was liberalized, a group of 900 Samoan men, women and children – about half of them Samoan-American navy men and dependants being transferred to Pearl Harbor – boarded a navy transport ship and set off for the

SUMO SAMOANS

Samoan Americans have become quite successful in sumo wrestling, especially in Japan. Some have even become Japanese citizens.

ripe and luscious mangos, bananas and other fruit growing on their private property.

Perhaps out of all the local Asian-Oceanic ethnic groups, Samoans have best retained their traditional cultural touchstones. When a Samoan "community" problem arises, elected chiefs, some of whom represent the various expatriate Samoan clans in Hawaii, call a special council called a *fono*. At these councils, the chiefs establish policy, mediate in the case of intra-Samoan grievances, and, if they feel a Samoan problem

Hawaiian islands. At the time, these emigrants from American Samoa represented 6 percent of American Samoa's total population.

In Samoa, life is communal and sharing precedes possession. Many of these Polynesian newcomers found it extremely difficult adapting to the faster lifestyles of modern Hawaii. Used to a place with mostly Western inclinations regarding possession and ownership, many Hawaii residents didn't understand when a neighborly Samoan bade them *talofa* (a Samoan *aloha*) and then helped himself to the

Left: Samoans are Hawaii's newcomers.
Above: Grand Sumo Tournament, Honolulu.

requires government attention, draft mutually agreed-upon statements for the appropriate outside individual or agency.

Most Samoan gatherings, however, are of a more celebratory nature: a wedding, or the investiture of a new chief, or Flag Day, an annual holiday that celebrates the raising of the American flag over Eastern Samoa.

Out come the *kava* cups and the colorful *lava-lava* sarongs and *puletasi* dresses, and the finely woven *lau hala* mats to be spread out on the ground. Joined by expatriates from Tonga, Fiji, Tahiti, and the Marquesas, the Samoans get together in fine *fia-fia* (feasting) fashion – *fa'a Samoa*, the Samoan way.

The Caucasians

As some Hawaiians explain it, their ancestors called the first Europeans *haole* because they could not believe that men with such pale skins and frail bodies could be alive. *Haole*, from *ha*, which means breath or the breath of life, connects with *ole*, which connotes an absence of the breath of life or, more simply, without life. Originally applied to any outsider, *haole* now refers to Caucasians, sometimes with neutral meaning, occasionally with negative meaning. Since the time of Cook, it has been fashionable in Hawaii for both *haole* and non-*haole* to put down *haole*.

For many years, the term was more of a slur than a synonym for Caucasian. *Haoles*, whether a *malihini* (newcomer) or *kama'aina* (long-time resident, old-timer), are now the fastest-growing ethnic group in the islands and are replacing the Japanese as the islands' main political force.

Since World War II, most *haole* coming to the islands more or less assimilated into the local lifestyle and rhythms, or at least made an attempt to. In recent years, however, new arrivals sometimes seem more interested in fashioning Hawaii into their own image of a paradise, or at least bringing a West Coast (from where a good percentage originate) attitude with them. It is not a new phenomenon. Since the first Polynesians arrived, every group has brought cultural baggage.

One distinct *haole* group that deserves special mention is the Portuguese, or *Portagee* in the local pidgin dialect, who immigrated in large numbers when Hawaii was still a kingdom, mostly to work in the cane fields. As early as 1872, there were perhaps 400 or so Portuguese in Hawaii, mostly sailors who had left whaling ships for life on land. These Europeans were well-received by both Hawaiians and *haole* merchants and planters, so in 1878 the Hawaiian government and sugar barons conducted an official labor recruitment campaign in Portugal's Azores and Madeira islands. Twenty years later, almost 13,000 Portuguese had made the rough voyage to the Hawaiian Islands, which, with their volcanic soils, offered very similar conditions for agriculture.

Many became *luna*, or foremen, on the sugar plantations, gaining a mid-level power foothold much more quickly than the Asian immigrants who worked alongside them. By the 1930s, the Portuguese community had a territorial supreme court chief justice, a territorial secretary and an acting governor, and the Catholic vicar apostolic of the Hawaiian Islands.

The Portuguese also introduced a small four-stringed instrument, known as the *braquino* or *cavaghindo* in Portugal, which became the *'ukulele* in Hawaiian. The Hawaiian word *'ukulele* literally means "leaping flea," and the story goes that it came from the nickname of Edward Purvis, an English expatriate who arrived in Hawaii in 1879. Purvis made friends with newly arrived Portuguese immigrants, and he soon learned to play the *braquino* with entertaining finesse. Purvis was small in stature and quick with his hands, so his Hawaiian friends nicknamed him *'Ukulele*, the Leaping Flea.

Local Portuguese, although more than two generations removed from the old country, still celebrate Portuguese traditions and religious festivals. A series of post-Easter *festas* are known as the Seven Domingas, or Holy Ghost festivals. During the seven weeks of *festa*, families participate in prayer and celebration. Traditional delicacies are prepared, such as *pao dolce* (sweet bread) and hot fried *malasadas* (a delicious light Portuguese donut). ❑

LEFT: a descendant of the *ali'i*, or Hawaiian aristocracy.
RIGHT: Hawaiian couple.

'OLELO HAWAII – THE LANGUAGE

It may take a while to catch the local linguistic nuances. Not only is there English,
but also Hawaiian and that special local style, pidgin, a mixture of many tongues

Until the 1970s, most linguists agreed that the Hawaiian language stood little chance of survival. In the background, however, local people of all persuasions could be heard chattering in pidgin English, a hybrid island language that flits in and out of conversations like a sassy mynah bird. A typical after-work

conversation between people of Hawaiian, Chinese, Japanese, Korean, Filipino, or Samoan backgrounds might include an invitation like this: "Hey, pau hana like go my hale for grind? Get plenty 'ono pupu – even pipikaula and poke in da fridge." Translation: "Hey, after work would you like to go to my house to eat? We've got plenty of tasty appetizers, even some beef jerky and raw fish marinated with seaweed in the refrigerator."

Today, pidgin continues to predominate among locals, but increasingly, true, grammatically correct Hawaiian is heard among part-Hawaiian members of many families and other individuals at social get-togethers. The startling

change can be credited to a renaissance of pride in being Hawaiian and the establishment of language immersion schools (funded by the Hawaii Department of Education with assistance from the Office of Hawaiian Affairs), where all classes are taught in the native language. Today, not only children take classes to *'olelo* (speak) Hawaiian, their parents do so too, in order to keep up with their multilingual kids.

Even a straightforward conversation in English will be peppered with Hawaiian words that are known to all residents of the islands, and that sometimes better describe something than an equivalent word in English. *Pau hana*, used in the example above, could superficially be translated as "after work." Yet, in Hawaiian it has a richer meaning and texture that, nonetheless, defies description. You have to be in the islands for a while for the subtleties to take effect.

To describe the Hawaiian language in English is problematical because it is a language of emotion, poetry, and nature-related sound and nuance. It is an ancient language that was not transliterated until after 1820, when American missionaries arbitrarily chose 12 English letters to represent the Hawaiian sounds they thought they heard. While any transliteration of one language into the letters and sounds of another isn't perfect, the romanization of Hawaiian works well, mostly.

A language of the Pacific

For hundreds of years, the language had thrived expressively and melodically as the exclusively spoken tongue of a Polynesian people who were rich in an unwritten literature; this included complicated poetic chants detailing history, genealogies, and mythologies set to memory and passed orally from generation to generation.

Historians have not determined all of the intricacies of the development of the Hawaiian language, but a fairly clear picture has emerged regarding its relationship to other languages. Hawaiian belongs to the Austronesian (formerly called Malayo-Polynesian) language family.

LEFT: translation not needed. **RIGHT:** newspaper, 1835.

These were the languages spoken by seafaring peoples who settled over a broader area of the globe than was covered by any other group until the 18th and 19th centuries, when Europeans began extensively exploring beyond their known world.

Hawaii is the furthest point of Austronesian expansion to the north, with Easter Island the eastern extent and New Zealand the most southern. From these points westward, Austronesian tongues are spoken through the Pacific to Indonesia, Malaysia, the Philippines, and parts of Taiwan. The furthest western point is the island of Madagascar off the coast of Africa.

More specifically, Hawaiian is classified as a Polynesian language closely related to the language spoken in Tahiti, the Marquesas, and the surrounding island groups of the South Pacific. Early ancestors of the Hawaiian race originated from these groups, sailing their outrigger canoes from Southeast or Indo-Malay Asia around the north coast of New Guinea, through the islands of Melanesia and into Polynesia.

Variations in the core language evolved along the way, but certain words and verbal inflections continue to reveal the ancient ties between them. Instead of the Hawaiian term *i'a* for fish, people

KE KUMU HAWAII.

HE PEPA HOIKEIKE I NA MEA E PONO AI KO HAWAII NEI.

"O ka pono ka mea e pomaikai ai ka lahuikanaka; aka, o ka hewa ka mea e hoinoia'i na aina."

Buke 1.   HONOLULU, OAHU, MEI 13, 1835.   Pepa 14.

HE ZEBERA.

Ua like kekahi ano o ka Zebera me ko ka Lio. Ua like ka heluna o kona mau niho, a ua poepoe ka mau iuu o kona mau wawae, aole hoi i maheleia, ua like no me ko ka lio.

O ka Zebera, o ka lio, ua nui ka lio. O ka Zebera, o ka hoki, ua nui ka Zebera. Ua olenalena ke oho o ka Zebera, a he onionio eleele nae. Ua kanawale ka olenalena, a me ka eleele. Nolaila ua like me ka mea i penaia. Ua like kekahi mau helehelena ona me ko ka lio, a me ko ka hoki kekahi. O kona kino a me kona uha

Makemake loa lakou e noho pu a hele pu, he ohana nui, nolaila, ua nui loa lakou i ikeia ma kahi hookahi.

I ka wa e ai ai kekahi mau mea, kiai no kekahi mau mea, o hiki mai auanei ka enemi, he kanaka paha, o ka ilio paha. Ina i ike mai ka poe kiai i ke kanaka, a i ka ilio huhu paha, alaila, hoike koke aku la lakou, i ka poe e ai ana; alaila, holo nui lakou, a no ko lakou mama, aole loa iki lakou i kekahi holoho-lona.

No ka hihiu o ka Zebera aole ia i hoolaka loa ia, no ka mea, ina i paa i kona wa uuku, hoowahawaha no ia i ka mea e hoohana mai ia ia.

Ina i malama pio ia oia i na makahiki he nui loa, a hanai mau ia i ka lima o ke kanaka hookahi, aole ia e oluolu ke noho ke kanaka ma

oi aku ka maikai o kona ai, a me kona poo, a me kona mau pepeiao mamua o ko ka Zebera.

He mama ka Zebera, he lohi ka lio. He lokomaikai nae ka lio, aoluolu i ke lawe i ke kanaka ma kona kua. Ina i ee ke kanaka maluna o ka Zebera, o kona pii no ia, a holo ino, i haule ke kanaka.

E hoomanawanui no ka lio ma na hana a pau a ke kahu e haawi aku ai ia ia. Aka, o ka Zebera, aole hiki ke hoolaka ia ia, no kona hihiu loa. Ma ka onionio maikai o kona mamua o na holoholona a pau. He onionio like, a maikai wale no.

I noonoo kakou i ka mooolelo no na holoholona a pau, maopopo no ko ke Akua lokomaikai. Ua hoonele ia kekahi holoholona i ka mea i loaa mai i kekahi. O ka Elepani, ina

of Southeast Asia say *ika* or *ikan*. Instead of *hale* for house, they say *fare*, *'are* or *vale*. Instead of *maka* for eye, they say *mata*. Na Pali, the name for the towering cliffs in Kauai's north shore, comes from the same root as the name of the Himalayan kingdom of Nepal.

By 1819, Calvinist Christian missionaries had succeeded in converting several adventurous Hawaiian seamen who had sailed on various trading ships to America's east coast.

The first missionaries to Hawaii knew that the Hawaiian language was a spoken language only, but they were eager to set it to writing to facilitate the translation of the Bible.

ABOUT THE SPELLINGS OF PLACES

Two symbols can be added to Hawaiian words to assist pronunciation: a glottal stop *(')*, called an *'okina*, and a macron, which is a horizontal line over a vowel, indicating it is drawn out. *Insight Guide: Hawaii* uses the *'okina*, but not the macron. The *'okina*, which gives a "hard edge" to a vowel or separates two adjoining vowels with distinct sounds, is necessary for basic pronunciation in normal conversation; the macron offers a more subtle pronunciation.

All place names in this guide that need them use a glottal stop, with three exceptions: Hawaii, Oahu and Kauai, also written as Hawai'i, O'ahu, Kaua'i. But the non-glottal spellings are so common and ubiquitous that most cartographers delete the glottal stop for these islands. Two islands requiring glottal stops for pronunciation are Ni'ihau *(nee ee how)* and Kaho'olawe *(kah ho o lah vay)*. We use these forms.

By 1823, three years after their arrival, the various missionaries established the Hawaiian alphabet, although not without disputes. Some argued that the *k* sound was closer to *t*, or that the flapped *r* sound was more of an *l* sound. When the final vote was taken, *k* was adopted over the *t*, and *l* was chosen over the flapped *r*. The consonants were established as *h, k, l, m, n, p*, and *w*, while the vowel sounds were recorded as the five distinctive *a, e, i, o* and *u* sounds of Western romance languages. These 12 letters remain the official Hawaiian alphabet today.

For some time after Westerners began settling in the islands, Hawaiian continued to be spoken and written in government, business, and social circles of the Hawaiian kingdom. For years, it was used almost exclusively in newspapers. Then, as the the outside culture came to predominate, with missionary schooling widespread and Hawaii emerging as the Pacific's key port, the use of Hawaiian fell into disfavor. It was forbidden in public schools by 1896, and by the start of the 20th century, it had been replaced by English in the territorial legislature.

Many Hawaiian households suppressed the use of the language in an attempt to conform to the standards of the day, and the art of chanting, which is the oral preservation of history and genealogy, diminished. The last Hawaiian language newspaper, *Ka Hoku O Hawaii (The Star of Hawaii)*, printed in Hilo on the Big Island, stopped its presses in 1948. In 1992, a monthly paper called *Na Maka O Kana*, aimed at Hawaiian-language students and published by the University of Hawaii, Hilo, began to offer news about sports, movies, and other activities in the Hawaiian language.

In the 1980s, it was estimated that only 2,000 native speakers of Hawaiian – about 300 of them residents of the privately owned island of Ni'ihau – remained in Hawaii. Today, the picture has brightened considerably. In 1979, the state legislature approved funding for the Office of Hawaiian Affairs (OHA), run for and by Hawaiians for the betterment of Hawaiians. The OHA assists the Department of Education in running language-immersion schools for children from kindergarten through 12th grade. Slowly, besides a few remaining *kupuna*, or elders, who are fluent enough to teach their native tongue, a younger generation of teachers is emerging.

Pronunciation guidelines

Every letter in Hawaiian is pronounced distinctly. Vowels have just one sound: *a* sounds like ah, *e* like ay (as in hay), *i* like ee, *o* like oh, and *u* like oo. Likelike Highway, for example, is correctly pronounced *lee-kay lee-kay*, not *like-like*. Keep these simple rules in mind when you see signs such as Kalaniana'ole Highway or Kapi'olani. Glottal stops, called *'okina*, often separate strings of vowels and indicate that each vowel should be pronounced distinctly. For example, Ka'a'awa makes considerable sense, but Kaaawa not so much. ❏

MUSIC AND HULA

The missionaries nearly erased the ancient forms of music and dance from the islands. They failed, and today both the old and new forms are celebrated

Few other types of music have girdled the earth more smoothly, more often, and more completely than Hawaiian music, and few musical genres have remained so popular with so many for so long. Say "Hawaiian music" to a banker in Bangkok, an army captain in Amsterdam, or a housewife in Minneapolis, and all get the same romantic, dreamy look. They're thinking of swaying palms and hips... the hula... the sultry slack-key guitar... a chilling, tremulous falsetto voice... the sassy plunky-plunkiness of a *'ukulele*... the keening notes of a steel guitar.

Hawaii has been described as a melting pot, historically quick to accept whatever comes to its golden shores. Nowhere is this phenomenal rate and degree of cultural assimilation more apparent than in the music. Listening to Hawaiian music is like listening to the islands' history.

Musical legends

In ancient times, Hawaiian music sounded simpler, consisting of long, monotonous chants recited either without accompaniment or against a percussive background of drums made from coconut trees, gourds, bamboo rattles and pipes, sticks, and pebble castanets. The ritualistic aspects of the music were complex and played a vital part in daily life and a significant role in religious beliefs and services. Chants, for example, were the means of establishing contact between humans and gods. Entering a *halau* (hula school) was equivalent to entering a monastery. Today, the hula is both a spiritual and an artistic expression of Hawaiian culture.

Legends say that the goddesses of dance were Laka and Hi'iaka. (If not actually worshipped, both are still revered today.) At first, both men and women performed the dance, but only men could perform the hula during temple worship services. It was believed that by pantomiming an action, that action could be controlled in the future. Thus there were many dances for desired

events, such as a successful hunt, fertility, or other successes. The hula later engulfed all of Hawaiian society and became many things – teaching tool, popular entertainment, and a basic foundation for *lua*, an art of self-defense promoted by the Hawaiians. As the dance became widespread and society increasingly

complicated, wars and governing duties kept the men too busy for the years of training required to be a performer. Thus, the women began to share equally in the performance of the hula.

Then an odd thing happened. After uncounted hundreds of years, King Kamehameha II overthrew the *kapu* (taboo) system in 1819 and with it went the ancient religion, of which hula was a part. This left the Hawaiian people spiritually disoriented, and ripe for newly arrived, enthusiastic Christian missionaries from New England.

These devout and dedicated settlers built churches amid the Hawaiian huts, held services, and sang hymns. Hawaiians had never heard melody and four-part harmony before, and they

PRECEDING PAGES: hula dancers performing at the water's edge. **LEFT:** *'ukulele* player in Palolo Valley, Oahu. **RIGHT:** tattooed dancer in bark-cloth skirt.

collected by the hundreds outside the small churches to listen to these exotic combinations. Thinking that the quickest way to a Hawaiian's soul might be through the ears, the missionaries enrolled the Hawaiians in church choirs. Progress was slow; the broader tones required by church hymns were new to Hawaiians, so songs had to be learned by rote as the missionaries sang the hymns, called *himeni* by the Hawaiians, over and over and over again, and the Hawaiians copied as best they could.

VAUDEVILLE

Hula dancers were popular in vaudeville. They were called "cootch" dancers because many non-native performers adapted the movements lasciviously.

today. He also reversed the traditional order of the *mele*, or song, by composing the music before the words. Hawaiians began doing the same, and before the 1870s ended, they were composing lyrics and music simultaneously. Heinrich Berger also served as inspiration and teacher for two generations of Hawaiian musicians, some of whom later went on to local, if not national or international stardom.

Other influences arrived: the guitar, for instance, was brought by early whalers or per-

Royal Hawaiian Band, H.

Outside influences

Hawaiian music's other most dominant influence came in the form of a single man and reflected a Hawaiian king's wish to be Westernized. King Kamehameha V decided that he wanted a royal band like those in Europe, and so the brisk, mustachioed Heinrich Berger was imported from Germany in 1868 to be bandmaster. Berger, who is known today as the father of Hawaiian music, served as director of the Royal Hawaiian Band from 1872 until 1915. During this time, he conducted more than 32,000 band concerts, arranged more than 1,000 Hawaiian songs, and composed 75 original Hawaiian songs, including several still popular

haps by traders from Mexico and California, but not, as is popularly believed, by Mexican cowboys, who arrived later in the early 1830s. In time, the traditional style of playing changed as the Hawaiian musicians loosened their strings, and tunings became whatever the player wished them to be. This style of playing came to be known as *ki ho'alu*, or slack key, and is as uniquely Hawaiian as flamenco is Spanish.

From Madeira came a small, four-stringed instrument called the *braquino*, or *cavaquinho*. It was brought to Hawaii by laborers imported to work in the sugar-cane fields, in 1878. As with so much else in Hawaiian musical history, there is disagreement as to how the *braquino* became *'ukulele*, which, in Hawaiian, roughly translates as "jumping flea".

Scholars also continue to argue about who invented the steel guitar. Some say a Hawaiian student discovered the sound in the 1880s when he dropped his pocket knife upon the strings of a guitar, and holding it there with one hand, plucked the strings with the other, moving the steel knife to "slide" the sound.

Others think the inventor once visited India, where he could have seen a stringed instrument, the *gottuvadyam*, played in a similar fashion. While the steel guitar has since been much identified with country-and-western music, it remains the single most identifiable part of the Hawaiian instrumental sound.

Royal inspiration

The descendants of the ancient *ali'i* ruling Hawaii in the final years before annexation to the United States were among the most talented and prolific composers of song that the island culture ever produced. The best known of these was King David Kalakaua, a complex and jovial man whose reign was also an inspiration for a genuine renaissance of music and dance.

Kalakaua was a gifted politician, world traveler, and patron of the arts. He promoted the *'ukulele* and steel guitar, and formed his own musical group, entering into competitions with relatives and friends. He collected the legends and myths of Hawaii into a definitive and literate book, and co-wrote with Heinrich Berger Hawaii's national anthem, "Hawaii Pono'i," a song that's still sung at ball games and public assemblies. The hula, long suppressed by the Christian missionaries, was revived under his personal direction. Much music is played today on the birthday, 16 November, of this bewhiskered king; the state's biggest hula competition, the Merrie Monarch (named for his nickname) takes place annually on the Big Island. His sister, Lili'uokalani, came even closer than the king to understanding and synthesizing ancient Hawaiian and Western musical traditions and form. Probably the most gifted Hawaiian of her time, she composed a song that has appeared in at least half the Hawaiian movies ever made, and it has been a certifiable "hit" for almost a century, "Aloha 'Oe."

The sound of Hawaiian music changed again after Lili'uokalani's kingdom was made a territory of the United States. This focused mainland interest toward Hawaii, and in 1915 a group of Hawaiian musicians, singers, and dancers were the runaway sensation of the Panama-Pacific International Exposition in San Francisco, sparking a craze that swept North America and spread to Europe. Soon after, the best or most adaptable Tin Pan Alley song writers were writing so-called Hawaiian music, too.

Even if most of those new songs had little to do with true Hawaiian musical tradition – and often double-talk served as Hawaiian, as in

"Yaaka Hula Hickey Dula" (a hit for Al Jolson) – the influence was immediate and significant. The craze propelled authentic Hawaiian musicians across America for many years. They, in turn, accepted the phony Hawaiian songs to satisfy requests, eventually turning them into Hawaiian "classics." At the same time, they began arranging traditional, more authentic Hawaiian songs with the newly popular jazz beat that they heard everywhere they went.

In Hawaii, the first hotels were going up in Waikiki, and dance bands were formed for the growing number of tourists. Ragtime, jazz, blues, Latin, and foxtrot rhythms were interspersed with Hawaiian themes and English lyrics. The

LEFT: Heinrich Berger and the Royal Hawaiian Band, 1910. **RIGHT:** *Hula halau* on Oahu, 1852.

purists were appalled, as always, but by 1930 the *hapa-haole* (half-Caucasian) song was an entrenched and accepted part of Hawaiian music, soon to become a staple on what was eventually the most widely heard radio program in the world. In 1935, Hawaii's music caught the ears of the mainland's West Coast listeners via "Hawaii Calls," a radio program broadcast from under a banyan tree in Waikiki beach and other exotic locales. Today, many of the more than 300 Hawaiian musicians who were on that radio

HOLLYWOOD BECKONS

Bing Crosby introduced two songs in the 1937 movie *Waikiki Wedding.* "Sweet Leilani" won the Oscar, so Hollywood began churning out musical romances.

hands/graceful as the birds in motion," the arms are extended and the hands move gracefully to simulate the wings of swooping birds. In "The Hukilau Song," which is about fishing, you see the hands throw out and pull in the net.

The period from 1930 to 1960 is regarded as Hawaiian music's "golden age," as the music of the islands circled the world on television and in radio and film.

Then came the Beatles, changing Hawaiian music just as they changed so many things. In fact, they nearly killed it.

program are legends of the state's musical past, among them Danny Kaleikini, Alfred Apaka and Benny Kalama.

The call of Hollywood

Then Hollywood called. The hula was revived again and cleaned up a bit for Hollywood as authentic island practitioners were featured in many films: the swaying hips and graceful limbs of the grass-skirted dancer would be the foremost symbol of Hawaii's image of carefree sensuality.

When a songwriter urged visitors to Hawaii to keep their eyes on the performers' hands, it was good advice, for the hands tell the story in hula. When the singer says, "Lovely hula

For 10 years, young Hawaiians were uninterested in the traditional island sound. Hawaiian music on local radio dropped to a low 5 percent. Rock dominated, and crooners like Kui Lee and Don Ho emerged as top Hawaiian stars, rendering songs such as "One Paddle, Two Paddle," "Days of My Youth," and "I'll Remember You."

Traditional sounds are revitalized

The most important figure among those responsible for keeping the flame of traditional Hawaiian music alive was the slack-key guitarist Gabby Pahinui. He made his first solo recording, "Hi'ilawe," in 1947, and in the late 1950s formed the Sons of Hawaii group with 'ukelele virtuoso Eddie Kamae, a keen musicologist who hunted out long-forgotten Hawaiian-language songs from all the islands. In the early 1970s, their reunion album, "The Folk Music of Hawaii," was hugely influential among younger musicians, many of whom began to write their own songs, celebrating the poetic resonance of the Hawaiian language and also addressing contemporary social realities.

During this so-called "Hawaiian renaissance," all the traditional Hawaiian arts experienced a rich revival, as islanders with Hawaiian blood discovered a renewed sense of ethnic awareness and pride. Many were influenced by

Gabby Pahinui left the Sons in the mid-1970s, and, thanks in part to his collaborations with guitarist Ry Cooder, went on to achieve international acclaim before his premature death in 1980. Meanwhile, new stars were emerging in Hawaii, such as guitarist Keola Beamer, who honed his techniques on an album called "Hawaiian Slack Key in the Real Old Style." Beamer says, "There's power in our music which is drawn from the environment. If you sit and watch a waterfall or listen to the trade winds for a while, you begin to feel a rhythm. You can be far away from Hawaii and hear a song and instantly be transported."

the cultural changes taking place in the rest of the United States, and some of the Hawaiian music of the era, it has to be said, sounds awfully like Californian-style rock.

However, there was also a great resurgence of interest in the more traditional Hawaiian sounds. As Moe Keale, who also played *'ukulele* with the Sons of Hawaii, put it, "Music is not something you just hear with your ears. It's something you hear with your heart. I can tell when Hawaiian music is being played right, because it makes me cry."

LEFT: Makaha Sons of Ni'ihau, with Israel Kamakawiwo'ole, 1979. **ABOVE:** hula dancers relax.

Among other new names on the scene were the Sunday Manoa, who included the Cazimero brothers; Hui Ohana, a trio featuring Ledward and Nedward Ka'apana and Dennis Pava'o; Palani Vaughan; and a young group from Gabby's hometown of Waimanolo, Oahu – the Makaha Sons of Ni'ihau, featuring the brothers Skippy and Israel Kamakawiwo'ole.

By the early 1990s, Hawaiian music was at the forefront of the political struggle for Hawaiian sovereignty. Dennis Pava'o recorded the popular "All Hawaii Stand Together," but it was Israel Kamakawiwo'ole, by now a solo artist and universally known as "Iz," who gave the movement its greatest anthems, in the form of songs like "Hawaii 78." Plagued by the chronic ill-health problems that had already killed his brother – his weight is said to have exceeded a phenomenal 1,000 lbs (454 kg) – but blessed with a voice of astonishing power and delicacy, Iz became a much-loved superstar. He died in 1997, and was honoured with a state funeral. His legacy was albums such as "E Ala E," and, especially, "Facing Future," which was still high in the world music charts a decade after his death, while his million-selling medley of "Somewhere Over The Rainbow/What A Wonderful World" has become a staple of Hollywood soundtracks.

Sisters are doing it

Women have always played a crucial role in Hawaiian music. Queen Lili'uokalani composed many of the islands' most enduring classics, while chanter/dancer Edith Kanaka'ole was the 20th-century's greatest repository of the Polynesian heritage. Female vocalists have been especially significant as performers of the unique Hawaiian tradition of falsetto singing, which is characterized by audible breathing for extra effect. Lena Machado, known as "Hawaii's Songbird," championed the form from the 1930s until the 1960s, while Auntie Genoa Keawe, who first recorded in the 1940s and established her own record label, was still performing regularly in Waikiki when she celebrated her 89th birthday in 2007. The latest divas in the genre are Amy Hanaiali'i Gilliom, known for her entertaining live performances with guitarist Willie K, and Molokai's Raiatea Helm. Popular falsetto vocal groups include the trio Na Leo Pilimehana, responsible for albums like "Anthology I" and "Colours," and Na Palapalai. It's worth mentioning too that there have been some fabulous male falsetto singers, such as Bill Lincoln Ali'iloa, and the phenomenal Mahi Beamer.

Hawaiian music today

New generations of young entertainers continue to emerge, sending out Hawaiian vibes to the mainland, Japan, and beyond, combining music with showmanship that draws on early Hawaiian traditions. On stage, composer, chanter, dancer, and singer Keali'i Reichel stands bare-chested, hair streaming about his shoulders, carved bone fishhook nestled at his neck. His body tattoos run from his ankle to disappear under his brief *malo* (loincloth). In the bright spotlight, he sings in sweet, resonant tones, switching from ballads like "Ku'u Pua Mae 'Ole" (about lasting romance and calming waters), to a poetic chant "Maika'i Ka 'Oiwi O Ka'ala" with *ipu* (gourd) accompaniment.

Albums such as "Kawaipunahele" and "Lei Hali'a" have been met with critical acclaim. Reichel explains why he believes his music has such appeal: "In order to compose music, words, poetry, you have to be inspired; you have to speak from experience."

Other names to watch out for these days include the duo Hapa, who, as their name suggests, consist of a *haole* and a native Hawaiian; Edith Kanaka'ole's great-grandson Kaumakaiwa; and the *'ukulele* prodigy Jake Shimabukuro.

Where to hear it

If you'd like to catch some live Hawaiian music, Honolulu is the best place to head for, with big-name concerts at such venues as the Hawaii Theatre and the Waikiki Shell; top-class nightly music at Chai's Island Bistro in the Aloha Tower Marketplace; and Genoa Keawe's weekly stint at the Waikiki Beach Marriott. On Maui, the Ritz-Carlton hotel in Kapalua plays host to an award-winning weekly slack-key recital, presided over by George Kahumoku, Jr.

The Royal Hawaiian Band too are still going strong after all these years, appearing in several public concerts each week, notably at noon nearly every Friday at the 'Iolani Palace Coronation Bandstand. Popular radio stations KHUI (99.5 FM) and KINE (105.1 FM) broadcast contemporary and traditional Hawaiian music.

Return of hula

Not since the beginning of the 19th century, when missionaries labeled many hula dances obscene and banned them, have such powerful and erotic movements been seen in Hawaii. Indeed, the suppression of hula had been so suc-

male hula now in a period of rich revival, the dance has become a symbol of the islanders' newly rediscovered sense of Hawaiian identity.

Prestigious events

Hawaii's most prestigious hula event is the Merrie Monarch Festival, which pays homage to King David Kalakaua, Hawaii's last king. It has been held every April since 1964 at the Edith Kanaka'ole Stadium in Hilo. The highlight of the week-long festival, which includes a parade and musical celebrations, is the two-day competition of *kahiko*, or ancient hula, and *'auwana* or modern hula.

cessful that by the 1850s it had nearly disappeared. Forty years later, after King Kalakaua revived the hula, a great deal had already been lost forever.

Today, hula has regained much of its serious heritage. Contemporary students heed ancient ritual religiously, although they are not asked to give up sex in order to be a hula performer, as was true in ancient times. Different *hula halau* (hula schools) compete fiercely; hula masters, or *kumu hula*, are revered figures. And with the

LEFT: children performing the hula.
ABOVE: proud state *keiki* hula (children's hula) champions.

Every island has its signature hula events. On Oahu, the Queen Lili'uokalani Keiki Hula festival draws 500 children to perform every July, and in the same month, the Prince Lot Hula Festival is played out under the giant monkey pod trees of Moanalua Gardens. At Princeville, Kauai, local entertainers meet mainland musicians at the Prince Albert Hula Festival every May. On Maui, the Na Mele O Maui Song Contest and Hula Festival takes place annually in Ka'anapali, while Molokai's Ka Hula Piko Festival is celebrated each May close to hula's supposed birthplace, near Maunaloa. If you are in Hawaii when any of these events is being celebrated it will be well worth attending. ❏

AN ART OF FLOWERS, FEATHERS AND *ALOHA*

Found throughout Polynesia, lei *were once almost sacred symbols. Today,* lei *retain some of that aura, but are also used to convey* aloha *and respect*

In ancient times, *lei* were offered to the gods during sacred dances and chants, taking the form of head wreaths and necklaces, as well as the long, open-ended strands of *maile* (vines) that are draped around the necks of grooms and prom escorts today.

Lei are made of flowers, leaves, shells, and paper, and of anything else that can be fashioned by six basic techniques. If a *lei*-maker uses *wili paukuku*, she is winding roses and begonias in a certain style. *Humuhumu* is a *lei* sewn onto a backing. *Wili* is a *lei* that is wound or twisted, *hili* is braided with leaves and *haku* is braided with flowers. *Kui* is strung on a thread.

Before needle and thread were introduced to Hawaii, stiff grass blades from Nu'uanu Valley were used as needles, and strands of banana bark were utilized as string. For the more elaborate feather *lei* reserved for the royalty of old Hawaii, strips of *olona* bark were twisted into a cord that was flexible and strong enough to invisibly secure hundreds of feathers.

Prices may range today from less than $5 up to $50 for the fragrant *maile* and multiple strands of *pikake*. Many *lei*, like the woven ginger *lei* or the complex maunaloa orchid *lei*, are intricate works of art. Others, such as a simple plumeria *lei*, can be strung by anyone with a needle and thread.

△ **FOR THE TOURISTS**
Makers of *lei* produce hundreds if not thousands of *lei* daily for the islands' tourism industry. Most common is the plumeria *lei*.

▽ **ECLECTIC DIVERSITY**
Nearly any flower or nut can be fashioned into a *lei*, including bougainvillea, ginger, and plumeria with its luscious scent.

▽ *LEI HULU*
Red and yellow feathers were used in the *lei* of royalty. *Lei hulu* also means a dearly beloved child or person.

A KINGLY *LEI*

n Kamehameha Day, the
onolulu statue of
amehameha the Great, who
nified the Hawaiian islands,
 draped with a floral cape of
cores of long *lei*, or *lei ali'i*, a
i for royalty or the chief.

LEI FOR HULA

he hula, both traditional and
odern, uses *lei* as an
nportant adornment. Often
 hula, *lei* are not made from
owers, but leaves and other
arts of flora considered to
npart importance.

AROUND THE NECK

lei for the neck is known as
i 'a'i, also an expression for
ecktie or scarf.

◁ **EQUESTRIAN *LEI***
A *pa'u* rider and horse on
Kamehameha Day are
exquisitely adorned with *lei*.
(A *pa'u* is a skirt or
sarong for female
horseback riders.)

DRAPED BY *ALOHA* AND RESPECT

In Hawaii, as in some other Pacific island cultures, a *lei* is a special symbol or gift given as a sign of respect, welcome (or departure), or good feeling. *Lei* are also draped over the statues or images of important people in Hawaii's history, such as Kamehameha the Great *(above)*, Queen Lili'uokalani or Father Damien.

Each island has its own special material for making *lei*. The delicate orange *'ilima* blossom represents Oahu. Feathery red *lehua* blossoms from gnarled *'ohi'a* trees symbolize the island of Hawaii. Pink *lokelani* (an introduced Castilian rose) make up Maui's *lei*, while Molokai is adorned by silver-green leaves from the *kukui* tree and decorated with tiny white blossoms.

Oblong leaves and dark berries from the *mokihana* tree are fashioned into a *lei* for Kauai. On Lanai, *lei* are woven from slim strands of *kauna'oa*, an orange, mossy beach vine. Even uninhabited Kaho'olawe has a *lei* from *hinahina*, a beach plant with narrow green leaves and little white flowers. Ni'ihau is the only island not represented by a flower, but by shells: the rare and very tiny *pupu* that are treasured by *kama'aina* as much as valuable gems.

FOOD OF AN ECLECTIC SORT

With ethnic influences from Polynesia, Asia, Europe and
North America, Hawaii's cuisine is among the world's most eclectic

sland menus read like a United Nations lunch order: *sushi*, pasta, crispy *gau gee*, *kim chee*, tortillas, tandoori chicken, *wienerschnitzel*, spring rolls – you name it, they eat it. Within a relatively small geographical area, visitors find a universe of dishes served in surroundings both down-home and haute, from casual eateries that serve two scoops of rice for a "plate lunch," to candlelit lairs with *chateaubriand* and chocolate mousse on the menu.

Hawaii has many to thank for its tasty diversity. To begin with the Chinese, who taught islanders that rice goes just as well with eggs at breakfast as with lunch and dinner. Supermarkets of all stripes stock supplies of *cilantro*, lemongrass and ginger, and restaurants turn out everything from Mandarin, Sichuan, and Cantonese to Mongolian barbecue and stir-fry. For an energizing assault on the senses, go to a house of *dim sum*, where waitresses load your table with little plates of bite-sized dumplings until hands are held up in surrender.

From the Japanese came the gifts of *shoyu* (soy sauce), *sashimi* (thinly sliced raw fish), and *tempura* (battered, deep-fried vegetables and meats, introduced to Japan from Portugal, actually). Almost every street has a sushi bar for swigging *sake* while chefs with lightning-fast hands fashion edible fantasies out of rice, seafood and *wasabi* (hot green-horseradish). Japanese culinary sensibilities are best summed up by the *bento*, a lunch box with tidy compartments for morsels of chicken, shrimp, pork cutlets, fishcake, pickled plums, rice, and other artful treats.

Wafts of garlic and grilled specialties lure hungry diners through the doors of Hawaii's Korean restaurants, which generally assume the form of Formica-tabled eateries. Therein await *kim chee* (pickled vegetables), *kalbi* (marinated short ribs), *jun* (foods fried in an egg batter), and the musical *bi bim bap*, which is a bowl of rice, with vegetables, fried egg, and a sweet sauce.

LEFT: Hawaii is a fruit-lover's paradise, with pineapples, mangos, and nectarines to name just a few.
RIGHT: lunch offerings.

A more recent influx of people from Thailand has introduced spring rolls, *mee krob* (noodle salad), and a coconut milk/hot pepper-flavored dish called Evil Jungle Prince, best followed by Thai iced tea with sweetened condensed milk. Vietnamese food – less spicy than Thai – is particularly popular for its *phô*, a broth with

noodles and beef or chicken slices. Portuguese influence makes itself known in *pao dolce* (sweet bread), *chorizo* (spicy sausage), *vinha d'alhos* (marinated meat) and a robust bean soup, while from the Philippines comes *lumpia* (fried spring rolls), *pancit* (noodles, vegetables and pork), *pork guisantes* (pork rump), *bagoong* (fish sauce) and *bitsu bitsu* (sweet potato scones).

Stir into this pot the creativity of classically trained chefs from France, Switzerland, Germany, North America, and Italy who have been imported to work in some of Hawaii's upscale restaurants. The state's continental ideas of the 1970s have evolved into today's more health-conscious cooking, but without too much effort you can still find an authentic veal *scaloppini* or a slab of salmon drenched in dill sauce.

The most recent take on island food is called Hawaii Regional Cuisine – a variation of what's known elsewhere as Pacific Rim Cuisine, New Australian Cuisine, or fusion cuisine – which begins with a sort of culinary word association. Think of a papaya and one thinks of the prolific trees of Puna on the Big Island. Onions conjure up images of cool upcountry Kula on Maui, where the sweetest variety is grown. Guava thrives in Kilauea on Kauai, and Molokai is known for its sweet potatoes, while fresh fish are pulled from the waters round all the islands.

she mingled in flavors of Filipino, Chinese, Japanese and Hawaiian dishes."

Inevitably, the blending of cooking styles occurred in Hawaii's plantation villages. When Japanese contract laborers were imported in the 1880s, they lived side-by-side with Hawaiian and Chinese workers in simple, single-walled wooden houses. The Chinese built community cookhouses, the Japanese added mom-and-pop tofu (soybean curd) factories. People grew their own *bok choi* and lemongrass in backyards.

When Hawaii's classically trained chefs saw they could infuse their own food with an exciting new range of flavors by learning Hawaiian-

The regional cuisine movement gained momentum in 1992, when a dozen curious, creative and congenial chefs began getting together to share their ideas as well as their wish lists for a wider variety of fresh produce and other more varied ingredients. In the kitchens of their own elegant restaurants, their sous-chefs and *gardemangers* were feasting on interesting, flavorful treats they had learned to make at home.

Alan Wong, whose Oahu Restaurant is the perennial winner of the in-state Hale 'Aina Award for Best Restaurant (eight times between 1996 and 2007), explains, "While I was growing up in Hawaii, my grandfather cooked Chinese and my mother cooked Japanese, but

style cooking from each other, while supporting local agriculture, they gave their group a formal name, Hawaii Regional Cuisine, Inc.

Their presence has made a difference on Hawaii's culinary scene. Today, any number of farmers are growing crops to the specifications of chefs who visit the fields and make known what they want for their own restaurants. Tomatoes are vine-ripened; arugula and baby lettuces fill Upcountry fields on Maui and the Big Island. Several hotels grow their own fresh herbs. One hotel in Waikiki has its own rooftop hydroponic garden, and a Maui resort harvests fresh tropical fruit and other produce from an organic garden that surrounds its parking lot.

A host of professional chefs were inspired by the daring dozen, and Hawaiian regional cuisine has become a palate-pleasing password even beyond island shores. Who hasn't seen or heard of Hawaii's own Sam Choy, or the equally renowned Roy Yamaguchi, both of whom own several restaurants, have published cookbooks, and host their own television cooking shows? The current pantheon of greats includes George Mavrothalassitis, Peter Merriman, David Paul and Daniel Thiebaut, each with their own signature restaurants.

> **PERPLEXING POI**
>
> A staple of the traditional diet, *poi* is a thick, viscous paste-like food. It is made from the taro root.

Passion and pineapple

Local products have become as intrinsically linked to Hawaii's lifestyle as the ebbing and flowing of the tides. Residents and visitors alike have easy access to an abundance of fresh fruit, and we're not just talking pineapple and coconut. Equally common are the apple banana, the golden papaya, the pungent *liliko'i*, and the guava, a yellow lemon-sized gem with a shockingly pink interior.

The lychee, prized for its juicy white flesh, can be spotted hanging in grape-like clumps on trees

Enthusiastic practitioners of Hawaii regional cuisine collaborate closely with farmers and fishermen to get the products they need, then infuse those foods with cooking techniques from around the world. The result is a menu that reads like this: *'ulu* (breadfruit) *vichyssoise*, Manoa greens with Waimea vine-ripened tomatoes and Puna goat cheese, *tempura*-style Keahole shrimp and apple banana, sesame-cured boar loin with guava dressing, and a slice of *liliko'i* (passionfruit) chiffon pie. If so inclined, enjoy the meal with a wine from Tedeschi.

in Manoa Valley, while *poha* (cape gooseberry) thrives on bushes near Kilauea Volcano. The markets of Honolulu's Chinatown district are a good source of these and lesser-known fruits, like the tamarind, kumquat, starfruit, *rambuton* (sweet white fruit in a red, spiky shell), and *cherimoya* (with tart white flesh).

Visit Hawaii during the summer and you'll discover the joys of the mango. When mango trees start to blossom in May, it's as big a deal as seeing the first whales of winter. By July, the fruit is weighing down the branches, and neighbors distribute free bags of sweet, juicy mangos. Leftovers that aren't picked drop on the road, get squashed by traffic, and ferment.

LEFT: planting taro, used for *poi*, and ripening bananas.
ABOVE: actor Robert De Niro, co-owner of Nobu, Waikiki.

Ocean harvests

What is harvested by land is matched only by the bounty of the sea. The king and queen of Hawaiian fish are the *mahimahi* (dolphin fish) and *'opakapaka* (pink snapper), but *ulua* (jack crevalle), *ono* (wahoo), *'ahi* (yellow-fin tuna), *onaga* (red snapper) and *tako* (octopus), which is served raw and marinated as *poke*, are equally impressive, whether blackened Cajun-style or baked in wafer-thin layers of crisp phyllo pastry.

Local people have been known to scamper crab-like across shorelines, hanging on when the big waves roll in (not recommended; deaths are reported each year when waves overpower

promoting its own special grade of lamb. Lanai axis deer has become a popular entrée laced with plum sauce, and Molokai venison makes for a tasty stew or toothsome sausage.

If all of these choices sound a little overwhelming, start with the basics. Try a "plate lunch" – sold at carryout restaurants and lunch trucks – the statewide institution defined by a few simple elements. You'll get a paper plate loaded with "two scoop rice," plus a mound of heavily mayonnaised macaroni salad. Order one with *teriyaki* beef, breaded pork, or chicken *(katsu)*, fried fish or Spam, an unexpected passion among local people.

harvesters), in order to pick a bunch of quarter-sized shells off the lava rocks. Called *'opihi,* limpets are Hawaii's answer to French *escargots* and are rarely found on restaurant menus. In the world of aquaculture, the Big Island, Kauai and north shore of Oahu are creating miniature ocean tanks and fishponds teeming with prawns, lobsters, abalone and other delicacies.

Two-scoop rice

Hawaii's homegrown extends to grain-fattened beef, grass-fed lamb, and free-range game. *Paniolos* (cowboys) on Maui and the Big Island saddle up in the pre-dawn mist to round up the beef that ends up on dinner plates. Ni'ihau is

Next, try some snacks – maybe shave ice, a snowcone soaked in neon-colored tropical syrups like mango, guava and coconut. Those in the know order it with vanilla ice cream and sweet *azuki* beans on the bottom. Or try *manapua*, the tennis ball-sized steamed Chinese dumpling filled with pork or curried chicken. Enjoy a bowl of *saimin*, an Asian noodle soup topped with an encyclopedia of garnishes like sliced *char siu* (roast pork), fishcake, and green onions. Or pick up a bag of crack seed, pickled plums and *pipi kaula* (beef jerky).   ❏

ABOVE: the day's catch of tuna, Hilo. **RIGHT:** preparing the pig, the staple of *lu'aus*.

The *Lu'au*

It's late afternoon when the *lu'au* table is finally set under the big banyan tree. The salmon has been chopped *lomilomi* style, with onions and tomatoes, and it sits next to a big bowl of *poi*, or pounded taro root, a staple of the old Hawaiian diet. Aunties chatter as they carry out the rest of the dishes: *laulau* (pork and fish steamed in ti leaves), *poke* (seasoned raw fish), yams, squid *lu'au* with coconut milk and taro tops, *haupia* (coconut pudding), and fresh fruit.

The boys have already pulled out the pig from the *imu* (underground rock oven), and now the moist, smoky meat is shredded and piled on a big platter as the centerpiece of the meal. Friends and family pick up a plate.

If you're lucky, you might just stumble upon the real thing at a community benefit, or be invited to one by an island friend. More likely though, the *lu'aus* you'll discover will be the commercialized variety, complete with the comic hula and *maitais*. While purists may find this a shallow version of the real thing, the *imu* ceremonies, hula, Hawaiian music, kalua pig and other culinary specialties and good cheer are all rooted in Hawaiian tradition. If you can let go of prejudices about "authenticity," you're very likely to have a rollicking good time.

These modern *lu'aus* are a far cry from the *aha 'aina*, or feasts of old, when women dined separately from men and were prohibited from eating some of the choicest of *lu'au* fare. Finally, after 1819, when Liholiho (King Kamehameha II) abolished the old *kapu* (taboo) system of restrictions, *lu'aus* became a lively tradition enjoyed by all. Today, an Island wedding, baby's first birthday, or junior's graduation just wouldn't seem the same without a backyard bash for friends and family.

The most popular way of preparing food in old Hawaii was to *kalua* the meat, chicken, dog or fish in an earthen oven lined with stones. Today, the heart of any *lu'au*, commercial or private, continues to be the preparation and unearthing of the *imu*. Although dog is no longer part of the menu, current *lu'au* food is reasonably authentic, except for such items as macaroni and potato salads or *teriyaki*-beef, added to suit all tastes.

You'll still find pig roasted to juicy tenderness in the *imu*, accompanied by *poi*, sweet potatoes, marinated *lomilomi* salmon with chopped tomatoes and onions, and sometimes *'opihi*, a Hawaiian shellfish plucked from wave-washed rocky shorelines and eaten raw as a special delicacy. For uninitiated taste

buds, it's best to sample *poi* with salty *kalua* pig or *lomilomi* salmon to enhance the flavors and textures. Many *lu'aus* ladle out chicken long rice, a dish of chicken cooked with translucent noodles made of rice flour and garnished with green onions. Frequently you'll find *laulau*, little green bundles of taro leaf, which taste like spinach, steamed with pork and fish. For dessert, coconut cake is a new addition, but *haupia*, a coconut-milk pudding, has long been served as a sweet finale.

The entertainment at one of these modern feasts is like taking a mini-tour through the island cultures of Hawaii, Tonga, Samoa, New Zealand, and Tahiti. Hawaii's contribution includes the haunting chants

that perpetuate the genealogies and legends of the past, as well as the graceful hula. Some *lu'aus* include pageantry with participants dressed like early Hawaiian royalty.

Whether visitors will get their money's worth from a commercial *lu'au*, which might cost from $60 minimum, depends upon the individual, and the *lu'au*. If you are ready to throw yourself into the spirit of the night by donning your most colorful aloha shirt, taking off your shoes, and getting up on stage to learn a Tahitian *tamure* while your traveling companions cheer, and if you find unfamiliar foods intriguing, you'll have a good time. *Lu'au* range from tacky to traditional, and you'll just have to look around for your style. ❑

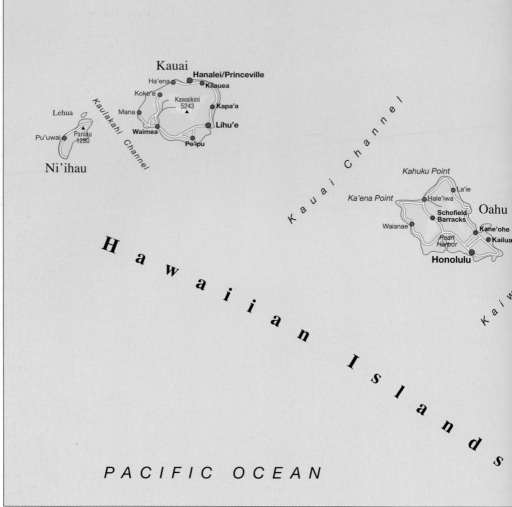

Kauai

Hanalei/Princeville
Ha'ena
Kilauea
Koke'e
Kawaikini
5243
Kapa'a
Lehua
Mana
Lihu'e
Waimea
Pu'uwai Paniau
1280
Po'ipu
Ni'ihau

Kahuku Point
La'ie
Ka'ena Point
Hale'iwa
Oahu
Schofield
Barracks
Waianae
Kane'ohe
Pearl
Harbor
Kailua
Honolulu

H a w a i i a n   I s l a n d s

PACIFIC OCEAN

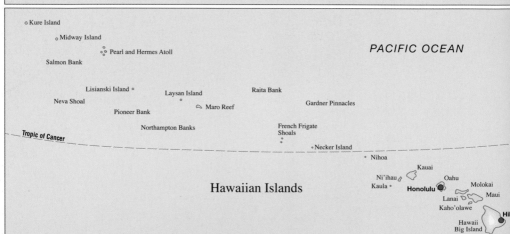

Kure Island

Midway Island

Pearl and Hermes Atoll
PACIFIC OCEAN
Salmon Bank

Lisianski Island
Laysan Island
Raita Bank
Neva Shoal
Maro Reef
Gardner Pinnacles
Pioneer Bank
Northampton Banks
French Frigate
Shoals
Tropic of Cancer
Necker Island

Nihoa

Kauai
Ni'ihau
Oahu
Molokai
Kaula
Honolulu
Hawaiian Islands
Lanai
Maui
Kaho'olawe
Hilo
Hawaii
Big Island

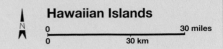

Hawaiian Islands

0   30 miles

0   30 km

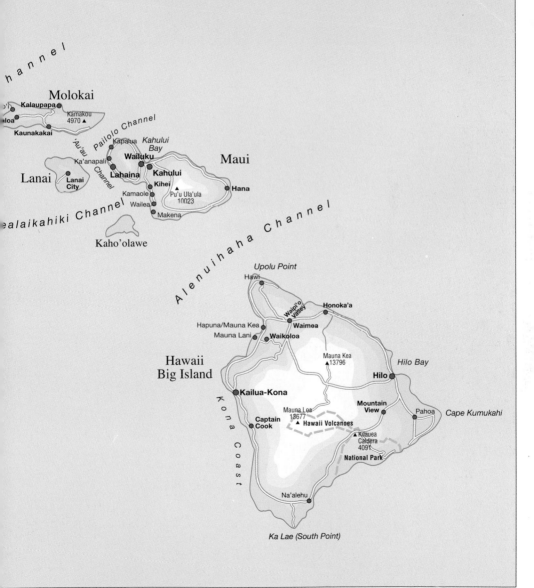

PACIFIC OCEAN

Channel

Kalaupapa

Molokai

loa

Kamakou
4970 ▲

Kaunakakai

'Au'au

Pailolo Channel

Kapalua

*Kahului
Bay*

Ka'anapali

Wailuku

Channel

Lanai

Lanai
City

Lahaina

Kahului

Maui

Kihei

Kamaole

Pu'u Ula'ula
10023

Hana

ealaikahiki Channel

Wailea

Makena

Kaho'olawe

Alenuihaha Channel

Upolu Point

Hawi

Honoka'a

*Waipi'o
Valley*

Hapuna/Mauna Kea

Waimea

Mauna Lani

Waikoloa

**Hawaii
Big Island**

Mauna Kea
▲13796

Hilo Bay

Hilo

Kailua-Kona

Kona Coast

Mauna Loa
13677 ▲

Hawaii Volcanoes

**Mountain
View**

Pahoa

Cape Kumukahi

**Captain
Cook**

▲ Kīlauea
Caldera
4091

National Park

Na'alehu

Ka Lae (South Point)

THE HAWAIIAN ISLANDS

A look at all the islands and important destinations, with cross references to detailed and comprehensive maps

Pull out a map and run a finger along the islands of Hawaii, strung across the Pacific like a series of jade stepping stones. The islands line up in order of age, with the youngest, the Big Island, in the southeast and the oldest islands – or what's left of them – 1,500 miles (2,400 km) away to the northwest. The oldest are atolls, shoals and seamounts now home to seabirds, turtles, and Hawaiian monk seals.

Scientists say the Hawaiian islands are "drifting" northwest on a tectonic plate a few inches per year. As each island drifts, it is also eroding and sinking under its own weight. Oahu, for example, has sunk over 1,000 feet (300 meters) since its birth three million years ago. Remaining stationary beneath the tectonic plate is a hot spot, where magma leaks through to create the islands.

This well-defined and orderly progression gives each of Hawaii's seven inhabited islands distinct geographical dispositions. The island chain encompasses a total of 6,423 sq miles (16,635 sq km) of land area, roughly the size of Connecticut and Rhode Island combined. The Big Island, aptly enough, accounts for close to two thirds of that. Hawaii ranks 40th among the states in population, with approximately 1.2 million people – about 75 percent of whom reside on Oahu.

Kauai is the oldest of the main islands, its ancient shield volcano deeply eroded into primal contours. Next comes Oahu, its two extinct volcanoes nearly unrecognizable as such. Younger still is Maui, a coupling of old and new, the older West Maui volcano worn down but Haleakala still looking like the active volcano it was (and may still be). Molokai, Lanai and Kaho'olawe hover off Maui as small volcanic siblings. All were once linked to Maui. And then, visible from Haleakala's summit, is the Big Island, formed by five volcanoes and with a landscape still largely rounded, pristine, and still growing. Some 18 miles (29 km) off the Big Island's South Point is Lo'ihi, a seamount that has yet to see the sun. Lo'ihi (meaning "long, tall") has given scientists an opportunity to study island formation. It is about 3,000 feet (900 meters) below sea level. Experts predict that a momentous event will occur in about a thousand lifetimes from now.

Notes on directions

Islanders share a common vernacular for directions – the two most common are *mauka* and *makai*. *Mauka* means "upland or towards the mountains," and *makai* means "towards the sea." In Honolulu, directional words take on an even greater sophistication. Directions are also given in relation to Diamond Head, the volcanic cone east of Waikiki, and to 'Ewa, a district west of Pearl Harbor.   ❑

PRECEDING PAGES: Waimea Canyon, Kauai; Waikiki Beach, Oahu; board walk.
LEFT: flying over the waterfalls on Kauai.

OAHU

Most of Hawaii's residents live on Oahu, hence its urban prominence. Still, much of the island remains rural and wild

Scour the globe and you won't find another island quite like Oahu. One *kama'aina* (long-time resident) compares Oahu to a Chinese restaurant. "There are plenty of enticing options, there's something to suit everyone's tastes, and yet after you leave you somehow wind up hungry for more." Oahu's pleasures are diverse. Where else can you find monstrous surfing waves, a multi-billion-dollar skyline, high tea at the beach, striptease at a downtown bar, and waterfall-defined, mist-shrouded, rainbow-blessed mountains? Every day, more than 70,000 visitors explore the island coast to coast, tip to tip, from Wai'anae in the west to Hale'iwa in the north, Pearl Harbor and Waikiki in the south, and Makapu'u in the east.

Like Polynesian tales about the lost lands of Mu and Hawaiki, the meaning of the word *o'ahu* has been lost. Nowadays, it is often, probably incorrectly, said to mean "the gathering place," but that was, perhaps, an early tourism catchphrase. In ancient Hawaii, scholars note, Oahu did not have a large population, and the powerful chiefs "gathered" not on Oahu but on the Big Island and Kauai.

There is no doubt that Oahu is a gathering place. Its 800,000-plus residents make up around 75 percent of the state's population. Honolulu is the seat of island and state government, and in terms of geographical reach, it is the longest city in the world. Technically, the city and county of Honolulu are one and the same, covering all of Oahu and extending 1,400 miles (2,250 km) northwest up the Hawaiian chain to Kure Atoll, near Midway Island.

Honolulu proper lies on Oahu's southern coast, backed up against the Ko'olau Range. Its two best known neighborhoods, downtown Honolulu, and Waikiki, 3 miles (5 km) to the east, hold almost all its facilities and attractions for tourists. Waikiki is virtually a separate destination in itself, and many visitors to Hawaii never leave it except to reach the airport on the other side of Honolulu. Still, only a fool would fly to one of the most remote island chains in the world just to sit in Waikiki. On the other side of the Ko'olau mountains is the windward side, green and wet. There are several commuter bedroom communities here, but farther north, the narrow corridor between mountain and ocean becomes exceedingly rural. Cresting the northern tip of the island, the highway shifts westward along the North Shore, whose waters are placid in summer but violent in winter with surfing's best waves. Between the North Shore and Honolulu lies the fertile central plateau, home to much of the state's military activity. On the south coast to the west of Honolulu and Waikiki is Pearl Harbor, encircled by military bases and housing. Further to the west are the 'Ewa plains and the dry, sunny Wai'anae coastal valleys, probably Oahu's most "local" area.   ❏

LEFT: Oahu's North Shore, above Waimea Bay.

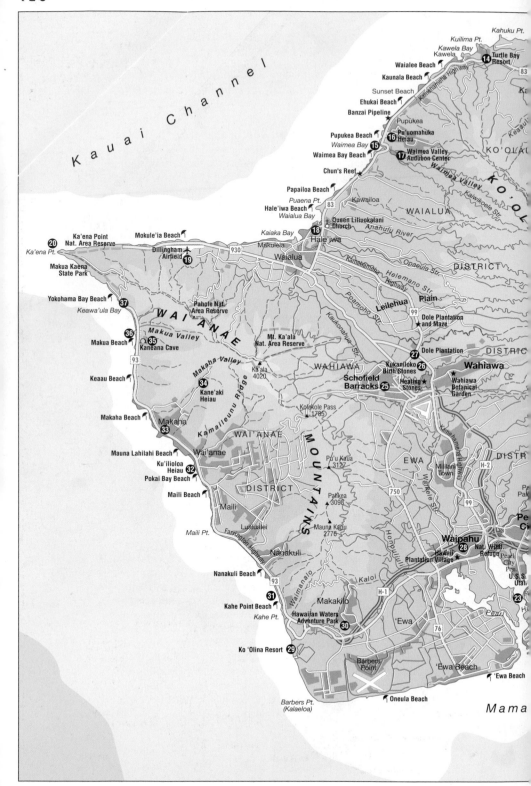

K a u a i   C h a n n e l

Kahuku Pt.
Kuilima Pt.
Kawela Bay
Kawela
Waialee Beach
14 Turtle Bay Resort
83
Kaunala Beach
Sunset Beach
Ehukai Beach
Banzai Pipeline
Pupukea
KO'OLA
Pupukea Beach
16 Pu'uomahuka Heiau
KO'OLA
Waimea Bay
15
Waimea Bay Beach
17 Waimea Valley Audubon Center
Chun's Reef
Waimea Valley
Papailoa Beach
Puaena Pt.
Kawailoa
WAIALUA
Hale'iwa Beach
83
Waialua Bay
Queen Liliuokalani Church
Anahulu River
DISTRICT
Kaiaka Bay
18
Hale'iwa
Mokule'ia Beach
Ka'ena Point Nat. Area Reserve
20
Ka'ena Pt.
Makaleha
Waialua
Opaeula Str.
Dillingham Airfield
19
930
Kamehameha Helemano Str. Highway
Makua Kaena State Park
Poamoho Str.
Leilehua Plain
99
Dole Plantation and Maze
Yokohama Bay Beach
37
W A I ' A N A E
Pahole Nat. Area Reserve
Keawa'ula Bay
Kaukonahua Str.
DISTRIC
Makua Valley
36
35
Makua Beach
Kaneana Cave
Mt. Ka'ala Nat. Area Reserve
Ka'ala 4020
WAHIAWA
Kukaniloko Birth Stones
27 Dole Plantation
26
Wahiawa
Keaau Beach
34
Kane'aki Heiau
Schofield Barracks
25
Healing Stones
Wahiawa Botanical Garden
Makaha Beach
Makaha
33
Makaha Valley
Kamaileunu Ridge
WAI'ANAE
Kolekole Pass 1785
DISTRIC
Mauna Lahilahi Beach
Wai'anae
DISTRICT
Pu'u Kaua 3127
EWA
Mililani Town
H-2
DIST
Ku'ilioloa Heiau
32
Pokai Bay Beach
M O U N T A I N S
Pa
Pak
Maili Beach
27
Maili
Palikea 3098
750
99
Pe
Ci
Maili Pt.
Luaiualei
Farrington Highway
Mauna Kapu 2776
Honouliuli
Waikele Str.
Waipahu
28
Nat. Wildl. Refuge
Pearl City Pen.
U.S.S. Utah
Nanakuli
Kamehameha Highway
Hawaii Plantation Village
Nanakuli Beach
Waimanalo
Kaloi
23
93
Kahe Point Beach
31
Makakilo
H-1
Pearl
Kahe Pt.
Hawaiian Waters Adventure Park
30
'Ewa
76
Ko 'Olina Resort
29
'Ewa Beach
'Ewa Beach
Barbers Point
Oneula Beach
Barbers Pt. (Kalaeloa)
M a m a

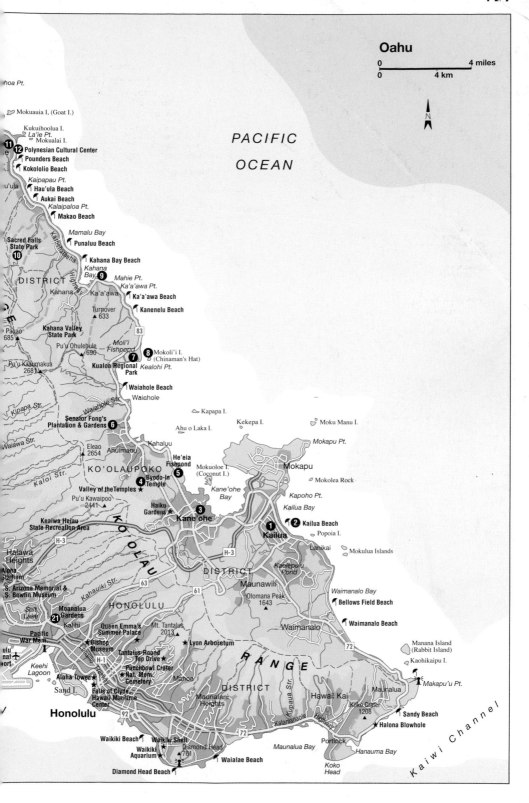

Oahu

0   4 miles
0   4 km

N

PACIFIC

OCEAN

hoa Pt.

Mokuauia I. (Goat I.)

Kukuihoolua I.
La'ie Pt.
Mokualai I.

u'ula

e
11
12   Polynesian Cultural Center
Pounders Beach
Kokololio Beach
Kaipapau Pt.
Hau'ula Beach
Aukai Beach
Kalaipaloa Pt.
Makao Beach
Mamalu Bay
Sacred Falls   Punaluu Beach
State Park
10
Kahana Bay Beach
Kahana
Bay
DISTRICT   9   Mahie Pt.
Ka'a'awa Pt.
Kahana   Ka'a'awa   Ka'a'awa Beach
Turnover
▲ 633   Kanenelu Beach
Pa'ao   Kahana Valley
685 ▲   State Park
Pu'u Ohulebule
690 ▲
Moli'i
Fishpond
Pu'u Kaaumakua   7   8   Mokoli'i I.
2681 ▲   Kualoa Regional   (Chinaman's Hat)
Park   Kealohi Pt.
Kipapa Str.   Waiahole Beach
Waiahole
Waiawa Str.   Senator Fong's
Plantation & Gardens   6
Eleao
▲ 2654   Ahuimanu
Kaloi Str.   KO'OLAUPOKO   Kahaluu
He'eia
Fishpond
Byodo-In   4   5   Temple
Valley of the Temples ★
Pu'u Kawaipoo   Haiku
2441 ▲   Gardens ★   3
Keaiwa Heiau   Kane'ohe
State Recreation Area
Halawa   H-3
Heights
Aloha
Stadium
S. Arizona Memorial &
S. Bowfin Museum   HONOLULU   63
Salt
Lake   Moanalua
Gardens
Pacific   21   Kalihi
War Mem.
Bishop   Queen Emma's   Mt. Tantalus
nal   Museum   Summer Palace   2013
al   Tantalus-Round   Lyon Arboretum ★
ort   Keehi   H-1   Top Drive ★
Lagoon   Punchbowl Crater
Aloha Tower   Nat. Mem.   Manoa
Cemetery
Sand I.   Falls of Clyde
Hawaii Maritime
Center   Maunalani
Honolulu   92   Heights
Waikiki Beach   Waikiki Shell
Waikiki   Diamond Head
Aquarium ★   761 ▲
Waialae Beach
Diamond Head Beach

Kapapa I.
Kekepa I.   Moku Manu I.
Ahu o Laka I.
Mokapu Pt.
Mokapu
Mokuoloe I.
(Coconut I.)   Mokolea Rock
Kane'ohe
Bay   Kapoho Pt.
Kailua Bay
Kailua   2   Kailua Beach
1   Popoia I.
Kailua
Lanikai   Mokulua Islands
Kaelepulu
Pond
DISTRICT
Maunawili   Waimanalo Bay
Olomana Peak   Bellows Field Beach
1643
Waimanalo   Waimanalo Beach
72
Manana Island
(Rabbit Island)
RANGE   Kaohikaipu I.
Makapu'u Pt.
DISTRICT   Maunalua
Hawaii Kai   Koko Crater
1208   Sandy Beach
Halona Blowhole
Portlock
72   Maunalua Bay   Hanauma Bay
Koko
Head

Kaiwi Channel

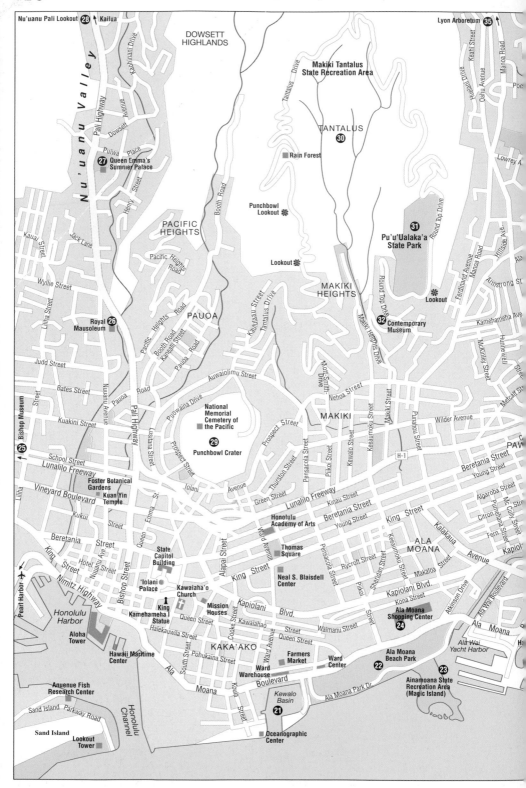

Nu'uanu Pali Lookout 28 ↑ Kailua

Lyon Arboretum 35 ↑

DOWSETT
HIGHLANDS

Makiki Tantalus
State Recreation Area

Manoa Road

Keahi Street

Tantalus Drive

TANTALUS
30

Huelani Drive

Poe

Lowrey A

Oahu Avenue

■ Rain Forest

Punchbowl
Lookout ❋

Round Top Drive

Pu'u'Ualaka'a
State Park 31

Hillside Ave.

Ala

Lookout ❋

Ferdinand Avenue

Manoa Road

Armstrong St.

PACIFIC
HEIGHTS

Pacific Heights Road

Kauai Street

Jack Lane

Henry Street

Kaohinani Drive

Avenue

Pali Highway

Dowsett

Puiwa Place

Queen Emma's
Sumner Palace 27 ■

Booth Road

Kamehameha Ave.

MAKIKI
HEIGHTS

Makiki Heights Drive

Round Top Drive

Lookout ❋

McKinley Ave.

Wyllie Street

PAUOA

Kalihi Street

Liliha Street

Pacific Heights Road

Booth Road

Kawaiilii Street

Pauoa Road

Contemporary
Museum 32 ■

Metcalf St.

Street

Royal
Mausoleum 26 ■

Kaeliilii Street

Makiki Street

Keeaumoku Street

Punahou Street

Wilder Avenue

Judd Street

Auwaiolimu Street

Tantalus Drive

Kaluanu Street

Mott-Smith Drive

Nehoa Street

Bates Street

Bishop Museum

Kuakini Street

Pauoa Road

Pali Highway

Nuuanu Avenue

Puowaina Drive

National
Memorial
Cemetery of
the Pacific ■

Prospect Street

MAKIKI

25 ◄

School Street

Lunalilo Freeway

Lusitana Street

Punchbowl Crater 29

Iolani Avenue

Pensacola Street

Piikoi Street

Kewalo Street

Keeaumoku Street

Makiki Street

H-1

Beretania Street

Young Street

PAV

PAV

Liliha

Vineyard Boulevard

Foster Botanical
Gardens ■

Kuan Yin
Temple

Prospect Street

Green Street

Thurston Street

Lunalilo Freeway

Kinau Street

Beretania Street

King Street

Algaroba Street

Citron Street

Fern Street

McCully Street

Street

Kukui

Street

Beretania

Street

Emma St.

Queen St.

Honolulu
Academy of Arts

Young Street

Pensacola Street

Rycroft Street

Keeaumoku Street

Sheridan Street

King Street

ALA
MOANA

Kalakaua Avenue

Kapiol

Pearl Harbor ✈

Nimitz Highway

Hotel Ave.

King Street

Bishop Street

Nuuanu Ave.

State
Capitol
Building

'Iolani
Palace ■

Kawaiaha'o
Church

Thomas
Square ■

Neal S. Blaisdell
Center ■

Piikoi

Makaloa Street

Kona Street

Kapiolani Blvd.

Atkinson Drive

Ala Wai Boulevard

Honolulu
Harbor

Aloha Tower

Hawaii Maritime
Center

King Street

1 King
Kamehameha I
Statue

Mission
Houses

Cooke Street

Kapiolani

Kawaiahao

Queen Street

Blvd.

Street

Waimanu Street

Queen Street

Ala Moana
Shopping Center 24

Ala Moana

Ala Wai
Yacht Harbor

Queen Street

Halekauwila Street

KAKA'AKO

South Street

Pohukaina Street

Ala

Moana

Knona

Street

Farmers
Market ■

Ward
Warehouse ■

Ward Avenue

Ward
Center ■

Ala Moana
Beach Park

22

Ala Moana Park Dr.

Ala Moana

23

Ainamoana State
Recreation Area
(Magic Island)

Anuenue Fish
Research Center

Sand Island Parkway Road

Honolulu Channel

Boulevard

Kewalo
Basin

21

Sand Island

Lookout
Tower ■

Oceanographic
Center ■

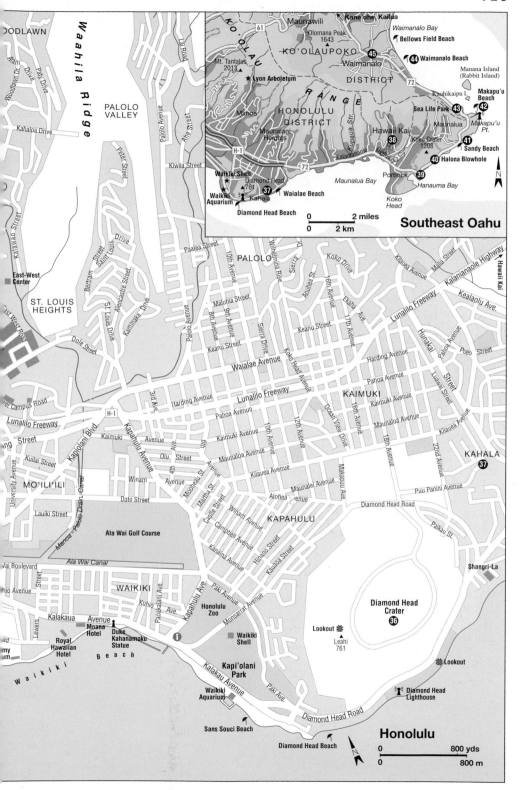

Southeast Oahu

Maunawili
Kane'ohe, Kailua
Olomana Peak 1643
Waimanalo Bay
45 Bellows Field Beach
Mt. Tantalus 2013
Lyon Arboretum
KO'OLAUPOKO
Waimanalo
44 Waimanalo Beach
Manana Island (Rabbit Island)
DISTRICT
72
Kaohikaipu I.
Makapu'u Beach
Makapu'u Pt.
42
KO'OLAU
RANGE
Manoa
HONOLULU
DISTRICT
Sea Life Park **43**
Maunalua
Maunalani Heights
Hawaii Kai
Koko Crater 1208
41 Sandy Beach
H-1
38
40 Halona Blowhole
Kalanianaole Hwy
72
Portlock
39
Waikiki Shell
Diamond Head
761
37
Kahala
Waialae Beach
Maunalua Bay
Koko Head
Hanauma Bay
Waikiki Aquarium
Diamond Head Beach

0 — 2 miles
0 — 2 km

N

Honolulu

WOODLAWN
Waahila Ridge
Pali Drive
Alani
Woodlawn Dr.
Lai Road
PALOLO VALLEY
Kahaloa Drive
Palolo Avenue
Alae Street
Peter Street
Kiwila Street
PALOLO
Paalea Street
10th Avenue
Wilhelmina Rise
Sierra Dr.
Koko Drive
Anuhea St.
Koko Head Avenue
16th Avenue
Ekaha Ave.
Kilauea Avenue
Malia Street
Kalanianaole Highway
Hawaii Kai
East-West Center
ST. LOUIS HEIGHTS
Bertram Street
Saint Louis Drive
St. Louis Drive
Alencastre Street
Kaiminaka Drive
8th Avenue
9th Avenue
Maluhia Street
Keanu Street
17th Avenue
Harding Avenue
Lunalilo Freeway
Kealaolu Ave.
Dole Street
East West Road
Keanu Street
Sierra Drive
Pahoa Avenue
Hunakai Street
Pahoa Avenue
Pueo Street
Waialae Avenue
KAIMUKI
Kilauea Street
er Campus Road
Harding Avenue
3rd Ave.
Lunalilo Freeway
Pahoa Avenue
10th Avenue
12th Avenue
Ocean View Drive
18th Avenue
Kaimuki Avenue
Maunaloa Avenue
Kilauea Avenue
22nd Avenue
KAHALA
37
Lunalilo Freeway
Kapiolani Blvd
Kaimuki
Kapahulu Avenue
Avenue
Olu. Street
4th Ave.
Kaimuki Avenue
Maunaloa Avenue
Makapuu Ave.
18th Avenue
Puu Panini Avenue
Street
University Avenue
Kuilai Street
MO'ILI'ILI
Winam Avenue
Dato Street
Michean St.
Castle Street
Kilauea Avenue
Maunalei Avenue
Alohea Avenue
Diamond Head Road
Paikau St.
Lauiki Street
Winam Avenue
KAPAHULU
Campbell Avenue
Kanaina Avenue
Hinano Street
Kaiulua Street
Shangri-La
Manoa · Palolo Drain · Canal
Ala Wai Golf Course
Ala Wai Canal
Ai Boulevard
hio Avenue
Street
WAIKIKI
Kalakaua Avenue
Kuhio Ave.
Paokalani Ave.
Kapahulu Ave.
Paki Avenue
Monsarrat Avenue
Honolulu Zoo
Diamond Head Crater
36
Lookout
Lewers
Moana Hotel
Duke Kahanamoku Statue
Waikiki Shell
Leahi 761
Lookout
Royal Hawaiian Hotel
Beach
Kapi'olani Park
Diamond Head Lighthouse
w a i k i k i
Waikiki Aquarium
Kalakau Avenue
Paki Ave.
Diamond Head Road
Sans Souci Beach
Honolulu
0 — 800 yds
0 — 800 m
Diamond Head Beach
N

HONOLULU

This city seems out of place in the middle of the Pacific Ocean. But, then again, maybe not. Residents originate from places around the globe, creating an ambiance that is distinctively island-style

Map, page 135

Honolulu – the word rolls off the tongue like a soft wave breaking off Waikiki. There's no mystery about this word's origin: *hono*, a bay, and *lulu*, protected. It explains why Honolulu has been the commercial, political, and cultural center of the Hawaiian Islands since the 1800s. Until Pearl Harbor was made navigable in the mid-19th century, Honolulu Harbor was the largest protected body of water within 2,000 miles (3,200 km) of Hawaii.

Three miles (5 km) west of the beaches of Waikiki, downtown Honolulu is a walker's delight. A stroll through downtown with its grid of side streets, shops, oddball bars and historic buildings can consume hours or days. The key to unlocking Honolulu is to treat it not like a city, but like the small gem that it is. You're on Hawaiian time now, so take it slow and easy.

Palace in paradise

Grand old **'Iolani Palace ❶** (364 S. King St; open Tues–Sat 9am–3pm; guided tours 9–11.15am only; entrance fee; tel: 522-0832; www.iolanipalace.org) is the only royal palace on US soil. It was built in a Victorian-era style its architects called American Composite or American Florentine. Completed in 1882 during King Kalakaua's reign, it took three years and $350,000 to finish.

King Kalakaua and his successor-sister, Queen Lili'uokalani, lived in the palace, holding royal court from 1882 until 1893, when a group of American businessmen staged a coup d'état and abolished the monarchy. 'Iolani – Hawaiian for heavenly hawk – was renamed the Executive Building after the monarchy's overthrow, but the humiliation did not end there. In 1895, following a futile counter-revolution led by royalists, Lili'uokalani was convicted of misprision of high treason and was returned to 'Iolani Palace, where she spent most of the year living on the second floor under house arrest as a prisoner of the provisional government.

The palace was used as a capitol for the provisional, territorial, and state governments of Hawaii. In 1969, the state legislature and administration moved out of the palace and into the new capitol building and grounds just *mauka* (towards the mountains) of the palace. The state and a private non-profit-making group then began a $6-million effort to restore the palace to its former splendor. Original furnishings were tracked down and recovered and the palace proper now glows as it did when Kalakaua and Lili'uokalani hosted formal banquets and grand balls. 'Iolani's splendor includes Corinthian columns, etched-glass door panels, chandeliers, the mirrored and gilded Throne Room, and the spectacular three-story *koa* (an indigenous hardwood)

LEFT: Capitol Building.
BELOW: entrance of 'Iolani Palace.

Every June, the King Kamehameha festival opens with a colorful lei-draping ceremony at the statue of Kamehameha the Great, with lei up to 18 ft (5 meters) long.

BELOW: the grounds of 'Iolani Palace.

stairwell with carved balusters. Also back in operation are the first flush toilets known to have been installed in any palace anywhere in the world, and Hawaii's first internal telephone and electric-light systems. A worthwhile museum of royal Hawaiiana is housed in the basement.

On the palace grounds are some other intriguing sites. The **Coronation Stand** was built in 1883 for King Kalakaua and Queen Kapi'olani's coronation. The stand's foundation was rebuilt in 1919, but the copper dome is the original and now plays host to free public concerts (every Friday at noon) by the Royal Hawaiian Band.

The **'Iolani Barracks** is a stone structure that served as headquarters and home to the Royal Household Guards from 1871 until the overthrow of the monarchy. The small building now includes a gift shop and the palace ticket office.

The **Royal Burial Ground and Tomb** is an inconspicuous, grass-covered mound surrounded by *ti* plants in the Diamond Head-*makai* (towards Diamond Head and toward the ocean) corner. It was the site of the first Royal Mausoleum, built in 1825 to house the remains of King Kamehameha II and Queen Kamamalu, who died of measles when they visited England in 1823. Later Hawaiian *ali'i* (royalty) were also buried there. But in 1865, with the tomb overcrowded with royal remains, all were moved to a new Royal Mausoleum in Nu'uanu Valley.

On the *makai* (toward the ocean) side of King Street, across from 'Iolani Palace, is the **King Kamehameha the Great Statue ❷**. Although this heroic bronze probably bears little resemblance to Kamehameha the Great, it's a Honolulu monument and a prime spot for camera-wielding tourists. The statue shows the king holding a barbed *polulu* (spear) in his left hand as a symbol of peace and his right arm outstretched in a welcoming gesture of *aloha*. Hanging

Map, page 135

from the king's shoulders is a large feather cloak and on his head is a *mahiole*, or feather helmet. Around his loins and chest he wears a feather *malo*, or loincloth, and a sash. When the Hawaiian kingdom's 1878 legislature commissioned this statue, King Kalakaua chose John Timoteo Baker, a local businessman, to serve as its primary model, as he was the most handsome man in court circles. Baker was mostly Anglo-Saxon, and only about one quarter Tahitian. Photos were taken wearing ancient clothing, and these plus copies of painted likenesses of Kamehameha were sent to Thomas B. Gould, an American sculptor in Florence. Unveiled during Kalakaua's 1883 coronation, the statue is a copy of the original, which is in Kapa'au, on the Big Island.

Behind the statue is the old **Judiciary Building** (open Mon–Fri 9am–4pm; free; tel: 539-4999), originally designed by Australian architect, Thomas Rowe, to be King Kamehameha V's palace. The king's household plans changed, however, and after the building was completed in 1874, it was used instead as a courthouse and legislative building. The building – also known as Ali'iolani Hale (*hale* means house, and *ali'iolani* translates as "chief of heavenly repute") – is now home to the state's supreme court and the Judiciary History Center .

Kawaiaha'o Church

Towards Diamond Head up King Street from the Judiciary Building is Hawaii's most famous Christian structure, **Kawaiaha'o Church ③**. On Sunday mornings, or when the church's Hawaiian choir is in rehearsal, the royal palms and hala trees in its grounds seem to sway with the lyrics of *"He A-kua he mo-le-le* – God is Holy," or *"E Ha-wai-i e ku'u o-ne ha-nau e,"* the opening words of "Hawai'i Aloha," which translates as, "Oh, Hawaii, my own birthplace, my own land."

Sculptor Thomas Gould's first statue of Kamehameha was cast in Paris in 1880, then shipped from Germany to Hawaii. The ship carrying it caught fire and sank off Port Stanley in the Falkland Islands. The statue was later recovered, and is now in Kapa'au, on the Big Island.

BELOW: Kawaiaha'o church.

For years this was the gathering place of missionaries and Christian Hawaiian *ali'i*. Even today, the church often serves as a meeting place where matters of serious Hawaiian interest are discussed. Designed by Rev. Hiram Bingham, who led the first Congregationalist mission to Hawaii in 1820, Kawaiaha'o Church was constructed in the late 1830s and early 1840s of some 14,000 large coral blocks cut from nearby reefs. Although the present Kawaiaha'o structure was dedicated in 1842, it was preceded by four thatched churches also built under Bingham's direction, the first in 1821.

It was at Kawaiaha'o Church that Kamehameha III spoke what has become the State of Hawaii's motto – Ua mau ke ea o ka'aina i ka pono, or "The life of the land is perpetuated in righteousness." He spoke after the restoration of Hawaiian sovereignty following a brief 1843 British takeover of the islands.

Kawaiaha'o, the "water used by Ha'o," was named after an ancient sacred spring that still flows in the church grounds. The grounds also hold a cemetery for early missionary *haole* (Caucasians) and faithful Hawaiian members of the congregation. It is estimated that as many as 2,000 Hawaiians were buried here in the 1800s, many the victims of diseases unwittingly introduced by the early sailors and settlers. Missionaries and their descendants were buried at the back of the church, while native Hawaiians and others were segregated in death on the harbor-side of the church.

One Hawaiian, however, received special exemption from Kawaiaha'o's congregation: King William Lunalilo, the popular "Prince Bill" whose Gothic tomb stands just to the right of the churchyard's main entrance. Lunalilo, who died in 1874 after a one-year reign, requested on his deathbed that he be buried "among his people" at Kawaiaha'o, away from the "clannish" Kamehameha kings and queens who rested in vaults at the Royal Mausoleum in Nu'uanu.

BELOW: tomb of Lunalilo, and the Mission House.

It was at **Likeke Hale**, an adobe schoolhouse built on Kawaiaha'o's grounds around 1836, that early Congregationalist missionaries taught Hawaiian children the *palapala*, or Bible, and literature in general. Built of mud, limestone,

and coral, the schoolhouse is the only survivor of the many adobe structures that were constructed during the early 1800s. It is still used today for Sunday-school classes and smaller church meetings.

The Mission Houses museum complex

Across from the schoolhouse is the yard where the missionaries lived, prayed and printed the first of their many 19th-century publications. Now a museum complex, the **Mission Houses ❹** (553 S. King St; open Tues–Sat 10am–4pm; entrance fee; tel: 531-0481; www.missionhouses.org) rank among the oldest surviving Western-style structures in Hawaii.

The main white Frame House still stands as it was the day it was erected in 1821 of New England timbers, which were cut and fitted in Boston and shipped to Hawaii aboard the brig *Thaddeus*. It is the oldest wooden house in Hawaii, and was for many years home to several prominent missionaries. The Coral House, where the first printing in the north Pacific was made, was built in 1823. A third building, the Chamberlain House, used as a storehouse and home for the mission's purchasing agent, was built in 1831. All three structures belong to the Hawaiian Mission Children's Society, an exclusive *kama'aina* (long-time residents') club made up of missionaries' descendants. If you fail to coincide with a guided tour of the actual houses, you can settle instead for the museum in the separate visitor center.

From the front entrance of Kawaiaha'o Church, *mauka* (towards the mountains) across King Street is **Honolulu Hale ❺**, the city's California-Spanish-style city hall built in 1927. Adjacent is a red-brick structure in a burst of Americana with white pillars, opposite the Mission Houses, which was

Map,
page 135

Urban biker with parasol.

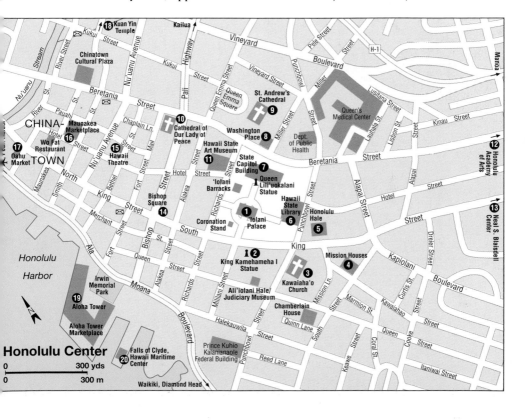

Queen Lili'uokalani, Hawaii's last monarch, with a fresh flower.

dedicated in 1916 as the Mission Memorial Building to honor the original New England missionaries. Since 1947, it's been used as a city hall annex. *'Ewa* (to the west) is the Greco-Roman **Hawaii State Library ❻** (478 S. King St; open Mon, Wed 10am–5pm; Tues, Fri, Sat 9am–5pm; Thur 9am–8pm; free; tel: 586-3500), which has an extensive Hawaiian and Pacific Isles collection. Built in1911–12, it was restored and modernized in the late 1980s.

State capitol and surroundings

Behind 'Iolani Palace is contemporary Hawaii's center of power – the **State Capitol Building ❼**, dedicated in 1969 and completely renovated in the mid-1990s. The structure's architectural lines were designed to suggest Hawaii's volcanic and oceanic origins. Its high and flaring support pillars represent royal palms. Paneling made of *koa* in offices and conference rooms gives the structure a distinctly Hawaiian touch. On the *makai* (sea) side of the building stands a majestic, bronze **statue of Queen Lili'uokalani**, the last monarch of Hawaii *(see page 43)*. An outstretched hand holds fresh flowers, placed there daily by admirers and supporters.

On the *mauka* (mountain) side of the capitol, along Beretania Street, fly the American and Hawaiian flags, and a blue, red, and starred governor's flag. Visitors to the islands are sometimes surprised to see the British flag in the upper left corner of Hawaii's red, white, and blue flag, designed in 1816 for Kamehameha the Great. It is thought that this flag includes the Union Jack out of consideration for the British sea captain George Vancouver, who presented Hawaii with its first flag when Kamehameha temporarily placed his islands under the protection of Great Britain. Other historians say Kamehameha adopted the Jack-and-

BELOW: *pau* riders on the state capitol grounds.

Stripes flag so that Hawaiian ships at sea would look both American and British, hereby discouraging pirates from pillaging his kingdom's vulnerable vessels.

On the same side, take a moment to study the bronze **sculpture of Father Damien Joseph de Veuster**, the self-sacrificing priest who lived and died among sufferers of leprosy (now called Hansen's disease) at Kalaupapa, Molokai in the 1870s–80s. This blockish statue, created by Venezuelan sculptor Marisol Escobar, is a duplicate of one that stands in Statuary Hall at the US Capitol building in Washington, DC. Unveiled in 1969, the statue ignited controversy because the bold and tragic likeness was based on a photograph taken of the priest shortly before he died of Hansen's disease in 1888; his formerly handsome features were grossly disfigured. Controversy regarding the statue has subsided, but Escobar's Damien remains a powerful artistic statement, and a telling memorial.

The official residence of Hawaii's governor is a white Greek Revival mansion on Beretania Street, **Washington Place** ❽ (320 S Beretania; free tours by appointment only, Mon–Fri; tel: 586-0248). It was built in 1846 for American sea captain John Dominis. His daughter-in-law, Lydia Kamakaeha, lived here between her marriage in 1862 and her accession to the throne as Queen Lili'uokalani in 1891, and returned just two years later following the overthrow of the Hawaiian monarchy. Washington Place remained a center of courtly social proceedings until Lili'uokalani's death in 1917, at the age of 79, and the deposed queen regularly sang her own compositions for visitors at the massive *koa* grand piano in her Music Room. The current governor, Linda Lingle, lives in a separate new building in the grounds.

Interior of Washington Place.

Peek in next door at **St Andrew's Cathedral** ❾, an English-Norman structure built at a snail's pace between 1867 and 1958 of imported English sandstone.

BELOW: Washington Place.

Another block *'Ewa* (west) up Beretania Street is the **Cathedral of Our Lady of Peace ⑩**, built by Roman Catholic missionaries from France. This coral building at the top of the Fort Street Mall was dedicated in 1843. Father Damien was ordained here in 1864.

The historic Richards Street YMCA building, immediately west of 'Iolani Palace across Richards Street, now houses the **Hawaii State Art Museum ⑪** (250 S. Hotel; open Tues–Sat 10am–4.30pm; Sun 1–5pm; entrance fee; tel: 532-8701). This highlights the state's impressive collection of art, purchased over a 25-year period as part of the Art in Public Places program. Exhibits are loosely divided between large-scale landscapes and natural-history displays in the eastern wing, and quirkier multi-media works in the western wing.

Culture to the east

Down Beretania Street from Washington Place and the Capitol, towards Diamond Head, is the superb **Honolulu Academy of Arts ⑫** (900 S. Beretania; open Tues–Sat 10am–4.30pm; Sun 1–5pm; entrance fee; tel: 532-8701; www.honoluluacademy.org). Housed in a magnificent Japanese-influenced former private home, built in 1927, the academy holds galleries of Asian and Western art, plus inner courtyards rich in flora and sculpture. There are works by Modigliani, Picasso, Gauguin, van Gogh, Monet, and Rodin, and some fascinating displays on how Hawaii has been depicted, and imagined, by the rest of the world. The true highlight, however, is one of the finest Oriental collections in America, including a wonderful range of artefacts from ancient China, statues and religious carvings from throughout southeast Asia, and the writer James Michener's collection of Japanese woodblock prints.

BELOW: downtown.

A block *makai* (towards the ocean) of the academy is the **Neal S. Blaisdell Center** ⓭, named for a former Honolulu mayor who served from 1955 to 1968. The complex encompasses an 8,000-seat arena, 2,100-seat concert hall, and a spacious exhibition hall. Performances of the Honolulu Symphony are first rate, with international stars of the classical world taking part during the symphony season, which runs from September to May.

Big business and wealthy families

Anchoring downtown is **Bishop Square** ⓮, a refreshing plaza with fountains at the intersection of Bishop and King streets. Named after Charles Reed Bishop, who established both the Bishop Estate and the Bishop Museum, **Bishop Street** carries financier and fun-seeker alike past the graciously porticoed suites of the "Big Five" *kama'aina* corporations – conglomerates built on sugar in the 19th century by business and missionary families.

Today, a bronze statue of the royalist Robert Wilcox shares their turf. Every Friday is Aloha Friday, when nearly every man on the street – Big Five type, banker or otherwise – wears a crisp aloha shirt. A necktie on Friday is truly an odd sight, as is a sports coat or sweater.

Be sure to check a special events listing before heading downtown. You just might be able to catch a show at the historic **Hawaii Theatre** ⓯ (1130 Bethel; tel: 528-0506; www.hawaiitheatre.com), located at the corner of Bethel and Pauahi streets, two blocks *'Ewa* (west) of Bishop Street. The 1,400-seat theater, which opened in 1922 and closed in 1984, was reopened in 1996, restored to its original glory: gold metallic leaf adorns the columns and grillwork moldings inside the theater; the lobby has new marble floors and counters. Lionel

Map, page 135

The Neal S. Blaisdell Center, then known as the Honolulu International Center, opened in 1964. It was the venue for Elvis Presley's legendary "Aloha From Hawaii" concert in 1973, beamed to a global audience of over 2 billion.

BELOW: slow day at Bishop Square.

Just mauka *(towards the mountains) of Nimitz and 'Ewa (west) of Chinatown is an area called Iwilei (pronounced ee-vee-lay), formerly the locale of the Dole Pineapple Cannery. Hawaii's once prosperous pineapple industry is in decline, however, and the operation shut down in the early 1990s. Attempts to keep the site going as a tourist attraction soon fizzled out.*

BELOW: images in Kuan Yin Temple and shopping in Chinatown.

Walden's *Glorification of the Drama*, a stunning mural that presides over the proscenium arch, has been fully restored. Today, the theater showcases a wide range of musical and theatrical acts.

Chinatown and Hotel Street

Historic buildings vie with rising glass towers throughout Honolulu. Perhaps the most interesting of the historic structures outside of the capitol district are in an area near the harbor. This brick-rococo neighborhood is a pleasant four-block stroll from the Federal Post Office Building, down Merchant Street, Honolulu's old "Financial Boulevard." Many of the structures in this area escaped the demolition ball: some have been restored, while others add a somewhat seedy edge to parts of Chinatown.

Between Bethel Street and Nu'uanu Avenue, two immense stone lions flank **Hotel Street** to announce **Chinatown**, an area bounded by the harbor waterfront and Nu'uanu, Beretania and River streets. In the late 1860s, Chinese plantation workers, after paying off their indentured labor contracts, gathered here and established new lives.

In 1900, a 12-block area in Chinatown burned down when a fire, set by the board of health to eradicate bubonic plague, went out of control. Once the rambunctious venue for sailors on liberty and characters on the loose, if not on the run from the law, Hotel Street is being transformed, mostly for the better, in a long-evolving urban renewal effort. Most of the area's unseemly past has been scrubbed over or pushed out, although a few louche peep shows and bars still remain.

Just beyond them, however, Chinatown comes into its own in a medley of Asian markets, noodle factories, shops, and art and antique galleries. Side streets

cutting across Hotel Street and extending from King Street to Beretania tempt the curious. The **Maunakea Marketplace** (1120 Maunakea St; open Mon–Sat 6am–6pm; Sun 6am–3.30pm) is a modern, open plaza nestled amid the old – look for the clock tower with Chinese numbers. Down on King Street, towards the waterfront, the **Oahu Market** ⓘ will rekindle a traveler's Asian memories with its early-morning hubbub of mongering and bargaining.

Hotel Street ends at River Street, which parallels the lower **Nu'uanu Stream** descending from the Ko'olau Mountains. On the *mauka* (mountain) side of Chinatown, on Vineyard Boulevard, is the **Kuan Yin Temple** ⓘ, where Buddhist and Daoist images gleam and a 10-ft (3-meter) statue of Kuan Yin, the Buddhist goddess of mercy, dominates.

A quiet respite can be found beneath hardy tropical trees in the spacious **Foster Botanical Gardens** (50 N. Vineyard Blvd; open daily 9am–4.30pm; entrance fee; tel: 522-7065) on Vineyard Boulevard, just beyond the Kuan Yin Temple. Several plants, such as the fragrant and ever-blossoming cannonball tree, are the only specimen of their genus and species in Hawaii.

Along the harbor

Towards the waterfront, Fort Street Mall empties into **Ala Moana Boulevard**, an oceanside artery that starts as Nimitz Highway near the Honolulu International Airport and turns into Ala Moana (Ocean Street) when it reaches downtown. Near here stood the old "fort" – Ke Ku Nohu, *circa* 1816 to 1857 – that gave Fort Street its name. Cross Ala Moana and hop on the elevator to the top of the **Aloha Tower** ⓘ (observation deck open daily 9am–5pm; free) for views that span downtown, with Waikiki to the east and the Wai'anae Mountains to

The herb garden at Foster Botanical Gardens was the site of Hawaii's first Japanese-language school. During Japan's attack on Pearl Harbor, an errant shell exploded in a classroom of students.

BELOW: Aloha Tower.

the west. This pleasing 1925 structure is only 10 stories high – or 184 ft (56 meters) – but it was once the tallest building in Hawaii. It is now dwarfed by the skyscrapers of downtown Honolulu.

As recently as the 1950s, Aloha Tower smiled down upon Hawaii's famous "Boat Days," when luxury Matson liners would arrive and depart at piers 10 and 11 in a hail of flowers and *hapa-haole hula*. On and off the ships would go huge steamer trunks and travelers in white linen suits and ribboned hats. At pier side, local boys would dive for coins tossed into the water. Something of that spirit has returned as increasing numbers of cruise ships make Honolulu port-calls, with Boat Day arrivals reinstituted in the process. The half-hour long mix of hula, music, confetti launches and waterboat displays provides a festive atmosphere, with Aloha Tower as the centerpiece of an open-air shopping, restaurant, and entertainment complex. For the Boat Day schedule, call 528-5700.

A museum modeled after King Kalakaua's boathouse

Immediately adjacent to Aloha Tower is the **Hawaii Maritime Center** [20] (open daily 8.30am–5pm; entrance fee; tel: 536-6373; www.bishopmuseum.org), a museum modeled after the boathouse of King Kalakaua. Completed in 1988, it celebrates Hawaii's 2,000-year-old seafaring heritage, from ancient Polynesian canoes to modern surfboards, sleek passenger liners and military submarines. Docked next to the Hawaii Maritime Center is the ***Falls of Clyde***, the world's only surviving full-rigged, four-masted sailing ship. Built in Scotland in 1878 (the Clyde is the river running through Glasgow, Scotland, which was the site of major shipyards) it spent 20 years in the India trade before entering the Hawaii trade routes. Its last voyage was in 1921.

TIP

In Honolulu, locals speak of a place as being *'Ewa* or *Diamond Head* of something else, not east or west. For example, Waikiki is *'Ewa* of Diamond Head. You'll catch on.

BELOW: bow of the *Falls of Clyde*.

Next to the *Falls of Clyde*, and so small you might miss it, is the ***Hokule'a***, a double-hulled, 60-ft (18-meter) modern replica of an ancient Polynesian voyaging canoe. Several times since the 1970s, including a 1999 voyage to Easter Island, it has followed ancient Polynesian ocean routes between Hawaii and the South Pacific. Only traditional navigation techniques – stars, ocean swells, rhythm – are used to make the *Hokule'a*'s modern-day voyages.

Map, page 135

Discovering Honolulu Harbor

European explorers didn't find Honolulu Harbor for more than 14 years after Captain Cook's arrival in 1778, probably because the navigable channel leading into the harbor was only about 550 ft (165 meters) wide, and also because in those early post-contact days the Big Island and Maui were greater centers of Hawaiian power than Oahu. However, in late 1792 or early 1793, Captain William Brown, then busy in both the Pacific Northwest-China fur trade and a new Hawaiian gun trade, accidentally came across this nameless inlet. He described it in his logbook as "a small but commodious basin with regular soundings from 7 to 3 fathoms clear and good bottom, where a few vessels may ride with the greatest safety." Brown named it Fair Haven, which in an unusual reversal was translated into Hawaiian to become "Honolulu."

While Oahu's chiefs had always preferred Waikiki, with the arrival of sailing vessels and a new concept called money, other *akamai* (smart) Hawaiians, including Kamehameha, began moving to Honolulu's harbor. In Kamehameha's hands, Honolulu became the most important stopover point in the mid-Pacific ocean, with hundreds of ships making use of the harbor every year. Although Kamehameha eventually returned to the Big Island around 1812, he closely

BELOW: the fishing fleet in Kewalo Basin.

Map,
page 128

monitored commerce at Honolulu until his death in 1819, as did his sons, Kame
hameha II and Kamehameha III. Later, during the whaling era, the Kamehame
has moved Hawaii's capital to the booming town of Lahaina, on Maui
Eventually the Hawaiian elite recognized that the future would play out in Hon
olulu, and in 1845, Kamehameha III moved back to Honolulu where he officiall
declared it the capital of the Hawaiian Kingdom in 1850.

Toward 'Ewa

From Aloha Tower, heading *'Ewa* (west) along the Nimitz Highway lead
towards the airport and *'Ewa*, while traveling *Diamond Head* on Ala Moan
Boulevard leads to Waikiki. Nimitz Highway is an unattractive gateway t
Waikiki, a mess of traffic amid light industry and warehouses – an unfortunat
introduction to Oahu's beauty, partly revealed on the crowded H-1 Freeway tha
also links the airport to Waikiki.

Toward Waikiki and Diamond Head

Along Ala Moana Boulevard, past the **Prince Kuhio Kalaniana'ole Federa
Building**, the harbor and ocean disappear behind walls and buildings, includ
ing Restaurant Row, where a theater complex plays art films not offered else
where in Hawaii.

BELOW: yachts in a
trans-Pacific race.
OPPOSITE: Magic
Island, with Ala
Moana and
Honolulu behind.

A mile or so farther on there's **Kewalo Basin** ㉑, where Honolulu's fishing
fleet returns with the day's catch, and which serves as a departure point for coastal
cruises and sport fishing. Opposite Kewalo Basin and on the other side of Ala
Moana Boulevard, there are two popular shopping, restaurant and cinema malls
all part of the Ward Centers complex, **Ward Warehouse** and **Ward Center**.

On the *makai* (ocean) side, just past Kewalo Basin
begins the **Ala Moana Beach Park** ㉒, 100 acres (40
hectares) of open space and beaches with good swim
ming and decent surfing beyond the reef. The adjacen
artificial peninsula, known locally as **Magic Island** ㉓
or **'Ainamoana State Recreation Area**, is popular with
joggers, cyclists, skaters, and walkers. Created by infill
ing a coral reef, this spot was originally intended as the
site for a collection of new luxury hotels, but they were
never built, and instead it holds a peaceful little sand
fringed lagoon.

Directly *mauka* (towards the mountains) from Ala
Moana Beach Park you come to the **Ala Moana Shopping Center** ㉔, a huge development and Hawaii's
largest shopping mall, with more than 250 stores and
eateries. Ongoing renovations and expansions mean tha
it now stands four stories tall, and holds a roster of top-
name retailers that includes Neiman Marcus, Dior
Gucci, Prada, and Louis Vuitton.

On the extreme *Diamond Head* end of Ala Moana
Beach Park, a bridge rises over the **Ala Wai Canal** and
into Waikiki. The Ala Wai is a favorite training area for
outrigger canoe paddlers. On the west side of the canal
rises the modernist Hawaii Convention Centre; to the
east looms the first of Waikiki's highrises. Oceanside
there are dozens of spindly sailing craft at the **Ala Wai
Yacht Harbor** and yacht basin, towered over by the
Hawaii Prince and Renaissance Ilikai hotels. ❑

WAIKIKI

There's nothing else like it in the Pacific Ocean: a perfect beach with crystal-clear water, backed by lush mountains laced with clouds and rainbows, luxurious hotels, plus some pure schlock

Map, page 151

A t 500 acres (200 hectares) in size, it covers less than 1 percent of Oahu's land area, yet Waikiki pumps $5 billion into Hawaii's economy annually, representing 40 percent of the state's total tourism dollars. It provides 40,000 jobs tending to Oahu's 88,000 tourists daily, while somehow finding the room to house its 20,000 residents.

World-famous **Waikiki Beach**, actually a series of connecting beaches – Sans Souci, Queen's Surf, Kuhio, Waikiki, DeRussy and Duke Kahanamoku – extends for more than a mile in a crescent of sand. The city has spent millions upgrading Waikiki beachfront promenade, adding landscaped gardens, statues, historic story boards and tourist facilities. Additional upgrades to Kapi'olani Park, Fort DeRussy and along the Ala Wai Canal have greatly enhanced Waikiki's appeal, with extensive redevelopment still underway in the heart of Waikiki, along Lewers Street, and Kalakaua and Kuhio avenues, Waikiki's two commercial thoroughfares. The central showpiece of all this revitalization is the new Beach Walk development on Lewers Street, which opened in 2007.

Early Hawaiians named this 1.5-mile (2.5-km) long coastal strip *Waikiki,* or spouting water, because its inland section was a wetland nurtured by mountain streams and springs. As early as the 1400s, Hawaiians capitalized on this water with a sophisticated irrigation system that fed aquaculture ponds and taro fields.

Until the 1920s, when completion of the Ala Wai Canal diverted water from the swamps and created dry land for future hotels, Waikiki's somewhat smelly interior was still a boggy place of fish ponds, taro patches, and rice paddies populated by quacking waterfowl and other damp creatures. The area's beaches, coconut groves, and fish-rich reefs, however, have long made this area a favorite spot among *ali'i*, or the Hawaiian royalty. All Hawaii's royals had homes here, as did the island's ruling chiefs before them.

Transport comes to Waikiki

In the 1860s, a dirt road was built to link Waikiki's cool surf with hot and dusty Honolulu. Two decades later, a mule-drawn omnibus began making daily round trips to Waikiki; by 1888, a regular tram service was initiated, which was motorized in 1895. Most visitors stayed with friends or in one of downtown Honolulu's hostelries – notably the long-gone Hawaiian Hotel – until the 1880s and early 1890s, when a few Waikiki homes and cottages were converted into guest houses.

In 1884, Allen Herbert opened one such guest house near Diamond Head and named it **Sans Souci** (in French this means "without a care"), and later hosted the noted Scottish author Robert Louis Stevenson.

PRECEDING PAGES: looking towards Halekulani across Waikiki Beach. **OPPOSITE:** sun and sand. **BELOW:** a man who knows how.

To this day, the "heavenly sunsets" that Stevenson loved take place off Sans Souci Beach, where the New Otani Kaimana Beach Hotel has replaced Stevenson's bungalow. Waikiki's first world-class hotel, the Moana, an eclectic structure geared for steamer-set tourists, opened in 1901 *(see page 152)*, followed in 1927 by the elegant **Royal Hawaiian**.

Reminders of the past

"If anyone desires such old-fashioned things as lovely scenery, quiet, pure air, clear sea water, good food, and heavenly sunsets hung out before his eyes... I recommend him cordially to the Sans Souci," wrote author Robert Louis Stevenson.

Once home to Oahu's chiefs, today's Waikiki offers intriguing hints of its past. Take, for example, the **Stones of Kapaemahu Ⓐ**, four imposing boulders at Kuhio Beach adjacent to the Honolulu Police substation. Approach the stones with respect, because according to Hawaiian oral traditions, they possess the *mana*, or spiritual powers, of four *kahuna* – priests or wizards – who were renowned throughout Polynesia for their wisdom and healing abilities. These four wizards – Kapaemahu, Kahaloa, Kapuni and Kinohi – came to Oahu from Tahiti in the 16th century, then left. A metal plaque notes that "before vanishing, the wizards transferred their powers to these stones."

A stone's throw away is the bronze **Statue of Duke Kahanamoku Ⓑ**. The statue includes a bronze surfboard representing Duke's classic 24-ft (7.5-meter) long *koa* board. Short boards are the norm today, but some of the old long boards still in use can be found nearby in storage racks wedged between the Moana Hotel and the Honolulu Police substation. Duke Kahanamoku *(see page 154)* was a swimming world-record holder in three Olympics. He also brought surfing into the modern age, introducing Hawaii to the rest of the world. Beach boys still paddle oversized surfboards out to surf spots like Queens, Populars, or Canoes.

BELOW: International Market Place.

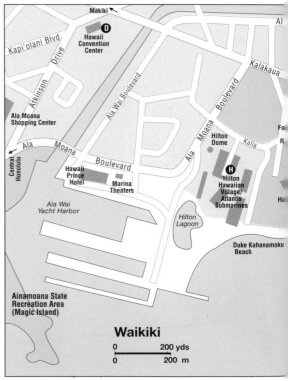

Waikiki

0   200 yds
0   200 m

A block beyond Duke is a statue of Prince Kuhio, royal champion of Hawaiian rights in the US Congress for 20 years after annexation. A statue of King Kalakaua graces Gateway Park, at the *'Ewa* (west) end of Waikiki. A statue of his niece, Princess Kaiulani, is located on the street that bears her name, while statues of Mahatma Gandhi and Queen Kapi'olani are to be found in Kapi'olani Park.

Family fun and shopping opportunities

The section of beach fronting the statue of Price Kuhio is known as Kuhio Beach. Almost entirely enclosed by stone breakwaters, the inshore waters here offer Waikiki's safest swimming, and are therefore good for families. At dusk nightly at the beachside hula stand at Kuhio Beach, torchlighting begins an hour of music and dance. On select evenings, movies are shown beachside at the Kalakaua entrance to Kapi'olani Park.

A block *'Ewa* (to the west) from the twin 40-story towers of the Hyatt Regency Waikiki (which has a top-floor ocean view to die for) is the **International Market Place C**. This acre or so of souvenir shops and kiosks selling everything from shave ice to gold jewelry was a pleasant, open place full of birds, a banyan tree and a good share of curious local folk. In recent years, however, with Waikiki space becoming an increasingly precious commodity, the Market Place has become rather overcrowded and tacky. It remains a worthwhile stop on any itinerary however, and it's still a challenge to leave without purchasing some curious trinket.

In the early 1990s, there was talk of replacing the Market Place with a massive convention center. However, the $350-million **Hawaii Convention Center D** – which was completed in 1997 – was built on the outskirts of Waikiki, on the

Map below

TIP

If you are renting a car, be aware that Honolulu's roads can be a little confusing. Entrances and exits for the H-1 freeway defy logic – they often don't come in pairs – and the routes into Waikiki are very convoluted and fussy.

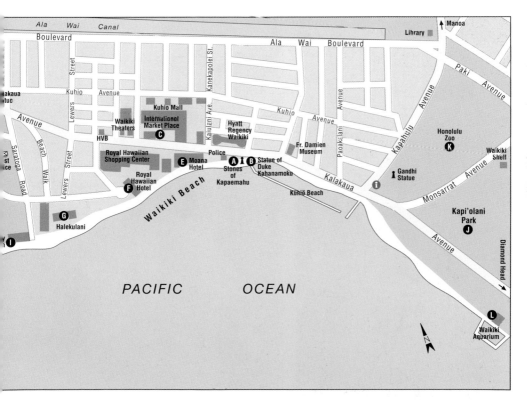

From the Banyan Courtyard, Hawaii Calls' MC would end the show with *"All of us wish you were here with us here in Hawaii on this beautiful day. Come over and see us sometime! Aloha, aloha nui loa."*

BELOW: Moana Surfrider Hotel.

mauka (towards the mountains) side of the Ala Wai Canal and bordered by Atkinson Drive, Kapi'olani Boulevard, and Kalakaua Avenue.

Visiting Hawaii a number of years ago, Russian poet and journalist Yevgeni Yevtushenko (b. 1933) wrote *The Restaurant For Two*, about a small tree-house office in a banyan tree at the entrance to the International Market Place. He wrote of "mermaidenly thighs… heedless brown hands… pilings of palm… baked shark's fin steeped in pineapple… the samba's throb… and flat champagne." Then, he recalled, a man stepped up to the banyan tree, threw a switch and turned on "the bird song tape-recorded to lend the illusion of Paradise." Such is the artificial charm of Waikiki.

The first luxury hotel

Since the mid-1950s, hotels in Waikiki have risen in escalating waves of concrete and steel, a Great Wall of Waikiki. At last count, there were more than 30,000 hotel rooms in Waikiki. However, for most of the 20th century, three Waikiki hotels anchored the beach, luxurious locales that are still regarded with respect by *kama'aina* (long-time residents) who knew them way back when.

The **Moana Surfrider Hotel** ⓔ, on the beach along Kalakaua Avenue near the Duke Kahanamoku statue, is the *tutu-kane,* or granddaddy, of them all. At its center is Hawaii's first luxury hotel, the **Moana**, which is what it is commonly called even today. Opened in 1901 with 75 rooms, it offered Hawaii's first electric elevator, and a 300-ft (90-meter) wooden pier with a bandstand at its far end; unfortunately, the pier was dismantled in 1930.

In 1918, two wings were added, forming the **Banyan Courtyard**, which is still popular today for its ambiance and nightly music beneath a majestic banyan

tree planted in 1885. It now stands at 75 feet (23 meters high). Another extension was added in 1952, and in 1969 the **Surfrider Tower** was built.

From 1935 to 1972, the Moana's Banyan Courtyard was known internationally as the favorite home of *Hawaii Calls*, a Hawaiian music program hosted by Webley Edwards (1902–77), who had previously been a World War II news correspondent, and the first to anounce the attack on Pearl Harbor on air. *Hawaii Calls* was once regarded as the most widely listened-to radio show on earth. Some 1,900 shows, broadcast by as many as 600 different radio stations around the world, were broadcast live from Hawaii *(see margin, previous page)*.

In 1989, after a two-year, $50-million restoration by its Japanese owners, the Moana Surfrider reopened its doors looking every bit as charming as it did when it first opened almost nine decades earlier. On the hotel's second floor, above the open-air lobby, is a museum with artifacts and nostalgic photographs.

The Royal Hawaiian

When the Matson Navigation and Territorial Hotel companies unveiled the $4-million, shocking pink **Royal Hawaiian Hotel ⑤** in 1927, Honolulu's *kama'aina* elite shifted their focus from the Moana to this Moorish-Spanish-style structure just down the beach. Social Honolulu and San Francisco were positively atwitter as the Royal Hawaiian's completion date neared. An advance *Honolulu Advertiser* story promised that the Royal's opening would be "one of the greatest social events in the history of Hawaii…." And indeed it was; 1,200 guests turned out to witness a "semi-barbaric pageant" produced by Princess Abigail Kawananakoa, the hotel's first official guest and wife of the late Prince David Kawananakoa. From the Royal's pink balcony, the princess hand-directed

BELOW: the Royal Hawaiian Hotel.

Duke Kahanamoku

In his lifetime, he was an Olympic champion, a Hollywood celebrity, a local sheriff and one of Hawaii's pre-eminent ambassadors of goodwill. Duke Kahanamoku's most enduring legacy, however, lives on through thousands of surfers in Hawaii and all around the world. Through it all, Kahanamoku was first and foremost a beachboy. He helped popularize surfing in places like California, Australia, and New Zealand. Kings and queens once governed Hawaii's lands, but it was a Duke who ruled its ocean waves.

A full-blooded Hawaiian, Duke Paoa Kahanamoku was born in Honolulu in August 1890. The Kahanamoku family moved to Waikiki three years later, and young Duke was never far from the beach he would help make famous. In 1911, in his first timed swims, he broke three free-style world records at Honolulu Harbor. Kahanamoku, in fact, shattered the 100-meter record by 4.6 seconds. When word was sent to Amateur Athletic Union (AAU)

officials in New York, they replied sternly, "Unacceptable. No one swims this fast!"

A year later, at the Summer Olympics in Stockholm, Kahanamoku made believers the world over by capturing the gold medal in the 100-meter free-style, and a silver medal as part of the American 200-meter free-style relay team. The handsome Olympic star became an international celebrity. In the 1920 and 1924 Olympics, Kahanamoku again came home a medalist.

In the 1920s, Kahanamoku tried his hand at acting. In all, he appeared in nearly 30 movies, sharing the screen with Hollywood giants like Dorothy Lamour, Ronald Coleman, and another Duke, John Wayne.

Kahanamoku's most impressive performance, however, came in 1925, when he used his longboard to rescue eight drowning men off Newport Beach, in California. The local police chief called his act of heroism "the most superhuman rescue act and the finest display of surfboard riding that has ever been seen in the world."

After returning to Oahu, he married Nadine Alexander in 1940 (who died in 1997 at the age of 92.) Kahanamoku was elected Honolulu's sheriff and was re-elected 12 times, finally giving up his office in 1960 when the position was abolished.

In January 1968, Kahanamoku suffered a heart attack in the parking lot of the Waikiki Yacht Club and died at the age of 77. An estimated 10,000 people attended his funeral at Waikiki Beach. From outrigger canoes, family and friends scattered his ashes in the waters off Waikiki Beach. Reported the *Honolulu Star-Bulletin*: "There is a strange sound in the booming surf in Waikiki today, like the anguished cry of a mother at the loss of her favorite son."

In 1990, on the centennial anniversary of his birth, an imposing bronze statue of Kahanamoku, sculpted by local artist Jan Fisher, was unveiled at Waikiki Beach. Some beachboys lament the fact that the statue is facing *mauka* (the mountains) instead of the ocean. Perhaps only the Duke could safely ignore the rule of the surf never to stand with one's back to the ocean. ❑

LEFT: Olympic champion Duke Paoa Kahanamoku taught surfing to anyone who was willing.

the movement of a fleet of 15 outrigger canoes and dozens of Hawaiians in warrior regalia, a re-staging of the 1795 landing at Waikiki by Kamehameha.

During the next 15 years, the six-story, 400-room Royal Hawaiian became the place in Hawaii where the Hollywood likes of Mary Pickford, Douglas Fairbanks, Al Jolson, and Ruby Keeler joined various Duponts, Rockefellers, Fords, and presidents and royalty over green turtle soup Kamehameha, and medallions of sweet breads Wilhelmina, in the tapestry-filled Persian Room.

With bush-jacketed bellhops tending to guests' needs, the Royal cruised through the Great Depression. But in 1941, World War II hit Pearl Harbor, and barbed wire was rolled across the sands of Waikiki. So the Royal mothballed its tapestries and was leased to the US Navy until 1945. Postwar, the Royal prospered once again and in 1959 was purchased by Sheraton, which, in 1975, sold it to the Japanese conglomerate, Kyoya, although Sheraton has continued to manage the hotel.

The house befitting heaven

The **Halekulani** , *'Ewa* (west) along the beach, was another pioneering hotel in Waikiki, where in the early 1900s, American author Jack London drank hard, chain-smoked, and spun stories on his typewriter. It was here, too, that writer Earl Derr Biggers created the fictional detective Charlie Chan. The Halekulani's bar, The House Without A Key, takes its name from the title of the first Charlie Chan novel, published in 1925. Opened in 1907 as the Hau Inn, the bungalows of the Halekulani ("The House Befitting Heaven") were eventually replaced with 450 modern but exquisite rooms (some of Waikiki's finest) in wings terraced back from the beach. A quartet and hula dancer perform nightly under the

Map, page 151

BELOW: board paddlers.

beachside banyan tree. With one of Waikiki's superlative trademark sunsets as a backdrop, and no cover charge for a stage-front table, it's the perfect way to round off a day in paradise.

Diamond Head's distinctive uplifting shape came from the steady trade winds 150,000 years ago that piled erupting ash higher on the ocean, or leeward, side of the tuff cone.

Hilton Hawaiian Village

At the far western end of the Waikiki Beach Waterfront, golden Kahanamoku Beach, once the home of the legendary surfer's family, is now dominated by the mighty towers of the **Hilton Hawaiian Village** Ⓗ. At the landscaped Ala Moana gateway you won't be able to miss the larger-than-life depicitions of hula dancers. Take the time to wander through the Village's landscaped grounds, enjoying the collection of rare birds and the king's ransom of giant *koi* (Japanese carp). Beachside, look up at the 30-story rainbow murals (the largest in the world) that make the Rainbow Tower a Waikiki landmark. On Friday nights there's an hour-long show of music and dance and a grand fireworks finale.

The Hilton Hawaiian Village is also the base of operations for **Atlantis Submarines** (tel: 973-9811), which offers fabulous underwater excursions to submerged shipwrecks a mile or so offshore.

Army Museum

A short walk east of the Hilton, the oceanfront **US Army Museum** ⒤ (at Fort DeRussy on Kalia Road; open Tues–Sun 10am–4.15pm; free; tel: 438-2819) displays warfare artifacts including weapons of ancient Hawaii, the American Revolution, Spanish–American War, World Wars I and II, and the Korean and Vietnam wars. Even for the pacifist, this is an interesting and underrated museum, located inside Battery Randolph, a massive bunker built in 1911 with

BELOW LEFT: pedestrian surfers. **BELOW RIGHT:** Hilton Hawaiian Village.

walls on its seaward side made of 22-ft (7-meter) thick concrete. When the military tried to demolish the football-field-size bunker in the late 1960s, they couldn't do it – hence the museum. The battery had two disappearing 14-inch (35-cm) shore guns, cut up in the late 1940s, capable of firing a 1,600-pound (726-kg) shell 14 miles (22 km) out to sea.

**Map,
page 151**

Kapi'olani Park

Kapi'olani Park ❶, a complex of beaches, grassy picnic and play areas, amphitheaters, jogging courses, gardens, a zoo, and aquarium, at the eastern end of Waikiki, was dedicated on June 1, 1877, Kamehameha Day, as Hawaii's first public park. Opening day was celebrated with a slate of high-stakes horse races held on a new track laid out just below Diamond Head. King Kalakaua named the park after his wife. The park's Kamehameha Day races in the early years of the 20th century were outlawed by temperance and anti-gambling forces.

Kapi'olani Park remains one of Oahu's favorite recreational areas, and whether you're seeking tennis, soccer, kite flying, surfing, or long tranquil walks under monkeypod and ironwood trees, you'll find it here.

The Aquarium in Kapi'olani Park.

Kapi'olani Park is also the finishing point for one of the running world's biggest and best-known marathons. The Honolulu Marathon takes place each December and draws competitors from around the world. The race, which was first run here in 1972, draws more than 30,000 runners annually, many of them from north Asia, and particularly Japan, where marathon-running has become extremely popular. In 2003, a young Japanese woman, Eri Hayakawa, was the first runner from her country to win the Honolulu race; and in 2006, some 60 percent of the runners were from Japan.

BELOW: on the waterfront.

Map, page 151

In 1927, world swimming records were set at the Waikiki Natatorium by Buster Crabbe and Johnny Weissmuller, the future Hollywood Tarzan.

Across the street at **Queen's Surf Beach** – Lili'uokalani's beach house once stood here – beach boys gather for volleyball, and to listen to impromptu conga drum, guitar, and flute concerts held under a banyan tree, especially at sunset. The nearby **War Memorial Natatorium**, built to commemorate World War I veterans, and designed by the same architect who did the beautiful California Academy of Sciences in San Francisco, was dedicated in 1927 as a world-class swimming facility. Although the pool, long in a state of disrepair, was approved for an $11-million restoration program in the 1990s, that plan drew substantial opposition from the community and sparked legal challenges. To date, only the decorative arch and entry have been restored, while the pool remains off limits.

Beasties galore

At the **Honolulu Zoo** ⓚ in Kapi'olani Park (open daily 9am–5.30pm; entrance fee; tel: 971-7171; www.honoluluzoo.org), you can enjoy the typical antics of assorted primates, lions, elephants, giraffes, and hippos. The zoo is the only place in Hawaii where you can see a live snake: there are no wild snakes in Hawaii, you may be pleased to learn, and strict control is maintained on their import to keep it that way.

Except for sea birds, virtually all the birds you will see nowadays in Hawaii are introduced species. This is probably the only place a visitor to Oahu – and most residents, as well – can see indigenous mountain birds, including the exquisite *'apapane* (Hawaiian honeycreeper) at the Manyara Bird Sanctuary and the South American Aviary.

The Tropical Forest section here is filled with flowering plants, trees and gardens, and there is a Children's Zoo where youngsters can pet a llama or touch a monitor lizard. Over the past decade or so, the zoo has made significant improvements, including the opening of the expansive African Savanna exhibit.

BELOW: life guard.
OPPOSITE: under the palms.

Yet more exotic creatures can be found just a few minutes away at the small **Waikiki Aquarium** ⓛ (2777 Kalakaua Ave; open daily 9am–5pm; entrance fee; tel: 923-9741; www.waquarium.org), established in 1904. Affiliated with the University of Hawaii since 1919, the Waikiki Aquarium is the third-oldest aquarium in the United States. Probably the rarest inhabitants here are the monk seals. The monk seal and hoary bat are the only two mammals known to have been native to Hawaii when the first Polynesian settlers arrived. There are also some fascinating exhibits on the nautilus and the spawning of the *mahimahi*, perhaps the most popular fish for eating in the Hawaiian islands.

If you are more interested in local art than flora and fauna, there is plenty around if you know where to look. Not far from here, at the Waikiki branch of First Hawaiian Bank (2189 Kalakaua Avenue) you will find the huge fresco mural *Early Contacts of Hawaii with Outer World*, by Jean Charlot.

If you're still feeling energetic after all this activity, it's possible to continue walking around the front of Diamond Head – there are spectacular views from the road overlooking the ocean – and into Kahala. It's quite a hike, and you can be pretty sure that none of the millionaires in Kahala will invite you inside their mansions for a cool drink. Too bad. ❑

GREATER HONOLULU

There's more to Honolulu than the resort frenzy of Waikiki and the bustle of downtown; besides the museums and sites you'd expect, there is superb wilderness hiking close to the most built-up areas

Map, page 128

W hat can loosely be called Greater Honolulu stretches for around 15 miles (24 km) along Oahu's southern shoreline. Its single most attractive feature has to be its physical setting, squeezed between the ocean and the soaring Ko'olau Mountains. Although the sharp, green-velvet ridge of the *pali* (cliffs) is often just three miles from the beach, the mountains are repeatedly indented by lush valleys. Several such valleys cradle characterful city neighborhoods, like Kalihi, Nu'uanu, and Manoa. Two major roads cross the mountains close to downtown, the Likelike and Pali highways, while a meandering 8-mile (13-km) route along Tantalus and Round Top drives enables visitors to enjoy some superb rainforest scenery.

The Bishop Museum

The working-class neighborhood of Kalihi, 2 miles (3 km) northwest of downtown, makes an unlikely setting for the world's greatest repository of Pacific and Polynesian artifacts: the **Bernice Pauahi Bishop Museum** ㉕ (1525 Bernice St; open daily 9am–5pm; entrance fee; tel: 847-3511; www.bishop museum.org). It was established in 1889 by Charles Reed Bishop as a memorial to his wife Bernice, a princess and the last of the Kamehameha family.

The Bishop Museum is considered one of America's most important multi-disciplinary museums, a Smithsonian Institution in microcosm. The museum maintains natural history collections of nearly 20 million animal and plant specimens. Among the highlights of its central building, the cavernous and recently restored *koa*-paneled Hawaiian Hall (1903), are carved and feathered icons, capes and many other remnants of pre-contact Hawaii; brilliant regalia from the time of Kamehameha the Great; the monarchical crowns, thrones, and court costumes used in 'Iolani Palace by King Kalakaua and his sister, Queen Lili'uokalani; and important pieces reflecting the experiences of Hawaii's many immigrant groups.

Further galleries explore the many differing cultures of the South Pacific, from Micronesia to Papua New Guinea. Across the lawns, a new addition, the Science Adventure Center, explains vulcanology and Hawaiian natural history in an entertaining way.

Nu'uanu

Just a half-mile or so inland from Chinatown (along Nu'uanu Avenue), and a mile east of the Bishop Museum, near the foot of the Pali Highway, **Nu'uanu** is perhaps Honolulu's prettiest valley. Even the name is beautiful – Nu'uanu, meaning the "cool height." There

PRECEDING PAGES: Hanauma Bay. **OPPOSITE:** view from Nu'uanu Pali Lookout. **BELOW:** main hall of the Bishop Museum.

*The Bishop Museum
also manages a
planetarium and
astronomical obser-
vatory, the* Falls of
Clyde, *a four-masted
sailing ship in
Honolulu Harbor,
and the adjacent
Hawaii Maritime
Center.*

was no doubt among early *haole* (Caucasian) settlers that Nu'uanu was the best place to live. Nu'uanu was the first suburb in which they built their Victorian mansions with broad *lanai*, and where they planted the monkeypods, banyans, Norfolk Island pines, bamboo, eucalyptus, African tulips, and golden trees that now tower over the valley's indigenous ferns, hibiscus, *koa*, and ginger. Many of these estates are still occupied by wealthy missionary descendants, but most have been sold or leased to institutions, churches, or Asian consulates.

Before stalking through the valley's lush rainforest, listen for the "oms" vibrating out of the **Soto Zen Mission** of Hawaii (1708 Nu'uanu Avenue), a duplicate of a major Buddhist *stupa* at Bodhgaya, India, where Gautama Buddha gave his first sermon. This temple's Indianesque towers would appear most at home on a Himalayan crag, but a few Japanese influences – gardens of tinkling water, sand, and bonsai – give its authenticity away. Built in 1952, the temple is somewhat similar to an even larger shrine, the nearby and hard-to-miss **Honpa Hongwanji Mission** (1727 Pali Highway), which was built in 1918 to commemorate the 700th anniversary of the Shin Buddhist sect.

The man who invented baseball

Nearby is the old **Oahu Cemetery**, where many names of rich or famous *haole* residents can be seen on tombstones. One in particular merits the attention of serious American sports fans: the layered, pink granite tomb with the inscription, "Alexander Joy Cartwright Jr. Born in New York City April 17, 1820. Died in Honolulu July 12, 1892." This austere monument, located at the center of the cemetery, marks the remains of the man who invented the game of baseball. After inventing the game – the first baseball contest played under Cartwright's

BELOW: the Soto Zen
Mission.

Map, page 128

rules took place in 1846 in Hoboken, New Jersey – Cartwright drifted west and eventually ended up in Hawaii. He founded Honolulu's first volunteer fire department and served as its fire chief from 1850 to 1859.

A few hundred yards/meters further up Nu'uanu Avenue is the **Royal Mausoleum ㉖** (2261 Nu'uanu; open Mon–Fri 8am–4pm; free), where the bodies of Kamehameha II, Kamehameha III, Kamehameha IV, Kamehameha V, Kalakaua, Queen Lili'uokalani, and other members or favored friends of those royal Hawaiian families are buried. The only two Hawaiian monarchs not buried here are King Lunalilo, who at his own request was buried in the grounds of Kawaiaha'o Church, and Kamehameha the Great, whose bones were hidden away in a secret burial place on the Big Island. The mausoleum, which lies on a 3-acre (1-hectare) site chosen by Kamehameha V, was prepared in 1865 to replace an overcrowded royal burial tomb on the grounds of 'Iolani Palace.

Nu'uanu Valley is thick with plants and trees today, planted decades ago by residents of the valley. Before this, Nu'uanu had no dense vegetation.

Queen Emma's Summer Palace

Half a mile (1 km) up the Pali Highway from its intersection with Nu'uanu Avenue stands **Queen Emma's Summer Palace ㉗** (2913 Pali Highway; open daily 9am–4pm; entrance fee; tel 595-3167; www.daughtersofhawaii.org). This royal bower with a ginger- and *ti*-lined driveway was built in the late 1840s and later sold to John Young II, an uncle of Queen Emma and son of Kamehameha the Great's chief *haole* adviser, the Englishman John Young. Queen Emma and Kamehameha IV in turn bought it from Young and named it Hanaiakamalama, "the foster child of the moon," after a favorite Hawaiian demi-goddess.

Until Emma's death in 1885, the royal family used this home as a summer retreat, salon, and courtly social center. In 1890, the summer palace was bought

BELOW: Queen Emma's Summer Palace.

by the Hawaiian government, while the Daughters of Hawaii organization has
maintained it as a museum since 1915.

The palace's rooms have been restored with many of the royal family's
belongings. Among the items are a spectacular triple-tiered *koa* sideboard of
Gothic design presented to Emma and Kamehameha IV by Britain's Prince
Albert, the husband and consort of Queen Victoria; a heavy gold necklace
strung with tiger claws and pearls given to Emma by a visiting maharajah;
and various opulent wedding and baby gifts, which were given to the royal
family by Queen Victoria, who was godmother to Emma's son, the Hawaiian
Prince Albert. Among the most fascinating Hawaiian pieces is a stand of
feather *kahili* (royal standards) in the queen's master bedroom. Behind and
around the corner from the palace, off Pu'iwa Road, is a lovely little retreat,
Nu'uanu Valley Park, favored by lovers and daydreamers who like to lounge
under its gigantic trees.

Nu'uanu Pali Lookout

Nu'uanu Pali Drive winds through the hanging vines, bamboo, wild ginger, jas-
mine, and cool air in two separate sections, east of the Pali Highway inland from
Queen Emma's Palace. Along this wending path you'll spot stately mansions
hidden away in the bushes, and, on rainy days, dozens of tiny waterfalls run
wherever wrinkled Ko'olau ridges let them flow. **Waipuhia Valley Falls**, on
the left side of Nu'uanu Valley just before you reach the Pali Lookout, is nicknamed "Upside Down Falls" because its waters are often blown straight back
up a cliff and turn into mist before they can reach the precipice below. Waipuhia
means "blown water."

BELOW: view from
Nu'uanu Pali
Lookout.

The **Nu'uanu Pali Lookout** ㉘, just off the Pali Highway, is one of the most popular scenic attractions on Oahu, offering panoramic views of the *pali* and the Windward Coast. Gale-force winds rush up this Ko'olau palisade and literally stand one's hair on end. The view from the lookout is spectacular: sawtooth peaks rise like a great rampart, with lush flatlands facing a sea of all shades of blue.

Several spectacular trails start to the left of the lookout, including one atop an abandoned stretch of the old Pali Highway. From here, the Pali Highway continues down to the windward side and the bedroom communities of Kailua and Kane'ohe.

Punchbowl Crater and the National Memorial Cemetery

Another relaxing Honolulu adventure includes two areas above town between Nu'uanu and Manoa valleys, known as Punchbowl and Tantalus-Round Top. **Punchbowl Crater** ㉙, once a site of human sacrifices, was known to Hawaiians as Puowaina, or "the hill for placing [of sacrifices]." Like Diamond Head and Koko Head craters to the east, Punchbowl emerged during an eruption phase about 150,000 years ago. It was pushed upward by volcanic action through a vast coral plain that had built up around this side of the Ko'olau Mountains.

Today, Punchbowl is the site of the **National Memorial Cemetery of the Pacific**, where more than 40,000 war veterans and family members are buried. The small, flat, white headstones, set level with Punchbowl's expanse of grass, stretch across the crater's 112-acre (45-hectare) floor.

Perhaps the most famous person buried here was Ernest Taylor "Ernie" Pyle (1900–45), not a conventional war casualty but a journalist whose ability to write about the average foot-slogging GI during World War II made him one of

Map, page 128

BELOW LEFT: memorial at Punchbowl. **BELOW RIGHT:** view of the city from Punchbowl.

the most widely read combat correspondents, and earned him the Pulitzer Prize in 1944, the year before he was killed by Japanese gunfire on a small Pacific islet. Pyle's burial here was allowed because he had served in the US Navy during World War I. More than 60 years after his death, cemetery officials have estimated that as many as 50,000 people a month visit his grave.

Tantalus

From Punchbowl's mountain-side entrance, Puowaina Drive crosses a bridge over Prospect Street and drifts along a steep valley through Papakolea, one of Oahu's few Hawaiian homestead communities. At the top of Puowaina Drive, turn right onto Tantalus Drive, a winding mountain road that twists and turns through some of Oahu's largest *kama'aina* estates. **Tantalus** ③⓪ has some of the coolest and most panoramic vantage points on this side of the island. You can hike one of the marked trails near the mountain's 2,013-ft (610-meter) peak into groves of bamboo and fern. At the top, Tantalus Drive connects with Round Top Drive, which descends down the ocean side to Makiki and Punahou.

There are at least a dozen knock-out viewpoints on Tantalus, but locals agree that the best one, a panorama extending from Diamond Head to Pearl Harbor and the Wai'anae Mountains, is from **Pu'u'Ualaka'a State Park** ③①, on Tantalus's Diamond Head flank.

A few hairpin turns below this peak is a straight stretch of Round Top Drive beside a lava rock wall, with an unobstructed postcard view of Diamond Head, the University of Hawaii, and broad Manoa Valley. Down below in Makiki Heights is the **Contemporary Museum** ③② (2411 Makiki Heights Drive; open Tues–Sat 10am–4pm; Sun noon–4pm; entrance fee; tel: 526-1322; www.tcmhi.org),

After they were tossed from power in the Philippines, Ferdinand and Imelda Marcos found themselves in exile, living in a pleasant villa just off Round Top Drive, with stunning views of Honolulu.

BELOW: bamboo trail around Mt Tantalus.

beautifully maintained contemporary art museum hosting top-class, regularly changing temporary exhibitions, with a gift shop and an appealing café that is a good place for lunch.

Manoa

Manoa Valley , meaning "vast," has long been preferred by islanders as a residential refuge from the heat and hassle of Honolulu's coastal flatlands. Indeed, residents of both Manoa and Nu'uanu consider their valleys the closest one can get to Eden – both are verdantly green and consistently wet – and still manage to be near shopping centers and bus routes.

At the mouth of this easy-going valley is the center of higher education in Hawaii, the large **University of Hawaii** Manoa campus, attended by some 18,000 full-time students. This institute has the academic and post-adolescent aura typical of any university in the world, except that its student body, like Hawaii itself, is generally more diverse and casual – loud T-shirts, shorts and sandals – and more ethnically mixed than the typical university campus. The university's sports teams are nicknamed the Rainbows.

At the **East-West Center** – a federally funded institute on the university campus that promotes understanding in the Pacific Basin – are a Thai pavilion personally presented and dedicated by King Bhumibol Adulyadej of Thailand in 1967; a Center for Korean Studies building hand-painted in the busy and intricate style of Seoul-area Yi dynasty palaces; and the center's main building, Jefferson Hall, which is fronted by large Chinese dog-faced lions and backed by a Japanese garden rich in sculptured grass, bonsai trees and a lily pond full of nibbling *koi* (Japanese carp).

Map, page 128

BELOW: University of Hawaii campus.

Arboretum and falls

Half a mile or so beyond Punahou School and beyond the university is the junction of Manoa and East Manoa roads. Branching left, Manoa Road leads to the back of the valley and the University of Hawaii's **Lyon Arboretum** ❸❺ (3860 Manoa Road; open Mon–Fri 9am–4pm; free; tel: 988-0456), established in 1907 Nearly 6,000 plants grow on the arboretum's 120 acres (48 hectares), on land rising from 300 ft (90 meters) to 1,800 ft (550 meters) above sea level. Tropical and native Hawaiian plants, conservation biology, and Hawaiian ethnobotany are the major themes here.

Cool **Manoa Falls**, accessed via a steep nearby trail that climbs through spectacular rainforest for just under a mile, is fed by 160 to 200 inches (4,065–5,080 mm) of rain a year (bring insect repellent and wear long sleeves).

A red cap cardinal.

SOUTHEAST OAHU

Mighty Diamond Head, towering to the east of Waikiki, is simply the most conspicuous of the chain of ancient volcanic cinder cones that elongate the coastline of Southeast Oahu. A driving tour of the district will take you beyond Honolulu's most luxurious residential neighborhoods to some dramatic beaches and scenery, including the popular snorkeling site of Hanauma Bay.

Diamond Head

You can actually drive into the extinct volcanic tuff cone of **Diamond Head** ❸❻, and hike up the inner walls to its sea-side rim 761 ft (231 meters) above the beach. It's well worth the short but steep hike. The view of Waikiki and Oahu's south shore is one of the island's best, and atop one of the abandoned World War

BELOW: Diamond Head Lighthouse.

Map, page 129

I gun emplacements there is a comfortable picnic spot. The crater's interior and exterior slopes are part of the 500-acre (200-hectare) Diamond Head State Monument. Inside the crater there's a visitor center, as well as civil defense and National Guard facilities, and an air traffic control facility of the Federal Aviation Administration.

Diamond Head is a nickname given the crater in 1825 by British sailors who mistook worthless calcite crystals found on its slopes for diamonds. Its original Hawaiian name was Lae'ahi, which means "brow" *(lae)* of the yellow-fin tuna *('ahi)*. Hawaiian legends say that the fire goddess Hi'iaka, Pele's younger sister, noticed the resemblance between Diamond Head's profile and that of the *'ahi* and named it Lae'ahi. In later years this was shortened by map-makers to Leahi. Its steep slopes were favored for *holua* sliding, a tropical form of tobogganing over dry ground.

Long before this tuff cone became Hawaii's most famous landmark, Lae'ahi was the site of the Papa'ena'ena *heiau*, an important temple. According to historical accounts, some of the last human sacrifices ordered by Kamehameha the Great took place at this *heiau* following the decisive Battle of Nu'uanu Valley, in 1795. Early descriptions indicate that the *heiau* was located below Diamond Head's jutting brow. A lovely estate called La Petra, now the Hawaii School for Girls, is built on the site.

Kahala and Hawai'i Kai

Beyond Diamond Head, at the eastern end of the H-1 highway, stands the high-priced neighborhood of **Kahala** ❼. Following Hawaii's statehood in 1959, this part of the island became increasingly residential as Honolulu proper began

TIP

The drive between Hanauma Bay and Sandy Beach is stunning. It is also the perfect time to watch the road, not the scenery, as the road is narrow and twisting, with many blind spots.

BELOW: lush Kahala bungalow.

running out of living space. Today, Kahala is one of Oahu's most desirable postal codes. At the end of ritzy Kahala Avenue is the Kahala Hotel, formerly known as the Kahala Hilton and the Kahala Mandarin Oriental. Built in 1959, the hotel has become the Hawaiian escape for those with money and status. A walk along Kahala Beach toward Diamond Head leads past immaculate beach-front estates. In the other direction is the Wai'alae Country Club.

Further along Kalaniana'ole Highway, toward Oahu's southeastern tip, is the sprawling **Hawai'i Kai** ❸, created by the late billionaire industrialist Henry J. Kaiser during the early 1960s. The development included converting Kuapa, once Hawaii's largest fishpond, into a marina for Kaiser's master-planned sub-urb, now home to more than 30,000 people. Check out the variety of water activities, from parasailing to snorkeling, offered by Hawaii Water Sports Center located in Hawaii Kai's Koko Marina complex (tel: 395-3773; www.hawaiiwatersportscenter.com); they will take you out into the neon-blue waters of Maunalua Bay. Once past Hawai'i Kai the Kalaniana'ole Highway cuts over a saddle ridge at **Koko Head**, yet another cinder cone, named either for the red earth common in the area or for the blood *(koko)* of a man bitten by a shark long ago.

Hawai'i Kai Marina.

Hanauma Bay and Sandy Beach

Even beach-loving tourists who otherwise never leave Waikiki during their entire trip emerge at least once to make the pilgrimage to gorgeous **Hanauma Bay** ❸ (open Wed–Mon 6am–6pm; entrance fee; tel: 396-4229). Famed since Elvis Presley's 1961 movie *Blue Hawaii* as Oahu's premier snorkeling spot, Hanauma is also exceptionally pretty in its own right. Its name, meaning "the curved bay," is an understatement. Cradled in what remains of an eroded extinct volcanic tuff

BELOW:
body boarding,
Sandy Beach.

Map,
page 129

one, the bay is all but circular, fringed on one long side by palm trees and luxuriant soft sand, and inhabited by enough protected but bold Hawaiian fish to seduce any snorkeler.

Daily visitor numbers are carefully regulated to minimize environmental harm – if you arrive any later than 9am you may not be allowed in – and the entire site remains closed every Tuesday. Snorkeling equipment is available for rent, and all visitors are obliged to watch an educational film. No food or water is sold at the beach, but if you bring your own supplies this is a great place to spend the whole day. Note that the park remains open until 10pm on the second and fourth Saturday of each month in summer, and the second Saturday only in winter, offering a great opportunity to snorkel at night.

After Hanauma Bay, the feeling of a city evaporates. At the next cliffside turn, *makai* (the ocean side) of Koko Crater, tourists wait at a parking lot lookout to hear the **Halona Blowhole 40**, a lava formation that emits a geyser-like wheeze when incoming sea swells push up through its underwater entrance.

Appropriately, *halona* means "peering place." Just along the coast, before you round Makapu'u Point to Oahu's windward side, is **Sandy Beach 41**, a local favorite for body surfing, people watching and, in season, an occasional whale sighting. On weekends especially, the beach is often crowded with daredevil Oahu kids; come during the week if you're looking for peace and serenity. And watch those waves – in winter, they're lethally dangerous to all but experts.

Makapu'u

Beyond Koko Head and Sandy Beach, the highway cuts inland, northward, and upward. At the crest, windward Oahu unfolds in one of the more beautiful

Elvis Presley and co-star Joan Blackman. Blue Hawaii *popularised Hanauma Bay.*

BELOW: Sandy Beach.

Map,
page 129

Celebrities such as James Cagney, Henry Fonda, and Chet Atkins used to drive to Waimanalo from Waikiki just to hear Gabby Pahinui (above) play his guitar.

BELOW: Sea Life Park.
RIGHT: Halona Blowhole.

Hawaiian vistas. Continue northward from Sandy Beach along winding Kalaniana'ole Highway and watch for this scenic lookout at the top of the rise and on the ocean side of the road. Directly below the lookout's parking area is **Makapu'u Beach Park** ❷, bounded by rough open seas, sheer lava-rock cliffs and hill-sized dunes. Makapu'u is prized for its bodysurfing waves. Lifeguards are stationed on the beach, but inexperienced bodysurfers should take extreme caution when in the water.

The rocky summit on the right is **Makapu'u Point**, where a white lighthouse is perched on the craggy black-lava palisade. A paved road leading up to the lighthouse is closed to automobiles but is accessible by foot; the view of the coastline is well worth the hike, especially during whale-watching season in winter. The wild lands adjacent are a future park.

Off Makapu'u are two small tuff-cone islands – a small, greenish-black one in the foreground called **Kaohikaipu Island**, and a larger, adze-shaped one named **Manana** but more commonly known as **Rabbit Island**, not because of its slight rabbit's head shape, but because it was formerly a rabbit-raising farm. The 67-acre (27-hectare) island is now a state-protected, off-limits bird sanctuary.

On Makapu'u's *mauka* (mountain) side, if wind conditions are amenable, brilliantly colored hang gliders may be seen floating in thermal currents that sweep up the face of sheer 1,200-ft (360-meter) cliffs. Below that neck-twisting focal point are perhaps more intelligent animals: the false killer whales, dolphins, penguins, sea lions, and other aquatic creatures at **Sea Life Park** ❸, smaller than, but similar to, such complexes in Florida and California. Among the highlights is a 300,000-gallon (11,350-hectoliter) Hawaiian reef tank, filled with sharks, rays, sea turtles, and teeming with fish of every color. The park also maintains a wildlife rehabilitation unit, and is called upon when marine animals are found in distress.

Waimanalo

If you are looking for a beach with plenty of empty space, an awesome mountain *pali* (high-cliff) backdrop and warm waters to soak in, **Waimanalo Beach** ❹ has few peers, but it's one of those gems that are often overlooked by visitors. **Waimanalo** ❺ is as local a town as anywhere in Hawaii, a place where the rural Hawaiian lifestyle is sustained. Perhaps the area's most notable resident was Gabby Pahinui (1921–80), a slack-key guitarist and one of Hawaii's finest musicians. Another famous son of Waimanalo is Chad Rowan, born here in 1969, a sumo star who fought in Japan under the name Akebono (Sunrise). In 1993, he became the first *gaijin* (foreigner) ever to ascend to the rank of *yokozuna*, or grand champion, in sumo.

Beyond Waimanalo and **Bellows Air Force Station** rises 1,643-ft (499-meter) **Olomana**. Named for a giant who jumped from Kauai to Oahu, Olomana casts morning shadows over **Maunawili**, an emerald vale where two parting lovers inspired Queen Lili'uokalani to write her timeless song *Aloha 'Oe*. Just minutes past Maunawili's pastures and farms are Oahu's second and third most-populated towns – Kailua and Kane'ohe *(see Windward Side, pages 179–83)* – which unfurl in a hybrid of modern suburbia and natural setting. ❑

Windward Side

*In Hawaii, "windward" signifies mountainous, wet and lush.
Oahu's windward coast follows the rule, even in suburban Kailua
and Kane'ohe, by offering primal contours and rural textures*

For the next 30 miles (50 km) or so northward, prepare to be overwhelmed by the majestic **Ko'olau Mountains**. Like a massive curtain that parts now and then to expose lone spires, fluted columns, crystal falls and deep green valleys, these sheer cliffs dwarf everything in their vicinity. Meaning "windward," the Ko'olau wear mist as a *lei* (garland), rainbows like jewels, and rainfall like running tears, or as the Hawaiians like to poetically say, *lei i ka noe*. On and on they stretch, from Makapu'u in Southeast Oahu nearly to the North Shore, like a chain of otherworldly cathedrals crowned by mist.

Kailua

Take the Pali Highway up from Honolulu, and, dropping down the sheer flank of the Ko'olau Mountains beyond the Nu'uanu Pali Lookout, you will reach Oahu's second largest town, Kailua. This unremarkable suburb is only worth visiting for its magnificent beaches, but if you're entering **Kailua ❶** around sunset, pause under the banyan tree on the corner of Oneawa Street and Ku'ulei Road. Scores of mynah birds will be gathering to roost for the night, kicking up a squawking fuss. A fine beach stretches the length of **Kailua Bay**, but the most convenient access to this swathe of sand is at **Kailua Beach Park ❷**, just before the cul-de-sac community of **Lanikai**. Blessed with fine winds and glorious turquoise water, Kailua ("Two Seas or Currents") is the site of international windsurfing competitions. Offshore are the small sanctuary islands of Mokuluas and Popo'ia, swimmable from Kailua Beach Park.

Kane'ohe

Kane'ohe ❸ town, immediately north of Kailua, is a bedroom community for Honolulu and the nearby marine base, with residential subdivisions that hug shimmering **Kane'ohe Bay** and the *pali* (steep cliffs). The large Kane'ohe Marine Corps Air Station dominates scenic Mokapu Peninsula. Just offshore, Mokuolo'e, better known as Coconut Island, is the site of the Hawaii Institute of Marine Biology, run by the University of Hawaii.

Stunning Kane'ohe Bay is a popular recreation area, protected by outlying reefs and good for most watersports. Several catamarans offer day trips to the bay's central sandbar. Kane'ohe means "bamboo husband." One interpretation says that a woman of ancient times compared the cruelty of her husband with a sharp bamboo knife; others suggest the name refers to one of his physical attributes.

Cultural attractions in the area include the serene **Byodo-In Temple ❹** (47–200 Kahekili Hwy; open

Preceding Pages: riding horses in the hills near Kualoa.
Opposite: snorkeling in Kane'ohe Bay.
Below: outrigger on Kailua Beach.

daily 8.30am–4.30pm; entrance fee; tel: 239-4724), a termite-proof cement replica of Kyoto's famous Byodo-In Temple of Equality. It is the major structure in the **Valley of the Temples Memorial Park**. A 7-ton bronze bell, a 2-acre (0.8-hectare) reflecting lake, peacocks, swans, ducks, meditation niches, and tinkling waterfalls enhance its imported architecture.

Of cultural and historical importance is a series of ancient fishponds that pepper windward shores north of Kane'ohe. The splendid **He'eia Fishpond ❺**, on the Kane'ohe side of **Kealohi Point**, is Oahu's biggest. It has a wall 12 ft (3.6 meters) wide and 5,000 ft (1,500 meters) long, and once enclosed an area of 88 acres (35 hectares).

Another worthwhile stop is **Senator Fong's Plantation and Gardens ❻** (47-285 Pulama Rd; open daily 10am–2pm; entrance fee; tel: 239-6775; www.fong garden.com), a 725-acre (293-hectare) attraction owned by the former US Senator Hiram Fong, with gardens of exotic flowers, scenic views of windward Oahu, and guided tram tours.

Waterfowl heaven

At **Kualoa Regional Park ❼**, heads usually crane seaward for lingering looks at a small, distinct island known to Hawaiians as **Mokoli'i ❽** (which means the little *mo'o*, or lizard). Long ago, the conical island was nicknamed Chinaman's Hat. At low tide, one can easily wade out on the reef to this island (reef shoes are recommended), bask under palm trees, and photograph the graceful Hawaiian stilts *(ae'o)* and frigate birds *(iwa)* that soar overhead. On shore, the 124-acre (50-hectare) **Moli'i Fishpond**, easy to spot with a 4,000-ft (1,200-meter) long retaining wall, has been in cultivation for 800 years. This is also a

Oahu once had nearly 100 fishponds used by Hawaiians to grow seafood. Now, only five are left intact. Four are on this windward coast: He'eia (north of Kane'ohe), Kahalu'u, Moli'i (off Kualoa Point), and Huilua (Kahana Bay). The fifth is at Oki'okiolepe, in Pearl Harbor.

BELOW: Byodo-In Temple.

very good place to see endangered Hawaiian waterfowl. Kualoa has long been sacred to the ancient Hawaiians and was favored as a royal residence.

Inland is the **Kualoa Ranch** (tel: 237-7321; www.kualoa.com), the largest of the few working cattle ranches still left on Oahu. In recent years, the enterprising owners have developed it as a film location, notably for the television series *Lost*, and as a popular tourist destination, offering activities like horseback riding, snorkeling, and jet-skiing at the beach park just across the street, plus helicopter tours that take in this spectacular stretch of coast and mountains. Equally impressive is a sailing trip in a catamaran to Kane'ohe Bay's sweeping sandbar. Set in the middle of the bay's waters and backed by the towering *pali*, this is Hawaii at its most beautiful. For information call Captain Bob's Picnic Sail (tel: 942-5077).

Kahana and Hau'ula

Beyond Ka'a'awa is **Mahie Point**, which overlooks the *hala* (screwpine) groves, reedy lagoons, and whistling ironwood that rim the silent beauty of **Kahana Bay ❾**. There is a rock formation at the Point called **Kauhi**, although it is better known as Crouching Lion, after an entrepreneur renamed it to give his nearby restaurant a romantic hue. From a certain angle, the rock does look like a lion. Local legend, however, offers a different explanation *(see margin)*.

Kahana Bay itself shelters a fine beach of grayish sand, while the valley behind, which is still farmed in the traditional manner by native Hawaiians, offers a couple of good hiking trails.

Straw baskets bulging with plump papayas, avocados, and Chinese bananas hanging inside weathered wooden stands compete with shell chandeliers for the

Map, page 126

Local legend has it that Kauhi, a demigod from Tahiti, was imprisoned on the rock by the goddess Pele. But Kauhi fell in love with Pele's sister Hi'aka and tried to break out of his prison to be with her. He was frozen into stone in a crouching position, which is why the rock is called the Crouching Lion.

BELOW: Kahana Bay.

Map, page 126

traveler's dollar along this stretch to **Hau'ula**. Further hiking trails enable adventurous walkers to explore the hillsides behind the little residential community of Hau'uh.

Nearby **Sacred Falls Park ⓪** is known as **Kaliuwa'a Falls** in Hawaiian. Kaliuwa'a, the "canoe leak," was said to be a hangout of the legendary pig god Kamapua'a, who could assume the form of either a man or a pig, depending upon his intentions. Due to a landslide that claimed eight lives in 1999, the trail to Kaliuwa'a has been closed indefinitely. However, helicopter tours still offer visual access to the area.

Polynesian Cultural Center

Three miles (5 km) north of Hau'ula is **La'ie ⑪**, a predominantly Mormon community that's home to the Hawaii campus of Brigham Young University, as well as the chaste-looking **Mormon Temple**, built in 1919 by descendants of missionary Mormons living in this area since 1864. The temple is closed to non-Mormons; however, its visitor center is open to all.

La'ie is very much on the tourist map, thanks to the **Polynesian Cultural Center ⑫** (open Mon–Sat noon–9pm; entrance fee; tel: 293-3333; www.polynesia. com), which manages to educate more than a million visitors each year about the history and culture of the Pacific islands, despite its decidedly theme-park presentation. Your hosts are native islanders whose enthusiasm and warmth are infectious, and the activities range from the serious to the comical, with plenty to keep you occupied and entertained; an IMAX theater adds a high-tech element to the experience.

The center's main shows – performed nightly by young Mormon students from Fiji, Samoa, Tahiti, Tonga, the Marquesas, New Zealand, and Hawaii – are designed, according to brochures, to give visitors a "pure cultural view of Polynesia." Exactly how much you pay for the experience depends on which of the many possible packages, including meals and shows, you choose to buy, but it can easily run into hundreds of dollars. The center runs special buses from Waikiki if you'd rather not drive.

Just north of the cultural center is **La'ie Point**, at the end of Anemoku and Naupaka streets and where windward waters running hard from the north pound two little offshore isles – **Kukuiho'olua** and **Mokualai** – with a frightening and beautiful force, especially in winter.

Kahuku ⑬ is an ex-plantation town where the only landmark is a former sugar mill (it closed in 1971). The site is now a rather run-down shopping mall, though sadly its towering chimney stack, deemed a health and safety hazard, had to be demolished in 2004. Here you will discover a place where workers' cafés, grocery stores, karate *dojo* and tiny homes survive much as they did when residents awoke to the mill's morning steam whistle. A walk around this village, where ferns and orchids hang in bleach-bottle planters, is pleasant and usually highly rewarding.

Aquaculture is very big business in the Kahuku area. Shrimp, shellfish, and edible seaweed are all cultivated in large ponds. Roadside stands offer the freshest and best catches of the day's harvest. ❑

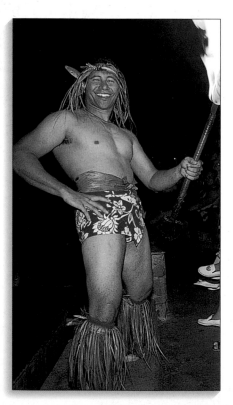

Bᴇʟᴏᴡ ᴀɴᴅ Rɪɢʜᴛ: showtime at the Polynesian Cultural Center.

Map,
page 126

NORTH SHORE

The ground along the North Shore fairly rumbles in winter as the world's finest surfing waves arrive from the north. This shore is also a rural counterpoint to Oahu's urbanized southern coast

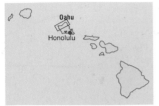

A drive along the North Shore is as far away from Waikiki as one can get without leaving Oahu. The fragrance of plumeria and coconut oil are replaced by the salty aroma of the pounding surf and Waikiki's wall of hotels gives way to the raw, unencumbered beauty of the North Shore.

Oddly enough, the first major landmark encountered on the North Shore, continuing from the windward side, is the recently upgraded **Turtle Bay Resort ⓮**, on a dramatic point extending into the ocean with dramatic vistas of storms and waves. A few miles farther, the world's finest surfing waves crash onto offshore reefs and sandbars: Sunset, Rocky Point, Banzai Pipeline, Waimea Bay, Chun's Reef, Hale'iwa, and Avalanche. Calm in summer and for much of the year, **Waimea Bay ⓯** hosts monster waves when the North Shore feels the fury of winter storms in the Arctic that drive rough seas toward Hawaii. In December 1969, more than 30 homes between Kahuku Point and Hale'iwa were reduced to tinder as monstrous 50-ft (15-meter) waves pounded the North Shore. The most jaded surfer will agree that a tubing, top-to-bottom wave off one of those reefs generates enough adrenaline to keep anybody going through at least a few nervous lifetimes, especially when Waimea Bay is

BELOW: Turtle Bay Resort.

breaking with waves so big that hundreds of people line the road like spectators at a gladiator show. The waves are so thunderous that the ground trembles underfoot. Only the best surfers paddle out towards the 20- to 30-ft (7- to 10-meter) winter swells lifting like glossy black holes on the blue-gray horizon.

A good place to take in Waimea Bay, most of the North Shore, and the distant Wai'anae Mountains is from the **Pu'uomahuka Heiau State Monument** ⑯, on a 250-ft (75-meter) bluff above the **St Peter and Paul Church**. Turn off from the main road onto Pupukea Road, at the fire station and supermarket.

At the very top of the bluff, on a marked side road, is an ancient *heiau*, or temple. It is one of Oahu's largest, and Hawaiians still leave offerings for the gods, usually lava stones wrapped in *ti* leaves, on its walls. It was known as Pu'uomahuka, the hill of escape, although historically not for some. In May 1792, two crew members (some accounts say three) of Captain George Vancouver's ship HMS *Daedalus* were offered in sacrifice at this *heiau* after being captured while filling water barrels at the mouth of the Waimea River. During that period, the Hawaiians had an insatiable desire to procure guns and ammunition.

When Vancouver was informed of what had happened, he pledged to track down and punish the culprits, and eventually he did. Three Hawaiians were executed with a pistol by their own chiefs in full view of islanders and crewmen. There is some debate as to whether the trio were the actual offenders. Some historians believe Oahu's wily ruler, Kahekili, rounded up three innocent people and "sacrificed" them to assuage the British captain. Whatever the truth may be, the *heiau* is a somber, foreboding place.

Where Waimea River enters Waimea Bay, on the *mauka* (mountain) side of the road, just east of the beach park, look for the entrance to **Waimea Valley**,

In 1899, Hale'iwa, not Waikiki, opened the island's first hotel: the Victorian-style Haie'iwa Hotel, now long gone.

BELOW: Waimea Bay.

Map, page 126

Ka'ena Point, Oahu's westernmost tip.

BELOW: Hale'iwa.

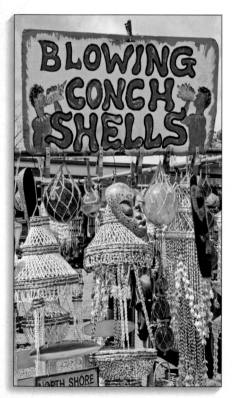

home of the **Waimea Valley Audubon Center** ⑰ (59-864 Kamehameha Hwy; open daily 9.30am–5pm; entrance fee; tel: 638-9199; www.audubon.org). This 1,800-acre (728-hectare) botanical garden used to be run as a theme park, but now serves as a nature preserve, under the auspices of the National Audubon Society. Trails leading well over a mile back into the valley, and culminating at a spectacular waterfall, enable visitors to enjoy more than 6,000 varieties of native and imported plants, many of which have magnificently colorful flowers.

Summer and shave ice

Further westward along the North Shore's surfing grounds, a small cement bridge funnels traffic over a little stream into **Hale'iwa** ⑱ (House of the Frigate Bird), an arty and funky outpost – but the biggest town on this side of Oahu – where people of all ethnic backgrounds and lifestyles mingle. An eclectic mix of trendy cafés, art galleries, boutiques, and shops mix with remnants of the old plantation days. Fujioka's Supermarket is one of the town's more familiar establishments. Founded in 1910, the family-run business carries the usual groceries and knick-knacks, along with, as a sign of the times, the North Shore's finest selection of wines and imported cigars. No visit to Hale'iwa would be complete without a stop at Matsumoto General Store (66-87 Kamehameha Hwy; open 8.30am–6pm), famous for shave ice in a rainbow of flavors, complete with *azuki* beans and ice cream at the bottom.

A mid-summer visit to Hale'iwa coincides with the height of the Japanese *Obon* season, when the **Hale'iwa Jodo Mission** has its annual lantern festival, *toronagashi*, with dozens of flickering lanterns – each a farewell light for an ancestor's spirit – floating on the dark sea to the east side of **Kaiaka Bay**. Hale'iwa also hosts the **Hale'iwa Festival** in July and the **Hale'iwa Taro Festival** in September, two celebrations that offer a hometown glimpse into Hawaiian culture.

Northwest Oahu

From Hale'iwa, continue south down the Kamehameha Highway through central Oahu and back to Honolulu, or head further east past taro and banana patches to the old plantation town of **Waialua**.

Beyond Waialua, on the *mauka* (mountain) side of Farrington Highway, is the **Mokule'ia Polo Farm**, where visiting teams from around the world battle through chukkas of polo against local pony teams (most Sundays from March to July); bring a picnic and settle in. Further down the road is the **Dillingham Airfield** ⑲, where Honolulu Soaring (tel: 637-0207; www.honolulusoaring.com) take to the skies alongside the 2,000-ft (610-meter) Wai'anae *pali*. The more courageous can skydive with Skydive Hawaii (tel: 637-9700; www.hawaii-iskydiving.com), which also departs from Dillingham. At the end of the road beyond Mokule'ia, a foot trail continues to **Ka'ena Point** ⑳, the westernmost tip of O'ahu where the Hawaiians believed the souls of the dead departed to the afterlife. The surrounding area is now a wildlife conservation district. Beyond, on foot, is the Wai'anae Coast. In winter, waves as high as 50 ft (15 meters) have been witnessed off Ka'ena Point. No one has surfed them. Yet. ❑

Surfing

Some historians believe that a primitive form of surfing originated somewhere in the Pacific around 2000 BC. It is likely that when the first Polynesians migrated to the Hawaiian Islands around AD 400, they were already well-versed in the sport.

Early Hawaiians called surfing *he'e nalu*, which literally translates as "wave sliding." Hawaiian chants dating from the 15th century recount surfing exploits, indicating that *he'e nalu* had become so developed that competitions were held among famous surfers, usually royalty, or *ali'i*. These were widely heralded affairs, sometimes pitting chiefs against each other; crowds of supporters would indulge in high-stakes gambling by placing property bets on a favored wave rider.

One Hawaiian legend tells the story of Kawelo, whose wife was taken by his brother, the ruling chief 'Aikanaka. Full of anguish, Kawelo was plotting his revenge when he suddenly noticed a crowd on the beach, enjoying *he'e nalu*. Overcome with desire, Kawelo at once forgot completely about his wife and 'Aikanaka and headed for the beach to engage in his favorite pastime. No wonder one long-time surfer says, "Perfect waves are miracles. When they come, everything else stops, including romance."

WAVES OF CHANGE

Gone are the days when *ali'i* rode on large *koa* boards weighing 150 lbs (70 kg). Also gone are early 20th-century Waikiki-style boards made of California redwood. And just as extinct are the balsa "pig boards" that were popular in the early 1950s. Thanks to modern technology, today's surfboards are made of foam and fiberglass, and can weigh less than 5 lbs (2 kg). The serious surfer today maintains not just one surfboard, but an all-purpose "quiver" of boards, ranging in function and size. Short-boards are slightly more than 6 ft (2 meters) in length, while long-boards (more buoyant and stable, they permit the surfer to perform more creative maneuvers) are about 9 ft (3 meters) in length.

Learning to surf is relatively easy. There is a handful of surfing instruction schools on Oahu, but one can usually get informal lessons from willing beachboys in Waikiki.

Of course, you can't become a true surfing aficionado without first knowing the language. Here are a few useful surf terms to be mastered:

- **breaks**: waves.
- **gonzo**: highly enthusiastic, raring to go.
- **hang ten**: usually performed on long boards, this maneuver entails placing all 10 toes over the nose or front of the board.
- **lull**: when waves aren't coming in.
- **rights/lefts**: the direction a wave breaks as you face the shore.
- **sets**: groups of arriving waves.
- **wipe out**: crash and splash, and it should be only on a big, big wave.

The best time to watch big-wave surfing is in November and December, when the **Triple Crown of Surfing** is held on Oahu's North Shore. The Triple Crown consists of three separate competitions featuring professional surfers from around the world. ❑

RIGHT: Banzai Pipeline.

CENTRAL OAHU

*Central Oahu is wedged between the mountains of the old Wai'anae
and Ko'olau volcanoes. At the southern end of this fertile land of
pineapples is Pearl Harbor, Hawaii's number-one visitor site*

Map,
page 126

Urbanized travelers who are so inclined will find the freeways
slicing across central Oahu to their liking. Indeed, with all the
housing subdivisions sprouting up in parts of Oahu's interior, a
mainlander could feel quite at home. From Waikiki and downtown
Honolulu, travel west along the Lunalilo Freeway, more commonly
called the H-1, then cut north on the H-2 freeway. But before heading
into central Oahu itself, there are several places of interest worth a visit.

Ancient Moanalua

Just off the H-1 freeway is **Moanalua Gardens ㉑**, a tranquil retreat graced with
huge, umbrella-like monkeypod trees. A popular picnic spot and site of July's
Prince Lot Hula Festival, the gardens are privately owned but are open to the
public. A country home built by Kamahameha V in Victorian Chinese detail
graces the setting. Behind is **Moanalua Valley**, an even more spectacular wilderness area where there are tall white hibiscus trees shading a stream, and Hawaiian petroglyphs and an ancient medicinal pool surrounded by colorful morning
glories, gardenias, ferns, and fragrant vines. The valley has recently been purchased by the state, which has pledged to ensure continued access for hikers.

OPPOSITE: USS
Missouri in Pearl
Harbor.
BELOW: preparing
flowers for sale.

The Moanalua area was probably named for two
ancient encampments where travelers between Honolulu
and 'Ewa could rest. A nearby field called Pueohulunui
("Much-feathered Owl") was said to be a place where
owls from Kauai and Ni'ihau arrived for a big battle.

In the early 1970s, Moanalua Valley was the focal
point of a bitter controversy between the state government and local activists. Plans for a freeway connecting central and windward Oahu called for a portion of
that freeway to wend through the valley. When petroglyphs were discovered, the valley was entered into the
National Register of Historic Places. In 1977, a US
Supreme Court ruling forced the state to reroute the
freeway to circumvent the valley. The resulting H-3
Freeway, completed in 1998, winds its way through the
lush heart of Halawa Valley, descending to the Windward Coast at Kane'ohe.

Medics and sport

Conspicuously set on a ridge overlooking the freeway
is the **Tripler Army Medical Center**, a pink structure
built in 1948, the largest military hospital in the Pacific.
The 14-story building was named after General Charles
Stuart Tripler, a major-general who served as army
medical director of the Potomac in the Civil War.

As you approach Pearl Harbor, you'll easily spot the
50,000-seat **Aloha Stadium ㉒**, Oahu's prime but
plagued-by-rust outdoor venue for major sports and

special events like the annual State Fair. Home of the annual Pro Bowl football game, which features National Football League all-stars, the stadium was built in 1975 and can be realigned into baseball or football configurations. Concession workers here sell Chinese crack seed and *saimin* noodles along with the usual hot dogs and burgers.

Aloha Stadium's parking lot is the site for one of Oahu's biggest attractions, when some 30,000 residents and visitors flock to the **Aloha Stadium Swap Meet** (open Wed, Sat and Sun 6am–3pm; entrance fee; tel: 486-6704). Here are row upon row of vendors hawking everything from aloha shirts to zucchini.

Just *mauka* (towards the mountains) of the stadium is **Stadium Mall**, a retail complex, unremarkable except that it is home to **The Ice Palace** (tel: 487-9921). Yes, there is ice skating even in balmy Hawaii, and it's a favorite activity for many youngsters. The Ice Palace occasionally hosts hockey competitions.

Beyond the stadium lie the east, middle, and west lochs of Pearl Harbor – named for the pearl oysters once found here – and the towns of **'Aiea**, **Pearl City** and **Waipahu**, largely bedroom communities for Honolulu.

'Aiea is the only town or city in the United States whose name is made up entirely of vowels.

Pearl Harbor

One of the major reasons why the US annexed Hawaii, at the end of the 19th century, was to acquire control of **Pearl Harbor ㉓**. This vast inlet, at the heart of Oahu's southern coast, is the finest harbor for 2,000 miles (3,200 km) in any direction. As the base of the US Pacific Fleet, it became the target of the notorious Japanese surprise attack on the morning of December 7, 1941. Denounced by President Roosevelt as a "date which will live in infamy," it immediately precipitated US entry into World War II.

BELOW: inside the Arizona Memorial.

Map, page 126

Japanese torpedoes and dive-bombers, launched from an armada 200 miles (320 km) northwest, destroyed a total of 18 warships that day. Their most famous victim is now the focus of the **USS *Arizona* Memorial** ㉔ (visitor center open daily 7.30am–5pm; tel: 422-0561; www.nps.gov/usar; shuttle boats run between 8am–3pm, weather permitting). US Navy boats ferry a constant stream of visitors to stand on the dazzling white platform that straddles the wreck of the USS *Arizona*, still visible, indeed still leaking oil, where it sank beneath the waters, carrying almost 1,200 of its crew to their deaths.

Designed by Honolulu architect Alfred Preis, the memorial was made possible in part by a benefit concert staged in 1961 by Elvis Presley, as his first public performance after leaving the US Army. It's the most popular free attraction on Oahu, with more than a million visitors annually, so you may have to wait for an hour or two before the next available shuttle service. The visitor center has a museum and book shop to keep you occupied.

USS *Bowfin* and USS *Missouri*

A few minutes' walk from the USS *Arizona* Memorial visitors center, across the parking lot, brings you to the privately operated **USS *Bowfin* Submarine Museum and Park** (open daily 8am–5pm; entrance fee; tel: 423-1341; www.bowfin.org). Would-be submariners and the curious can check out defused torpedoes, and descend into and walk through a completely refurbished World War II diesel-electric submarine, the USS *Bowfin*, which is credited with 44 ship sinkings in nine patrols, many of them well inside Japanese waters.

Shuttle buses run from the *Bowfin* across a slender road bridge to reach Ford Island, which is otherwise barred to non-military personnel. Their destination

Commissioned on 7 December 1942, The Bowfin *was later mothballed in the Middle Loch of Pearl Harbor until it was brought out of retirement.*

BELOW: USS *Bowfin*.

Refreshments at the Battleship Missouri *Memorial.*

is a decommissioned World War II battleship, moored a short way along from the USS *Arizona* Memorial – the **USS *Missouri*** (open 8.30am–5pm; entrance fee; tel: 973-2494; www.ussmissouri.org). Known affectionately as the "Mighty Mo," this was the last battleship ever built by the US, in 1944, and the last still in use by any nation when she was finally retired in 1992. You can visit the *Missouri* by yourself or take one of the guided tours – both 60-minute guided walking tours and in-depth tours are available. Whichever you choose to do, the highlight will be the precise spot on deck where Japan's surrender was signed in Tokyo Bay in September 1945.

Another monument, considerably lower in profile and cost, can be found on **Ford Island** alongside the rusting hulk of the USS *Utah*. Civilians, however, can visit the site only if accompanied by a member or dependent of the United States military. At neighboring **Hickam Air Force Base**, a plaque marks the spot where the *Apollo 11* astronauts first touched earth after their walk on the moon in 1969.

Central plateau

On the drive north and inland on the H-2 freeway, Oahu's central plateau rises gradually until it reaches the **Schofield Barracks ㉕** army post and **Wahiawa**, the highest residential community on Oahu. Wahiawa ("Place of Noise") can be bypassed altogether by staying on Highway 90, which separates the town from Schofield Barracks. But military enthusiasts will enjoy a stop at Schofield's **Tropic Lightning Museum** (open Tues–Sat 10am–4pm), which houses artifacts, photographs, and archival materials documenting the history of Schofield Barracks and the famed "Tropic Lightning" 25th Light Infantry Division.

BELOW: offerings at the stones of Kukaniloko.

Others, more interested in a place of quiet than a place of noise, might care to stop in Wahiawa to take a look at the visually unspectacular **Healing Stones**. The stones sit on a simple altar inside a concrete shelter on California Street. Until the late 1920s, pilgrims regularly visited these stones, which, according to legend, were two sisters from the island of Kauai who were petrified by greater powers. Other myths attribute alternative origins to the stones but, whatever the explanation, they are still thought to emanate healing powers. Offerings are regularly left here. Also in Wahiawa is the **Wahiawa Botanical Garden** (1396 California Avenue; open daily 9am–4pm; tel: 621-7321).

Birth stones

On the north side of Wahiawa, to the left of Kamehameha Highway and just beyond Whitmore Avenue, are sacred stones of a different sort. These are the **birth stones of Kukaniloko ㉖**. This eucalyptus-fringed clearing in a pineapple field has been venerated by Hawaiians as far back as the 12th century. The wives of high-ranking chiefs bore their children on the gently curved surfaces of these stones. Attendant chiefs, high priests, and physicians would gather around the newborn infant and, during an impressive ceremony marked by great drum rolls, chants and offerings, the royal child would be named and the umbilical cord cut and ritually hidden away.

From this open-air site, to the west in the direction of the Wai'anae Range, you can look up the side of Leilehua Plain to the broad **Kolekole Pass**, which was used by low-flying Japanese bombers as a convenient cover and western approach for their sneak attacks on Schofield Barracks and adjacent **Wheeler Army Air Field**. In 1969, when the joint American-Japanese movie *Tora! Tora! Tora!* was being filmed, the sight of Japanese Zeros, Kates and Vals roaring through Kolekole and raining simulated bombs and machine-gun fire on Schofield Barracks and Wheeler Air Force Base produced a chilling sense of *déjà vu* for anyone who had been here during World War II.

Pineapple world

Although the Dole company no longer grows pineapples on Oahu on a significant commercial scale *(see box for more on the Dole company background)*, its former headquarters, just north of Wahiawa, have been converted into a flourishing tourist attraction known as the **Dole Plantation** (Kamehameha Highway; open daily 9am–5.30pm; free, entrance fee to specific attractions; tel: 621-8408; www.dole-plantation.com). The central building is a large store that sells all kinds of pineapple-related products, along with coffee, Hawaiian plants, and T-shirts displaying the company logo. There's a little yellow train, the Pineapple Express, that makes regular 20-minute tours of the fields, accompanied by a helpful narrative. There is also what's claimed to be the world's largest maze (it was featured in the 2001 edition of the *Guiness Book of World Records*), an intricate tangle of hedgerows with six distinct "centers," and more than 10,000 colorful plants, including varieties of hibiscus, the state flower. ❑

TIP

Throughout the islands you will encounter *leis* or *ti*-covered objects at sacred sites. These are religious offerings of Native Hawaiians and should be left undisturbed. They are not tourist souvenirs.

BELOW: pineapples in abundance.

PINEAPPLES

Pineapple fields spread across central Oahu, stretching from the Wai'anae Mountains on one side to the Ko'olau Range on the other. Europeans first came across pineapples in South America and the West Indies. Quickly adopted as a crop, they were transplanted throughout the world, and were reportedly grown in Hawaii as early as 1813. However, the commercial selling of pineapple in Hawaii did not begin until 1899, when an Oahu entrepreneur, James D. Dole, planted 60 acres (24 hectares) of Wahiawa land with the fruit. Two years later, Dole organized the Hawaiian Pineapple Company, and by 1906 he had begun building a cannery at Iwilei, near Honolulu Harbor. Dole's father was a cousin to Sanford Dole, president of the Hawaiian Republic from 1893 to 1900 and one of the group of businessmen and landowners responsible for overthrowing the monarchy *(see page 49)*.

WAI'ANAE COAST

Oahu's western coast is one of the sunniest places on the island, and the locals tend to keep this a secret. They also fiercely guard their lifestyle, which sustains the coast's island feel

Map, page 126

The Wai'anae Coast is perhaps the most misunderstood and maligned area of Oahu. It is true that this 20-mile (32-km) coastline is hotter, dustier, and drier than the rest of the island. And with the exception of the Ko 'Olina Resort at the southern end, and Makaha's golf club, it does lack the usual tourist attractions. But dig deep, and you'll find that West Oahu has considerable natural and cultural beauty to offer the enlightened, respectful and adventurous traveler. Even on this side of the island, however, changes are unavoidable. At its southern end, where Wai'anae meets the flat 'Ewa plains west of Honolulu, a so-called second city – Kapolei – has risen, an ambitious attempt to relieve urban Honolulu's congestion, and to offer Oahu a resort area outside of Waikiki.

PRECEDING PAGES:
rinsing surfboards.
OPPOSITE: fisherman
inspects his net
catch.
BELOW: local coffee
house.

Local eulogies

Question any long-time resident of Nanakuli, Ma'ili, Wai'anae, or Makaha about the West Side, and they may just spend hours explaining why it's paradise: "It's the closest thing to an unspoiled Hawaiian place on this island," says a truck driver from Lualualei. A Nanakuli elder states flatly that "You've never been to a real *lu'au* until you've been to a big one on this side." Indeed, wedding or first-birthday *lu'au* (feasts, *see page 113*) on this side of the island are legendary, remembered by participants by the number of *kalua* pigs and kegs of beer consumed.

Just over 35,000 people live along Wai'anae's jagged shorelines and dry mountain slopes. Before the arrival of Captain Cook, the west coast of Oahu was a major center of Hawaiian civilization, probably because of the rich fishing grounds in the clear offshore waters between Nanakuli and Ka'ena Point. It was here, according to oral traditions, that the demigod Maui lived and first learned to make fire after he arrived in Hawaii. Also along this coast, several myths refer to the infamous man-pig Kamapua'a, renowned throughout Hawaii as a god who both charmed and harassed mortal worshipers with his capricious antics.

As island-style a place as any to prepare for the Wai'anae Coast is **Waipahu** ㉘, which is just past Pearl City and a quick dash off the H-1 Freeway. Waipahu, over a century old, is a town in transition. Until the mid-1970s, Waipahu was devoted to growing sugar-cane. But today cane has been phased out, and employment is provided by other industries, such as tourism and leisure.

In the heart of Waipahu, just off Waipahu Street, is **Hawaii Plantation Village** (open Mon–Sat 10am–2pm; entrance fee; tel: 677-0110; www.hawaiiplantationvillage. com). Plantation-era houses reveal the diverse cultures of eight ethnic groups in Hawaii that were a part of the sugar industry's century-long flowering. Guided tours of the 3-acre (1.2-hectare) site are offered.

BELOW: wet feet at Kahe Point Beach.

The Southwest Corner

The **Ko 'Olina Resort** ❷ has the requisite golf course plus a spa and a series of beach-lined lagoons. Anchoring the resort is the **Marriott 'Ihilani Resort and Spa**, perched on one of the lagoons and white-sand beaches. The spa is as elegant and comprehensive as any in the world. Although upscale timeshares dot the vicinity, the 'Ihilani has long been the only hotel here. However, the Disney corporation recently announced plans to construct a large new beachfront hotel, the first Disney hotel not to adjoin a theme park. Several large *luaus* (feasts) are held adjacent to the resort (there's a bus link to Waikiki). Each Wai'anae coast beach has its own character and devotees. 'Ewa Beach Park, for example, is famed for its abundance of *limu* (also called *ogo* in Japanese), or edible seaweed.

Just outside Ko 'Olina is **Hawaiian Waters Adventure Park** ❸ (400 Farrington Way; opening times vary; entrance fee; tel: 674-9283; www.hawaiianwaters.com), with 25 acres (10 hectares) of water-slides and wave pools. Favored by surfers, **Kahe Point** ❸ is a beach past Ko 'Olina, opposite an electric power plant on the main road, which parallels the western coastline. This spot is called the Kahe Point Beach Park, but locals call it Tracks because remnants of the old narrow-gauge train tracks still parallel the highway northward.

Ku'ilioloa Heiau ❸, on the extreme fingertip of Kane'ilio Point on the south side of Poka'i Bay, is surrounded by water on three sides. This *heiau*, or temple, of coral and lava rock was built in the 15th or 16th century in honor of Ku'ilioloa, a giant dog that often protected travelers in the area.

Protection by giant dogs was appreciated here. This area is said to have been populated in ancient times by cannibals preying on passers-by. According to J. Gilbert McAllister, who wrote a 1933 Bishop Museum survey entitled

Archaeology of Oahu, these highwaymen apparently hid behind high ridges and ambushed unwary victims who came their way. The largest town on this coast, Makaha, meaning fierce or savage, takes its name from these marauders.

"For many years these people preyed upon the traveler," McAllister wrote, "until at one time men from Kauai, hairless men *(olohe)* came to this beach. They were attacked by these cannibals but defeated them, killing the entire colony. Since then, the region has been safe for traveling."

Surfing the waves

Several reefs and points of land along this coast have long been favored as surfing spots, but perhaps the most famous is Kepuhi Point in **Makaha ㉝**, where the annual Makaha International Surfing Championships were once held. In recent years, however, most major big-wave surfing contests have been held on Oahu's vicious North Shore, particularly at the Banzai Pipeline and Sunset Beach surf breaks. Nevertheless, an oldie-but-goodie surfing event at Makaha has caught the fancy of wave-riding old-timers: the annual Buffalo's Longboard Contest, which began in 1978. Makaha Beach commander Buffalo Keaulana and other *kama'aina* (long-time residents) organized it to renew interest in the style of surfing that was in vogue during the 1950s and 1960s.

Wander into the back reaches of **Makaha Valley** to the impressive **Kane'aki Heiau ㉞** (open Tues–Sun 10am–2pm; free), which has been restored by the National Park Service, Bishop Museum, and the Makaha Historical Society. This 17th-century *heiau*, one of the best-preserved on Oahu and tucked away in a spectacular setting alongside Makaha Stream, was rebuilt entirely by hand, using indigenous *pili* grass, *'ohi'a* timber and lava stones much as they were

Map, page 126

BELOW: surfers at Makaha's Buffalo Longboard Contest.

Map,
page 126

utilized by ancient craftsmen. Originally, this was an agricultural *heiau* dedicated to the god Lono, but archeologists speculate that it may have been reconditioned in 1796 by Kamehameha the Great as a *luakini heiau*, or *heiau* of human sacrifice, in honor of his war god Kukailimoku. At the time, Kamehameha was amassing a huge fleet in the Makaha area in preparation for an invasion of Kauai. The fleet was forced back to Oahu by gale-force winds and raging seas, and perhaps people were sacrificed near here to appease the angry and unhelpful gods. Head up into Makaha Valley toward the Sheraton Makaha Golf Club and continue through the golf course to the gate for Mauna 'Olu Estates. The guard will direct you to the *heiau*.

Mt Ka'ala, just east of Makaha in the Wai'anae range, is Oahu's highest point at 4,020 ft (1,225 meters) above sea level.

Half human, half shark

Another famous site you can walk into is about 3 miles (5 km) north of Makaha: **Kaneana ⑤**, the Cave of Kane. Although this cave is 100 ft (30 meters) high in places and about 450 ft (135 meters) deep, it is not a lava tube. Rather, it was carved out by the sea 150,000 years ago when its entrance was at or below sea level. According to a local story, this cave was occupied by a fierce character, Kamohoali'i, who was able to alternate at will between being a human and a shark. Kamohoali'i had a fondness for human flesh, so in his guise as a mortal, he would periodically jump on people and drag them into this cave for dinner. Eventually, this human disguise was discovered and Kamohoali'i had to flee into the sea, but he was captured and destroyed later by vengeful Makua residents.

BELOW: gospel shoes at a gospel church.

Makua Beach ⑥ is the photogenic area where much of the epic motion picture *Hawaii*, based on James Michener's novel of the same name, was filmed in 1965. Film producers recreated an entire set on this beach representing the old Maui whaling town of Lahaina. That set has long since been carted away, but the same spectacular backdrop remains.

Moments later, Farrington Highway ends and briefly becomes a modest road that terminates at **Keawa'ula Bay ⑦**, a favorite board- and body-surfing spot known to residents as **Yokohama Bay**. This sandy playground received the Japanese name at the turn of the 20th century when the Oahu Railway train between 'Ewa and Hale'iwa would stop here to let off Japanese fishermen, who favored the fishing at Keawa'ula. Nobody knows who actually coined the term Yokohama Bay, but the name stuck and later became well-known in surfing circles because of popular left-slide waves that leap off a shallow reef on the bay's south side.

Beyond Yokohama Bay, the landscape loses its sandy character and turns into a jangle of black lava, thorny scrub brush, and sand dunes at **Ka'ena Point**. Like an arrow, Ka'ena points slightly to the northwest and the island of Kauai. It can be traversed on foot or bicycle. Continuing further on and around Ka'ena Point would lead you to the North Shore. Ka'ena Point is now a state wildlife preserve, home to nesting albatross, the occasional Hawaiian monk seal and rare flora.

Ka'ena is said to be named for the brother or cousin of Pele, the fire and volcano goddess, and ancient Hawaiians were reluctant to cross it, for it was a place from which souls departed the earth – the good to the right, and the not-so-good to the left. ❏

GOSPEL SHOES
OF
CHRIST JESUS
~WELCOMES YOU~
SERVICES
SUNDAY- 10:00A.M.-12:00 NOON
YOUNG PEOPLE'S SERVICE-SUN. 1:00-1:45P.M.
MEN'S WORSHIP-TUESDAY 6:30P.M.
BIBLE STUDY-WEDNESDAY- 6:45P.M.
WOMAN'S WORSHIP-THURSDAY-6:30 P.M.

The Leeward Islands

For most travelers, Honolulu ends at the sharp, beaky tip of Ka'ena Point on northwest Oahu. Unknown to many, however, including most Honolulu residents, is that Honolulu is the most far-flung city in the world. The city's jurisdiction not only includes Oahu, but also dozens of smaller points of land that stretch some 1,400 nautical miles (2,200 km) to the northwest.

These shoals, atolls, and desert isles have names like Nihoa, Necker, French Frigate Shoals, Gardiner Pinnacles, Maro Reef, Laysan, Lisianski, Pearl and Hermes Reef, and Kure Island. The better-known Midway Islands are also within Honolulu's sprawling city limits, but they were placed under military jurisdiction at the start of the 20th century.

Collectively, these islands are often referred to as the Leeward Islands, although, officially, they are the **Northwestern Hawaiian Islands**. Eight of these islands and reefs have been combined to form the Hawaiian Islands National Wildlife Refuge.

Some 2,000 US Navy personnel and dependants – as well as hundreds of thousands of goony birds – live at Midway, but the other islets are uninhabited, except for Tern Island at French Frigate Shoals, which supports an airstrip and Loran navigation station maintained by the US Coast Guard. Midway, partially converted to ecotourism in the 1990s, is no longer open to visitors, pending a new management contract.

Largely because of their remoteness, these isles are a favorite breeding ground of the Hawaiian monk seal, an endangered species. This sea mammal prefers solitude over congregating in groups, hence the name "monk" seal, and can grow to over 7 ft (2 meters) in length and weigh nearly 500 lbs (230 kg).

Each spring, adult green sea turtles – Hawaiians called them *honu* – migrate to the wildlife refuge, where the females lumber ashore to lay eggs. The turtles can grow up to 4 ft (1.2 meters) in length and weigh up to 400 lbs (180 kg). They are known to bask on the beach on these uninhabited Hawaiian islets, an activity rare among sea turtles. The monk seals and green sea turtles are federally protected and should not be disturbed.

Among the interesting birds that populate these islands and excite ornithologists are Hawaiian noddy terns, sooty terns, red-footed and blue-faced boobies, Laysan albatrosses, shearwaters, frigate birds, wandering tattlers, Pacific golden plovers, Laysan honey eaters, bristle-thighed curlews and Laysan teals (said to be the rarest ducks in the world).

The two islands closest to Oahu, **Nihoa** and **Necker**, are located about 250 miles (400 km) northeast of Honolulu. They once supported small groups of pre-contact Hawaiians. On Necker, archeologists have found beautifully carved stone images, stone bowls, adzes, and other evidence of an early human presence. Nihoa is about a mile long, a quarter of a mile wide, and rises to an elevation of 900 ft (270 meters). Necker is 3,900 ft (1,200 meters) long, and has an elevation of 276 ft (84 meters). ❑

RIGHT: blue-faced boobies consider their next move, Lisianski Island.

MAUI

Maui is a playful island, attracting a young, cool crowd.
Nearby Molokai and Lanai keep their own company

Booming as a vacation destination, especially among younger, more active and often more affluent travelers than visit Oahu, the island of Maui is very much dominated by a single landmark – mighty Haleakala. This massive dormant volcano offers the adventure of lofty, sometimes snowbound, heights. In ancient times, Maui was a strong and stable island kingdom. It was the only one to complete a "king's highway," a paved walkway 9 ft (3 meters) wide that completely encircled the island. For a period in the late 1800s, the Maui town of Lahaina was capital of the newly united Hawaiian kingdom.

Nowadays, Maui, bolstered by a strong economy, has emerged as a strong competitor to Waikiki with a thriving tourist industry. In addition, the economic diversification needed to compensate for declines in the production of sugar and pineapple, has sparked alternative industries, such as floriculture and information technology.

For a relatively small island – if it were square, it would only be 27 miles (43 km) on each side – Maui possesses an amazing natural diversity. The island is composed of two entirely different volcanic masses. Eastern Maui is Haleakala, an enormous three-sided shield volcano capped with a Manhattan-sized *caldera*, a national park, and a space-age research facility. On Haleakala's western slopes, Upcountry offers farming and cattle ranches worked by skilled Hawaiian cowboys, or *paniolos*. Its windward slopes include one of the best windsurfing spots in the world, ancient taro-growing fields, and the scenic Hana Road. Leeward boomtown Kihei, flanked by the landscaped resort of Wailea, includes long stretches of beach where spectacular winter views include humpback whales offshore.

West Maui is anchored by the island's older and second volcano. On the lee, colorful Lahaina and the two resort areas of Ka'anapali and Kapalua draw many of the island's visitors. The "downtown" communities of Kahului and Wailuku punctuate the windward side.

Adding to this diversity are two other neighboring islands that comprise the County of Maui – Molokai and Lanai. Together with uninhabited Kaho'olawe, this row of sheltering islands forms one side of the 'Au'Au Channel, which protects Maui's dry shores and creates a haven for the humpback whales.

Maui's population has doubled in the past two decades, bringing serious concerns about water, traffic congestion, and the risk of compromising the fragile beauty that makes it one of the most popular destinations in the Pacific. ❑

PRECEDING PAGES: red sails off West Maui.
LEFT: the lush cane fields and mountains of West Maui.

Kanounou Pt.

Poelua Bay

Honolua Bay

Kapalua **10**

Napili Bay

Napili

Kahana **30**

Honokōhau **11**

Honolua

Honolua

Pōhaku Kāni ★ (Bellstone)

★ Blowhole

Kahakuloa Head

12 Kahakuloa

Mokeehia I.

Honokōwai Beach

★ West Maui Airport

Honokōwai

LAHAINA

West Maui

Kahakuloa Section

Hulu I.

Waiheʻe River

★ Waiheʻe Beach

Waiheʻe

Waiehu Beach

Hoʻokipa Beac **19**

Kuau

Mantok Buddhi Mission

Black Rock

Kaʻanapali **9** Whaler's Village ★

Hanakaoo Beach

Honokōwai Section

Natural Area

Eke Crater ▲4480

Puʻu Kukui ▲5788

Maui Jinsha Shinto Shrine ★

H.P. Baldwin Beach

Paʻia

Holy Rosary Church

18

Union

Panaewa Section

ʻIao Needle 2250

ʻIao Valley

Wailuku

3

Kahului Bay

2 Kanaha Pond

Kahului Airport

Lahaina **8**

Lahaina Harbor

Courthouse, Banyan Tree ★

ʻIao Valley State Park ★

5

4

kaʻahumanu Church (1837)

1 Kahului

Alexander & Baldwin Sugar Museum

Reserve

DISTRICT

Kepaniwai Heritage Gardens

Hale Hoʻikeʻike Museum

WAILUKU

Puʻunene **6**

Haleakala Highway

Hal

Maluʻulu O Lele Beach

Puamana Beach

Lihau Section

Wailuku Heights

Waikapu

DISTRICT

350

Haiku

Lowei Ditch

Pukala

Sugar Mill Ruins ★

Olowalu

Mopua

Hawaii Tropical Plantation

Hanaula ▲4616

380

Mokulele Highway

Hekili Pt.

30

Ukumehame Beach

Maʻalaea

Maui Ocean Center

7

Kealia Pond Nat. Wildlife Refuge

MAKAWAC

Papawai Pt.

★ Kapoli Beach

Maalaea Bay

Mai Poina Oleau Beach

Capt. Vancouver Monument

David Malo's Kilolani Church

Kihei **13** 31

Waipuilani

Kalama Beach

Kamaole

Kamaole Beach

Keawakapu

Keokea

Wailea **14**

37

Makena **15**

Keawalai Church (1832)

ʻUlupalakua Ranch **22** **23** Tedeschi Wine

ʻUlupalakua

Oneloa Beach

Kanahena Ahihi Bay

Last Lava Flows on Maui (1790) ★

Ahihi-Kinaʻu Natural Area Reserve

Kanaio

Kanaio Area P

La Pérouse Bay **17**

Cape Kinaʻu

Cape Hanamanoia

Kamanamana Pt.

Pohakueaea Pt.

Molokini Island **16**

Kahoʻolawe

0 —— 2 miles
0 —— 2 km

Cape Kukui

Kuheʻeia Bay

Ahupu Bay

Lua Makua 452

Ahupu Gulch

Honokoa Bay

Lae Paki Pt.

MAKAWAO DISTRICT

Kanaloa

Kanapou Bay

Kealaikahiki Pt.

Wai Honu

Kamohio Bay

Kuakaiwa Pt.

Kaka Pt.

Waikahalulu Bay

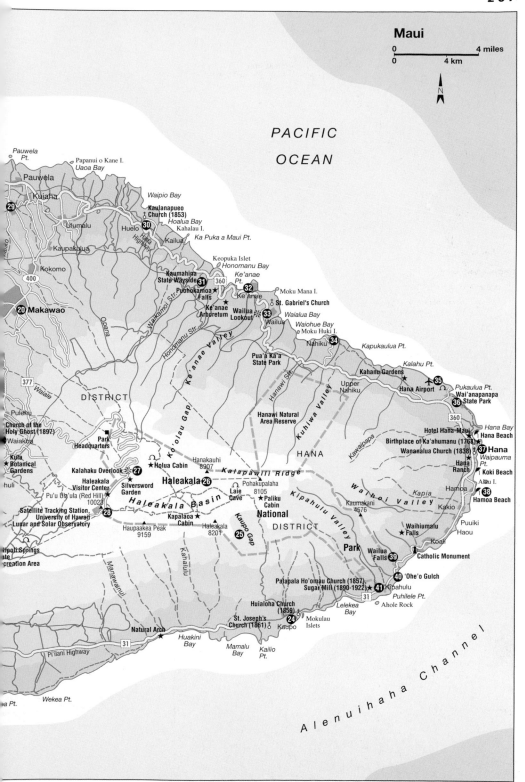

Maui

0 ——————— 4 miles
0 ——————— 4 km

N

PACIFIC

OCEAN

Pauwela
Pt.
Papanui o Kane I.
Uaoa Bay
Pauwela
Kuiaha
29
Waipio Bay
Kaulanapueo
Church (1853)
Hoalua Bay
Ulumalu
Huelo
30
Kahalau I.
Kailua
Ka Puka a Maui Pt.
Keopuka Islet
Kaupakulua
Honomanu Bay
Kokomo
400
Kaumahina
State Wayside
31
360
Ke'anae
Pt.
32
Moku Mana I.
Puohokamoa
Falls
Ke'anae
St. Gabriel's Church
20 Makawao
Ke'anae
Arboretum
Wailua
Lookout
33
Waialua Bay
Wailua
Waiohue Bay
Moku Huki I.
Nahiku
34
Kapukaulua Pt.
Pua'a Ka'a
State Park
Kalahu Pt.
377
Waiale
DISTRICT
Kahanu Gardens
Upper
Nahiku
Hana Airport
35
Pukaulua Pt.
Wai'anapanapa
State Park
36
Pulehu
Hanawi Natural
Area Reserve
360
Church of the
Holy Ghost (1897)
Waiakoa
Park
Headquarters
Hotel Hana-Maui
Hana Bay
Hana Beach
Birthplace of Ka'ahumanu (1768)
37 Hana
Kula
Botanical
Gardens
huli
Kalahaku Overlook
27
Holua Cabin
Hanakauhi
8907
HANA
Wananalua Church (1838)
Hana
Ranch
Waipauma
Pt.
Koki Beach
Haleakala
Visitor Center
Pu'u 'Ula'ula (Red Hill)
10023
Silversword
Garden
Haleakala
26
Kalapawili Ridge
Pohakupalaha
8105
Hamoa
Alau I.
38 Hamoa Beach
Satellite Tracking Station,
University of Hawaii
Lunar and Solar Observatory
28
Haleakala Basin
Kapalaoa
Cabin
Laie
Cave
Paliku
Cabin
National
Kaumakani
4576
Kapia
Kakio
Puuiki
Haou
Haupaakea Peak
9159
Haleakala
8201
25
Kaupo Gap
DISTRICT
Waihiumalu
Falls
Koali
Ipoli Springs
ate
creation Area
Kahalului
Park
Wailua
Falls
39
Catholic Monument
Manawainui
40
'Ohe'o Gulch
Palapala Ho'omau Church (1857)
Sugar Mill (1890-1922)
41
Kipahulu
Puhilele Pt.
Ahole Rock
Natural Arch
31
Huialoha Church
(1859)
St. Joseph's
Church (1861)
24 Kaupo
Mokulau
Islets
Lelekea
Bay
Huakini
Bay
Mamalu
Bay
Kailio
Pt.
Pi'ilani Highway
a Pt.
Wekea Pt.

Alenuihaha Channel

CENTRAL AND WEST MAUI

The urban center of Kahului anchors the isthmus connecting the island's two volcanoes. But it is the sun and surf of the west coast – and Lahaina's whaling history – that seduce visitors

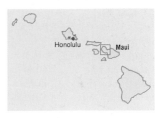

Map, page 206

The central isthmus connecting Haleakala with the West Maui Mountains is Maui's prime agricultural region. It was created when lava flows from the Haleakala volcano filled in the gap between it and the much older West Maui volcano. Erosion of the West Maui Mountains blanketed the isthmus with fertile soil. Although agriculture is declining in importance elsewhere in Hawaii, the production of both pineapples and sugar-cane remains important here today.

Anchoring central Maui is **Kahului ❶**, Maui's deep-water port on the north side and the site of the island's primary airport. Kahului is Maui's commercial hub, with shopping malls, a community college, and the **Maui Arts and Cultural Center** (Kahului Beach Road; tel: 242-2787; www.mauiarts.org). Created by an heroic grass-roots fund-raising campaign, the center includes the elegant, 1,200-seat Castle Theater, several smaller performance spaces, an amphitheater, and an art gallery and public installations by local artists. Other than shopping in Kahului and going to the cultural center, travelers have little reason to linger in the town, and most don't stay long. Just off the highway between the airport and downtown Kahului is **Kanaha Pond ❷**, the state's most important waterfowl sanctuary and the home of several endangered species of native birds.

Wailuku

Wailuku ❸ is perched in the western foothills above Kahului like an older and wiser sibling. Once centered around a now-defunct sugar mill, Wailuku is the seat of the Maui County government, administering not only Maui, but the islands of Molokai, Lanai, and the contentious but uninhabited Kaho'olawe.

In Wailuku's historic district in the heart of town is **Ka'ahumanu Congregational Church**, built in 1876 of white-painted wood and plastered stone to honor Queen Ka'ahumanu, who played an important role in establishing Christianity in the islands. The church is often closed except when services are being held, but if you attend one of the services you will hear hymns sung in the Hawaiian language.

An early example of Western architecture touched with Hawaiian influences is the stone- and timber-built **Hale Ho'ike'ike** (open Mon–Sat 10am–4pm; entrance fee; tel: 244-3326; www.mauimuseum.org), a small museum operated by the Maui Historical Society. Previously called the Bailey House, it was built in 1841 for Edward Bailey, headmaster of the former Wailuku Female Seminary. The museum conveys the spirit of missionary life and exhibits paintings of old Maui by Bailey himself.

OPPOSITE: 'Iao Needle and stream.
BELOW: interior of Hale Ho'ike'ike.

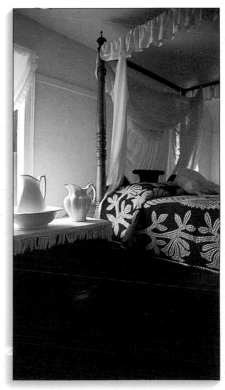

West Maui Mountains

Beyond Wailuku at the end of the road are the wet, lush remnants of the West Maui crater and **'Iao Valley** ❹ (pronounced *ee-ow*, meaning "cloud supreme"). At the valley's mouth is **Kepaniwai Heritage Gardens**, a country park with gardens and pavilions representing the many ethnic groups that have settled in Maui. It was established in counterpoint to an historic and vicious Hawaiian battle waged in the area. During the battle of 'Iao Valley, Kamehameha's forces pushed Maui warriors back into the valley and slaughtered them, choking the river with their lifeless bodies. Kepaniwai means "water dam."

Next to Kepaniwai is the **Hawaii Nature Center** (open daily 10am–4pm; entrance fee; tel: 244-6500; www.hawaiinaturecenter.org), an environmental education project with particular emphasis on programs for children. The Interactive Science Arcade offers 30 hands-on natural history exhibits and daily guided nature hikes in the afternoons.

Further up, the scenic road ends in **'Iao Valley State Park**, a lush mountain terrain dominated by **'Iao Needle**, the exposed core of an old cinder cone that rises 1,200 ft (365 meters) above the stream at its base. There is a parking lot at the end of the road, and a path leads down to the stream and up to various sheltered spots for a view of the valley.

Surrounding this compact, spectacular valley are the 5,788-ft (1,764-meter) walls of **Pu'u Kukui** ❺, the summit of the eroded remains of the West Maui volcano and one of the wettest places in the islands, with more than 400 inches (1,000 cm) of rain annually. The summit is a natural wonderland, as it has one of the greatest selections of native species in Maui, but unfortunately it is totally inaccessible to visitors.

If the heat and slow traffic get to you, especially on the cliffside highway into Lahaina, watch for the remnants of the old stagecoach road, which parallels the highway in some places; the trip to Wailuku used to take all day.

BELOW LEFT:
Kepaniwai Heritage Gardens.
BELOW RIGHT: 'Iao Valley State Park.

On the isthmus

Just to the east of Kahului is the plantation town of **Pu'unene** ❻ and a sugar mill that is still in operation. The former plantation manager's house next to the mill is now the **Alexander & Baldwin Sugar Museum** (open daily 9.30am–4.30pm; entrance fee; tel: 871-8058; www.sugarmuseum.com), with working exhibits and an informative look at the lives of early migrant laborers on Hawaii's sugar plantations.

On the south side of the central isthmus is **Ma'alaea** ❼, a small coastal village and harbor, and a departure point for fishing and whale-watching charters, with one of the best surf breaks on the island. Ma'alaea's star attraction is the **Maui Ocean Center** (open daily 9am–5pm; entrance fee; tel: 270-7000; www.mauioceancenter.com), a brilliantly designed aquarium dedicated to the Hawaiian marine environment. Exhibits include a gigantic walk-through open-ocean tank, a turtle pool, and a touch pool.

Lahaina

After Honolulu, **Lahaina** ❽, on the western coastline of West Maui, is Hawaii's best-known town, partly for the nearby beaches of Ka'anapali, partly for its history, and nowadays for its party atmosphere. In the early 1820s, King Kamehameha III made Lahaina the capital of his kingdom, and it remained so until 1845. By then, New England whaling ships had begun visiting. Missionaries followed in 1823, sponsored by Queen Keopuolani, mother of Kamehameha II and Kamehameha III. She helped the missionaries establish a grass church called Waine'e, the site of today's Waiola Church. Keopuolani is buried at the site, on Waine'e Street in Lahaina.

Map, page 206

Print of sperm whaling, 1839.

BELOW: Pioneer Inn and *Carthaginian II.*

Humpback Whales

The estimated 600 to 800 humpback whales that visit Hawaii each winter spend their summers in Alaska, where the rich waters fatten the whales with krill, a type of shrimp. Around November, the whales start heading for Hawaii's warmer waters, where they mate and give birth. By the end of May, they have disappeared again, having eaten little in Hawaii's nutrient-poor waters.

Although humpback whales tend to congregate in large numbers off Maui – in the protected waters between Maui, Lanai, and Molokai – they are found throughout the islands. The number of whales that winter in Hawaii is steadily increasing each year, though precise figures are not known. In fact, only recently have researchers undertaken detailed studies of the whales' local behavior, previously having spent more time studying larger Pacific migratory patterns.

Male humpbacks sing songs in a behavior possibly related to mating. (Not all whale

species, however, have songs.) It is not known whether the information contained in the songs is simple or complex. What is known is that during the winter season, males repeat the song in precise sequence. Over time, the whale song changes and evolves.

The songs are composed of thematic sets sung repeatedly in a specific order. The average song session lasts maybe a quarter of an hour, although they have been known to last as long as 22 hours. Whale songs sound like creaks and groans of different lengths in many pitches. Because sound travels well underwater, it's easy to hear these enchanting tunes if the whales are singing nearby.

When the humpbacks leave Hawaiian waters in spring, the singing stops, to resume again the following winter in almost exactly the same spot in the song as where they broke off months earlier. Humpbacks in Hawaii sing the same evolving song as humpbacks in Mexico, indicating communication between regional whale "cultures."

Humpbacks give clues regarding their moods. Slapping the long front flippers – called pectoral fins – on the water is affectionate behavior, perhaps a whale hug or a kind of caress. A tail, or fluke, slapping the water is defensive or aggressive behavior indicating a boat, a low-flying airplane, or another whale that may be too close. Whale fact: each fluke is unique, a whale "fingerprint." Researchers photograph the flukes to track the mammals.

No one knows why humpback whales (and some others) leap from the water in displays called breaches. But if whales breach offshore, keep watching the spot; they often do it several times before quitting. Around January, it's common to see baby whales breaching over and over next to their mothers.

Whales can be seen from the shore or from charter boats, and are easily located when they spout – inhaling and exhaling on the surface – and when they fluke, spy hop, (spin vertically into the air), and breach.

Humpback whales like privacy. Federal and state laws require 300 ft (90 meters) in distance for whale watchers in Hawaii. The law is strictly enforced by arrest. ❑

LEFT: humpback whales are able to dive to great depths, but must eventually surface for air.

By the 1840s, Hawaii had become the principal forward station of the American whaling fleet. All the actual hunting of whales took place in the northern Pacific; humpback whales were never the prey. Lahaina was a favorite port-of-call because of its protected offshore waters in **'Au'au Channel** that are sheltered by nearby Molokai and Lanai. Seamen took liberty from their ships and prowled the streets of Lahaina. The whaling ships have long disappeared from Lahaina, but this waterfront town continues to preserve the lively spirit and look of the salty 1800s – although sometimes with a decidedly commercial or Hollywood veneer. It's a superb walking town, nonetheless, compact and manageable for any traveler, whatever their condition.

The heart of Lahaina lies along **Front Street**, between Shaw and Papalaua streets, parallel to the waterfront. The narrow streets that Mark Twain and Herman Melville walked are now lined with cafés and restaurants (some perched over the water in weathered buildings), art galleries, T-shirt boutiques, and fashionable shops. In 1962, the town was designated a National Historic District, and since then, the Maui County Historic Commission and the non-profit Lahaina Restoration Foundation have worked to encourage the preservation of older buildings and the construction of harmonious new ones. The result is a blend of seaport nostalgia and contemporary living (peppered nonetheless with some gaudy schlock), found nowhere else in Hawaii.

Herman Melville, author of Moby Dick, *unsuccessfully looked for work in Lahaina. He finally found a job in Honolulu as a store clerk and then as a pin-setter in a bowling alley. He later went home to Boston, never to return to the Pacific.*

Exploring the town

The **Pioneer Inn A**, built on the harbor in 1901 and wedged between Wharf and Front streets, is nothing if not nostalgic. On its walls are fading photographs of early ships and sailors, whaling equipment, and other memorabilia, including the original house rules: "Women is not allow in you (sic) room; if you burn you bed you going out; only on Sunday you can sleep all day." Downstairs is a veranda restaurant and a popular and noisy bar.

Kamehameha's Brick Palace once stood nearby; it is thought to have been Hawaii's first Western-style building. Built around 1798 of locally produced brick, it was commissioned by Kamehameha the Great, using the labor of two ex-convicts from a British penal colony in Australia. Unfortunately, all traces of the ruins have now disappeared.

In a plaza next to the Pioneer Inn is the expansive **Banyan Tree**, planted in 1873 by the town sheriff. It is the largest known banyan tree in the islands: more than 60 ft (18 meters) high and covering ⅔ acre (0.25 hectares) with its canopy. Next to it is the old courthouse building, now an art gallery and information center. Opposite the Pioneer Inn on Front Street is the **Baldwin House B** (open daily 10am–4pm; entrance fee; tel: 661-3262). Formerly the home of Dwight Baldwin, a Protestant medical missionary, it was a focus of Lahaina missionary life in the mid-19th century. The house has been fully restored and is now a museum.

Hale Pa'ahao C ("Stuck-in-Irons House") is the old prison, located a few blocks up – where else? – Prison Street. It's a worthwhile stop just for its cool, quiet courtyard. Step inside one of the whitewashed cells and imagine a confined life in paradise. The prison had

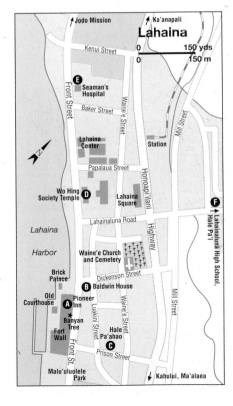

inmates convicted of the usual perfidy, including some convicted of "furious riding" – 89 in 1855 but just 48 in 1857. In that same year, one person was imprisoned for "neglect of parent to send children to school."

A few blocks to the east is **Malu'uluolele Park**, once a pond with an island where Maui chiefs lived. Kamehameha III enjoyed showing visitors the ornate coffins and burial chamber embellished with mirrors, royal feather standards, and velvet drapes. A well-known *mo'o*, or lizard god, inhabited the pond. Today, the place is a ball park.

Further north along Front Street, the **Wo Hing Society Temple ⓓ** (open daily 10am–4pm; admission fee; tel: 661-3262) is a fascinating museum of early Chinese life in the islands. The early 1900s-era building was a cultural and social home for Chinese immigrants, mostly male and single. In the former cook house next door, old Thomas Edison movies are shown amongst the pots and pans. Farther up Front Street is the restored **Seaman's Hospital ⓔ** (closed to the public), built in 1833 as a retreat for Kamehameha III. It was leased to the American government in 1844 as a hospital for seamen from the visiting whaling ships. At the north end of Front Street is the seaside **Jodo Mission Buddhist Cultural Park**, with the largest Buddha outside of Asia.

Lahainaluna High School ⓕ is located up Lahainaluna Road and behind the now defunct Pioneer Sugar Mill. It opened as a general academic school in 1831 under the name "Lahainaluna Seminary." This is the oldest American high school west of the Rockies. Californians once sent their children here rather than to the East Coast schools, which ran the risk of Indian attack. The original printer's shop, **Hale Pa'i** (visits by appointment only; donation suggested; tel: 661-3262), is where the first Bible in the Hawaiian language was published.

Door to one of the prison cells at Hale Pa'ahao, the "Stuck-in-Irons House."

Ka'anapali

When the **Ka'anapali Resort ⓭** began to be developed during the early 1960s, less than 5 miles (8 km) north of Lahaina, Maui entered the global tourist industry, starting the expansion that has since doubled the island's population. This complex of hotels, shopping centers, golf courses, and condominiums also lays claim to what some people consider to be Hawaii's finest beaches: two 1-mile (1.6-km) long stretches of sand separated by a promontory made of lava rock. Hotels already line the South beach, with the less-urbanized North beach poised for future development.

The **Whaler's Village** shopping center includes the **Whaler's Village Museum** (open daily 9am–10pm; free; tel: 661-5992), a small but sophisticated museum with wonderful exhibits, including one of the country's best collections of baleen and scrimshaw.

A rebuilt 1890s-vintage sugar-cane train, the **Lahaina Ka'anapali Railroad** (tel: 667-6851; www.sugarcane train.com), regularly puffs over a 6-mile (10-km) route between Lahaina and Ka'anapali, transporting tourists through the cane fields. Narrow-gauge tracks follow the haul-line road that was used by the Pioneer Mill until the early 1950s.

The first of Ka'anapali's hotels, the Sheraton Maui, opened in 1963, sits at the northern end of Ka'anapali Beach at a rocky point called **Black Rock**, or **Pu'u**

Keka'a ("The Rumble"). This *'uhane lele*, or sacred place, was where the souls of the dead departed for ancestral spirit worlds. Whether you are staying at one of the Ka'anapali deluxe resorts lining the beach – which include the Hyatt Regency Maui, Westin Maui, and Maui Marriott – or not, enjoy a walk along Ka'anapali Beach, timed to coincide with the sunset, if possible, for the spectacular, torch-lighting, cliff-diving ceremonial that ends the Ka'anapali day.

Northward

From Ka'anapali, Honoapi'lani Highway passes through **Honokowai**, **Kahana** and **Napili**, a clustering of condos and apartment hotels. Just beyond Napili Bay is **Kapalua Resort** ❿, renowned for its golf courses and beautiful setting at the base of the West Maui Mountains, along with its luxury accommodations such as the Kapalua Bay Hotel (currently being rebuilt), the Ritz-Carlton Kapalua and the Kapalua Villas.

Beyond Kapalua, the road arcs eastward over the northern end of the West Maui Mountains, passing the beach at the **Honolua/Mokule'ia Marine Preserve**, a hugely popular surfing destination that is also great for snorkeling (visited by catamaran). Park roadside (the long line of cars makes the site obvious) and it is then only a short hike down to the beach.

Situated nearby is the small bay of **Honokohau** ⓫. Beyond the Marine Preserve, the landscape becomes wilder, with beautiful panoramic coastal and mountain views. Although the road has some rough passages, it is possible to navigate all the way to **Wailuku**. Make sure you stop in the rustic town of **Kahakuloa** ⓬, a scenic rural enclave where taro is still grown and the lifestyle is quintessentially Hawaiian. ❏

Maps pages 206 & 213

BELOW: Whaler's Village Museum, Lahaina.

Map, page 206

SOUTH MAUI

South Maui is hardly pretty in itself, but it is handily poised near the center of the island, and offers a wide range of accommodations to suit all budgets, plus some great beaches

In the past 25 years, the area known as South Maui has come to rival West Maui as the island's main resort destination. The name is somewhat misleading; South Maui is not along the island's southern coast, but at the foot of the west-facing slopes of Haleakala. This region is nothing like as green as West Maui, in fact it used to be a virtual desert, but what it lacks in scenic beauty it makes up for in reliable sunshine, and, crucially, sheltered sandy beaches. Roughly half of Maui's guest rooms are now located in the neighboring communities of Kihei and Wailea, which are not so much towns as simply elongated strips of low-rise hotels, condos and restaurants.

Kihei

Stretching for 7 miles (11 km) along the shoreline of Ma'alaea Bay, **Kihei** ⓫ consists largely of endlessly repeated condominium rentals and shopping centers with little esthetic appeal. They are at least here for a good reason: the adjacent beaches are actually quite decent, and offer spectacular sunset views and whale-watching during winter months. Some of the best deals in accommodations can be had here. Broadly speaking, the more northerly beaches, where

BELOW: outriggers at Kihei Canoe Club.

the swimming is poor, are mainly used by windsurfers heading out into the sheltered waters of the bay, while the further south you go, the better the beaches become for bathing.

Wailea and Makena

Immediately south of Kihei lies the far more upscale resort of **Wailea ⑭**, home to a succession of glorious crescent beaches – Wailea and Polo beaches are the best of all – a fancy, luxury-oriented shopping mall, and several extravagant oceanfront hotels. As elsewhere throughout Hawaii, you don't have to be a hotel guest here to visit any beach you like. Higher up the landscaped slopes of Haleakala, there are five 18-hole golf courses.

South again from Wailea, little **Makena ⑮** has just one hotel, the Maui Prince. Makena did at least exist before the tourist boom, so it retains one or two vestiges of the past, in the shape of the pretty Keawala'i Church, and the remains of its former harbor. There's yet another lovely beach in front of the Maui Prince, but the finest of all South Maui's beaches lies another mile (½ km) further south. Known to everyone as "Big Beach," but officially named both Oneloa Beach and Makena State Park, this magnificent 1-mile (½-km) long expanse of broad golden sand is a wonderful place for walking and taking pictures, but unless you're an expert boogie-boarder the waves are too dangerous for swimming.

Molokini and Kaho'olawe

Looking out seawards from the resorts of South Maui, it's easy to spot the small crescent island of **Molokini ⑯**, an eroded tuff cone whose submerged crater offers spectacular snorkeling. Daily diving and snorkeling boats to Molokini depart from several points along the shore, especially from Ma'alaea.

BELOW: Wailea Beach.

Beyond Molokini, looming low and red on the horizon, lies uninhabited **Kaho'olawe**, the smallest of Hawaii's eight major islands. The ancient Hawaiians used Kaho'olawe as a center of religious practices and a navigational school. Sites on the island have been placed on the National Register of Historic Places.

During World War II the US Navy appropriated the island for use as a gunnery range. Native Hawaiian Rights activism from the 1970s onwards resulted in the eventual return of the island to the state in 1994. A major rehabilitation program, involving the removal of debris and unexploded ordinance, has been underway for several years, and is not likely to be completed in the foreseeable future.

La Pérouse Bay

You can drive another 3 miles (5 km) beyond Big Beach on a road that finally ends at **La Pérouse Bay ⑰**, another popular snorkeling and kayaking spot. The first Westerner to land on Maui, the French explorer Jean-François de La Pérouse (Captain Cook had earlier sailed past without stopping), wrote in 1786 that "during our excursion we observed four small villages of about 10 or 12 houses each, built and covered with straw." Shortly after his departure, around 1790, the whole area was covered by lava from Haleakala's last volcanic eruption. Much of the landscape here remains a lava desert to this day. ❑

Map, page 206

HALEAKALA AND UPCOUNTRY

Think "Hawaii" and tropical weather comes to mind. But on the slopes of Maui's main volcano, the air is cool and often crisp. At the summit, it can be frigid, but the beaches below are usually in sight

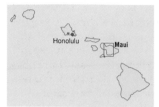

Honolulu   Maui

O f the sunrise from atop Maui's Haleakala, Mark Twain wrote: "It was the sublimest spectacle I ever witnessed, and I think the memory of it will remain with me always." Travelers continue to be awed by dawn at the 10,023-ft (3,055-meter) summit of **Haleakala**, which means "House of the Sun." But from a distance, this gently sloping shield volcano, which is dormant, not extinct, lacks pretension. The first European to sight Haleakala, Captain James Cook, who did not land on Maui, described it as simply "an elevated hill… whose summit rose above the clouds."

Indeed, as with the Big Island's Mauna Kea and Mauna Loa, also shielding volcanoes, Haleakala carries its enormous size – 2 miles (3 km) above sea level and another 3½ miles (6 km) below – with modesty. The exact dimensions of Haleakala weren't fully known until 1841, when an American expedition surveyed the summit basin: 3,000 ft (915 meters) deep and 19 sq miles (49 sq km) in area, with a circumference of 21 miles (34 km).

The island's namesake, the demigod Maui, was a magician and mythical figure in Polynesia long before the Hawaiian Islands were inhabited. According to legend, the sun was fond of sleeping late and then racing across the sky to

BELOW: windsurfing at Ho'okipa Beach.

make up time. With the short days, Hina, Maui's mother, had trouble drying *kapa* cloth that she pounded from the bark of the mulberry. Noticing that the sun appeared each morning over Haleakala, Maui wove a rope of coconut fiber and climbed up to the summit basin's edge one night to await dawn. When the sun awoke, Maui lassoed its rays and threatened to kill it. The sun begged for mercy and promised to behave more responsibly. For most contemporary travelers watching the sun rise or set from the summit of Haleakala, it still moves too fast. To witness the sunrise or sunset from atop Haleakala, one must first ascend the lower slopes of the volcano, an area commonly called **Upcountry**.

Upcountry

Say that you're heading Upcountry and envious listeners will know that shortly you'll be smelling eucalyptus suspended in cool air and following rolling grassy contours reminiscent of Ireland. Upcountry is the lower-slope area of Haleakala that overlooks the isthmus connecting the volcano with West Maui. Far below one can see the white ribbons of beaches, but in Upcountry, there are farms, flowers and fireplaces. There are two gateways to Upcountry: from Kahului on the Haleakala Highway or, preferably, through Pa'ia and Makawao.

Once a sugar town, **Pa'ia** 🔞 has been changed in large part by the winds and waves at **Ho'okipa Beach** 🔟, one of the world's finest windsurfing places. Pa'ia now reflects a demographic shift from plantation worker to windsurfer and artisan. Just outside of Pa'ia is the **Mantokuji Mission**, a Japanese Buddhist temple with an oceanfront cemetery of more than 600 burial markers, most of them traditional Japanese. Higher up, **Pukalani** (Heavenly Gate) and **Makawao** 🔟 (Forest Beginning) lie at the geographical entrance to Upcountry. Makawao and

TIP

It can be quite cool in Upcountry – many homes have fireplaces – and it's increasingly colder as one ascends the slopes of Haleakala. In the morning and late afternoon, the winds atop Haleakala are often cold if not frigid.

BELOW: Makawao Rodeo and *paniolo* cowboy.

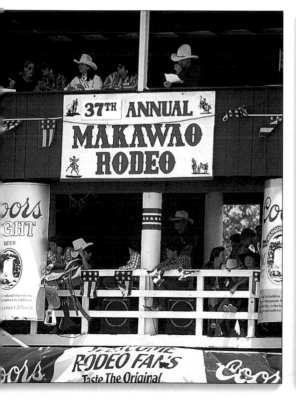

surrounding villages were once home for both sugar plantation laborers and cattle cowboys. Previously in decline, Makawao has been resuscitated by a diverse collection of newcomers, ranging from upscale professionals to counterculture refugees. Even with the influx of cafés and boutiques, Makawao has retained a rough-hewn rustic feel from its days as a ranch town. On the July 4th weekend, a wide variety of people turn out for the annual Makawao parade and rodeo.

Beyond Makawao and Pukalani, the **Kula** area is blessed with a mild climate and rich, deep soil. As a result, its agriculture is probably the most diversified in Hawaii. During the California gold-rush days of the mid 1800s, Kula farmers grew potatoes, corn, and wheat for export to California. Nowadays, farmers harvest lettuce, cabbage, turnips, carrots, and peas. Most delectable, claim the gourmets, are the extra-sweet Kula onions, which are said to be unparalleled. Flowers of all colors and purposes are yet another Upcountry product, including many of the exquisite tropicals like heliconia, bird-of-paradise, and protea.

There is a high road in Kula that leads to the turn off for Haleakala National Park. This road ascends from Upcountry to the summit of Haleakala in more than 30 switchbacks, with exquisite scenery. Continuing onward through Upcountry on the main road, on the other hand, near **Waiakoa** is the **Church of the Holy Ghost ㉑**. This octagonal church, dating from the late 1890s, was

BELOW LEFT: a rare silversword plant.
BELOW RIGHT: Church of the Holy Ghost.

built by Portuguese families who had settled on Maui two decades earlier.

Beyond Kula and **Keokea** (a good place to stop for coffee) on a narrow two-lane road, the 18,000-acre (7,300-hectare) **'Ulupalakua Ranch ㉒** marks a terrain shift from green and cool to brown and hot. Started as a sugar plantation in the 1850s, 'Ulupalakua is a working cattle ranch of about 5,000 head, with additional

sheep and elk. The ranch's general store offers *paniolo* gear and a deli. 'Ulupalakua Ranch is also home to Hawaii's only commercial vineyard, **Tedeschi Winery** ㉓ (open daily 9am–5pm; tel: 878-6058; www.mauiwine.com), which produces a rather diverse collection, from pineapple wine to champagne. A 20-acre (8-hectare) vineyard of Carnelian grapes thrives here. The vineyard offers free tastings, tours, and a small museum.

From the winery at 'Ulupalakua Ranch, the view downslope south to the coast and **La Pérouse Bay** *(see page 217)* is as unobstructed as one could want.

The back side of Haleakala

Beyond 'Ulupalakua Ranch, the Pi'ilani Highway begins a slow descent, rounding the southwest slopes of Haleakala and cutting across dry, open range where cattle roam. Pastures are scarred by lava flows and abandoned stonework. Now parched and uninhabited, this vast leeward side of Haleakala once supported dryland forests and a population of Hawaiians. Sandalwood cutting and ranching have bared these rugged slopes to steady winds, creating a landscape of dramatically stark panoramas that are well worth a visit.

In **Kaupo** ㉔, 5 miles (8 km) of the road are unpaved, and most rental car contracts prohibit driving the unpaved sections. The road *is* driveable, however, and rental cars do make their way each day without problems. Kaupo is about 1½ miles (2½ km) past pavement's end (coming from Upcountry) just beyond **St Joseph's Church**, built in 1861. A well-defined trail winds up the southern slope and through the 8,200-ft (2,500-meter) **Kaupo Gap** ㉕ into the basin atop Haleakala. Assuming it's clear, the road beyond Kaupo continues to Kipahulu and the Hana Coast, and eventually back to Pa'ia. Even if you were planning to

Map, page 206

Wine from Tedeschi.

BELOW: Kaupo cowhands.

Map, page 206

Although the vast depression atop Haleakala is usually called a crater, it is actually a basin or caldera created by the collapse and erosion of the summit rim.

OPPOSITE: paragliding in Upcountry.
BELOW: hiking the Sliding Sands Trail.

turn around here, consider going a little further to the eternally windswept setting of **Huialoha Church**, which was built in 1859 and still in use.

Atop Haleakala

More than half a million people visit **Haleakala National Park** ㉖ annually, many venturing into the basin either by foot or on guided horseback trips along a 30-mile (50-km) system of trails. As far as visitors are concerned, the park consists of two distinct and mutually inaccessible sections, extending down Haleakala's southeast flank to the Hana Coast and the 'Ohe'o Gulch (Seven Pools), embracing along the way the **Kipahulu Valley**, a research reserve of indigenous plant and animal species that is closed to the public. The National Park Service maintains two campgrounds and three cabins in the basin for visitors, and another coastal campsite adjacent to 'Ohe'o, which is approximately 10 miles (17 km) past Hana.

Park Headquarters (open daily 8am–4pm; tel: 572-4400; www.nps.gov/hale) offers information and a telephone, but no gas or food, and the **Visitor Center** (open daily sunrise–3pm) at the summit has displays, restrooms, and shelter from the high-altitude cold winds. There are good overlooks of the summit basin itself at several spots along the way to the summit. At the **Kalahaku Overlook** ㉗, one may be lucky enough to see the striking Haleakala silversword, a native member of the sunflower family *(see below)*.

Pu'u 'Ula'ula ㉘ (Red Hill), the summit of Haleakala, now has a space-age tenant. Here at **Science City**, scientists track satellites across the sky and bombard the heavens with laser beams, while University of Hawaii researchers operate lunar and solar observatories. Both military and civilian facilities are closed to the public.

Crater hikes

To drive yourself to the summit of Haleakala in time to see the dawn, you'll need to leave almost any hotel in the island by around 3am. Commercial tours pick up passengers even earlier than that; some offer the option of rolling back down the mountain on a bicycle.

If you have the time and energy, it's well worth venturing down into the caldera itself, an extraordinarily desolate yet compelling wilderness of cinder cones and ash. After even the shortest of hikes, you'll have to walk steeply uphill in order to exit the crater, at an altitude of 10,000 ft (3,000 meters), so prepare for a serious physical challenge. The most obvious route is to take the Sliding Sands Trail, which drops down from close to the visitor center. Distances are very deceptive once you're in the caldera, but you need to allow three or four hours for the round-trip if you want to descend at all far. A full day's hike will take you right into the heart of the caldera, and out again via the other major route, the Halemau'u Trail. If you're lucky, you may be rewarded with one of the rarest sights on earth – a unique silversword plant in full bloom. When fully mature, a silversword stands from 3 to 8 ft (1 to 2.4 meters) high, its central stem covered with yellow and reddish-purple florets. After flowering just once at the end of its life, between June and October, the plant dies. ❑

THE HANA COAST

Map,
page 206

Tucked away on the rainy side of Haleakala is Hana. It is so removed from the rest of Maui that in ancient times it was often the domain of Big Island chiefs. A famous road winds its way there

Both geography and climate have conspired to keep the Hana district, the east-facing bulge of Haleakala, a separate world. Between Hana and the rest of Maui stretches the windward face of the mountain, and in Hawaii that means the rainy side of the island. Hana is so separate from Maui proper that ruling chiefs from the Big Island often claimed it as their own and defended it successfully against the challenges of Maui chiefs. Lovely, rounded Hana Bay, backed by lush grasslands and a mountainous wilderness of rain forest and waterfalls, was the site of some fierce fighting in the old days.

The road to Hana twists through jungle, over bridges, past waterfalls, and along cliff-edges for 35 miles (56 km), finally straightening out in the town itself. It slices through a landscape scoured by water, cut with deep gulches, and choked with the enthusiastic flora of the rainforest. Recently repaved, it remains a stomach-churning drive of twists and turns, lasting a minumum of two hours, more if you divert to picnic or explore.

It's another 30 minutes to Haleakala National Park at 'Ohe'o Gulch, promoted, erroneously, as the "Seven Sacred Pools." At that point, one can turn back, or else, assuming the highway is currently clear, continue on through Kaupo to completely encircle Haleakala. Either way, start early and plan to put in a long day. Remember that local people drive the road every day. They know every twist and turn, and they usually have a good reason to keep moving. It's polite to use the passing places and let *kama'aina*, or residents, go by.

Today, the road to the Hana side is well maintained, and although narrow, twisting, and demanding of the driver's constant attention, it's easy enough to travel in any car.

The road to Hana

Properly speaking, the **Hana Road** begins at the one-mile marker (look for the green rectangular signs on the roadside) at the bottom of Kaupakalua Road in **Ha'iku** ㉙. The gateway to the Hana Coast and the winding road is the quiet community of **Huelo** ㉚, with its small Congregational church, **Kaulanapueo** ("Owl Perch"), built in 1853. Maui's mood and *'aina* – land – begin to shift here, slipping away in the tropical wetness. From this point on, you'll be driving pretty slowly for most of the way, as pasture and open forest give way to ever-thickening jungle. Many of the bridges offer easy turnouts and places to swim. The best of these is the pool at mile 11, with the added bonus of a waterfall and covered pavilion.

Another good resting spot is at **Kaumahina State Wayside** ㉛. The park's carefully tended grounds, with restrooms and picnic tables, include labeled examples of plants common to this coast. You can retrace your steps a few hundred yards/meters for a refreshing swim at **Puohokamoa Falls**. Or from the Kaumahina parking lot, hike to the upper left side of the park and experience a spectacular view of the **Ke'anae Peninsula**. The view here is due east, which may explain the name Kaumahina, or Rising Moon.

The road next drops into spectacular **Honomanu** (Bird Bay), with a rocky, black beach and canyon walls choked with flowering trees. Just after Honomanu,

TIP

Souvenir T-shirts promote the drive to Hana as if it were a transcontinental expedition. It's not; it's just a slow, winding road. It Is narrow, with several one-lanc bridges. If cars pile up behind you, pull over and let them past.

PRECEDING PAGES: kayaking along the Hana Coast.
LEFT: beachless coast of Hana.

*Flowering vines
cling to the cliffs
along the Hana
Highway.*

BELOW: Wailua
nestles in verdant
splendor.

at about mile 16, is **Ke'anae ㉜**, a community of taro farmers who still maintain *lo'i*, or irrigated fields, that were first established over 500 years ago.

A narrow road leaves the highway and curves ½ mile (800 meters) down to a scattering of houses, a tiny cemetery, and a Congregational church built in 1860. Decades ago, when only a horse trail connected Ke'anae and Hana, there were two country grocery stores here, and the field behind the church was a baseball diamond. The school building used to face in the opposite direction, but a lethal tidal wave in 1946 spun it around on its foundations. The shoreline down here consists of jagged black lava rocks, lashed endlessly by crashing white surf.

Near the turn off to Ke'anae is the **Ke'anae Arboretum**, which offers a look at taro cultivation and pleasant walks among tropical and Hawaiian native plants.

A Cultural Landscape area

Three miles (5 km) farther is **Wailua ㉝**, another traditional taro-growing region. The state has designated this entire area as a Cultural Landscape, and life here follows patterns established in pre-discovery Hawaii. Wailua's tiny **St Gabriel's Church** was one of the first to be built on this coast. The lookout on the Hana Highway above Wailua has picnic benches and a captivating view.

Continuing toward Hana, the highway offers another popular roadside stop, **Pua'a Ka'a** (Rolling Pig) **State Park**, between mile markers 22 and 23. Located here, where one least expects it, are a pay telephone, restrooms, and picnic tables, along with a natural waterfall and pool. Now you are approaching **Nahiku ㉞**, the wettest stretch of this coast. At the end of the 19th century, Nahiku was the home of America's first rubber plantation, with thousands of acres of rubber trees. The vigorous community was serviced by a small railroad and barges.

The most impressive accomplishment along this coast, however, is still active and clearly visible along the roadside as flumes, tunnels, engineered ditches, and watergates. In the late 19th century, the East Maui Irrigation Company built a water-delivery system that is arguably the boldest engineering accomplishment in post-discovery Hawaii, especially considering the awesome logistics of transporting all construction materials by horse, mule, and human power. The waterworks transformed Maui's arid central plain into verdant and extremely productive sugar-cane fields.

The road begins to relax at about mile 30. The **Hana Airport ㉟**, which has a limited commuter service to Honolulu and Kahului, is just beyond. One mile later, **Wai'anapanapa State Park ㊱** offers a lava coastline ornately sculpted by nature, including one of Maui's best campsites, hiking trails, cabins, and good swimming along a jet-black sand beach. Inland are some caves. Water in the caves of Wai'anapanapa ("Glistening Water") is said to run red with the blood of a cruel chief's errant wife, killed for her infidelity. In fact, the effect is caused by swarms of tiny red shrimp.

Nearby, visit the large **Pi'ilanihale** *heiau* (temple). The rock platform of the *heiau* overlooks the coast and is part of an escorted or self-guided tour of **Kahanu Gardens** (open Mon–Fri 10am–2pm; entrance fee; tel: 248-8912).

Hana

Finally, the tortuous road unravels into the rolling hills and ranch pastures of **Hana ㊲**. Hawaiians say that "the sky comes close to Hana," and, indeed, moody clouds often hang low off the hills here. A local legend tells of a deity who once stood atop **Ka'uiki Hill**, the prominent cinder cone that forms the right flank of

Map, page 206

BELOW: the black sands of Wai'anapanapa State Park.

Exploring the trails of the Hana Ranch.

Hana Bay, and who was able to throw his spear right through the sky. Ka'uiki ("The Glimmer") served as a fortress during the wars with Kamehameha the Great. A cave here, now marked with a plaque, was the 1768 birthplace of Queen Ka'ahumanu, later the favorite of Kamehameha's many wives.

Directly above the bay and to the right, the **Hana Cultural Center** (open daily 10am–4pm; donations accepted; tel: 248-8622) offers a brief, but thought-provoking glimpse into the area's history. Next to the museum is the small former courthouse dating to 1871, and a recently constructed *kauhale* – a compound of authentic thatch buildings constructed in the ancient style of this region. Several historic 19th-century churches add to Hana's appeal.

For a magnificent view of the Hana area, hike through the pasture above the town to the large stone cross on the hill; the cross is a memorial to Paul Fagan, founder of the 3,000-acre (1,200-hectare) **Hana Ranch**, which owns much of the land in these parts. Pedestrian access to the memorial is from the parking lot across from the **Hotel Hana-Maui**, a low-profile luxury retreat. A trail from the hotel's Sea Ranch cottages leads to the isolated red sands of Kahailulu. In addition to the hotel, camping and bed-and-breakfast accommodations are options for an overnight stay in Hana. It's well worth spending the night in Hana, for the place is bewitching in the morning and evening hours, when the day-trip visitors are long gone.

There are two markets in Hana. One of them is the well-known Hasegawa General Store. Rural Hawaii grew up on family-owned stores like this, established a generation or two ago by descendants of Japanese immigrants. Like most of these stores, Hasegawa Store employs a hall-closet system of inventory control, and the Hasegawa family is seldom stumped on unusual requests.

Beyond Hana

The road beyond Hana passes through several miles of grassy ranchland. Watch for the next big cinder cone, Ka'uiki's twin, **Kaiwio Pele** ("Pele's Bone"), site of a legendary battle to the death between Pele, the volcano goddess, and the earth deity Kamapua'a, a pig-man. Tiny **'Alau Island**, just offshore, marks the spot where Maui, the demi-god, fished the Hawaiian Islands out of the sea with a magic hook. The spur road that curves down to the sea here passes two of Hana's most accessible beaches. **Koki Beach**, at the foot of the cinder cone, is shallow and sandy for a long way, and great for body surfing, but watch for rip tides. As the road bends back to the main highway, it passes **Hamoa Beach** ❸, a favorite of James Michener. The Hotel Hana-Maui maintains facilities for its guests here, but the beach is open to the public.

From here to the Kipahulu district, the road encounters deep glades, sheer cliffs, and cascading waterfalls. **Wailua Falls** ❸ is the most accessible. Then, 13 miles (21 km) out of Hana, the road enters the lower portion of **Haleakala National Park** and crosses an arched, stone bridge that overlooks **'Ohe'o Gulch** ❹, a common turn-around spot for drivers heading back the way they came.

The parking lot, with restrooms, is just past the bridge. A trail leads down to the lower pools, which are wonderful swimming holes. Be aware that 250 inches (635 cm) of rain falls annually in the forests above, and the stream and pools can quickly become raging torrents. Near the bottom-most pools and along the cliffs fronting the ocean are the stone foundations of an ancient fishing village. Just south of this area is a campground, with tent sites along the dramatic basalt cliffs. Campers may stay for up to three days at a time. Fires are forbidden, but barbecue pits are provided, as well as restrooms. Bring your own water, however.

Map, page 206

TIP

If you like quiet, and you want a special place mostly for yourself, spend the night in Hana. After the tourist herds leave in late afternoon, Hana becomes even more heavenly.

BELOW: the stone foundations of 'Ohe'o fishing village.

Map, page 206

Polynesian mailbox.

BELOW: exposed roots of a young banyan tree.
RIGHT: the road bridge over the 'Ohe'o pools.

One of the most rewarding hikes on the island begins directly across the road from the parking lot: a 2-mile (3.2-km) jaunt inland to **Waimoku Falls**. Rangers have built two mildly spectacular bridges, and also a boardwalk to keep the ground virginal while passing through the heart of an enormous bamboo forest. Waimoku Falls is high (400 ft/120 meters), sheer, and powerful enough to keep observers at a distance. Afternoon showers in the hills can mean flash flooding.

Kipahulu and Kaupo

Beyond 'Ohe'o Gulch is the drier, grassy Kipahulu district and the village of **Kipahulu ㉑**. About a mile past the pools lie the ruins of the **Kipahulu Sugar Mill**, a relic of the early 20th century. Below the ruins, a narrow, paved road leads toward the ocean and to tiny **Palapala Ho'omau Church**, erected in 1857. This is the burial place of aviation pioneer Charles Lindbergh, the first person to fly solo from Paris to New York. The church is open to visitors who respect the surrounding property and homes. However, the Lindbergh family and local residents don't intend the area to become a major tourist destination.

The road beyond is paved except for about 5 miles (8 km) of rugged, jaw-rattling dirt toward Kaupo; driving on the unpaved sections of the road is prohibited by most car rental companies. It is always liable to be blocked by rock falls; check locally before you set off. As a rule, though it's all quite passable when dry, and the grand scenery keeps changing in climate as you move from the windward to leeward side around the mountain. The road breezes past the soft pastures of Kipahulu, touches a cove, then climbs a spine-tingling cliffside grade into the sterner landscape of Kaupo. Cattle guards mark the entrance to **Kaupo Ranch**, a large cattle operation since the late 19th century. A

windswept and surf-pounded peninsula juts out below the road, where **Huialoha**, a restored old Congregational circuit church is sited. Huialoha was built in 1859, when Kaupo was almost totally isolated, accessible only by sea and a primitive trail. The crumbling walls behind the church were once a school. Offshore is an ancient surfing area once known as **Mokulau** ("Many Islets"), named for the lava islets sprinkled just offshore. The winds here seem nonstop.

The small store in **Kaupo** was once the only local source of food and supplies on this part of the island, but it now caters mostly to travelers in rental cars and minivans. From here, the road continues to Upcountry.

Toward the mountain, the slopes of Haleakala rise to a deep slash at the top called the **Kaupo Gap**, 8,200 ft (2,500 meters) above sea level, which opens into Haleakala basin. In ancient times, the gap was the primary route taken by Hawaiians traversing Maui on foot. It was easier to climb the mountain than to bushwhack through the coastal jungle. Horseback trips are available; hikers also make the climb, though it's nearly all uphill and can be jarring on joints.

Kipahulu Valley, on the Hana side of the gap, is a protected natural science reserve (closed to the public). Untouched by introduced species of flora or fauna, the reserve shelters vast expanses of native trees like *koa* and *'ohi'a,* and endangered birds like the Maui parrotbill and Maui *nukupu'u*. ❑

MOLOKAI

*Overshadowed by nearby Maui, Molokai retains a distinctive
ambiance of "being Hawaiian." Still noted for its historic leprosy
colony, it is equally known for its rugged terrain and rural lifestyle*

Map,
page 239

ong overlooked by most travelers, Molokai has gained
prominence not because of its dramatic ocean cliffs (the world's
tallest) along the northern coast, but because of an historic
leprosy colony on its northern shores. Still, travelers have had varied
responses to the colony. For example, nowhere in his travel letters
from Hawaii in 1866 did Mark Twain mention leprosy, now called
Hansen's disease, or the colony on Molokai. Two decades later, however, Robert Louis Stevenson was not so timid. In a public letter,
written in 1890, Stevenson defended a Catholic priest, Father Damien, who had
been criticized by a Protestant minister in Honolulu as "a coarse, dirty man,
headstrong and bigoted... not a pure man in his relations with women." Father
Damien had died earlier, in 1888, of Hansen's disease, while helping the patients
at the Molokai colony to which people with leprosy were exiled. During those
early years of Damien's time Molokai certainly wasn't the "friendly island," as
it's now nicknamed in a public relations move.

Volcanic origins

On a map, Molokai appears to be shaped like a slender slipper, 37 miles (60 km)
long and 10 miles (16 km) wide. The island has three
geological anchors, each created by volcanic activity
millions of years ago. **Mauna Loa**, a 1,380-ft (420-
meter) tableland at the western end of the island (not to
be confused with the active volcano of the same name
on the Big Island), was noted in ancient times for an
adze quarry, *holua* slides (snowless sledding), and as a
source of wood for sorcery images.

Later, the east Molokai volcano erupted, and **Mauna
Kamakou** was pushed up to 4,970 ft (1,515 meters) to
become the island's highest point. Kalaupapa Peninsula,
properly called Makanalua, was born even more
recently, when 400-ft (120-meter) **Kauhako**, a small
shield volcano, poured forth its lava to shape a flat
tongue of land in the center of the northern coast. It is
separated from the rest of the island by a fortress-like
barrier of *pali,* or high cliffs, perfect for isolating a
colony of exiles.

Agricultural Molokai

Molokai's land is primarily agricultural, and development has been limited. And, perhaps best of all for the
adventurous traveler, tourists are few. Only a few paved
roads transit Molokai, and some of its more spectacular sights and places of archeological interest require a
four-wheel-drive vehicle, boat or helicopter to view.

Ho'olehua Airport ❶ is situated 7 miles (11 km)
away from the town of **Kaunakakai ❷**, which is on the

PREVIOUS PAGES:
Pelekunu Bay.
LEFT: just another
Molokai evening.
BELOW: fishermen
carrying hand nets.

southern coast. More than half of the island's 6,700 people live near Kaunakakai Ala Malama, the main street, contains ramshackle buildings that have probably changed very little since the "Cockeyed Mayor of Kaunakakai," who was made famous in a *hapa-haole* (semi-Caucasian) song popular during the 1930s strolled along its streets.

A wharf extends several hundred yards out to sea at Kaunakakai; barges were loaded with pineapples here until the plantations closed down in the 1970s and 1980s. The focus is now on crops such as corn, watermelon, soybeans, hay, coffee, and onions. Before becoming king in 1863, Kamehameha V spent his summers on Molokai. In the 1860s, he planted nearby **Kapuaiwa Coconut Grove** (Kapuaiwa means "Mysterious Taboo"), in which there were originally 1,000 coconut trees on 10 acres (4 hectares) of land. The grove that remains is a great spot for watching the sunset.

Kamehameha V.

The Rainforest

Shrouded as often as not by clouds, the summit of Molokai's eastern mountain Mauna Kamakou, holds a remarkable unspoiled expanse of Hawaiian rainforest The only route to the top is up a gravel road that branches east just south of the junction of Maunaloa Highway and the highway to Kaunakakai, and soon degenerates into muddy ruts that are only passable in a high-clearance four-wheel-drive vehicle. The easiest way to visit is on a tour organized through **Molokai Outdoor Activities** (tel: 553-4477; www.molokai-outdoors.com); if you decide to go it alone, call in first for advice at the **Nature Conservancy Office** (tel: 553-5236; www.nature.org), a mile or so south of the turn-off towards Kaunakakai, which also organizes monthly guided hikes.

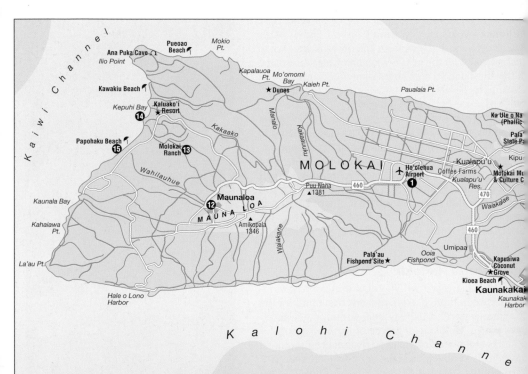

Nine miles (14 km) up from the highway, the curious **Sandalwood Boat ❸** is actually a hole in the ground roughly the size and shape of a 19th-century sailing ship's hold. Hawaiian laborers would fill this pit with the amount of sandalwood that such ships could carry, before selling it to Western traders. Sandalwood was once common throughout the Hawaiian islands, but demand from China, where it was appreciated for its fragrance, encouraged the Hawaiian king to harvest it until there was no more left.

Map below

Waikolu Lookout and the Pepe'opae Trail

A mile further on, the **Waikolu Lookout** offers a first glimpse of the beautiful and rugged cliffs of Molokai's northern shore, the highest sea cliffs anywhere in the world. It also marks the start of the Kamakou Preserve, which protects unique Hawaiian plants and birds. A little over 2 miles (4 km) further on, you reach the **Pepe'opae Trail**, one of Hawaii's greatest hikes, an hour-long stretch of springy boardwalk that leads through extraordinary high-altitude mountain boglands and stunted forest to reach further verdant views. The two deep valleys along this shore, Wailau and Pelekunu, cannot be reached on foot. The expensive and spectacular way to see them is by helicopter. Trips depart from Maui, or in summer you can also take a boat trip from Kaunakakai.

Central Molokai

Branching north off Maunaloas Highway, onto Kala'e Highway, just beyond the rainforest turn off, brings you to **Kualapu'u**, an old Del Monte company town; there are several unusual attractions en route, between Kaunakakai and the end of the road lookouts. **Coffees of Hawaii** (tel: 567-9241) offers tours and

Ka Ule o Nanahoa ("Penis of Nanahoa"), a rock once believed to cure infertility.

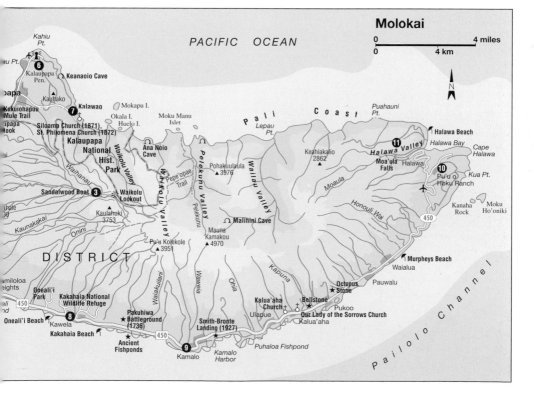

tastings from a vistor center (8am–4pm) adjacent to its fields, where coffee has replaced pineapple as the crop. A bit further down the road is the **Moloka** **Museum and Cultural Center**. Housed in the historic **R.W. Meyer Sugar Mil** (open Mon–Sat 10am–2pm; tel: 567-6436), the center provides a Molokai perspective on the Hawaiian past.

Pala'au State Park

Still heading north, you come to **Pala'au State Park** ❹, where the park road passes through an attractive forested area of *koa*, paperbark, ironwood, and cypress trees. A small arboretum with more than 40 species of trees and a picnic area await at the end of the road. From the parking lot, it's a short walk and a slight climb to **Ka Ule o Nanahoa** ("Penis of Nanahoa"), a phallic rock 6 ft (1.8 meters) high and once visited by those who believed it was a cure for infertility. The **Kalaupapa Overlook** ❺ offers a spectacular view from atop the 1,600-ft (485-meter) high cliffs above the former leprosy colony.

Kalaupapa

In his novel *Hawaii*, published in 1959, James Michener described the **Makanalua Peninsula** ❻ (often referred to as the **Kalaupapa Peninsula**, after the settlement) as "a majestic spot, a poem of nature… In the previous history of the world no such hellish spot had ever stood in such heavenly surroundings."

In 1866, the year of Mark Twain's visit to Molokai, the Hawaiian government began transporting victims of Hansen's disease, or leprosy, to Molokai. The exiles were literally pushed from the boat into the peninsula's rough coastal waters, with little care whether or not they would survive. Over the years, more

In 1936, as the Catholic Church considered Damien's candidacy for sainthood, the priest's remains were returned to Belgium. Sixty years later, a relic – his hand – was returned to Hawaii. After a ceremonial tour of the islands, it was reinterred at his former burial site in Kalaupapa.

BELOW: mule's eye view of Makanalua Peninsula and settlement.

than 8,000 people were exiled to Kalaupapa. During Father Damien's time, more than 1,000 exiles lived here. Now there are fewer than 40 residents in Kalaupapa. They all live there voluntarily.

Map, page 239

Father Damien

Father Damien (formerly Joseph De Veuster) arrived in the islands in 1864 from Belgium. He came to Molokai in 1873 and remained in the colony until his death 16 years later. Damien organized the colony into a true community, establishing a church and small clinic. Land was cleared, crops were grown, and a modern water system installed. By 1883 Damien had contracted Hansen's disease and six years later he died, just 49 years old. (It was not until the late 1940s that Hansen's disease was brought under control.) He was buried in Kalaupapa, but his body was returned to Belgium in 1936. In 1907, the writer Jack London traced the priest's footsteps around Kalaupapa, writing a number of short stories about Hansen's disease after his visit, including a chapter in *The Cruise of the Snark* about the Kalaupapa residents.

Molokai's population has Hawaii's highest percentage of Native Hawaiians.

Kalaupapa National Historical Park

Today, Kalaupapa is protected by the **Kalaupapa National Historical Park**, which was established in 1980 and is jointly administered by the National Park Service and the State of Hawaii. Permission to visit the historical park is easily obtained through airlines, through Damien's Tours (tel: 567-6171), which is what the majority of visitors do, or by contacting the Hawaii State Department of Health in Honolulu or Molokai. Children under the age of 16 are not permitted to visit Kalaupapa.

BELOW LEFT: altar at St Philomena church.
BELOW RIGHT: Damien's former grave.

There are two ways to arrive: by air, which takes you to a small airport on the peninsula, or from the top of the cliffs down the steep trail that Father Damien took in the late 1800s. The most colorful way to manage the trail, which drops 1,800 ft (550 meters) to the peninsula, is on the back of a nimble-footed mule, which you can organize with the **Molokai Mule Ride** (Mon–Sat departs 8.30am, returns 3.30pm; fee; tel: 567-6088; www.muleride.com). Visitors to Kalaupapa must be escorted by a resident of Kalaupapa, which usually means going with Damien's Tours.

State law prohibits photographing residents without their permission. Although some residents still suffer from Hansen's disease, they are no longer confined to the island; as previously mentioned, they live here by choice. The disease can now be controlled by medication, and, despite the fears that surrounded it for so many years, it is not contagious.

East across the peninsula is the abandoned settlement of **Kalawao ❼**, site of the original colony. **Siloama Church**, the Church of the Healing Spring, was built here by Protestants in 1871. The Catholic church nearby, **St Philomena's**, has a monument to Father Damien, marking his original burial spot. The plan is to preserve Kalaupapa as a living community until the last resident has died or departed, then to preserve it as a historic park.

Eastern Molokai

East from Kaunakakai, the Kamehameha V Highway runs for 30 miles (48 km) along the southern coast to Halawa. There is much to see along this road, the second half of which is a narrow lane twisting along the coast. It is a long drive, and a slow one. Just a few miles past Kaunakakai is **Oneali'i Park** (Royal

TIP

Molokai's biggest social event of the year takes place at Hale o Lono, a rocky harbor on the southwest coast. It is the starting point of the annual Molokai-to-Oahu outrigger canoe race, held in October. The 41-mile (66-km) race ends in Waikiki.

BELOW: Siloama Church.

Map, page 239

Sands), a beach with campsites. For a small daily fee, campers may stay here for two weeks but must renew their permit every three days.

Along this southern coastal road are numerous **ancient fish ponds** dating back as far as the 15th century. These were built in order to supply food for the families of chiefs. Such ponds are found on all of the Hawaiian islands, but the largest concentrations were on Oahu and the south coast of Molokai. A few of the ponds have been restored and stocked, an exercise in cultural revival with commercial potential, in the hope of developing aquaculture.

Above **Kawela ❽** is a battlefield where Kamehameha the Great won an early skirmish. It's been said that his war-canoe fleet landed upon the beach here in an assault wave 4 miles (6 km) long. In 1736, two decades before Kamehameha's birth, an invading war fleet from Oahu battled combined armies from Molokai and the Big Island here. The Oahu chief was killed and his army defeated. Appropriately, perhaps, Kawela means "the heat."

Visitors should stop at **Kamalo ❾**, where Father Damien built the second of his two churches on this side of the island. He constructed this white, wood-frame structure in 1876 and dedicated it to St Joseph. Nearby is the spot where Ernest Smith and Emory Bronte ended the first civilian flight from the main-land by crashing their plane into a *kiawe* thicket in 1927. An earlier military attempt at flying to Hawaii from the mainland fell, literally, 300 miles (480 km) short of Hawaii. At **Kalua'aha** is the restored **Our Lady of Sorrows Church**, built by Damien in 1874. There is a wooden statue of the famous priest in the pavilion, and the grounds are well kept. Also at Kalua'aha is the **Kalua'aha Church**, which was constructed by Congregationalist missionaries in 1844 but now lies in ruins.

Fishponds were enclosed by walls of coral blocks and basalt stones, rising up to 6 ft (1.8 meters) above water. Wooden gratings allowed small fish to enter from the sea. Once fattened, they were too large to escape.

BELOW LEFT: an ancient fish pond.

Hill of Stars

Three miles (5 km) beyond **Waialua**, the road twists inland and begins winding up to **Pu'u o Hoku Ranch ⑩**. Looking back down the mountain from Pu'u o Hoku ("Hill of Stars"), the scenery is spectacular. Across the **Pailolo Channel** is Maui, a little more than 10 miles (16 km) away, and in the distance the great dome of Haleakala. Closer is tiny 10-acre (4-hectare) **Moku Ho'oniki** (which means "Pinch Island," and apparently was meant in the sense that a lover would pinch). It is nicknamed Elephant Rock by inter-island pilots, because it looks like a pachyderm lying at rest in the ocean, its trunk stretched out toward Maui.

Just past the ranch entrance is the sacred *kukui*-tree grove of **Kalanikaula**, or the Royal Prophet. These silvery-leafed trees once encircled the home of Lanikaula, a local *kahuna* (priest) and seer or prophet who specialized in lizard-god-killing, who lived here. Hawaiian laborers once refused to help Del Monte clear the area because of Lanikaula's *mana*, and a non-Hawaiian grower who cut down some trees to plant pineapples here found that his crop wilted. Travelers speak of seeing torch lights moving through the grove at night, said to be spirits returning to Kalanikaula.

Halawa Valley

The road ends at a park and sandy shoreline on deep **Halawa Bay**, the mouth of 4-mile (6.4-km) long **Halawa Valley ⑪**. Although this is a beautiful spot, the ocean currents at the stream's mouth can be tricky, so exercise great caution. Additionally, Portuguese man-of-war jellyfish are occasionally swept into the bay by offshore winds, and they can give the unwary a very nasty sting. Hundreds of fishing and farming families once lived here, but only a handful remain.

BELOW: dunes and freshwater pool.

At the rear of the valley there are two waterfalls that feed a stream flowing into the sea. The highest is 250-ft (76-meter) **Moa'ula Falls**, the legendary home of a giant sea dragon. According to tradition, you will want to find out if the *mo'o* (dragon or lizard demi-god) is at home before you go swimming: you must toss a *ti* leaf into the water, and if the leaf sinks, the dragon is in, so you should come back later. At the time of Queen Emma's death in 1885, storms pushed beach sand right up the valley to the pool at Moa'ula's base. The only way to see the falls these days is to go on a guided hike; it is well worth the money (tel: 553-5926; www.molokai fishanddive.com).

Western Molokai

Back through Kaunakakai and up past Ho'olehua Airport, the Maunaloa Highway runs through a dry landscape for about 10 miles (16 km). **Maunaloa ⑫**, itself a former plantation town, lies at the end of the road.

Much of this dry leeward side of the island is composed of grazing land owned by the 40,000-acre (16,000-hectare) **Molokai Ranch ⑬**, the largest local landowner. When the Dole Company closed down its pineapple operations here in 1976, the firm returned almost 10,000 acres (4,000 hectares) to the ranch, much of which has been planted with hay, grown for commercial purposes. Cattle continues to be the mainstay of the ranch's operation, which currently runs as many

Map,
page 239

…s 8,000 head across its arid pasture lands. For visitors, they run the Paniolo Roundup, where ranch cowboys teach horsemanship and rodeo skills.

The Molokai Ranch operates an elegant lodge in Maunaloa itself (reservations on toll free number: 888-627 8082), and an upscale campground at Kolo Beach. Each offers a variety of activity options, including ocean kayaking, scuba diving and horseback riding, and there's an appealing sense of away-from-it-all relaxation. The town itself has been somewhat gentrified, and features the island's only movie theater.

Not far away, but hidden away from the gaze of casual visitors, is one of the most sacred spots in Hawaii. Dedicated to Laka, the goddess of hula, a difficult-to-find *heiau* (temple) is said to be the birthplace of this ancient dance form. *Halau hula* (hula school) students and their *kupuna* (elders) gather here before sunrise to make offerings before performing at the annual Molokai Ka Hula Piko festival in May.

Back to the beach

A number of spurs branch off the main highway and wind down to the coastline. Kaluako'i Hotel and Golf Resort, the island's only resort hotel, at **Kepuhi Bay ⑭** near the northwestern tip, is currently closed. Neighboring Papohaku Beach, a vast expanse of golden sand, is superb, and on clear nights the lights of Oahu and Diamond Head are visible across the 26-mile (42-km) wide Kaiwi Channel. Only the strongest swimmers should venture into the ocean along the beach. The treacherous current and pounding waves, nicknamed the Oahu Express, can sweep the unwary out to sea. Camping is allowed by permit at **Papohaku Beach Camp ⑮**. ❏

BELOW: Halawa Bay.

Map
below

LANAI

Privately owned but open to visitors, Lanai was once a plantation island with nothing to offer but pineapples. Pineapples are history now, replaced by exclusive hotels and the promise of adventure

Honolulu
Lanai

Seen from West Maui, the island of Lanai seems both close and far away. It's only 9 miles (14 km) from Maui, but the island presents a smooth-contoured, featureless face. Some 18 miles (30 km) long and 13 miles (20 km) wide, Lanai is the sixth-largest of the Hawaiian islands. It buckles upward along its windward, Maui-facing ridge, to the 3,370-ft (1,030-meter) heights of Lanaihale. From there, the land drops and tapers to the west, sloping gradually to the sea.

The Maui sun sets over Lanai, giving the island center stage at sunset. The ancient Hawaiians felt Lanai was inhabited by spirits and, according to legend, people stayed away from the island until one day a hero named Kaulula'au, the son of a chief from Lahaina, crossed the channel and rid the place of danger.

The first Western residents were Mormons, who in the mid 1850s arranged generous lease terms with chief Ha'alelea of Oahu. Agriculture thrived at first, but three years later drought and insects ruined the crops. The settlement was abandoned, only to be purchased by an idealist and adventurer named Walter Murray Gibson, who used church money for the purchase of the land to his own advantage. He eventually settled in Honolulu as the kingdom's prime minister, forced to leave Lanai just one day ahead of a lynching.

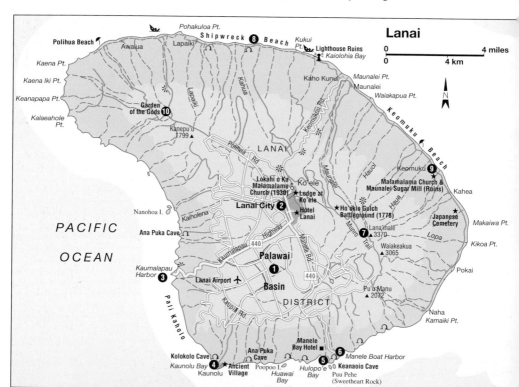

Pineapples arrive on the island

After James Dole, a persevering businessman from Boston, purchased Lanai in 1922 for $1.1 million, mules dragged anchor chains across Palawai Basin to clear it of cactus so that the land could be plowed and planted with pineapple. Using boulders from Palawai Basin, Dole then created a deep-water harbor at Kaumalapau and laid out a nearby town for the Japanese and Filipino immigrants who came to work on his Lanai plantation.

Dole's Hawaiian Pineapple Company prospered and was later purchased by one of Hawaii's original "Big Five" *kama'aina* (resident) corporations, Castle & Cooke, which kept Dole's name and operated the plantation as the Dole Pineapple Company. In 1987, California investor David Murdock bought controlling interest of Castle & Cooke. Like Dole, Murdock moved quickly, building two world-class hotels, two golf courses, new homes for the island's residents, and a recreational complex in the middle of Lanai City. Stunning the locals but acting pragmatically given the competition of cheaper Asian pineapples, he plowed up more than 13,000 acres (5,260 hectares) of what was once the world's largest pineapple plantation. Fewer than 500 acres (200 hectares) of pineapple land remain on Lanai – token fields to provide pineapples for the island's three hotels. Other fields are being replaced by experimental crops such as citrus, onions, papayas, macadamia, coffee, and grains used for cattle and other livestock feed.

To stay in either of the two luxury hotels (the island's third hotel, in Lanai City, is simple) is to vanish into Sybaritic privacy. The almost surreal isolation makes even nearby Maui seem like "the madding crowd" and tempts visitors to stick close to the resorts in oblivious retreat. But a rented four-wheel-drive vehicle opens the whole island for exploration – dirt roads, ancient sites, and remote beaches without a footprint in sight. There are only about 25 miles (40 km) of paved roads on Lanai.

The heart of the island is a lone volcanic crater, **Palawai**, long extinct and weathered into a subtle depression surrounded by a great saucer of fertile but dry farmland. The **Palawai Basin ❶** once sustained the largest pineapple plantation in the world; today, its grassy fields glimmer quietly in the soft, muted light.

Lanai City ❷, built by Dole in the early 1920s, is home to virtually all 2,600 residents of the island. Located inland at the base of the Lana'ihale ridge, it's a classic plantation town – quiet, modest, and orderly, designed around rectangular Dole Park edged with stores, the headquarters of the Lanai Company, and the vintage 10-room **Hotel Lanai**. Nearby is The Lodge at Ko'ele, one of the two award-winning luxury resorts that now sustain the island's economy. Three paved roads connect Lanai City with the coast. One, heading southwest, leads to the airport and **Kaumalapau Harbor ❸**. When the pineapple was king on Lanai, more than a million pineapples a day were loaded onto barges here for shipment to the Honolulu cannery 60 miles (100 km) away. Now, infrequent incoming barges are filled with supplies for the island.

A very rough road off the highway leads down to **Kaunolu Bay**, but you must hike more than 3 miles (5 km) on rocky trails; it is off-limits for rental vehicles, four-wheel-drive or otherwise. At the hike's end are the hard-to-locate ruins of **Kaunolu ❹**, an ancient fishing

Lanai's trademark tree, the tall and dark Cook Island pine, creates water for the thirsty island. Mists collect in the trees' tight branches and drip like rain. One tree can produce as much as 40 gallons (150 liters) a day.

BELOW: Kaumalapau Harbor's workers no longer load pineapples for export.

BELOW: affluent visitors now define Lanai, not farming.

village, Kamehameha's summer home. Kaonolu is rich with the *mana*, or spiritual power, of old Hawaii. Nearby is Kahekili's Leap, a scenic lookout named after the Maui chief renowned for diving into the waters below. The coastal views from here are breathtaking.

Hulopo'e marine life

It's a much easier 20-minute drive on a paved road from Lanai City to **Hulopo'e Bay ❺**. The bay, a nature conservation district that's off-limits to nearly all boats, is home to spinner dolphins, turtles, and an abundance of other marine life. Hulopo'e is the best place on the island to swim and snorkel. You can also hike along the eastern coast to reach the panoramic lookout that takes in Sweetheart Rock, with Maui rising majestically above the horizon. Conveniently, the Manele Bay Hotel stands in a commanding position directly over Hulopo'e Bay; a trail leads down from the hotel to the beach. Frequent shuttles carry people from The Lodge at Ko'ele, a 20-minute drive away. Visitors even come over for the day from Maui, and the state allows camping at six sites on the grass above the beach. Permits are available from Lanai Company for a maximum stay of seven days.

Just around an easterly point from Hulopo'e Bay is **Manele Boat Harbor ❻**. Here, sailboats can be seen bobbing at anchor during stopovers between Maui and Oahu. A ferry from Lahaina (45 minutes) stops here several times daily.

Off-road excursions

Lanai's most unusual touring route is surely the **Munro Trail**. This is a four-wheel-drive dirt track that climbs along the island's eastern ridge, cresting at **Lana'ihale ❼**, the high point at 3,370 ft (1,030 meters). On a clear day, all the

major Hawaiian islands except Kauai and Ni'ihau can be seen on the horizon. The Munro Trail continues down past **Ho'okio Gulch**, scene of a 1778 battle involving Kamehameha the Great, to Ko'ele and back to Lanai City. Start from Manele Road end, because descending is easier than ascending on the mushy, slippery Ko'ele side. The trail is impassable during rainy weather.

Another popular excursion heads out to the island's convex northeast coast. It can be reached by following Keomuku Road until it forks near the shoreline. To the left is a track to **Shipwreck Beach ❽**, so named because of the rusting hulk of the *Helena Pt. Townsend*, a tanker that has sat impaled on a reef in 12 ft (4 meters) of water for over 50 years (the shipwreck is a 15-minute coastal hike once the road ends). To the right is a better road to the abandoned village of **Keomuku ❾**. The trip to Keomuku takes about 45 minutes, with the restored church the main attraction. Keomuku village was abandoned after the 1901 collapse of the Maunalei Sugar Company. A short distance down the road is an oblong stone marker, a sad memorial to the Japanese immigrant workers who died of a plague during Keomoku's plantation days.

The **Garden of the Gods ❿** can be reached by driving northwest along the Polihua Road, which turns into a dirt track that passes through grasslands. This is a strange playground of strewn boulders and disfigured lava formations that look spectacular at sunset, when they glow an unearthly orange. The route to the Garden of the Gods also passes one of the largest examples of a dry-land forest in Hawaii at **Kanepu'u**. Protected by high fences, it has been donated to the Nature Conservancy to preserve its vegetation. Beyond the Garden of the Gods, magnificent Polihua Beach stretches along the north coast. With its fearsome currents, it's no place for swimmers, but the views across to Molokai are stunning. ❑

Map, page 246

Shipwreck Beach is at the end of a track and can only be reached on foot.

BELOW: Garden of the Gods.

THE BIG ISLAND: HAWAII

Appropriately named, the Big Island seduces with its Sybaritic resorts and with the hot passion of Kilauea

The island of Hawaii, more commonly called the Big Island, reveals its fiery soul slowly, distracting mere mortals with its intense beauty and the startling diversity of its landscape. Ride a bike on empty roads around steaming cinder cones or through crumbling fields of black lava, hike into a misty rainforest filled with towering tree ferns, ride on horseback across a spreading plain where cattle roam untethered, or strike a dimpled golf ball across the greenest-of-green golf courses.

Geologically the youngest of the Hawaiian islands and twice the size of all the others combined, the Big Island is a geological exhibit of considerable proportions. In Hawaii Volcanoes National Park, since 1983 the volcano goddess Pele has brought Kilauea to life, pouring ribbons of crimson lava from rifts and vents on the southeastern coast. Amidst billowing clouds of steam, lava hits the ocean, bursting into glistening fragments that pile up black sand into new beaches.

On the dry western side, upscale resorts stretch from Kohala in the north to Kona in the south. Save for the lushness of North Kohala, where Kamehameha the Great was born, most of the land on the western side is dry and expansive, and peppered with petroglyphs, ancient fish ponds, and other archeological treasures. It was here that Kamehameha the Great planned his conquests in the 18th century.

To the south in Kona, Kailua is the Big Island's center of tourism and play. Once the playground of Hawaiian royalty, the sun-washed town today is crowded with boutiques, hotels, condominiums, and tourists. Down by the waterfront, delve into history at Hulihe'e Palace, 'Ahu'ena Heiau, and Moku'aikaua Church – built of black stone from an abandoned *heiau* (temple) and cemented with white coral.

Continuing south, the highway rounds the island at South Point, or Ka Lae, the southernmost point in both Hawaii and the United States. When the wind whistles across the grasslands, one can easily picture the original Polynesian seafarers landing at this point, a feat that archeologists think may have occurred more than 1,500 years ago.

On the wetter eastern coast, a half-hour's drive to the northeast of Kilauea, is rustic Hilo, the island's seat of government. Hilo is a tranquil town, with much of its charm originating in its quiet, unassuming residents. North of Hilo is the lush Hamakua Coast, where sugar plantations once reigned. One can continue beyond Hamakua and cross over through the highland town of Waimea to Kohala and the western coast. ❑

PRECEDING PAGES: Pu'uhonua 'O Honaunau National Historical Park; flow from Kilauea entering the ocean.
LEFT: honeymoon couple at St. Peter's Church, in Kona.

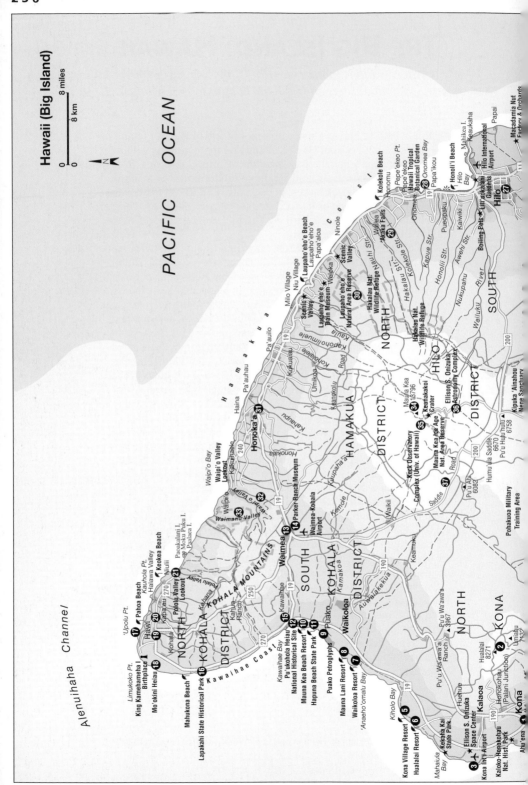

Hawaii (Big Island)

PACIFIC OCEAN

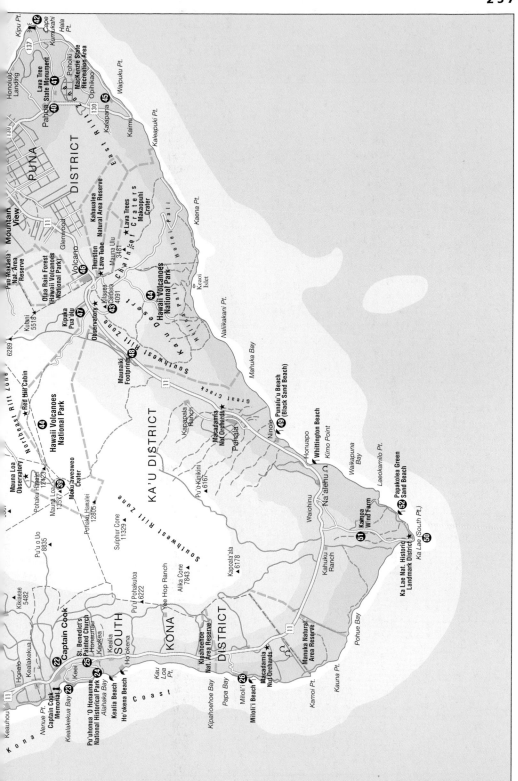

Kipu Pt.
Cape Kumukahi
Hala Pt.

42

137

Lava Tree State Monument **41**
MacKenzie State Recreation Area
Pohoiki
Ophikao
45

Honolulu Landing

Pahoa **10**
130

Waipuku Pt.

Kalapana

PUNA

130

Kaimu

DISTRICT

Kaleapuki Pt.

Mountain View
111

Glenwood

Pu'u Maka'ala Nat. Area Reserve

Ohia Rain Forest (Hawaii Volcanoes National Park)

Kaena Pt.

Kahaualea Natural Area Reserve
Lava Trees ★
Makaopuhi Crater

Thurston Lava Tube ★
Mauna Ulu

Lava Trees Craters ★

Kulani 5518▲

Kipuka Pua'ulu ★
Volcano

Keaoi Islet

Observatory ★
Kilauea ★
Caldera 4091
43

Hawaii Volcanoes National Park
47

44

Nalikakani Pt.

Hawaii Volcanoes National Park

6289

★ **Red Hill Cabin**

Mauna Loa Observatory ★

Mahuka Bay

Maunaiki Footprints ★
48

11

Great Crack

Punalu'u Beach (Black Sand Beach)
49

Ninole

Pohaku Hanalei 12325▲
Mauna Loa 13537▲
Maku'aweoweo Crater
38

Pohaku Hanalei 12805▲

Macadamia Nut Orchards
Pahala

Kapapala Ranch

Honuapo
Whittington Beach
Kirmo Point

Sulphur Cone 11329▲

KA'U DISTRICT

Waikapuna Bay

Laeokamilo Pt.

Pu'u o Uo 8835▲

Pu'u Kiikini 6167▲

Waichinu

Na'alehu

Papakolea Green Sand Beach
52

Pu'u Pohakuloa 6222▲
Yee Hop Ranch

Alika Cone 7843▲

Kapapala'ala 6178▲

Kapua Wind Farm
51

Ka Lae (South Pt.)
Ka Lae Nat. Historic Landmark District
50

Kikiaeae 5482▲

Captain Cook
22

St. Benedict's Painted Church
23
Honaunau
Ke'okea

25

SOUTH KONA DISTRICT

Kahuku Ranch

Pohue Bay

Honele
Kealakekua

Captain Cook Memorial
23
Keei
Kealakekua Bay

Pu'uhonua 'O Honaunau National Historical Park
24
Kealia Beach
Alahaka Bay
Ho'okena Beach

Ho'okena

Kipahoehoe Nat. Area Reserve

Kamoi Pt.

11

Keauhou
11

Nenue Pt.

Macadamia Nut Orchards
26

Manuka Natural Area Reserve

Kauna Pt.

Kau Loa Pt.

Kealakekua Bay

Milolii Beach **26**
Miloli'i

Papa Bay
Kipahoehoe Bay

Coast

Kona

KONA AND KOHALA

Map,
page 256

The Big Island's western coast is anchored by the town of Kailua-Kona, and peppered with some of the world's finest resorts. Still, there are ancient sites on this drier side of the island

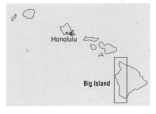

Honolulu

Big Island

The Kona and Kohala coasts of the Big Island are on its leeward side. This is the island's dry side because central mountains catch the moisture-rich trade winds from the northwest and release their rain on the island's windward side. To put it simply, west coasts in Hawaii are usually the dry and sunny coasts. On the Big Island, this makes Kohala and Kona prime destinations with some of the world's finest resort hotels. The northern part of this side of the Big Island is called Kohala, while the southern part is known as Kona. In the past, the only way to drive from Kohala to Kona was along a narrow road far uphill from the ocean. Today, however, a highway named for Kamehameha's wife Ka'ahumanu connects Kawaihae in Kohala with Kailua-Kona. The highway passes through some of the driest land in Hawaii, where beaches and archeological sites are strung along the coast. Expansive views range inland and along the coast, the landscape scarred by lava that flowed as recently as the 19th century.

The main town on this side of the island is known to locals as **Kailua**; with the district being called **Kona ❶**, it is known to the post office as **Kailua-Kona**. Generally, they're interchangeable, but Kona is commonly used for the town, the district, and the coast. Dominating North Kona is 8,271-ft (2,521-meter) **Hualalai ❷**, an awesome volcano that last erupted in 1801. The **Kona International Airport ❸** lies on one of its lava flows at Keahole. Legend has it that an 1801 eruption of Hualalai was initiated by Pele, the fire goddess, because she was jealous of the successful Kamehameha the Great. When Kamehameha followed the advice of a *kaula*, a seer, and made offerings to Pele, the eruption ceased. Today, Hualalai is home to game birds, and sheep, goats and pigs wander over its dormant heights foraging on dry shrubs and grasses.

Pu'uwa'awa'a, a pumice cone around 100,000 years old, rises sharply 4,000 ft (1,200 meters) on the flanks of Hualalai. The typical lava flow in Hawaii is 15 ft (5 meters) thick, but flows from Pu'uwa'awa'a reached 900 ft (270 meters) in thickness. Obsidian, used for making sharp tools and weapons, is found here. The only other place in the Hawaiian islands where obsidian is found is on the island of Kaho'olawe. On Hualalai's southwest flank, at about 1,500 ft (460 meters), is **Holualoa ❹**, home to those seeking refuge from the hectic pace of Kailua-Kona below. It sits on the high road surrounded by coffee plants and wonderful views. A growing number of visitors are discovering the town's small galleries.

Konane, a game resembling chess, that was played by Hawaiians before Captain Cook's arrival in Hawaii.

Kona

The town of Kailua-Kona is one of those places noted for sun and night life – with the sun outshining the night life by far. **Kailua Bay**, a harbor skirted by Ali'i Drive and a seawall, is the downtown focus. At the north end on the grounds of King Kamehameha's Kona Beach Hotel is an ancient temple or *heiau*, **Ahu'ena**, once used for human sacrifices. It was later restored by Kamehameha the Great and used as his personal *heiau*, when he settled here at the royal compound called **Kamakahonu**, or "turtle eye." This is where Kamehameha the Great retired and later died in 1819. Loyal attendants hid his bones, lest they be defiled by his enemies or the *mana* (spiritual essence)

LEFT: ancient foot trail and petroglyphs along the Kohala coast, near Mauna Lani.

*A child's depiction of
the fish found in the
waters off the Kona
Coast.*

abused. Occasionally, someone claims to have found the burial site – caves were traditional burial locations – but it remains undiscovered. Possibly it was sealed by a lava flow, or it may even be under water, as the island's west coast has sunk an average of 9 inches (23 cm) every 100 years for the past eight centuries. The Ahu'ena *heiau* site, which was partially demolished to build the Kona Pier, was later restored. The site provides a unique perspective for those on the nearby beach.

Ali'i Drive leads south along the harbor past the Royal Kona Resort, which is hard to miss as it juts into the ocean, and through a jungle of condominiums and apartments. The harbor area along Ali'i Drive, situated between the King Kamehameha and Royal Kona hotels, is a walking district for both shoppers and those interested in the history of the stretch.

The charming **Hulihe'e Palace**, built in 1838 by the brother of Queen Ka'ahumanu, sits right on the ocean just down from Ahu'ena *heiau*. Its grounds were once part of Kamakahonu. Restored in 1927, it is a wonderful museum evoking the old days when it served as a royal getaway. Opposite the palace on Ali'i Drive, **Moku'aikaua Church** was built in 1837. The original church, with a pandanus roof and foundations of old *heiau* stones, was dedicated in 1823 but destroyed in 1835.

Sheltered from the prevailing trade winds, the waters off the Kona Coast are home to game fish considered among the best in the world. Each summer, the Hawaiian International Billfish Tournament is staged here. Blue marlin weighing 1,000 lbs (450 kg) have been caught within an hour's run from the pier. *Ahi* (tuna), *ono* (bonefish), *ulua* (jack crevalle), *mahimahi* (dolphin fish), and swordfish are regularly caught.

BELOW: Hulihe'e
Palace and fragrant
plumeria.

North of Kona

About two miles north of town is the first of three access roads that are part of the Kaloko-Honokahau National Historic Park. This mile-long coast park has a visitor center (daily 8am–3.30pm; tel: 329-6881), which offers a self-guided tour made interesting by display boards. It's hot and dry, so bring some bottled water. A *heiau* (temple) platform, magnificent fishpond walls (restoration is underway), and an ancient *holua* (sled run) provide a rare insight into Hawaii's past.

Just north of Kaloko and south of the airport is the **Natural Energy of Hawaii** (Wed and Thur tours at 10am; entrance fee; reservations necessary, tel: 329-7341) where aquaculture and energy programs have been underway for more than 20 years.

North of the Kona International Airport is a one-of-a-kind among Hawaii's resorts: the low-profile **Kona Village Resort ❺**, wrapped in a mystique that's in sharp contrast to the mega-resorts built in Hawaii during the 1980s and the elegant properties built in the 1990s. From the main highway, a string of what look to be simple thatched huts lines the ocean. In fact, they are luxury *hale*, or bungalows, without TVs, phones, or anything else that disrupts the serenity of the setting. They originated in the 1960s as part of a re-creation of the old Hawaiian village of Kaupulehu that once stood on this site. In the early years, before construction of the Queen Ka'ahumanu Highway, visitors arrived by boat from Kailua-Kona. It remains an idyllic escapist resort, where days flow effortlessly by. The petroglyphs and beach-front *tikis* (carved Hawaiian god figures) add a sense of Hawaiian authenticity.

Modernity has, however, come to the area, in the shape of the elegant **Hualalai Resort ❻**, with its Four Seasons Hotel, 18-hole golf course and condominiums.

Map, page 256

Rock graffiti, or maybe a wistful valentine.

BELOW: Waikoloa hotel with Mauna Kea in background.

For further details of
Kona and Kohala
resorts *see pages
325–6* in Travel Tips.

Its lovely rooms, complex of oceanside swimming pools, and impressive cultural center make it as desirable a neighbor as Kona Village could have hoped for.

Another good collection of ancient petroglyphs can be found at the Waikoloa Resort at **'Anaeho'omalu ❼**, where they have been joined by both a golf course and relatively modern petroglyphs from the late 1800s that include English words, and figures bearing rifles. Also well preserved here are ancient fish ponds on the ocean side of the Outrigger Waikoloa Resort.

The grand-scale Hilton Waikoloa Village has 1,200 rooms. The hotel's three towers are connected by mechanically guided boats in a canal, a sleek electric train and a mile-long walkway lined with Asian and Pacific Island art. As the oceanfront here is very rocky, the hotel is laid out around an artificial lagoon with sand to create a pretty good approximation of a beach. This is the setting for the resort's popular "swim with a dolphin" program (tel: 886-1234, ext 2875), under which guests can pay to share a few minutes' water time with a brace of sleek dolphins.

Kohala

A few minutes further north is **Mauna Lani Resort ❽**, with two elegant hotels, The Orchid and Mauna Lani Bay Hotel and Bungalows. In earlier days, Mauna Lani was known as Kalahuipua'a, a site of aquaculture ponds that the Mauna Lani Hotel has preserved. A walking trail leads from the hotel toward Keawanui Bay and the palm-lined ponds. Of six major ponds, the largest is 5 acres (2 hectares) in size and 18 ft (6 meters) deep. A trail heads inland to a lava field, where caves have yielded an ancient canoe paddle and large fishhooks, probably for catching sharks.

Kamehameha the Great maintained a canoe landing here, marked by a replica of an old canoe shed; inside is a full-sized replica of an outrigger canoe. Beyond

BELOW: lobby of the
Mauna Lani Hotel,
and tuna catch.

is the Eva Parker Woods Cottage Museum, built in the 1920s and later moved to its current seaside location. Ancient Hawaiian artifacts are displayed inside.

A 5-minute walk up the coast, in **Pauoa Bay** fronting the Orchid at Mauna Lani, is a submarine freshwater spring. Ancient Hawaiians would dive to the spring's opening and fill gourds with fresh drinking water.

Map, page 256

Ancient petroglyphs

The shoreline trail to the south follows an ancient footpath that connected fishing villages in pre-contact Hawaii. Along the path are ancient fishing platforms, a house site, and some anchialine pools – low-sited caves that were once flooded with sea water. Brackish water now fills these natural depressions in the lava.

The west coast of the Big Island has a number of these ponds, unique in the United States. Some have been preserved, like these at Mauna Lani, where five shrimp species thrive. To the south at the sprawling Hilton Waikoloa Village, anchialine pools were intentionally destroyed during the resort's construction to make way for artificial lagoons, although others were preserved.

Just north of the Mauna Lani Resort is one of Polynesia's best collections of petroglyphs, the **Puako petroglyph field ❾**. Years ago, access was through the village of Puako. Now a well-marked road at the Mauna Lani Resort ends in a parking lot, where a self-guided trail leads to a field of several thousand petroglyphs etched into the lava. The age of these petroglyphs has not been determined. Many are of uncertain meaning; others, like the circles with a dot inside, called *piko* (navel) holes, are thought to have been receptacles for the umbilical cords of newborns. Most Hawaiian petroglyphs were chiseled into smooth *paho'eho'e* lava along major trails. Long sections of this rock-lined trail are still

The most profitable agricultural crop on the Big Island is marijuana, known in Hawaii as pakalolo *(lit. "numbing tobacco"). The so-called Kona Gold is a cash crop, estimated as surpassing coffee and sugar in net revenue. It is illegal in Hawaii.*

BELOW: Puako petroglyphs.

The lava flows of Kona and Kohala are rich with petroglyphs. Although carved in rock, they are fragile.

to be found along the coast, at Koloko and at each of the Kona and Kohala resorts.

The low roads in both North and South Kohala are lined with *kiawe* trees and prickly-pear cacti. The *kiawe* tree is burned into first-rate charcoal, and the cactus blooms develop into a tasty fruit. On land found too dry for cattle, Laurance Rockefeller commissioned a luxury resort in the 1960s, the **Mauna Kea Beach Resort** ⓾, piping in water for its grounds and golf course all the way from Waimea. For 40 years, Mauna Kea was the standard by which other Hawaii resorts were measured. At present, however, it remains closed following earthquake damage in 2006.

Half a mile south lies **Hapuna Beach State Park** ⓫, with the island's largest natural white-sand beach. The Hapuna Beach Prince Hotel opened in 1994 at the northern end of Hapuna Beach, and local people continue to use the popular public beach side-by-side with visitors – which is not surprising, as this is one of the very finest beaches in all the Hawaiian islands. In summer, its warm turquoise waters offer truly superb swimming, but look for warning signs if you're here in winter, when the waves are so fierce that they scoop away enough sand to cut the beach into two separate halves.

A shrine to Kamehameha's war god

BELOW: hiking the trails of Lapakahi.

Continuing northward, hot, dusty, and dry South Kohala looks like parts of the western United States – rock-strewn grasslands but with a seacoast, and with fewer than 9 inches (23 cm) of rain a year. Where Highways 270 and 19 from North Kohala and Waimea meet and continue south stands the largest restored *heiau* (temple) in Hawaii: **Pu'ukohola National Historic Site** ⓬ (open daily 7.30am–4pm; tel: 882-7218; www.nps.gov/puhe), built in 1791 by Kamehameha the Great for

his war god, Kuka'ilimoku, a prelude to his military conquests. When it was finished, he invited his main Big Island rival and cousin, the high chief Keoua, to a ceremony at the *heiau*. As Keoua's canoe landed he was killed by Kahamanu's father, Ke'eaumoku. The temple was dedicated with Keoua's body on the altar. In 1991, at a re-dedication of the site, descendants of the once-warring clans were reconciled in an impressive *'awa* ceremony, complete with costumed pageantry.

Map, page 256

The gateway to Kohala and Kona

When coming from Hilo, **Waimea** ⓭ is the gateway to Kohala and to Kona beyond. Waimea, sometimes called **Kamuela**, is a cool and often misty town at nearly 3,000 ft (910 meters) above sea level. That mellow upland climate has made it hugely in demand as a residential community for rich local people, who, amazing as it may sound to most of us, weary of the endless sunshine on the coastal plain below. Waimea holds some of the most expensive real estate in the state.

Captain George Vancouver and other early Europeans introduced goats, sheep, and cattle to the newly united island kingdom of Kamehameha the Great. The traditional low stone walls of the Hawaiians were unable to contain these domesticated stock animals, and in less than a decade, feral herds were ravaging cultivated farmlands and gnawing down young indigenous trees and plants.

In 1815, a New England farmer named John Palmer Parker offered to round up the animals in exchange for homestead land. Kamehameha gave him 2 acres (1 hectare) in the Kohala. These 2 acres grew to become what was at one time the largest privately owned ranch in America. Today, the cowboys of **Parker Ranch** run some 50,000 head of cattle over 210,000 acres (85,000 hectares) of pasture. Although the ranch is now administered by a trust, the Parker name still crops up all over Kohala, the Big Island's northern district. At **Parker Ranch Museum and Visitor Center** ⓮ (open daily 9am–5pm; entrance fee; tel: 885-7655) in Waimea/Kamuela, visits can be arranged to the century-old family home, Mana, and a second, more modern home, Pu'uopelu, which has an extensive art collection.

Like the 19th-century sugar barons, Parker had to import workers for his ranch, primarily Spanish-speaking cowboys from Mexico who were called *paniolos* (derived from the word *españa*) by Native Hawaiians. Today, all cowboys in Hawaii are called *paniolos*, and ranchlands are known as *paniolo*-country. In later years, Portuguese joined them, and local men were trained as ranch hands, too, as were Asian immigrants. Today, *paniolos* have no racial or ethnic identity.

Parker Ranch supplied most of the locally produced beef in Hawaii, butchering it at a company-owned slaughterhouse in Honolulu. Until a port was built, cattle were herded to the surf at **Kawaihae** ⓯ and forced to swim through the ocean to waiting ships, which hauled them aboard in slings. Nowadays, they are driven through gates onto enclosed barges. In the 1960s, Parker's descendant Richard Smart sold large, unproductive coastal tracts in South Kohala to resort developers.

In 1968, archeologists excavated a 600-year-old Hawaiian fishing village, Lapakahi, near Highway 270 that skirts North Kohala's coastline. The area is protected as **Lapakahi State Historical Park** ⓰ (open daily

BELOW: rodeo at Waimea.

8am–4pm except holidays). The park, which offers self-guided tours, preserves the restored foundations and stone enclosures of this commoners' fishing village.

The northern tip of the Big Island, **North Kohala**, is one of those windswept, wide-open places enveloped in mysticism. Literally at the end of the road is the Big Island's northernmost point, **'Upolu Point** ⓲ (named for an island in Samoa). Past the small airfield is well-preserved and partially restored **Mo'okini Heiau** ⓳, built around 800, it's said, by a *kahuna* (priest) from Tahiti. Today, a *kahuna* from the Mo'okini family of North Kohala still maintains the *heiau*. Within sight of the *heiau* is the **birthplace of Kamehameha the Great**, *circa* 1752. Signs mark both Mo'okini Heiau and Kamehameha's birthplace, and the *heiau* in particular is well worth the short side trip on an unpaved road that's frequently rendered impassable by rain.

The backbone of North Kohala

Defining North Kohala are the **Kohala Mountains**, the remains of an extinct 700,000-year-old volcano. In addition to the coastal road on the west side, Highway 250 ascends from Waimea to the ridge line and then through ranch land and groves of trees planted decades ago as windbreaks. The winds, called *'apa'a-pa'a*, that whip across the Kohala ridge are powerful and persistent.

At the north end of the peninsula is **Hawi** ⓳, an old sugar town that's begun a modest, tourist-focused revival. In adjacent **Kapa'au** ⓴, in front of the town's historic civic center, is the original **Kamehameha the Great statue**. It was lost at sea off the Falkland Islands and later recovered and taken to the Big Island town of Kapa'au. Its replacement stands opposite 'Iolani Palace in Honolulu.

In the 1880s, Kohala led the island in sugar production. Chinese laborers were

BELOW: purple jacaranda trees.

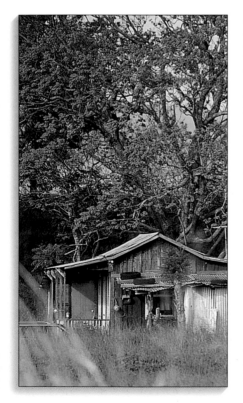

hired by a businessman to construct a narrow-gauge railway from **Niuli'i**, beyond Kapa'au, to the port of Mahukona, on North Kohala's western coast. Formally opened by King Kalakaua, the railroad was abandoned half a century later when trucks replaced trains. Chinese laborers founded the Kohala Tong Wo Society ("Together in Harmony") in 1886, the last of the Big Island's many Chinese societies. The Tong Wo Society had emerged in 16th-century China to overthrow the Manchus, and later flourished wherever Chinese settled. Sun Yatsen came to Hawaii in the 1880s, and again in the early 1900s, seeking help from the societies to overthrow the Qing dynasty.

The **Kohala Tong Wo Society building** was a social center for Kohala's early Chinese. At night, the men gambled or climbed a rope ladder for opium breaks in the loft. As a man neared death from old age, he moved to the "death house," where he would await death and be buried on the society grounds. The main building was restored and re-dedicated in 1971. Plaques engraved with proverbs and phrases surround the doors and windows.

Beyond the Tong Wo building the road continues until the **Pololu Valley Lookout** ㉑ with its expansive coastal views, alternating seacliffs and valleys leading to the **Hamakua Coast**. A steep trail leads down to Pololu Valley's rocky beach, partially visible from the lookout. You can join Hawaii Forest and Trail (tel: 800-

464-1993; www.hawaii-forest.com) on a memorable horseback and hiking excursion to waterfalls deep into the valley.

Dense forests cover the round, eroded highlands of Kohala, scarred by deep-cleft valleys and ravines. Along their eastern ocean faces, water seeps out of cracks in the cliffs and plunges 1,000 ft (300 meters) to the sea. At the turn of the 20th century, a technique for tapping this mountain water was established. Christened in 1906, the **Kohala Ditch** was a water course 18 miles (29 km) long that funneled the headwaters of Waimanu Valley to Honokane, terminating in an 850-ft (260-meter) artificial waterfall. Immigrant Japanese laborers bored and blasted 44 tunnels 8 ft (2.4 meters) wide and 7 ft (2 meters) high; the longest tunnel was nearly ½ mile (1 km) long. At least six men died and countless others suffered from exposure and chills while working in the icy darkness of the flooded tunnels.

South of Kona

Up above Kailua on the slopes of Hualalai and Mauna Loa, the climate is cooler. Moist air, bright sunshine, and porous volcanic soil produce one of the world's finest gourmet coffees. Schools in **South Kona** used to close during coffee-bean harvest season so that children could help their families fill burlap sacks of the bright-red beans for delivery to the local mill. The coffee industry expanded substantially in the 1990s, riding the wave of growth in coffee drinking in the US. There are numerous boutique mills throughout the Kona region that welcome visitors. All along the upcountry stretch of highway south of Kailua-Kona to the town of **Captain Cook** ⓦ are tasting rooms where various types of Kona coffee are sold; be sure to stop and sample a cup.

Map, page 256

TIP

Kona coffee is popular with *kama'aina* (locals) and visitors alike. A Kona blend, however, is legally required to contain only 10 percent Kona beans. One hundred percent Kona sells at premium prices, but it's well worth it.

BELOW: Kealakekua Bay.

Map, page 256

South Kona has diversified, both in spirit and in economics, since the 1960s, when the area was a haven for self-exiled counterculture types, then later for artisans and craftspeople. Other newcomers settled here to become farmers by leasing land from large estates and buying up farmlands. Much of that new farm land went not into coffee production, but into vegetables, citrus fruits, and cocoa, with beans that, when processed, compare with the finest European chocolate.

Higher up Mauna Loa's slopes are forests of native trees. Around their trunks, wild *maile* wraps itself. *Maile* is prized for making *lei*, but with an increasing population, *maile* has become scarce. Sandalwood once covered many of these slopes; today, few trees remain. Whole forests of the creamy, aromatic wood were cut and sold by Kamehameha the Great and his heirs for profitable shipment to China.

Carved image at the ancient place of refuge, Pu'uhonua 'O Honaunau.

BELOW: St Benedict's. **RIGHT:** northern coast.

The site of Cook's demise

Far below today's coffee farms, Captain Cook met his death at **Kealakekua Bay** ㉓, now a state marine conservation district. Visitors arrive on day-cruises from Kailua-Kona, or drive here on a paved road descending through relatively recent lava fields. A white obelisk, on a parcel of land that is officially British territory, marks the spot where Cook and some of his crew died. It is accessible only by water, or on foot via a strenuous trail. Archeological surveys between Kealakekua Bay and Kailua-Kona have mapped at least 40 temples in the area, with one of the best preserved at Napo'opo'o overlooking a rocky beach.

Travelers sailing south from Kealakekua Bay would be startled on reaching **Honaunau Bay** by the sight of fierce, hand-carved, wooden *ki'i* (sacred sculptures), and an immense stone platform with thick walls topped by thatched roofs. In this ancient *pu'uhonua*, or place of refuge, now known as the **Pu'uhonua 'O Honaunau National Historical Park** ㉔, (open daily 7.30am–5.30pm; entrance fee; tel: 328-2288; www.nps. gov/puho) Hawaiians pardoned violators of *kapu* (taboos) and war criminals who reached sanctuary here, but only if they vowed to do penance. Over the centuries, this *pu'uhonua* gained importance and accumulated *mana* (spiritual power), as more and more chiefs were buried here. Its *heiau* and the 1,000-ft (300-meter) long, 10-ft (3-meter) high and 17-ft (5-meter) wide Great Wall, have been meticulously restored.

Near the main road and up from the historical park, **St Benedict's Painted Church** ㉕ is one of Hawaii's special little places. The interior was painted with biblical scenes and motifs by a Belgian priest *c.* 1900. Outside stands a bust of Father Damien, the priest who worked in the Molokai leper colony *(see page 241)*.

South along this jagged Kona shore, the people of **Miloli'i** ㉖ still fish for a living. In few places is there a feeling of neighborliness so strong as in this little village of hand-built stone walls topped with night-blooming cereus. Further south along the highway, lava flows from the 1920s lift the road higher onto Mauna Loa's slopes and toward **Ka Lae**, or **South Point**, the southernmost tip of the Big Island and the United States. Too dry for farming, but with rich harvests from the sea, this was an early site of Polynesian settlement. Past South Point, the road turns northeast and ascends to Hawaii Volcanoes National Park and eventually to Hilo. ❑

HILO AND
THE WINDWARD SIDE

Map,
page 256

*On the Big Island's wet side, Hilo is a classic, friendly island town.
To its north is the lush Hamakua coast. To the south are the dry
Puna lands. Inland, volcanic heights beckon*

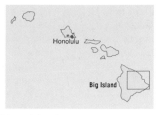

Honolulu

Big Island

Wet, warm, and sensuous in its appeal, **Hilo ②** is undeniably a tropical city. Unpretentious and subtle, it can yield its charm quickly or take forever, depending upon a traveler's receptiveness. Named for the first night of a new moon, or possibly for an ancient Polynesian navigator, Hilo has been a center of trade since ancient Hawaiian times. At the **Wailuku River**, which spills into **Hilo Bay** at the northwest end of today's Hilo, ancient Hawaiians shouted their bargains across the rapids and gingerly made their exchanges. Later, foreign ships found deep anchorage between the coral heads of its wide bay, and eventually a channel was dredged so that larger steamships could anchor. Blacksmiths, missionaries, farmers, jewelers, tailors, teachers, and dentists dropped anchor in Hilo, opening shops and churches, offices and schools.

Japanese foundations

The Japanese especially embody Hilo's growth. The first generation that came as sugar-cane laborers raised English-speaking children, the *nisei,* or second generation, who flocked not to the plantations for work but to government service and free enterprise. Respectful of their parents, the *nisei* and later *sansei* – third generation – descendants have run the island with particular sensitivity to the needs of older people.

Hilo's importance once revolved around its sheltered harbor. While cruise ships, freighters, and kayaks still ply its waters, the heart of town has moved inland, along Kanoelehua Avenue. Hilo's downtown buildings are dilapidated, although several have been artfully restored, with wooden awnings overhanging the sidewalks. Along **Waianuenue Avenue**, iron rings to which horses were once tethered are still embedded in the curb.

Downtown Hilo once stretched along the black-sand harbor, so the town was nicknamed the Crescent City. But in 1946, a *tsunami* swept half the town inland, then dragged the debris seaward. Hilo was rebuilt, and a stone breakwater was constructed across the bay to shield the harbor. Then in 1960 another *tsunami* broke through and blasted the shore. This time there was no rebuilding. Lowland waters were drained and a hill of 26 ft (8 meters) was raised above sea level, where city planners built a new government and commercial center, calling it **Kaiko'o**, or the strong seas. The old buildings that survived form a historical downtown district with a time-worn veneer that makes Hilo unique; the so-called Renaissance-Revival style was obviously popular for buildings from the early 1900s.

LEFT: red ginger and Hawaiian-style house.
BELOW: friendly smile from a local.

Downtown Hilo has undergone a partial restoration, and a fine walk that mixes old plantation ambiance with trendy hipness awaits in the central area, bordered by Kino'ole Street, Furneaux Lane, Kamehameha Avenue, and Waianuenue Avenue.

The Pacific Tsunami Museum ⓐ (open Mon–Sat 9am–4pm; entrance fee; tel: 935-0926; www.tsunami.org) in the heart of old Hilo tells the dramatic story of the *tsunamis* that have hit the islands.

A few blocks inland is the **Lyman Mission House and Museum ⓑ** (276 Haili St; open Mon–Sat 9am–4.30pm; entrance fee; tel: 935-5021; www.lyman museum.org), a reminder of the island's early missionary days. Built in 1839, the restored house is the oldest frame building in Hilo. Next door, a newer museum complex features Hawaiian and other ethnic history exhibits; upstairs is a world-class shell and mineral collection. Contemporary arts are on view at the East Hawaii Cultural Center Gallery (tel: 961-5711) on Kalakaua Street.

A couple of miles further inland stands the innovative '**Imiloa Astronomy Center ⓒ** (600 'Imiloa Place; open Tues–Sun 9am–4pm; entrance fee; tel: 969-9700; www.imiloahawaii.org). This sets out to explain the work and discoveries of the various observatories atop Big Island's highest mountain, Mauna Kea, and also to acknowledge Hawaiian religious beliefs about the entire cosmos, as well as the sacred mountain.

At the other end of the harbor to the east is the venerable **Banyan Drive ⓓ**, a crescent road lined with voluptuous banyan trees shading most of Hilo's finer hotels. Japanese-style **Lili'uokalani Gardens ⓔ**, nearby and off Banyan Drive, have stone bridges, lanterns, and a tea ceremony pavilion.

From the Hawaii Naniloa Hotel, one of several Hilo hotels with superb harbor views, 13,800-ft (4,200-meter) **Mauna Kea** dominates the western horizon.

'I realize more fully the beauty of Hilo, as it appeared in the gloaming. The rain had ceased, cool breezes rustled through the palm groves and sighed through the foliage of the pandanus.'

– ISABELLA BIRD
19TH-CENTURY TRAVELER

BELOW: warm water, and Hilo Harbor.

Dark forests circle the mountain above bright-green sugar cane, thinning out as the altitude rises, and finally vanishing – along with shrubs, grasses, and bird life – at the alpine heights where snow in winter gives the mountain its Hawaiian name, White Mountain. A long and broad saddle separates Mauna Kea, the island's older main volcano, from Mauna Loa, or Long Mountain.

Perhaps once in a generation Mauna Loa erupts. In 1975, lava flowed to within a short distance of Hilo. It wasn't the first time lava had put Hilo at risk. In the late 1880s, a perilous flow from Mauna Loa headed toward Hilo, stopped only, it is said, when the volcano goddess, Pele, heeded pleas from a high princess. In 1942, American military aircraft dropped water and explosives on the leading edge of a similar flow to halt the lava. The danger remains very real; volcanic activity in 2007 was assessed as posing a potential threat to Hilo.

Like the town itself, nearby scenic sites are quiet and contemplative places. **Rainbow Falls** in the **Wailuku River State Park ❼** sport a prismatic halo in early mornings and late afternoons, when the sun is oblique to its cascade. Further upstream are the odd **Boiling Pots ❽**, a section of bubbling water at the base of Pe'epe'e Falls.

North of Hilo

When sugar was king along the **Hamakua Coast** north of Hilo, a railway carried cane, freight, and commuters between the sugar mills of Hamakua and Hilo. A simple, winding road between the workers' camps carried cars and horse-drawn carts, with palm trees for fence posts along the sea cliffs. After the 1946 *tsunami* undercut most of the railway bridges, the tracks were torn up. Trucks took over, clogging the old road until a new highway was built.

Map below

TIP

A note of caution if you are traveling to the Big Island in April, around Easter. Hilo is the site of the state's most popular hula competition and performance, the annual Merrie Monarch Festival. Hotel rooms for this week are reserved a year in advance. Book ahead if you can *(see page 105 for further details)*.

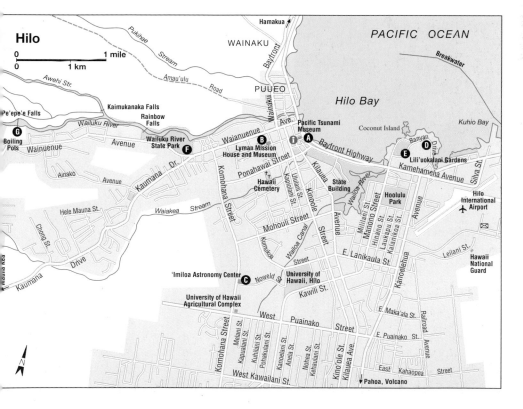

Honoli'i is said to be where the demi-god Maui came to his end while chasing a young maiden up a tree. He had turned himself into an eel during the pursuit, but a passing kahuna *killed him.*

You can return to plantation times and enjoy a glimpse of an old-fashioned part of Hawaii by driving along the deserted road, using the main highway to bridge its gaps. A turn-off leads to **Honoli'i**, a river estuary and beach park with the only reliable, year-round surfing waves in the Hilo vicinity.

After picking up the highway, a right turn past **Papa'ikou** marked "Scenic Drive" follows a beautiful 4-mile (6-km) stretch along the coast past **Onomea Bay**, once a major sugar port. **Hawaii Tropical Botanical Garden ㉘** (open daily 9am–5pm; entrance fee; tel: 964-5233; www.htbg.com) is a 17-acre (7-hectare) privately owned preserve with 2,000 species of plants and flowers, including palms, bromeliads, ginger, heliconia and orchids along shaded pathways in an oceanside rainforest.

The old road rumbles over single-lane wooden bridges covered with bright-red African tulip flowers in spring and squashed guavas in autumn. Plantation workers have, by and large, left the camps to buy homes on company land. Near **Pepe'ekeo**, their fine gardens and flower beds are turning old cane fields into lush, warm neighborhoods. At the town of **Honomu**, a spur road leads to the thin 400-ft (120-meter) **'Akaka Falls ㉙**, and their neighbor, **Kahuna Falls**, both of which can be seen on an undulating mile-long hiking trail. Somewhere in the area is a special rock, a stone of the fire goddess Pele, which causes the sky to cloud over and rain whenever struck by a branch of the *lehua 'apane*.

Easy living

BELOW: Honomu, on the Hamakua Coast, and weighing in for a cockfight.

Change comes so slowly to Hamakua that few people notice it. A new house, a new car, a new storefront appear, but never anything startling. Places like **Papa'aloa**, **Laupaho'eho'e**, **Pa'auilo**, and **Pa'auhau** look and feel much as they have for generations. On weekends, families secretly wager on the cockfights

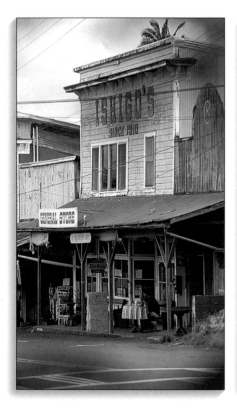

brought from their home islands in the Philippines. Fathers and sons take their dogs into the muddy forests on pig-hunting expeditions. Children and old men play softball in the parks. The paternal mills and the fraternal labor unions made Hamakua's plantation workers the highest-paid agricultural workers in the world. But as elsewhere in Hawaii, sugar died here. The largest mill and employer closed in 1996, and the fields of untended cane have rapidly vanished. What will replace the fields and the jobs remains to be seen. Some agribusinessmen have hedged their bets by planting macadamia trees, which mature late but bear nuts for decades. It is a lucrative market, but the competition from foreign producers is fierce. Another alternative to sugarcane is a fast-growing eucalyptus tree, which is harvested for paper, wall board, and as a source of fuel.

Slicing through the Hamakua coast are three great gulches: Maulua, Laupaho'eho'e, and Ka'awali'i. The streams that cut through these volcanic channels have their sources far uphill where few people venture. With permission from neighboring ranchers to unlock their gates, the occasional hunter or forester rides up into the high terrain of the **Laupaho'eho'e Natural Area Reserve ㉚**, which protects the watershed of the island's windward side, a landscape misty in summer and frosty in winter. Here, the tall indigenous *koa* and *'ohi'a* trees stand. Hidden in the reserve are some cold-weather trees that were planted in the 1920s by foresters: spruce, cypress, maple, Dutch elm, redwood.

The **Laupaho'eho'e Train Museum** (open Mon–Fri 9am–4.30pm, Sat–Sun 10am–2pm; small entrance fee; tel: 962-6300) is worth a stop, with historic images of what was an impressive bit of early 20th-century engineering.

Nine miles (14 km) beyond **Honoka'a ㉛**, a rustic former sugar town, lies the broad and deep **Waipi'o Valley ㉜**, the first of several windward valleys along

Map, page 256

Macadamia nuts have incredibly hard outer shells that enclose rich, sweet white flesh.

BELOW: Saturday conference at the local park.

TIP

You can get a tour to
Waipi'o valley with
Waipi'o Na'alapa Trail
Rides (tel: 775-0419;
www.naalapastables.
com) or Valley Wagon
Tours (tel: 775-9518;
www.waipiovalley
wagontours.com).

BELOW:
grass growing
on the slopes of
Mauna Kea.

North Kohala's wilderness coastline. Waipi'o was a population center before European contact, home to thousands, including fishermen and farmers who built irrigated terraces to grow taro in the rich earth, which was said to have become red when Kanaloa, one of the four primary gods, beat Maui against the rocks.

Waipi'o's **Hi'ilawe Falls** fed a river stocked with fish that skilled men and women would catch with their bare hands. The black sand beach knew the keels of dozens of canoes that crossed treacherous currents to trade with neighboring valleys, but by the early 20th century, young people had moved away to work on the plantations or to live in more accessible towns. In the valleys, rice replaced taro grown by Japanese and Chinese settlers. After World War II, two *tsunami* flooded the valley floor and it was largely abandoned. Today, a few families call Waipi'o home. Most visitors take in Waipi'o from the clifftop lookout. The valley is accessed via a steep dirt road, off-limits by rental car companies but open to hikers or on organized tours *(see margin tip)*.

In the 1960s, the Peace Corps, newly initiated by President Kennedy, trained volunteers here to prepare them for life in rural Asia. Today, the Peace Corps village is gone, but visitors may pitch a tent a short hike away from a natural swimming hole below 300-ft (90-meter) Hi'ilawe Falls. Dedicated hikers can cross the beach and scale the trail on the far side toward **Waimanu Valley** ㉝, 7 miles (11 km) north over mostly irregular terrain.

The highest point in Hawaii

The older of the two largest Big Island volcanoes, **Mauna Kea** ㉞, towers over the Pacific at 13,796 ft (4,185 meters). It is the highest point in Hawaii and the Pacific Basin. Measured from its base below the ocean's surface, it is the tallest

mountain on earth at more than 30,000 ft (9,100 meters). Now dormant, Mauna Kea last erupted 3,500 years ago. More than 15,000 years ago, a glacier chilled the slopes of Mauna Kea. Today, a continual layer of permafrost sustains **Lake Wai'au**, close to the summit. Poli'ahu, the snow goddess and enemy of the fire goddess Pele, is said to live atop the volcano. It is said that when the gods disapproved of someone's presence on the mountain, they would turn him or her into stone; there are a lot of stones on the mountain.

Supplies of a dense and steel-hard basalt for use in adzes attracted Hawaiians to the area. The Mauna Kea adze quarry, 11,000 ft (3,350 meters) above sea level, is a National Historic Landmark. It covers nearly 8 sq miles (21 sq km). The site contains 40 *heiau* (temples) and other shrines, and a trail leads to Lake Wai'au.

No site in the Northern Hemisphere is so high, so clear, so free from light and heat, and so easily accessible as Mauna Kea's summit. The University of Hawaii and the governments of the US, Canada, Japan, and the UK have built 13 giant telescopes on summit cinder cones. The **Keck Observatory** ❸ is the most powerful optical telescope in the world, with mirrored segments aligned by computer to create a light-gathering surface of 33 ft (10 meters). Four-wheel-drive vehicles are needed for the trek up a road that angles off Highway 20 toward the peak of Mauna Kea (off-limits to rental cars). Hawaiian Forest & Trail offers summit tours (tel: 331-8505; www.hawaii-forest.com). For details, call Mauna Kea Support Services (tel: 961-2180). Plans for additional observatories have been challenged by environmentalists, and those who consider the summit a sacred site. At a lower elevation is the **Ellison S. Onizuka Astronomy Complex** ❸ (variable hours; tel: 961-2180), with evening star-gazing and displays in honor of Hawaii's first astronaut, who was killed in the 1986 *Challenger* space shuttle disaster.

Map, page 256

BELOW: March skiing on Mauna Kea.

The Hilo and Kona sides of Hawaii have never been directly linked. The only overland road through the center of the Big Island, winding between Mauna Kea and Mauna Loa, is the **Saddle Road** ㉧, which connects Hilo with Kohala. (Most rental car companies prohibit travel on the Saddle Road.)

A direct Kona–Hilo road has long been in the pipeline. In 1849, Kamehameha III approved a plan to survey and build a road over Crown lands from Kona, the seat of government, to Hilo, the only deep-water port. Convict laborers began at the edge of the forest and followed a nearly straight line. After 10 years they had reached halfway to Hilo when Mauna Loa erupted. A broad river of lava poured down the mountain and covered part of the road; it was never completed.

A scant quarter-mile (400 meters) from the edge of that flow, high up in what is called the **Saddle**, stand the stone remains of a monument to a 16th-century king, 'Umi, the first known king of the Big Island. He completed his military unification of Hawaii here on a desolate plateau inland behind dormant Hualalai, which, at 8,271 ft (2,521 meters), is the island's third-largest volcano. At this location, Mauna Kea, Mauna Loa, and Hualalai appear nearly the same size. 'Umi, according to some stories, ordered a census. Stones were used to represent people, animals, and units of land. These heaps of stones were fashioned into a place of worship, Ahua 'Umi Heiau, and probably decorated with offerings.

It has been 500 years since ancient armies bivouacked on the plain in this geographical center of the island, but only a few miles away in the Saddle at **Pohakuloa**, the American military practices war games. Near the Saddle's high point is the **Kipuka 'Ainahou Nene Sanctuary** ㉨, one of the preserves where Hawaii's indigenous geese, or nene, are found. They can also be found in Haleakala National Park on Maui and Koke'e on Kauai.

The Hawaiian goose, or nene, never sets its clawed (not webbed) feet in water. It's found only in Hawaii at higher elevations on the Big Island and Maui.

BELOW: colors on the Saddle.

Mauna Loa

Unlike Mauna Kea, Hawaii's southern volcano, **Mauna Loa** ㉩, is not yet dormant. Indeed, the Big Island districts of Kona, Ka'u, Hilo, and Puna remain vulnerable to a possible major eruption. Mauna Loa's last eruption was a 1984 fountain inside the summit caldera of **Moku'aweoweo**, a name that refers to the *'aweoweo* fish whose red color has obvious volcanic parallels. Mauna Loa has erupted 36 times since European contact. Several times, it has threatened Hilo, situated on its northeast flank, most recently in 1984, when flows stopped just 5 miles (8 km) away.

Mauna Loa is a shield volcano, growing through the accumulative stacking of thin lava flows of 10–15 ft (3–4.5 meters). This process gives the shield volcano its gentle convex shape, in contrast to dramatically explosive volcanoes such as Mt Fuji and Mt St Helens. Lower than Mauna Kea, at 13,679 ft (4,149 meters), Mauna Loa ("Long Mountain") has more mass than any other mountain on the planet, with more volume (almost 10,000 cubic miles/40,000 cubic km) than the entire Sierra Nevada range in California. For most hikers, the trail to the summit is a two-day climb, with a cabin at Red Hill providing overnight shelter. With fog and sudden storms a possibility, the summit hike can be risky.

From the summit caldera, two prominent rift zones, which are fractured areas of weakness, extend deep into

he ocean. The first rift zone passes through South Point at the bottom of the
sland, and the second, the northeast rift zone, extends toward Hilo.

Map,
page 256

South of Hilo: Puna

Travelers often bypass the **Puna** area south of Hilo off Highway 130. The road
that once linked Puna to Hawaii Volcanoes National Park was closed in 1994
after lava covered it in several places. Scores of homes, the village of Kalapana,
and several historic sites have been destroyed by the slow flows of Kilauea.

The gateway to the Puna area is the town of **Pahoa** 40, once a major supplier
of *'ohi'a* wood to the railroads, which used the wood for ties. Its small Downtown is interesting, with raised wooden sidewalks and old buildings along its
main street. The historic Star of the Sea painted church was moved here after
lava covered its original site near the coast. The area surrounding Puna is known
for producing tropical flowers, papaya, and illegal *pakalolo* (marijuana).

In 1790, lava flows flooded then drained a rainforest, leaving shells of
solidified lava around now-vaporized trees. These lava-tree mold forests of **Lava
Tree State Monument** 41 are eerie, especially in early mornings before the
mists have lifted. Costal Route 137 leads to volcanically heated thermal springs
at Ahalanui Beach Park, and naturist sunbathing at Kehena. To the North lies
the island's westernmost point, **Cape Kumukahi** 42, which grew dramatically
after eruptions in 1955 and 1960. The Cape's namesake may have been one of
two men: a chief who mocked Pele or a migratory traveler from Tahiti. Either
way, Kumukahi means "first beginning." Partially covered by the recent flows
is a cemetery for Japanese immigrants. The coastline of Puna is volcanic and
rough, with few satisfactory beaches. ❑

*Cemetery marker
on Cape Kumukahi
that survived a
1960 lava flow
over the Japanese
cemetery there.*

BELOW LEFT: near
Lava Tree National
Monument.
BELOW RIGHT: palms.

VOLCANO AND KA'U

Near the community of Volcano, a real volcano – Kilauea – has erupted for more than two decades. To the southwest, South Point was where the first Polynesians landed

Maps, pages 256 & 283

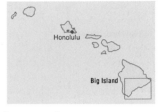

Honolulu

Big Island

Here on the Big Island is nature at its most awesome. Allow yourself time to absorb views of searing, red-hot lava flowing down the side of Kilauea; canopied, misty rainforests filled with giant tree ferns; barren lava flows; and the windswept deserts of Ka'u. Few visitors can ignore the primal pull originating on the southeastern slopes of **Mauna Loa**, still an active volcano. An 18-mile (29-km) trail to the summit of Mauna Loa is a difficult and unforgettable hike. It takes half a day just to reach the **Red Hill** cabin at 10,000 ft (3,030 meters), and most of the next day to attain the summit cabin that overlooks the steaming summit crater, Maku'aweoweo. Here, the unspoiled colors of the lava gleam brilliantly, snow glints from cracks in the rock – it is the only source of water – and the thin air makes sturdy travelers light-headed and the surroundings mystical.

A continually erupting volcano

On Mauna Loa's slopes is a rift zone, where lava that sometimes feeds the summit crater oozes from cracks lower on the mountain. This is the Big Island's biggest draw, along with the beaches of Kohala and Kona. All of the current activity is from **Kilauea ㊸**, the youngest of Hawaii's volcanic mountains, which has been erupting steadily since 1983, the longest continuously erupting volcano in the world. Like all Hawaiian volcanoes, Kilauea is a dome-like shield volcano with deceptively gentle slopes. It rises southeast of Mauna Loa, more than 20,000 ft (6,000 meters) above its base on the ocean floor.

All of this and much of the surrounding area is part of the **Hawaii Volcanoes National Park ㊹** (open daily; entrance fee; tel: 967-7311; www.nps.gov/havo). Created in 1916, the national park once included Maui's Haleakala, which was made into its own national park in 1961. At the **Kilauea Visitor Center Ⓐ** (open daily 7.45am–5pm), latest information about eruptions, road closures, and flow activity is displayed on maps, information boards and on film. Hikers should sign in here.

From the visitor center, the 11-mile (17-km) **Crater Rim Drive** passes over some of the Pacific's most bizarre scenery as it skirts past wheezing steam vents at **Steaming Bluff (Sulfur Banks) Ⓑ**, where seeping ground water hits hot rock; there are several breathtaking views of the caldera. Lava flows in the caldera just below the first stretch of road and the Volcano House hotel date from 1919.

The **Hawaiian Volcano Observatory Ⓒ** (closed to the public), operated by the US Geological Survey, is one of the world's premier volcanology and geophysical research centers. Next door, the **Thomas A. Jaggar Museum Ⓓ** (open daily 8.30am–5pm; tel: 967-7643) has informative exhibits and presentations. Near the

LEFT: a fountain from Kilauea.
BELOW: a tenacious plant takes root in lava.

observatory, but inaccessible to visitors, is the site of one of only two *heiau* (temples) believed to have been situated near the caldera, on the bluff of Uwe-kahuna, "the place of priestly weeping." Apparently a house was built over a pit here. A *kahuna* (priest) waited for unsuspecting visitors to enter the house, then he yanked ropes that opened up the floor to send visitors to their death. A timely hero set the house alight, causing the *kahuna* to weep.

The primary vent of Kilauea

The road slips into the Southwest Rift zone, crossing lava flows from 1971, 1974, and 1921 to an overlook of **Halema'uma'u Crater** Ⓔ, the collapsed depression within Kilauea Caldera. From the parking lot near the crater, whiffs of sulfuric gases escaping the earth along the short trail are reminders that all is not finished down below. Halema'uma'u is the primary vent of Kilauea. The crater of Kilauea is 2½ miles (4 km) by 2 miles (3.2 km) in size, its walls a set of step-like fault blocks that form cliffs as high as 400 ft (120 meters). From the early 1820s until 1924, Halema'uma'u was a lake of active lava, but today steam is more evident than molten lava. Still, Halema'uma'u is said to be the fire goddess Pele's current home. At the crater's rim, offerings of *lei*, *ti*-wrapped stones, and money are left for Pele's appeasement.

Compared to explosive volcanoes in the Mediterranean or around the Pacific Rim, Hawaii's volcanoes are relatively benign, allowing visitors "drive-through" access to eruptions and lava flows. Only twice in recorded history have dangerously explosive eruptions occurred in Hawaii. The latest was in 1924, when steam pressure expelled Kilauea volcano's plug and enlarged Halema'uma'u's diameter from 1,200 ft (360 meters) to 3,000 ft (900 meters), and left a hole 1,300 ft

*Heed the signs
and warnings at
Halema'uma'u
and elsewhere in
the national park.*

BELOW: crater of
Halema'uma'u.

(400 meters) deep. An eight-ton block of basalt was tossed 3,000 ft (900 meters) from Halema'uma'u's center. Dust clouds rose to 20,000 ft (6,000 meters).

A parasitical shield dome

The **Chain of Craters Road** ❻ cuts off the rim road and descends along the East Rift, passing prehistoric pit craters and heading toward the ocean down a fault scarp covered with lava flows that look like black molasses.

In recent decades, Kilauea's eruptions have been primarily along the Southwest Rift and the East Rift zones, structural weaknesses in the shield volcano. The Southwest Rift extends through Ka'u, and the East Rift to Puna. Since 1969, a number of eruptions on the East Rift have built a new "parasitic" shield dome called **Mauna Ulu** ❼, the "growing mountain." Among its achievements, Mauna Ulu has buried 12 miles (19 km) of park road, some of it under 300 ft (100 meters) of lava, and added more than 600 acres (243 hectares) of land to the Big Island.

Kilauea is famous for its "curtains of fire" – walls of flaming, gushing fountains that erupt along well-known rift zones. A typical eruption begins with a change in the pressure of the underground plumbing, then a crack or rift opens on top. Fountains dozens or hundreds of feet high squirt flaming rock into the air. Puddles collect and form a lake. Heat blasts from the surface, sucking up the colder air, which flings stinging cinders and sharp ashes into a whirlwind.

Kilauea Iki Crater ❽ was where a 2,000-ft (600-meter) volcanic geyser erupted in 1959, possibly the highest volcanic fountain ever recorded. Nearby, a popular stop is the **Thurston Lava Tube** ❾, where a short trail weaves through primal groves of fern to a short lava tube. Lava tubes, which are like perfectly round tunnels in a cooled lava flow, form when a *paho'eho'e* lava flow

Map below

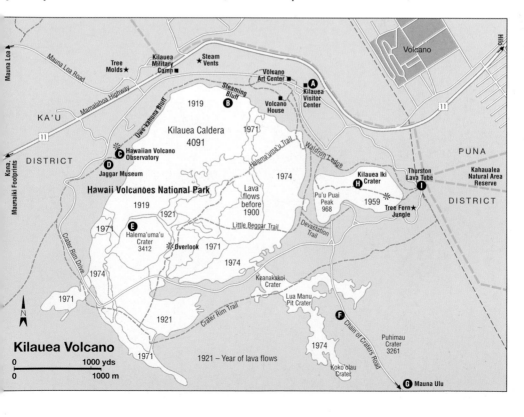

Kilauea Volcano

0 ___ 1000 yds
0 ___ 1000 m

1921 – Year of lava flows

starts to cool on its outer edges. A channel forms, through which flows continue to move while the surrounding flow cools. If Kilauea's active flows have reached the ocean, steam plumes rise ahead at the road's end.

The National Park Service maintains facilities at the roadblock on the Chain of Craters Road. From here it's a marked walk to safe viewpoints. Caution is required when hiking off the marked trail, as the lava cover can be unstable, and deaths have occurred here. Recorded updates are provided on the park's phone line.

It was once possible to continue along this road to Hilo. In the 1980s and 1990s, lava flows obliterated scores of homes, the village of **Kalapana** ⑤, archeological sites, the road itself, and the national park's Waha'ula Visitor Center. In 1997, the **Waha'ula** *luakini heiau*, once used for human sacrifices, was finally swallowed up. Waha'ula was first established by a Tahitian priest in the 13th century, and later used by Kamehameha the Great. According to legend, when a young chief passed through smoke coming from the *heiau* – a taboo, as the smoke was considered a shadow of the *heiau*'s god – he was killed and his bones were thrown in a pit. About 25 miles (40 km) out at sea, 3,000 ft (900 meters) below sea level, a new island-to-be, **Lo'ihi**, is developing on the East Rift. Thousands of years from now, it will surface as either a new island or an extension of the Big Island itself.

Volcano

BELOW: solidified lava covers a road near Kalapana.

Just outside of the national park boundary, on the road to Hilo and not far from the Kilauea Visitors Center, **Volcano** ⑥ is a small town set amid forests and mists situated 3,700 ft (1,100 meters) above sea level. There are several bed-and-breakfast guest houses in the town for those wanting to stay up here, rather than returning the same day to Hilo or Kona. The well-appointed Kilauea Lodge (tel:

967-7366; www.kilauealodge.com), with its popular restaurant, is well worth an overnight stay, as are the many village bed-and-breakfasts. Conard Eyre's Green Goose Lodge (tel: 808-985-7172; www.greengooselodge.com), Volcano Rainforest Retreat (tel: 800-550-8696; www.volcanoretreat.com), '20s vintage Hale Ohia (tel: 967-7986; www.haleohia.com), and Volcano Places (tel: 877-967-7990; www.volcanoplaces.com) are all good choices.

The Volcano area attracts artisans, writers, and craftspeople. Many of their works are offered for sale at the **Volcano Art Center** (open daily 9am–5pm; tel: 967-7511) next to the Hawaii National Park headquarters and housed in the old **Volcano House**, once perched on the caldera's edge (tel: 967-7321; www.volcano househotel.com). In 1877, a master carpenter was hired by a steamship company to build a real hotel, Volcano House. The original building was eventually moved back from the crater's edge and restored as the Volcano Art Center. The current hotel, overlooking Halema'uma'u and a short walk from the visitor and art centers, is comfortable though rustic. During the day, it's crowded with visitors, but in the evenings it's quiet and pleasant. The lunch buffet at the restaurant is tourist fare, but dinner is adequate.

From the main highway and still inside the national park, a side road leads to **Kipuka Pua'ulu** (Bird Park), an idyllic hideaway with a nature trail through meadows and one of the thickest concentrations of native plants in Hawaii.

A *kipuka* is an isolated ecosystem created when a lava flow shunts around an "island" of older growth or a habitat, isolating it. These *kipuka* are important biological research areas where native species continue to flourish independent of outside influences. Biologists often create artificial *kipuka* for research. In 1968, the National Park Service isolated an area near the coast with fences,

Map, page 256

TIP

If hiking in Hawaii Volcanoes National Park, don't be fooled by the visual ruggedness of the land. Its surface is fragile, as is the flora that grow from it. Please stay on trails.

BELOW: new beach near Kalapana.

Map,
page 256

protecting it from the wild pigs and goats that roam the Big Island. Something grew within the fenced *kipuka* that had never been seen before by modern scientists: a large bean plant with purple flowers. Until the fence was put up, island goats had eaten the bean plants before they could mature.

Ka'u

To the southwest of Kilauea and Volcano is **Ka'u Desert**, downwind from the summit and where noxious gases and dehydrated breezes inhibit vegetation. In 1790, an eruption of gas and dust suffocated a phalanx of warriors headed to battle Kamehameha the Great. Their footprints pressed into the hardening cinder, as they unsuccessfully sought to escape, are to be seen at **Maunaiki** ㊽, preserved under glass at the end of a mile-long trail, accessed from the main highway coming from South Point. There are other footprints to be found off the trail, but the environment is exceedingly fragile, as are the footprints, and a ramble through the bush may not only damage the delicate plants and soil, but also some of these ancient footprints that remain unprotected. Stay on the trail.

From the national park, the road descends along the Southwest Rift of Kilauea. **Punalu'u Beach** ㊾ is a black-sand beach near the small Sea Mountain Resort, complete with golf course. Beyond is **Na'alehu**, a traditional Hawaiian town billed as the southernmost in the USA, with a bakery renowned for its sweet bread.

Turning off the main highway, a dead-end road traverses 12 miles (19 km) of cattle range southward to **Ka Lae** ㊿ (The Point), or **South Point**. Along the way, the road passes three dozen immense electricity-generating windmills, spinning in the unceasing winds that whip this cape. Privately owned **Kamoa Wind Farm** ㊿ feeds electricity into the island's main power grid.

Somewhere along South Point, some of the first Polynesians landed in Hawaii, calling it Ka Lae. Modern-day visitors sense somehow that this is a special place. Clear, blue waters smash against the 50-ft (15-meter) high basalt cliffs. Small fishing boats are often tied up below. The ocean is tempestuous, the wind forceful, and the isolation nearly complete. The ancient Hawaiians built the **Kalalea Heiau**, a temple dedicated to fishing, right on the cliff's edge. Today, this is the southernmost place in the United States. Due south is Tahiti.

A 3-mile (5-km) hike east from South Point through a grassy plain leads to the unique **Papakolea Green Sand Beach** ㊿. Here, an entire cinder cone of olivine has collapsed into a little bay and been reduced into polished sand by the surf. Bring water; it's a dry, hot place.

Moving north through **Ka'u District**, one finds an increase in gray and black lava – the Mauna Loa flows of 1907, 1919, 1926, and 1950. Where the local microclimate has permitted, lichens, grass and *'ohi'a* – usually the first tree to appear in lava flows – sprout from the new earth. This is one of the least-populated places in Hawaii. During the 1950s and 1960s, however, unscrupulous real estate salesmen trafficked in these barren lava acres, hawking them sight-unseen to Americans as properties in paradise. Nevertheless, some of those living here came knowing full well how barren the land was going to be and they've come to like it, even if swaying palm trees and white-sand beaches are distinctly lacking. ❑

BELOW: perhaps a little too close for safety.
RIGHT: some of the youngest land on Earth.

A STATE OF FIRE IN THE PACIFIC OCEAN

Hawaii is one of the few places in the world where one may literally drive to a volcanic eruption and watch it in relative safety. It's not to be missed.

The islands of Hawaii sit almost in the middle of the Pacific Plate, a piece in the giant jigsaw puzzle that is the earth's crust. This Pacific Plate is moving slowly to the northwest. Each of the 132 islands in the Hawaiian chain, from the smallest atoll in the northeast to the Big Island, was formed as the plate moved over a "hot spot" 50 miles (80 km) deep in the earth's mantle and from where molten lava periodically welled up from inside the earth.

The oldest Hawaiian islands are in the northeast near Midway Island; erosion and sinking has reduced them to coral atolls. The process of island growth continues. Kilauea Volcano, on the Big Island, offers the world's most active continuing eruption, since 1983. Lo'ihi, an erupting seamount 20 miles (30 km) southeast of the Big Island and 3,000 ft (900 meters) below sea level, is growing and may one day surface.

VOLCANO CREATION

Hawaii's volcanoes, because they resemble the shield carried by medieval Germanic warriors, are called shield or dome volcanoes. Shield volcanoes form in massive but gently rising oval shapes because they are fed by lava flowing repeatedly through a conduit, slowly and benignly. Fuji and Vesuvius, with more classical conical shapes, arose through explosive eruptions.

Two Hawaii volcanoes, Mauna Loa and Kilauea, have summit calderas, created when lava drains from an underground magma chamber, causing the volcano summit to sink. In contrast, Maui's Haleakala has neither crater nor caldera, but rather a summit basin created by erosion.

Mauna Kea is the world's tallest volcano, measured from its base 18,000 ft (5,500 meters) below sea level. Mauna Loa, also on the Big Island, is the planet's most massive mountain, at 10,000 cubic miles (16,000 cu km) in volume.

△ **FOUNTAIN**
Most spectacular at the Kilauea Volcano, in Hawaii Volcanoes National Park on the Big Island, is when a rift opens and lava spurts into the air in a fountain. These happen sporadically and often don't last long, but if you are anywhere nearby when one does occur, rush, don't walk, to the national park.

▷ **SLOW MOVING**
The lava flows from Kilauea Volcano have a grace to them that betrays their heat and mass. An extremely dangerous reality to those who dare to explore these new fields is that beneath a thin crust of what seems to be solid footing is yet masses of uncooled lava.

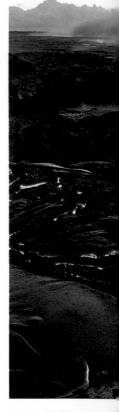

△ **GENTLE FLOWS**
The eruptions of Kilauea are quite benign and lacking the explosive destruction of other volcanoes. Still, lava flows such as this not only create new land, but also destroy nearly everything in their path.

◁ **PELE AT HOME**
Contemporary sculpture of Pele, the goddess of fire, carved out of lava from Kilauea.

PELE: GODDESS OF HAWAII'S FIRE

Stay in Hawaii long enough and you'll encounter the name of Hawaii's goddess of fire, Pele, probably the best-known of Hawaii's deities to contemporary traveler and resident alike.

Pele is responsible for the current eruptions of Kilauea. However, she did not create the Hawaiian islands, as many tend to believe. Nomadic by disposition, Pele arrived in Hawaii from Tahiti in a canoe provided by the god of sharks. After arriving in Ni'ihau, a small island to the east of Kauai, she traveled along the islands looking for a volcano to call home.

The only suitable location was the Big Island. Arriving there, she went after the reigning fire god, Aila'au, hoping to move in with him. Her reputation had preceded her, especially the stories about her awesome power and rather tempestuous personality. By the time Pele reached Kilauea, Aila'au had already fled.

A visit to Hawaii Volcanoes National Park will reveal the reverence that many contemporary Hawaiians have for Pele. Offerings pepper the caldera rim of Halema'uma'u. Even outsiders learn of her power. Tourists who've taken lava souvenirs home later return them to national park authorities, hoping to rid themselves of the bad luck that suddenly befalls them.

◁ NEW LAND, NEW LIFE
The ropy, smooth character of *paho'eho'e* lava, seen along the Chain of Craters Road near Kilauea, is easily distinguished from the jagged and rough textures of *a'a* lava. Both types are a challenge to the survival of flora.

▽ EXPLOSIVE SPRAY
Kilauea's usually passive flows can take on explosive force when reaching the cooler ocean or during the more spectacular fountaining.

◁ KALAPANA DESTRUCTION
Flows from Kilauea follow gravity to the ocean, destroying both modern housing estates and ancient *heiau* along the way. The destruction can be capricious: a house can go up in flames while a neighbor's is spared.

KAUAI

*Long the most reclusive and independent of Hawaii's islands,
lusciously sculpted Kauai bides its own time, welcoming hikers,
kayakers and others with its diverse and dramatic landscape*

The historian Edward Josting called Kauai a "separate kingdom"
when he detailed the history of this idyllic island, for it remained
stubbornly independent after all the other Hawaiian islands had
succumbed to Kamehameha the Great's conquest in the 1790s.

Kauai does not disappoint. Remember Elvis in *Blue Hawaii*, or
South Pacific, or *Jurassic Park* and *The Lost World?* Oldest and
northernmost of the main Hawaiian islands, Kauai is ringed by perfect, white-sand beaches that are strung like seductive gems from
Ha'ena Point on its northern coast to the ever-sunny resort of Po'ipu
on its southern shore, to broad and beautiful Polihale Beach lying
in indolent splendor in the west. The inaccessibility of Kauai's most
stunning terrain undoubtedly adds to its mystical appeal. Anchoring this nearly circular island, reportedly the wettest place on earth,
is the summit of Wai'ale'ale. (But not Kauai's highest point, which
is nearby Kawaikini.)

On the southeastern coast is Lihu'e, Kauai's largest urban center
and main airport. Northward from Lihu'e, the road passes through the
green and wet windward coast to the spectacular north shore, where
Hanalei Bay and Lumahai Beach seduce even the jaded traveler. The
road stops here. Beyond is the 14-mile (22-km) long Na Pali coast,
inaccessible except by foot or boat. Westward from Lihu'e is the dry
side of the island, along with some of Kauai's most important historical sites. At Waimea, Captain Cook first set foot in the Hawaiian
Islands. Nearby, an ascending road leads inward along spectacular
Waimea Canyon to Koke'e, where mists compete with the sun, providing stunning views from 4,000-ft (122-meter) lookouts.

The people of Kauai, some 60,000, are for the most part unassuming and hardworking individuals justifiably proud of their *'aina*, or
land. More than half of this 550-sq mile (1,430-sq km) island is
reserved for conservation and preservation. Alaka'i Swamp, a boggy
dwarf forest high in the verdant interior, provides safe harbor for a
number of endangered plants and birds. Elsewhere are many nature
preserves and botanical gardens. Retreat to the seemingly silent
places of Kauai, and sometimes you'll hear the song or catch a flash
of the red or yellow feathers of a rarely seen *'apapane* or *'akialoa*,
two types of Hawaiian honeycreepers.

Even more secluded is barren Ni'ihau, a small privately owned
island in the dry rain shadow of Kauai, and populated by a couple of
hundred people of Hawaiian blood. Life on the island is simple, lacking in the amenities taken for granted elsewhere. Boat and helicopter
tours provide a glimpse of what some call the Forbidden Island. ❏

PRECEDING PAGES: looking for easy fish, Hanalei Bay, on the northern shore.
LEFT: looking for an easier life, Princeville Resort, northern shore.

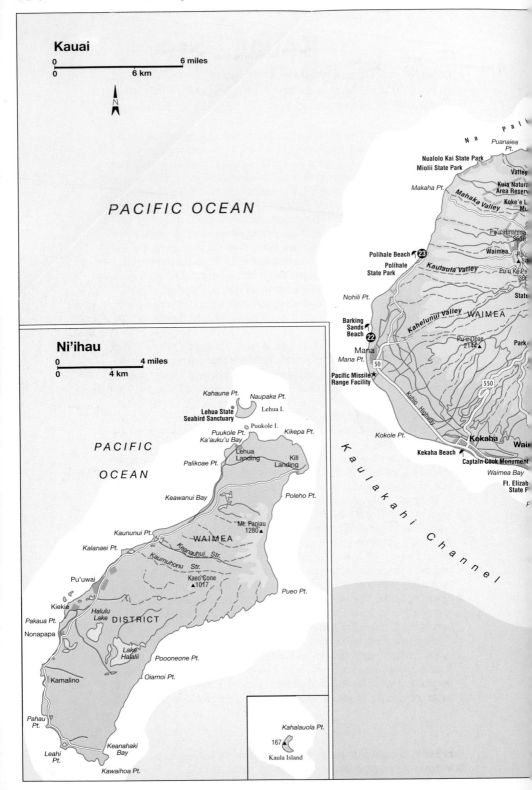

Kauai

0 ___ 6 miles
0 ___ 6 km

N

PACIFIC OCEAN

N a   P a l i
Puanaiea Pt.
Nualolo Kai State Park
Miolii State Park
Makaha Pt.   Mahaka Valley
Valley
Kuia Natura
Area Reser
Koke'e L
Mt.
Pu'u Hinahina
3636
Polihale Beach 23   Waimea   Pu'u
Polihale   Kaufaula Valley   ▲ 84
State Park   Pu'u Ka Pe
36
Nohili Pt.   State
Kahelunui Valley   WAIMEA
Barking
Sands   Pu'u Opae
Beach 22   2144 ▲   Park/
Mana
Mana Pt.   50
Pacific Missile ★
Range Facility   550
Kuhio Highway
Kokole Pt.   Kekaha   Wai
Kekaha Beach ♠   Captain Cook Monument
Waimea Bay
Ft. Elizab
State P

K a u l a k a h i   C h a n n e l

Ni'ihau

0 ___ 4 miles
0 ___ 4 km

PACIFIC
OCEAN

Kahauna Pt.   Naupaka Pt.
Lehua State ●   Lehua I.
Seabird Sanctuary
Puukole I.
Puukole Pt.   Kikepa Pt.
Ka'auku'u Bay
Lehua
Palikoae Pt.   Landing   Kill
Landing
Keawanui Bay
Poleho Pt.
Mt. Paniau
Kaununui Pt.   1280 ▲
WAIMEA
Kalanaei Pt.   Keanauhui Str.
Kaumuhonu Str.
Pu'uwai   Kaeo Cone
▲ 1017
Kiekie   Pueo Pt.
Halulu
Pakaua Pt.   Lake   DISTRICT
Nonapapa
Lake
Halalii
Poooneone Pt.
Kamalino   Oiamoi Pt.

Pahau
Pt.
Leahi   Keanahaki
Pt.   Bay
Kawaihoa Pt.

Kahalauola Pt.
167
Kaula Island

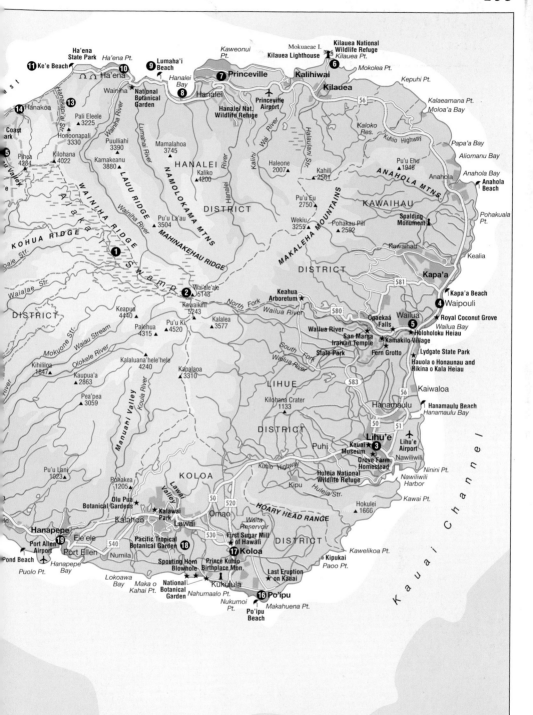

Kaweonui Pt.

Mokuaeae I.
Kilauea National
Wildlife Refuge
Kilauea Lighthouse   Kilauea Pt.

Ha'ena
State Park   Ha'ena Pt.
11 Ke'e Beach   **10**   Ha'ena   **9** Lumaha'i Beach   **7** Princeville   Kalihiwai   Kilauea National
Wildlife Refuge   **6**   Mokolea Pt.   Kepuhi Pt.

Wainiha   ★ National
Botanical
Garden   Hanalei Bay   **8** Hanalei   Kilauea   Kalaeamana Pt.
Moloa'a Bay

13   Hanalei Nat.
Wildlife Refuge   Princeville
Airport   56   Papa'a Bay

14 Hanakoa   Pali Eleele
▲ 3225   Hanalei   Kalihi Wai River   Kaloko
Res.   Kuhio Highway   Aliomanu Bay

Coast
Park   Honoonapali
3330   Puulliahi
3390   Mamalahoa
3745   Haleone
2007▲   Pu'u Ehu
▲ 1946   Anahola   Anahola Bay

15 Pihea
4284   Kilohana
▲ 4022   Kamakeanu
3880▲   HANALEI   Kaliko
▲ 4200   Kahili
▲ 2581   ANAHOLA MTNS.   Anahola
Beach

LAAU RIDGE   Pu'u La'au
▲ 3504   DISTRICT   Pu'u Eu
2750▲   KAWAIHAU   Pohakuala
Pt.

WAINIHA RIDGE   Wainiha River   NAMOLOKAMA MTNS   MAHINAKEHAU RIDGE   Wekiu
3255▲   Pohakau Puli
▲ 2592   Spalding
Monument   Kawaihau

1   Wai'ale'ale
▲ 5148   Keahua
Arboretum   DISTRICT   Kealia

2   Kawaikini
5243   North Fork   Wailua River   580   Ogaekaa
Falls   Wailua   **4** Waipouli
Kapa'a Beach
★ Royal Coconut Grove

DISTRICT   Keapua
4440▲   Kalalea
▲ 3577   South Fork   San Marga
Iraivan Temple   **5**   Wailua Bay
Holoholoku Heiau

Kihililoa
1847▲   Palehua
4315▲   Pu'u Ki
▲ 4520   Kalaluana'hele'hele
4240   Kapalaoa
▲ 3310   Wailua River
State Park   Fern Grotto   Kamakilo Village   ★ Lydgate State Park
Hauola o Honaunau and
Hikina o Kala Heiau

Kaupua'a
▲ 2863   Kilohana Crater
1133   LIHUE   583   Kaiwaloa

Pea'pea
▲ 3059   DISTRICT   Hanamaulu   56   Hanamaulu Beach
Hanamaulu Bay

Pu'u Lani
1023▲   Pohakea
1205▲   Manuani Valley   Koula River   Puhi   50   51   Lihu'e   Lihu'e
Airport

Olu Pua
Botanical Gardens   KOLOA   Lawai
Valley   Kuhio Highway   **3** Kauai
Museum   Nawiliwili

Kalaheo   Kalawai
Park   Kipu   Grove Farm
Homestead   Ninini Pt.

19 Hanapepe   Omao   520   Huleia National
Wildlife Refuge   Huleia Str.   Nawiliwili
Harbor

Port Allen
Airport   Ele'ele   Lawai   Waita
Reservoir   530   HOARY HEAD RANGE   Hokulei
▲ 1666   Kawai Pt.

Pond Beach   Hanapepe
Bay   Pacific Tropical
Botanical Garden   **18**   First Sugar Mill
of Hawai'i   DISTRICT   Kawelikoa Pt.

Puolo Pt.   Numila   **17** Koloa   Kipukai
Paoo Pt.

Lokoawa
Bay   Maka o
Kahai Pt.   Spouting Horn
Blowhole   Prince Kuhio
Birthplace Mon.   Last Eruption
on Kauai

National
Botanical
Garden   Nahumaalo Pt.   Kukulula   **16** Po'ipu   Makahuena Pt.

Nukumoi
Pt.   Po'ipu
Beach

Kauai Channel

KAUAI AND NI'IHAU

 Map, page 294

The most remote of the four main Hawaiian islands, Kauai has a natural beauty and friendly people that define this tropical refuge, which many consider to be Hawaii's most beautiful

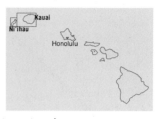

An island of exceptionally lush beauty, Kauai offers high valleys and remote forests and beaches that are an uncrowded refuge for endemic plants and native birds. Of all the islands, Kauai has lost the fewest of its native feathered creatures. At the heart of the nearly circular island of Kauai is a virtual jungle of vegetation and fauna unique in the world, nestled in a narrow bowl that is suspended a mile (1.6 km) high amid thin, jagged ridges that rim deep valleys and canyons. Within this depression is **Alaka'i Swamp ❶**, 10 miles (16 km) long and 2 miles (3 km) wide. It is a sanctuary for endangered species of flora and fauna. But the virgin interior of Kauai is vulnerable to invasions by alien plants and animals.

At the eastern end of the swamp is one of the wettest places on earth, **Wai'ale'ale ❷**, actually the second-highest point on Kauai at 5,148 ft (1,569 meters), exactly in the island's center, where 300–500 inches (760–1,270 cm) of rain falls annually. The highest point is nearby **Kawaikini** at 5,243 ft (1,598 meters). At the northern end are the precipitous ridges and valleys of the wilderness called Na Pali, meaning, literally, the cliffs.

Wet, warm trade winds that gather moisture from the vast Pacific are caught in a funnel over Kauai, formed by the **Anahola Mountains** lying to the northeast and the **Ha'upu Mountains** to the east. The breezes carry the clouds to Wai'ale'ale, where the altitude and the colder temperature make them surrender their moisture. The rains fall all along the slopes leading to Wai'ale'ale and then over the central area of Alaka'i Swamp northwest to Na Pali. By the time the winds reach the south and west sides of the island, they are dry. Thus, while Wai'ale'ale tends to be drenched, resort-filled Po'ipu, on the south east side, gets little more than 12 inches (30 cm) of rain each year. The road that circles most of the island terminates at either end of Na Pali, on the north coast. These isolated, roadless 13 miles (20 km) are flanked by Polihale Beach Park on the west and Ha'ena Beach Park on the north. Most of Na Pali is under state jurisdiction.

Ringing the entire island are beaches with names that roll off the tongue like a Hawaiian chant: Po'ipu, Kalapaki, Hanama'ulu, Waipouli, Kapa'a, Anahola, Kauapea, Lumahai, Ha'ena, Ke'e, Hanakapi'ai, Kalalau. These are only a few of the better-known white-sand beaches. Some are easily accessible, some require hiking, some can be reached only by boat or helicopter, and some require the permission of the owner of an adjacent property to gain access. But as everywhere in the state, all beaches are public and access can't be denied.

Mysterious little people

Theories differ as to how and when Kauai and Ni'ihau, Hawaii's oldest main islands, geologically speaking, were first inhabited. Fables regarding the *menehune,* a group of legendary Polynesian people *(see page 24),* provide fanciful explanations. Like leprechauns, *menehune* were seldom seen, working only after dark. In a single night, they would perform prodigious works, accepting in payment only a single shrimp per worker. Among the construction projects attributed to these pygmies are the Menehune Ditch near Waimea on the leeward coast, which exhibits a knowledge of stonework not seen elsewhere in Hawaii,

It is said that Kauai is one of the planet's wettest places, and the island's countless waterfalls suggest so.

LEFT: Hanalei Valley and Bay.

and the 'Alekoko Fishpond, also called the Menehune Fishpond, near Lihu'e's Nawiliwili Harbor on the southern coast.

Kauai remains a rural island, despite the increasing traffic congestion, and farmers and commerce provide a balance to tourism. Farmers grow taro at Hanalei, Waimea, and a few other places, and papayas and guava orchards are found along the highway between Anahola and Kilauea. Sugar-cane still waves in the trade winds over much of the dry southern and western sections of the island, but the wetter east-side fields are being abandoned. Tropical flowers and crops thrive on small farms, and local fresh produce is often sold in the weekly markets held across the island.

A few large commercial fishing operations remain in business, but the majority of Kauai's fishing is done by individuals with their own small boats who fish on days off from their regular jobs. Some of the commercial fishing docks have been taken over by sport-fishing boats, which take visitors out hunting for deep-sea prizes like marlin, *aku, kawakawa,* and *mahimahi*. But the newest form of fishing on Kauai follows the form of traditional Hawaiian fish ponds. In old Hawaii, large ponds were built along the shoreline to form enclosures in which fish were raised and harvested for eating. On Kauai, the best example of such a pond is a rare one built in a river instead of on the shoreline. The aforementioned 'Alekoko, or Menehune Fishpond, at Lihu'e was built by cutting off an elbow of the Hule'ia River with a stone dam. It is no longer farmed for fish, but it is a much-admired scenic spot. Kayakers, both escorted and on their own, make their way to the Hule'ia Nature Preserve and beyond.

Kauai's people are low-key and guarded about their lives and about the island's more private and especially beautiful places. But that doesn't mean that

TIP

The astounding amount of rainfall makes much of the area surrounding Wai'ale'ale nearly impassable to hikers. Stay on authorized trails – not because you might sink into the boggy ground, but because the ecosystem is fragile.

BELOW: Po'ipu Beach.

ourism is shunted aside. Indeed, Kauai is visited by around 1 million people annually. Some visitors arrive in the morning to climb into tour buses that stop t scenic areas, then leave for Honolulu in the evening. Most spend time becoming acquainted with the island. The primary tourist centers are Kauai Lagoons in Lihu'e, Po'ipu, Kapa'a/Wailua and Princeville/Hanalei.

The island has long attracted escapists – tourists, and travelers of limited resources who make Kauai their home in paradise, lured by Kauai's rugged beauty and langorous pace of life.

In the 1970s, Woodstock-generation drop-outs and wanderers were an established part of the scene, and several communities of transients settled on the island. The best known was Taylor Camp, on the far north side near Ha'ena: the mostly young visitors constructed houses of driftwood, bamboo, and plastic amid the trees. Sixty or more people lived in homes shaded by Java plum trees and flanked by the small, clear Limahuli Stream; their front yard was a magnificent white-sand beach. Taylor Camp took its name from the property's owner, Howard Taylor, the brother of actress Elizabeth Taylor. In the mid 1970s, the state bought the land to expand Ha'ena State Beach Park, but it took years of legal wrangling to move the transients, who claimed squatters' rights. People seeking to escape the pressures of modern life are still to be found here.

Lihu'e

On the island's southeast coast, **Lihu'e** ❸ is the seat of county government, the island's major business district and shopping area, and the site of Kauai's airport. Nearby, **Nawiliwili Harbor**, the island's major port, plays host to a growing number of cruise ships on inter-island and trans-Pacific itineraries.

Map, page 294

BELOW: planting taro, and a beach on the western coast of Kauai.

TIP

If you feel like being really indulgent, Gaylords restaurant offers a "Romantic Dinner" package that includes a bottle of champagne and is preceded by a carriage ride around the estate. For details, e-mail pcarriage@hawaii-antel.net.

BELOW: storefront lure, and Kauai Museum, Lihu'e.

The Lihu'e area is home to the **Kauai Lagoons Resort**, an elegant spread that includes two magnificently scenic golf courses and the Kauai Marriott, a large property featuring a grand classically Roman-style pool, impressive grounds and the sands of Kalapaki Beach, which faces the beautiful Hoary Head mountains and Nawiliwili Harbor.

Since the 1850s Kauai has been a sugar-producing island, and the history of sugar's heyday can be studied at two highly recommended museums in Lihu'e. In the center of town, on Rice Street, **Kauai Museum** (open Mon–Fri 9am–4pm, Sat 10am–4pm; entrance fee; tel: 245-6931) occasionally offers courses in such activities as *lau hala* weaving and *lei*-making. A gallery upstairs frequently displays the work of local artists, and many excellent books and maps may be found in its gift shop. Located off Nawiliwili Road (Hwy 58), also in Lihu'e, is the **Grove Farm Homestead** (Mon, Wed, Thur tours 10am and 1pm; entrance fee; reservations required; tel: 245-3202). For close to a century this was a plantation-owner's home; today it provides insights into the era of plantation agriculture in Hawaii. **Kilohana**, another restored plantation-era home, includes shops, and Gaylords, one of Kauai's best restaurants. You can also take a ride around the grounds in a horse-drawn carriage.

Both museums offer a good introduction to the contributions made by Kauai's elite *kama'aina* (long-time resident) families, with names that become more familiar during one's stay on the island: Rice, Wilcox, Sinclair, Gay, and Robinson. Many had missionary roots but later made their fortunes in sugar and ranching. Some of these *kama'aina*, such as William Harrison Rice and his son, William Hyde Rice, had a strong affinity for the Hawaiian people and their culture, and did a great deal to keep the language and legends alive. Kauai Museum

Map, page 294

vas founded by Rice's progeny, while Grove Farm Homestead was established y George N. Wilcox, whose parents were among the earliest American Protes- ant missionaries to Hawaii; they left a legacy of land and sugar.

The Wilcox holdings comprise some of the largest privately owned land on Kauai, including one of the few remaining plantations in the islands. With the lecline of the sugar industry, Grove Farm has branched into land development, ncluding Kukui Grove, Kauai's largest shopping mall. The Wilcox family also etains extensive holdings on the North Shore and developed a shopping cen- er in Hanalei. The Sinclair-Robinson-Gay clan, which purchased the tiny island of Ni'ihau in 1864, continues to be active in cattle ranching and sugar cultiva- ion. The Robinsons, who manage Ni'ihau, are perhaps the most secretive of he *kama'aina* families.

North from Lihu'e

Along the eastern shore from Lihu'e, sometimes called the Coconut Coast in its ower extent, a string of bays and beaches, resort hotels and condominiums runs rom **Waipouli ❹** to Kapa'a. Kauai legends and oral traditions are among Hawaii's richest. They often concern the activities of *kahuna,* a class of elite professionals, priests, or wise men. In the past decade or so, visible remnants hat embody ancient Hawaiian culture have become popular with travelers, ncluding a large gathering of rocks at **Wailua ❺**, a few hundred yards up Kuamo'o Road toward the mountains and Opaeka'a Falls. Here are the Wailua Golf Course, a municipal 18-hole facility; Wailua Beach; the Wailua River, which carries tour boats to the **Fern Grotto**, a natural though commercialized wedding site; and the modern Coconut Plantation Marketplace.

BELOW: Fern Grotto.

Two stones, a birthstone and a *piko* (navel) stone, make Wailua a sacred place Women of high rank bore their children at the birth stone to ensure their babies would become chiefs, then disposed of the umbilical cord at the *piko* stone, or *pohakuho'ohanau*.

According to widespread legend, the umbilical cords of new-born babies were wrapped up in a cloth and hidden in narrow cracks in the stone, a common practice throughout the islands. They were secreted in this manner because, according to ancient chants, if a rat were to steal away the cord, the child would grow up to be a thief.

Turning inland on Route 53, there's a turnoff for **Kamakilo Village**, where you can visit a reconstructed *hale*, a type of a traditional Hawaiian village house (open 9am–5pm; entrance fee; tel: 823-0559). Continue on past Opaeka'a Falls turning at Kaholalele Road to reach the **San Marga Iraiven Temple**, a Hindu retreat built on acres of lush, rainforested valley. Work is underway on a traditionally built Indian temple. Five tours are offered by warm and welcoming devotee-guides (tel: 822-3012).

Back on Kuhio Highway, heading northward, is the town of **Kapa'a** with a good selection of galleries, shops and restaurants. Next comes **Anahola**, a rural township that includes extensive Hawaiian Homelands beneficiaries. That state-owned program is mandated to providing homestead land for the dispossessed Native Hawaiians.

Further north is the small town of **Kilauea**. Sea birds are protected at the **Kilauea National Wildlife Refuge ➏** (open daily 10am–4pm; entrance fee; tel 828-0383), where visitors can follow trails around the refuge and tour the light house on the point. It was built in 1913 and is a National Historic Landmark

The coastline cliffs at the Kilauea National Wildlife Refuge make excellent breeding grounds for assorted birds.

BELOW: not a golf course, but an open range along Kauai's northern shore.

The lush Princeville area

A few miles beyond is **Princeville ❼**, a 2,000-acre (800-hectare) resort area containing several golf courses and a large clubhouse, airport, shopping center, private houses, several luxurious condominium projects, and the elegant Princeville Hotel. Princeville offers striking views of Hanalei Bay and the sheer mountains at Hanalei, which is one of the wettest and greenest parts of the island. When rain mists the mountains, countless waterfalls hang like strands of silk thread from the dark green cliffs. It was in these lush mountains that films such as *Jurassic Park* and *Raiders of the Lost Ark* were filmed. In the distance, near where the sun sets, is the so-called Bali Hai, a small peak that rises where the mountains enter the ocean. Beginning at Princeville and continuing to the end of the road at Ha'ena are several valleys, each fronted by a curved, white, and sandy beach.

Hanalei Bay ❽, the largest bay on Kauai, is a favorite spot for yachts in summer. In winter, when big surf from the north makes anchorage riskier, the Bay's outer reef provides a challenge for the island's surfers. Sheltered from the open sea, Hanalei is spared the largest surf that crashes against Kauai's north shore. Waves generated by storms in the north Pacific can reach 30 ft (9 meters), although surf of 10–20 ft (3–6 meters) is more common. From fall to spring, the huge waves create clouds of floating sea mist known as *'ehukai* all along the north shore. In late afternoon, the descending sun gives the mist a golden cast.

Beyond Hanalei is an 8-mile (13-km) stretch of scenic coast, a glorious mix of mountains, beaches and sea, renowned as the North Shore. Highlights include the photogenic series of beaches called **Lumaha'i ❾**, where brilliant white sands are interspersed with black-lava rock promontories. The blue of the sea shimmers beyond the sand, and the green of *hala* trees glows behind it. Access

Map, page 294

BELOW: Princeville resort, and Lumaha'i Beach.

to the beach is down a short dirt trail overhung with exotic *hala* trees (also known as *pandanus*). This is the beach where Mitzi Gaynor sang to the world in the movie *South Pacific* that she'd "wash that man right out of my hair." And there's the long stretch of reef-sheltered beach called Bali Hai, another stand-in for *South Pacific* – with good snorkeling as an additional reward.

Lumaha'i Beach, like the rest of Kauai, continues to be known for its dramatic, rich beauty, an attribute that justifiably adds to Kauai's reputation as the most romantic island of all. Botanically speaking, this is Hawaii at its most tropical, with waving palms, hibiscus, plumeria, ginger and a host of other flowers. The **Limahuli** section of the National Tropical Botanical Garden (open Tues–Fri, Sun 9.30am–4pm; entrance fee; tel: 826-1053; www.ntbg.org), 5 miles (8 km) on from Lumaha'i Beach, is dedicated almost entirely to native plants such as these and includes a 900-acre (360-hectare) natural preserve that encompasses much of this striking valley.

The Na Pali Coast

The volcano goddess, Pele, was associated with Kauai long before she established her current home at Kilauea on the Big Island. One story about Pele places her at beautiful **Ha'ena** ⑩, beyond Hanalei Bay and at the end of the road before Na Pali, during a big hula festival. In order to join the dancing, Pele took the form of a beautiful young woman, then fell in love with a handsome Kauai chief, Lohi'au. The remnants of the hula platform can still be found on the hillside, to the west of **Ke'e Beach** ⑪, where the road ends. This is a popular spot that marks the start of **Na Pali Coast** ⑫, perhaps one of the world's most exquisite places. A short oceanside trail leads to the ancient *hula heiau* (temple) plus spectacular scenic

BELOW: harvesting taro.

views. A far longer, 11-mile (18-km) foot trail starts at Ha'ena – there is no vehicular access to Na Pali – then rises on a ridge and drops into lush **Hanakapi'ai** ⑬, which has a lovely pool and waterfall at the back of the valley reached by a 2-mile (3-km) loop trail, and a crescent of white sand at its mouth during the summer months. The ocean here becomes extremely dangerous in winter, and numerous unwary visitors have drowned. Hiking to and from Hanakapi'ai usually takes at least three hours; only head any further if you have a permit to camp overnight *(see below)*.

From Hanakapi'ai, the Na Pali trail zigzags a heart-thumping course upward, scurrying in and out of valleys and across a sheer cliff face to **Hanakoa** ⑭, a "hanging" valley. Like several others here, Hanakoa sweeps from the heights in a flourish of vegetation and ends abruptly, hanging over the ocean, its stream turning into a misty waterfall that falls on the rocks and sea below. A rough trail shelter is well used by hunters at Hanakoa, and from it the jungle-shaded trail wanders out and along the shallow valleys and cliffs until it drops and then ends in **Kalalau Valley** ⑮, the largest of Na Pali's valleys and visible from an overlook in Koke'e.

A once-inhabited valley

Hikers can camp at Kalalau, Hanakoa, and Hanakapi'ai with a permit from the state parks office in Lihu'e. The state maintains portable toilets in Hanakapi'ai and

Kalalau, but there's no safe drinking water. It's advisable to bring some bottled water, if you are able to carry it, but if you plan to use stream water, remember to boil it first, or use purification tablets. There are no cabins and few places to set up a tent along the trail. Kalalau itself offers beachside camping sites.

Kalalau has a stream at one end of the valley mouth and a waterfall at the other joined by a beach. And at the back of Kalalau are fruit trees, creeks, and the remains of ancient house sites and stone-lined taro patches used by Hawaiians who lived here until the early years of the 20th century.

Today there is little to indicate the large numbers of people who once inhab-ited Na Pali's valleys. House platforms, stone walls, irrigation ditches, coffee, taro, and even the trail itself were built and planted by families that settled in what is now a wilderness.

Extensive stonework that formed the taro paddies of Nu'alolo-aina ('aina means fertile land), a hanging valley, and the remains of a fishing village at Nu'alolo-kai (kai means sea) survive. The people of Nu'alolo-aina had access to the sea, while the people of Nu'alolo-kai had little land or fresh water, so each group worked with what it had. They formed a trading relationship, a single community built, of necessity, in two valleys.

In centuries past, the people who lived here maintained the trails, but they are impassable today. A tree trunk that spanned a section of cliff between Honopu and Awa'awapuhi has rotted away, and a ladder that once connected the upper and lower sections of the Nu'alolo-aina and Nu'alolo-kai trail is gone. A hardy hiker can reach Kalalau Valley from Ha'ena in six to eight grueling hours, but you would need a kayak, boat or helicopter to get to the rest of Na Pali's val-leys and beaches.

Map, page 294

BELOW: sugar-cane fields, and making sandcastles, Po'ipu.

Westward from Lihu'e

On Kauai's southernmost point, **Po'ipu** ⓰ is the sunniest of the island's districts. It has several large hotels, plus many smaller hotels and condominiums; all of them face the ocean, some fronting sandy beaches and generally calm waters. There are several scenic spots in the area, such as the **Spouting Horn**, a water spout in the shoreline rocks of an old lava flow, and **Brennecke's Beach**, renowned for its great bodysurfing waves. This portion of the island suffered most from the wrath of 1992's Hurricane 'Iniki. Although many homes, especially those along the coastline leading to Spouting Horn, were destroyed, they have all been rebuilt, as has a visitor center for the National Tropical Botanical Garden.

Japanese immigrant working in a sugar plantation, c. 1910.

The coast westward from Lihu'e, the dry leeward side, might as well be a different island from the opposite side. Little rain falls past Kalahea, with moisture extracted from the air by the heights of Wai'ale'ale in the center of the island.

Kauai's "Hawaiianness" is obvious, but since 1835, when Hawaii's first commercial sugar plantation was started at **Koloa** ⓱, the island's ethnic character has gone through radical changes. As in other parts of Hawaii, sugar attracted a diverse set of people willing to work in its dusty, itchy fields and pungent mills. First came the Chinese, then the Japanese, Portuguese, Puerto Ricans and lastly, the Filipinos. Thus many of Kauai's communities developed as plantation towns, with the different races separated into camps. Koloa is one of these towns, welcoming visitors with rustic charm and a cluster of shops and restaurants. The town also has a monument to its plantation past, a Buddhist temple and several historic churches to add flavor to a visit. Today, many of the sugar firms that started the towns are gone or have merged with other companies, but the communities themselves persist. Waimea, Numila (the Hawaiian pronunciation

BELOW: sugar-cane plantation workers.

of New Mill), Puhi, Kealia, and Kilauea are a few of the towns that have lost the plantations which helped build them. Today, only Gay & Robinson grow sugar, with the company's mill at Makaweli the best on the island.

Map, page 294

Botanical Gardens

The prestigious **National Tropical Botanical Garden** ⓲ (open Mon–Sat 8.30am–5pm; entrance fee, reservations essential; tel: 742-2623; www.ntbg.org) in Lawa'i Valley is a congressionally chartered facility that saves endangered tropical plants, and locates and grows flora of medicinal and economic importance. In recent years, the garden has begun collecting and propagating Hawaii's endemic plants, which are found nowhere else on the planet. The gardens also include **Lawa'i Kai**, the verdant estate of John Gregg Allerton, who willed his estate to the nation upon his death. Lawa'i Kai is a wonderland of vegetation and statuary at the base of Lawa'i, where it meets the sea in a clean, white-sand beach. The estate's lovely gardens and buildings, including Queen Emma's summer home, were devastated by a 30-ft (9-meter) wave generated by Hurricane 'Iniki, but have been restored and re-opened to the public (tours at 9am, 10am, 1pm, 2pm; *see page 304* for details of the Gardens' Limahuli site on the North Shore).

John Gregg and his adoptive father Robert spent many years traveling all over the world, collecting art and botanical species. Robert died in 1964 and John Gregg in 1986.

On the ocean side of sleepy **Hanapepe** ⓳ town, still slightly derelict despite the growing number of galleries, are a group of pre-contact salt ponds that have been worked by local Hawaiian salt gatherers for generations. Here, along the seaside just off Highway 543, members of the Hanapepe Salt Makers Group still gather salt in the old Hawaiian way during the spring and summer months by filling small, mud-lined ponds with sea water and letting the sun cause the water to evaporate, leaving behind heavy salt crystals.

BELOW: an anthurium blooms.

Between Hanapepe and Waimea, just past mile marker 19, ancient monkeypod trees line the nameless road that leads to the Gay & Robinson mill and plantation tour. Kauai's only remaining sugar plantation (one of two left in Hawaii) was founded in 1889. The two-hour commentated tour includes a visit to the mill and canefields (open Mon–Sat, tours at 8.45am and 12.45pm; reservations required; tel: 335-2824; www.robinsonadventures.com). The small visitor center displays artifacts relating to the plantation's long history.

Waimea

The people of old Hawaii took full advantage of the island's often drastic climatic variations. Chiefs sometimes moved their courts from the warmth of leeward **Waimea** ⓴ to cooler Wailua on the east side of the island. When Captain Cook arrived at Waimea in 1778, there were no chiefs in residence. Historians suggest that the *ali'i*, or royalty, were holding court at Wailua on the other side of the island. Cook left Waimea before the chiefs could return to greet him. He eventually found his welcome, and end, on the Big Island.

On the south bank of the Waimea River is the old Russian **Fort Elizabeth** ㉑, now protected as a state park. In 1816, an agent of the Imperial Russian government came to Kauai to recover the cargo of a ship that had broken up on the island's shore. The agent, Dr Anton Sheffer, convinced Kauai's King Kaumuali'i that

Ni'ihau

Across the **Kaulakahi Channel** from Kauai's west side, Ni'ihau rises dimly through sea mists like some slumbering prehistoric creature 17 miles (27 km) away. It is denied rain because it falls in the lee of Kauai, whose mountains collect most of the moisture. The mystique of this windswept, privately owned island, whose estimated 160 residents are seemingly caught in a 19th-century time warp, has been perpetuated by the owner's patriarchal restriction on visitors.

Owned by the Robinson family since 1864, Ni'ihau has been cloaked in myth from the time the first Polynesian explorers came upon the 6- by 18-mile (10- by 29-km) sliver of arid land. Early chants relay that Ni'ihau and its tiny islet neighbors, **Lehua** and **Ka'ula**, were triplet siblings born to the ancestral gods Papa and Wakea.

Another chant postulates that Pele chose Ni'ihau as her first home. Interestingly, many volcanologists now theorize that Ni'ihau was the first of the current Hawaiian islands to break the surface of the ocean. Seventh largest in the chain, its highest point is 1,281 ft (390 meters) above sea level.

Ni'ihau was Captain James Cook's second stop (following Kauai) in the islands during his voyage of exploration in 1778. In 1864, King Kamehameha V sold it to Elizabeth (McHutcheson) Sinclair, widow of a Navy officer who had perished, along with their eldest son, in a shipwreck. Mrs Sinclair saw Ni'ihau lush after two years of abundant rainfall and believed it would make a good ranch home for her remaining five children. For her $10,000, she acquired not only an island, but also the 300 Hawaiians living on it. Today, family heirs Keith and Bruce Robinson manage the ranch and island. They continue to guard the privacy of Ni'ihau's Hawaiian populace to the extent that the island is one of the last true enclaves of a lifestyle that has long since disappeared elsewhere. Life on the island, however, is quite unembellished and without frills.

Ni'ihau is the only island in Hawaii where Hawaiian is the primary language. Today, children attend a grammar school with three classrooms in **Pu'uwai**, the island's only village. Though many homes do not have electricity and most do not have indoor plumbing or telephones, the school has solar-powered computers. Other schools for Ni'ihau's children are on Kauai, where kids go to live with relatives. They must go to Kauai or Oahu to attend high school.

State education officials and tax officers visit the island, and a couple of doctors make infrequent checks on the populace. Otherwise, access is limited to visitors who pay for an expensive helicopter tour (tel: 335-3500) or less costly day-long snorkeling tours to remote ends of the island, which do not allow passengers to set foot on the soil (tel: 335-0815). There are virtually no county services, no county roads, and no sewers. Few people use cars; horses and bicycles are more common.

Nearly all residents still work for the Robinsons, rearing cattle and sheep, making charcoal from *kiawe* trees and gathering honey. Twice a week a barge arrives at Ka'auku'u Bay to carry goods across the sea to market and to deliver mail and other necessities. ❑

LEFT: rare Ni'ihau-shell *lei* are made by Ni'ihau residents, who find the shells on the beach.

Map, page 294

together they could conquer the rest of the islands. Sheffer's Machiavellian bid for Hawaiian power failed miserably, but ruins of the fort, named after Czar Nicholas's queen, remain as a testimonial to Sheffer's adventurism and folly.

Kauai provided its residents with many avenues to the sea, as the island is ringed with sandy beaches. The largest is the stretch of nearly unbroken sand along the western coast, from Waimea stretching northward more than 15 miles (24 km) along Highway 50 through sugar plantations and shorefront property. Along the beach north of Waimea is the Pacific Missile Range Facility at **Barking Sands ㉒**, which remains the site of controversial military testing. At the end of the highway – and the end of this long stretch of sand and former cane-fields – is **Polihale ㉓**. A state park, the beach is Hawaii's longest at over 15 miles (24 km); it is usually empty, and often dramatically draped with the shifts of weather and ocean. Polihale offers campsites and showers; permits are available from the parks office in the state office building in downtown Lihu'e. Hidden in the cliffs at the Na Pali coast end are a couple of *heiau*, or temples. Unless you know exactly what you're looking for, however, you'll not find them. There is no public access trail from here to the looming cliffs of the Na Pali coast.

All along this western coast, the modest rise of **Ni'ihau** breaks the horizon less than 20 miles (32 km) offshore. Because the island sits on the leeward side, in the rain shadow of Kauai, desert-like Ni'ihau receives very little rain.

Barking Sands got its name from the sound made – something like a tired barking dog – when walked upon. The unusual structure of the grains of sand generates the sound.

Waimea Canyon

Back down the coast from Polihale, at both Kekaha and Waimea, roads lead up into the high central regions of the island. Winding upward into the interior is **Waimea Canyon ㉔**. This roseate canyon's headwaters are high in the bogs of the

BELOW: crescent-shaped Lehua and Ni'ihau.

Map,
page 294

Alaka'i Swamp. Waterfalls tumble from here into deep valleys carpeted in green. As the plum- and guava-dotted valleys converge into gorges, a change in flora occurs. The wetness of the swamp is left behind as the vegetation becomes sparse.

Downstream, the *'ohi'a* gives way to *kukui,* the candlenut tree. The gorges meet with the main canyon, and the *kukui* yields to dry country trees: the native *wiliwili* and introduced *kiawe* (mesquite) and *lantana.* The weather lower down is hot and dry, and the streambed holds the only moisture. Red dust blows from barren hillsides; by the time the **Waimea River** meets the sea at Waimea town, its currents carry a heavy suspension of red earth.

The scenery is still elegant and primal, but visitors should arrive early before the mists have cleared, before the rainbows have had time to form and before the caravans of other tourists in rental cars and tour buses gather. For the more experienced hiker, there is the **Kukui Trail**, which drops in a steep, zigzagging course down the side of the remarkable Waimea Canyon.

Koke'e

Just after the second canyon lookout, **Koke'e ㉕** is the only inhabited place in Kauai's higher elevations. There are a dozen state-owned cabins that anyone can rent as long as reservations are made well in advance. The cabins, which are basic and rustic, are managed from **Koke'e Lodge**, which offers facilities including a restaurant, bar, store, and information center. Educational activities are also run from here.

OPPOSITE: Waimea Canyon.
BELOW: water lily.

Next to the lodge is the **Koke'e Museum** (open daily 10am–4pm; donation requested; tel: 335-9975) with displays on the natural history of Kauai and the other islands. Prints and living examples of important plants are exhibited. Maps and guidebooks are also sold here. Located in the state park, the lodge and museum are fronted by a spreading lawn where protected *moa,* or wild Hawaiian chickens, strut.

Activities in the Koke'e area include a casual stroll around the **Iliau Nature Loop,** or if you're in the mood for less strenuous activity, a drive to **Kalalau Valley Lookout ㉖** at the end of the road reveals one of the world's finest views on a clear day: the panorama of Kalalau Valley, the largest valley along the Na Pali Coast.

The view from that 4,000-ft (1,200-meter) high lookout will more than reward the trials of the twisting drive to Koke'e. Low clouds sometimes obscure the view of the valley, but the lookout offers a fine opportunity to see some of Kauai's native birds, such as the red-and-black *'apapane* and vermilion-colored *'i'iwi,* which frequents the *'ohia* tree.

Koke'e also offers some of Hawaii's most magnificent **hiking**. From the Kalalau Lookout, an undulating trail follows the course of a former road along the ridge atop Kalalau Valley to reach further stupendous viewpoints, then plunges inland into the pristine **Alaka'i Swamp**. A round-trip trek of 8 miles (13 km) enables walkers to see remarkable native rainforest, alive with rare and colorful birds, as well as otherworldly high-altitude marshlands where only dwarf species can thrive, and culminates at yet another amazing overlook. Known as Kilohana, this commands long-range views along the North Shore as far as Hanalei Bay and Princeville. ❏

INSIGHT GUIDES

TRAVEL TIPS

HAWAII

TRAVEL TIPS

T RANSPORTATION

GETTING THERE AND GETTING AROUND

GETTING THERE

By Air

Hawaii is regularly serviced from the US mainland, Canada, Europe, the South Pacific and Asia. Arriving aircraft at **Honolulu International Airport** (tel: 808-836 6413; www.honoluluairport.com) on Oahu touch down on a reef runway, completed in 1977 on a shallow reef-lagoon between Honolulu Harbor and Pearl Harbor. The airport's interior is adorned with Hawaiian arts and crafts created by top local artists. (In 1967, a Hawaii legislative act designated one percent of all appropriated public works funds for the purchase of artwork for state buildings, including the airport.) Japanese, Hawaiian and Chinese gardens also enhance the terminal's promenade areas.

Located at the center of the airport's main concourse is the **Pacific Aerospace Museum** (tel: 808-245 2302; open daily 8am–10pm; entrance fee), a 6,500-sq-ft (604-sq-meter), $3.8-million museum that highlights the many aviation and aerospace achievements in Hawaii and the Pacific region. It's a worthwhile visit, especially if you have time to kill while waiting for a flight.

Maui's main airport, **Kahului Airport** (tel: 808-872 3893), handles some direct flights from the US mainland and many inter-island hops. There's a Visitor Information Center, major rental car counters, and taxi and shuttle stands. Maui also has two small airports served by a few local airlines, the **Kapalua-West Maui Airport** (tel: 808-669 0623) and **Hana Airport** (tel: 808-248 8208).

The Big Island has two main airports, **Kona International Airport** at Keahole (tel: 808-329 3423) on the popular west side and **Hilo International Airport** (tel: 808-934 5838) on the outskirts of Hilo.

On Kauai **Lihue Airport** (tel: 808-246 1448) has direct flights daily from San Francisco and Los Angeles on the US mainland, as well as numerous inter-island flights from Honolulu and other neighboring island airports. **Molokai Airport** (tel: tel: 808-567 6361) in south-central Molokai, handles inter-island flights only. The same is true at **Lanai Airport** (tel: 808-565 6757), ten miles from Lanai City. For airport information visit www.hawaii.gov/dot/airports.

If you're traveling on a full-fare round-trip ticket from the US mainland or Canada, inquire about discount tickets that allow travel from Oahu to any of the neighboring islands. Aloha Airlines, Hawaiian Airlines, and Go! are the main inter-island carriers, with commuter airlines Island Air and Pacific Wings linking a number of smaller neighbor island airports. Websites may offer the best fares.

Trans-Pacific Airlines

Air New Zealand
Tel: 800-262 1234
www.airnz.co.nz
Aloha Airlines
Tel: 800-367 5250
www.alohaair.com
American Airlines
Tel: 800-433 7300
www.aa.com
Continental Airlines
Tel: 800-523 3273
www.continental.com
Delta Airlines
Tel: 800-221 1212
www.delta.com
Hawaiian Airlines
Tel: 800-367 5320
www.hawaiianair.com
Japan Airlines
Tel: 521-1441
www.jal.com
Korean Air Lines
Tel: 926-8000 or 800-438 5000
www.koreanair.com
Northwest Airlines
Tel: 800-225 2525
www.nwa.com
Philippine Airlines
Tel: 800-435 9725
www.philippineairlines.com
Pleasant Hawaiian Holidays
(via American Trans Air)
Tel: 800-242 9244
www.pleasantholidays.com
Qantas Airways
Tel: 836-2461 or 800-227 4500

Distances from Honolulu		
	Miles	**Km**
Hilo	214	344
Kailua-Kona	168	270
Kahului, Maui	98	158
Lanai	72	116
Molokai	54	87
Lihu'e, Kauai	103	166
Midway Is.	1,309	2,106
Kure Atoll	1,367	2,200
Anchorage	2,781	4,475
Auckland	4,393	7,068
Equator	1,470	2,352
Hong Kong	5,541	8,915
London	7,226	11,627
Los Angeles	2,557	4,114
Manila	5,293	8,516
New York	4,959	7,979
North Pole	4,740	7,631
San Francisco	2,397	3,857
Papeete, Tahiti	2,741	4,410
Tokyo	3,847	6,190
Vancouver	2,709	4,359

www.qantas.com
United Airlines
Tel: 800-864 8331
www.united.com

Leaving the Airport

A yellow-brown-and-orange striped bus – **TheBus** (www.thebus.org) – departs frequently from Honolulu Airport to Waikiki via Downtown and Ala Moana Shopping Center where you can transfer to other buses. Exact change (currently $2) is required.

Baggage restrictions apply and passengers are limited to one carry-on bag small enough to be held on the lap or placed under the seat. No exceptions. If you have more than a small carry-on piece of luggage, forget the bus – you'll have to take a taxi into Waikiki and pick up a rental car from there, if you need one. Alternatively, you can rent cars from the airport, although the busy 20–30 minute drive into town can be tiring. Advance reservations are recommended for car hire.

By Sea

Numerous cruise ships including **Crystal Cruises** (www.crystalcruises.com), **Princess Cruises** (www.princess.com) and **Royal Caribbean** (www.royalcaribbean.com) now make Hawaii a port-of-call, stopping in Honolulu as well as the neighbor islands as part of their itinerary. A few lucky souls, of course, arrive by private yacht.

BELOW: traveling in style.

GETTING AROUND

Island Hopping

By Sea

For seafaring types, **Norwegian Cruise Line** (tel: 866-234 0392; www.ncl.com) offers weekly seven-day cruises that depart Honolulu for Kauai, Maui and the Big Island. Tours, in-port activities and rental cars are all optional.

For the latest information on whether the long-promised high-speed Hawaii Superferry service from Oahu to Maui and Kauai has finally started (its initial operations in 2007 were halted by court challenges) access www.hawaiisuperferry.com. The Maui Lanai ferry (www.go-lanai.com) makes daily runs from Lahaina on Maui to Lanai and Molokai.

By Air

Flights between islands are frequent, every half hour or hour. There are two primary carriers, **Aloha** and **Hawaiian Airlines**, using jets between all major airports.

A new arrival, **Go!**, is offering discounted fares on the same routes. In addition, **Aloha Island Air**, a subsidiary of Aloha Airlines, uses small prop craft to smaller airports like Princeville on Kauai. There are also fixed-wing and

helicopter flights for inter-island travel.

With the exception of morning and late afternoon commuter times, when local workers and business-people are returning to their home islands, you can usually get a seat at short notice. If one flight is full, there is another flight in about 30 minutes to an hour. However, weekends and holidays are busy times; reserve ahead if possible. Inter-island flights are short, from 20 to 45 minutes, depending on the route.

Both Aloha and Hawaiian Airlines offer hotel and rental car deals with their flights, again often on very short notice. The first couple of early-morning flights and the last couple of flights at night are sometimes also discounted.

Inter-Island Airlines

Aloha Airlines
Oahu, tel: 484-1111.
Maui, tel: 244-9071.
Big Island, tel: 935-5771.
Kauai, tel: 245-3691.
Toll free from the US mainland, tel: 800-367 5250.
www.alohaairlines.com
Go!
Toll-free tel: 888-435 9462.
www.iflygo.com
Island Air
Oahu, tel: 484-2222.
Toll-free from neighbor islands, tel: 800-652 6541.
Toll-free from US mainland, tel: 800-323 3345.
www.islandair.com

Hawaiian Airlines
Oahu, tel: 898-1555.
Toll-free from neighbor islands,
tel: 800-882 8811.
Toll free from US mainland,
tel: 800-367 5320.
www.hawaiianair.com
Pacific Wings
Oahu, tel: 833-4324.
Toll-free tel: 888-575 4546.
www.pacificwings.com

Public Transportation

By Bus

Oahu is the only Hawaiian island with a mass transit system. (On the neighboring islands, bus transportation, other than tour buses, is not an available option.) With more than 65 routes that cover the entire island, **TheBus** system is a convenient and affordable way to get around. TheBus Gazebo is at Ala Moana Center, and the staff here are very helpful. The open-air **Waikiki Trolley** leaves from the Hawaiian Shopping Center every 20 minutes from 8.30am–6.30pm and makes stops at visitor attractions including the Waikiki Aquarium, Iolani Palace and Bishop Museum.

Multi-day passes, which are available at the ubiquitous ABC stores, are recommended if you are likely to use TheBus to get around. Up-to-date maps and bus schedules are available free of charge.

Orientation

Local folks share a common vernacular for directions, which has nothing to do with cardinal directions or where the sun rises and sets. Rather, it deals with *local* geographical features.

The two most common directional terms are *mauka* ("upland" or "towards the mountain") and *makai* ("towards the sea"). In Honolulu, directions are also given in relation to *'Ewa*, a plantation town just west of Pearl Harbor, and to *Diamond Head*, the famous landmark to the east side of Waikiki. Those four orientations – *mauka, makai, 'Ewa* and *Diamond Head* – are regularly used among residents. Say north, south, east or west and you'll receive looks of bewilderment.

Printed schedules are also available at all satellite City Halls on Oahu.

Customer service, tel: 848-4500.
www.thebus.org
Schedule and route information, tel: 848-5555.
24-hour recorded information, includes information on attractions accessible by TheBus, tel: 296-1818 (then enter 8287).

Lost and found/bus pass, tel: 848-4445.

By Taxi

Although a taxi service is available on all islands, if you are traveling beyond local destinations it generally becomes cheaper to rent a car. All taxis are metered, although most are available for sightseeing at a fixed rate. Honolulu, of course, has the most taxis, but don't expect to flag one down on the street. If a taxi is required, go to a nearby hotel. Elsewhere on Oahu, call one of the companies listed below or check the yellow pages under the heading "Taxicabs."

Aloha State Cab, tel: 847-3566.
Charley's Taxi, tel: 531-1333.
Sida Taxi, tel: 836-0011.

Car Rental

Everywhere except Honolulu and Waikiki, renting a car is all but essential for visitors to Hawaii. The major rental companies have 24-hour counters at most airports. Book in advance for the best deals. Drivers generally are required to be 25 years or older, have a valid driver's license and a major credit card. Car rental agencies in Hawaii include:
Alamo tel: 800-462 5266; www.alamo.com
Avis tel: 800-230 4898; www.avis.com
Budget tel: 800-527 0700; www.budget.com
Dollar tel: 800-800 3665; www.dollar.com
Enterprise Rent-a-Car tel: 800-261 7331; www.enterprise.com
Hertz tel: 800-654 3131; www.hertz.com
National tel: 800-CAR RENT; www.nationalcar.com
Thrifty tel: 800-847 4389; www.thrifty.com

Driving

Driving in Hawaii is much like driving on the US mainland (right side of road). All passengers must wear seatbelts and infants must be strapped into car seats. Pedestrians, whether in a crosswalk or not, always have the right of way. Most roads are paved; highways are well maintained; signs are in English and/or international symbols; speed limits and distance are indicated almost exclusively in miles and miles-per-hour. One unnerving rule is that drivers can turn right from the right lane on a red light if there is no oncoming traffic (unless a sign forbids the turn).

BELOW: a North Shore road sign points the way.

HOTELS, YOUTH HOSTELS, BED & BREAKFAST

CHOOSING A HOTEL

Hawaii abounds in accommodations of every persuasion. There are several types of places to stay: hotels (including small, classy inns), rental condominiums, bed-and-breakfasts, hostels and campsites.

Many of the international luxury hotel chains have resorts in Hawaii. If you can afford them, you'll probably know what you're looking for. But for those on a budget or wanting to visit on an extended stay, the multitudinous offerings of economical and mid-range hotels can be intimidating.

Many hotels and condominiums are part of larger chains with universally high standards. Season and location determine price – off-beach and on-beach differences can be substantial. Hotel and condo specials abound, either direct to the property or via wholesalers. The best prices may be offered on-line.

If you are particular about the exact location of your accommodation, you should either confirm the location with the property or call the reservations company. Be aware that mailing addresses sometimes don't reflect the true location of a hotel or condominium. Lahaina, for example, is often the mailing post office for places across West Maui.

Hotel Companies

ResortQuest Hawaii
Tel: 866-774 2924
Toll free: 877-997 6667
www.resortquesthawaii.com
Well-priced hotels and rentals on all the major islands.
Castle Resorts & Hotels
Tel: 545-3510

Toll free: 800-367 5004
www.castleresorts.com
Hilton
2155 Kalia Road, Honolulu, HI 96816
Tel: 800-445-8667
www.hilton.com
With Waikiki's largest hotel (Hilton Hawaiian Village) and the Hilton Waikoloa on the Big Island.
Marc Resorts Hawaii
2155 Kalakaua Avenue, Suite 318, Honolulu, HI 96815
Tel: 922-9700
Toll free: 800-535 0085
www.marcresorts.com
Marriott
Tel: 888-236 2427
www.marriott.com
Resorts and timeshares on all the main islands.
Outrigger/Ohana Hotels & Resorts
Tel: 303-369 7777
Outrigger toll free: 800-688 7444
Ohana toll free: 800-462 6262
www.outrigger.com
www.ohanahotels.com
Starwood Hotels & Resorts
This, the world's largest hotelier, owns the Sheraton, Westin, Luxury Collection and W-Hotel brands in Hawaii.
Tel: 800-325 3535
www.sheraton.com

Bed & Breakfast

Bed-and-breakfast places have caught on in Hawaii. There is little regulation of B&Bs, so standards do vary, but they are are generally good. The reservation companies listed below book for most of the islands.
Affordable Paradise Bed & Breakfast
Tel: 261-1693
www.affordable-paradise.com

All Islands Bed & Breakfast
463 'Iliwahi Loop, Kailua, HI 96734-1837
Tel: 263-2342
Toll free: 800-542 0344
www.all-islands.com
Bed & Breakfast Hawaii
PO Box 449, Kapa'a, HI 96746
Tel: 822-7771
Toll free: 800-733 1632
www.bandb-hawaii.com
Bed & Breakfast Honolulu
3242 Ka'ohinani Drive, Honolulu, HI 96817
Tel: 595-7533
Toll free: 800-288 4666
www.hawaiibnb.com
Hawaiian Islands Bed & Breakfast and Vacation Rentals
1277 Mokulua Drive, Kailua, HI 96734
Tel: 261-7895
Toll free: 800-258 7895
www.lanikaibeachrentals.com
Hawaii's Best Bed & Breakfasts
574 Pauku St, Kailua, HI 96734
Tel: 263-3100
Toll free: 800-262 9912
www.bestbnb.com

Hotels and Condos

The following listings are not comprehensive and they do not carry endorsements. An establishment not listed – especially in bed-and-breakfasts and rental condominiums – could be just as satisfactory as those listed. For travelers wanting a more inclusive and comprehensive listing, telephone the **Hawaii Visitors Bureau** on 923-1811 for a current *Accommodations and Car Rentals* guide or visit www.gohawaii.com.

Notes on Room Rates
Nobody pays a full rack rate in Hawaii. Prices fluctuate with the

season and type of accommodation. An individual hotel can have rooms ranging from $100 to $1,000.

Our pricing notations – $ (budget) to $$$$$ (luxurious) – are intended only as a relative guide of a hotel's cost compared to others. Bargains, discounts, packages and seasonal deals abound and should be pursued through travel agents, airlines or brokers.

CAMPING

Campsites are run by the National Park Service, the State of Hawaii, and the four island counties. Plan outings ahead of time, as campsites are usually very popular.

Haleakala National Park, Maui

Haleakala National Park
PO Box 369, Makawao, HI 96768
Tel: 572-4400; Kipahulu: 248-7375;
www.nps.gov/hale
Island-wide weather forecasts
Tel: 877-5111
There is one drive-in campground near the summit, and one in Kipahulu, at 'Ohe'o Pools near Hana. For Hosmer Grove, near the summit, permits are required and are issued on arrival at the park. Sites are first-come, first-served. In Haleakala basin itself, there are three cabins available, accessible by hiking and assigned by lottery reservations. Book three months in advance.

Hawaii Volcanoes National Park, Big Island

Hawaii Volcanoes National Park
PO Box 52, Hawaii Volcanoes National Park, HI 96718
Tel: 985-6000
www.nps.gov/havo
There are two campgrounds. Permits are not required, as the sites run on a first-come, first-served basis. There are also rustic camper cabins available at the Namakani Paio campground; payment should be made at the Volcano House hotel in the park. Bedding provided.

State Parks

There are more than 60 state parks throughout Hawaii. Some are well developed, others primitive; many are true gems. Permits are required.
Camping permits, tel: 587-0300.
Hiking, tel: 587-0166.
Fishing licenses, tel: 587-0109.
www.hawaii.gov/dlnr

Regional Offices

Oahu
Department of Land and Natural Resources, Division of State Parks, 1151 Punchbowl, Honolulu, HI 96813
Tel: 587-0300.
Maui (includes Molokai)
Department of Land and Natural Resources, Division of State Parks, 54 High Street, Wailuku, HI 96793
Tel: 984-8109.
Big Island
Department of Land and Natural Resources, Division of State Parks,

PO Box 936, Hilo, HI 96720
Tel: 974-6200.
Kauai
Department of Land and Natural Resources, Division of State Parks, 3060 Eiwa, #306, Lihu'e, HI 96766
Tel: 274-3444; Koke'e State Park (cabins), Manager, Koke'e Lodge, PO Box 819, Waimea, HI 96796
Tel: 335-8405.

County Parks

Honolulu/Oahu
Department of Parks and Recreation, 650 S. King Street, Honolulu, HI 96813
Tel: 523-4525.
13 beach parks, tent and vehicle camping. Permits required, no fee.
Maui (including Molokai)
Department of Parks and Recreation, 1580 Ka'ahumanu Avenue, Wailuku, HI 96793
Tel: 270-7389.
Two county beach parks. Permits and fees are required. On Molokai: seven parks, permits and fees are required.
Hawaii (Big Island)
Department of Parks and Recreation, 25 Aupuni Street, Hilo, HI 96720
Tel: 961-8311.
13 county beach parks and 10 campsites. Both permits and fees are required.
Kauai
Department of Parks and Recreation, 4444 Rice, Suite 150, Lihu'e, HI 96766
Tel: 241-6660.
Seven county parks, both beach and inland. Permits and fees required.

BELOW: the unmistakeable pink facade of the Royal Hawaiian Hotel, Honolulu.

OAHU

HOTELS

$$$$$

Halekulani
2199 Kalia Road, Honolulu,
HI 96815-1988
Tel: 923-2311
Toll free: 800-367 2343
www.halekulani.com
Centrally located on Waikiki Beach, quiet, crisply elegant, chic and expensive, with stress on personalized service; 456 rooms, fitness center, large pool and beach services.

Hawaii Prince Hotel
100 Holomoana Street, Honolulu,
HI 96815
Tel: 956-1111
Toll free: 888-977 4623
www.princeresortshawaii.com
Luxury hotel overlooking Ala Wai Yacht Harbor. Within walking distance of Ala Moana Center. 521 rooms, most with ocean views, in two towers. Gourmet American and Japanese dining; don't miss the great buffets.

Hyatt Regency Waikiki
2424 Kalakaua Avenue, Honolulu,
HI 96815
Tel: 923-1234
Toll free: 866-333 8881
www.hyatt.com
Centrally located just across the street from Waikiki Beach. Large, 1,230-room hotel takes up an entire block along Waikiki's main street. Expansive lobby and shopping area.

J.W. Marriott 'Ihilani Resort & Spa
92-1001 Olani Street, Kapolei,
HI 96707
Tel: 679-0079
Toll free: 800-626 4446
www.ihilani.com
Located in West Oahu at Ko Olina Resort, about a 30-minute drive from Honolulu International Airport. 'Ihilani has 387 rooms. Spa placed third among world's best, according to *Condé Nast Traveller*. Area is quiet with a beach and lagoons adjacent to the hotel, and 36 holes of golf. Spacious rooms with private roofed verandas.

Kahala Hotel & Resort
5000 Kahala Avenue, Honolulu,
HI 96816
Tel: 739-8888
Toll free: 800-367 2525
www.kahalaresort.com
This 370-room hotel (formerly the Kahala Mandarin) is a 10-minute drive east of Waikiki. Tucked away in the upscale residential area of Wai'alae-Kahala, it is especially valued for its secluded oceanfront location away from Waikiki. The dolphin lagoon is home to Atlantic bottlenose dolphins and tropical fish.

'Ilikai Renaissance Waikiki Hotel
1777 Ala Moana Boulevard, Honolulu, HI 96815
Tel: 949-3811
Toll free: 800-245 4524
www.ilikaihotel.com
A 10-minute walk from Ala Moana Shopping Center, on the outskirts of Waikiki. Overlooks the Ala Wai Yacht Harbor. The complex includes hotel rooms and condominium rentals. Its tennis courts and golf practice range are unique for Waikiki. Many dining options in and around the hotel.

Moana Surfrider
2365 Kalakaua Avenue, Honolulu,
HI 96815
Tel: 922-3111
Toll free: 866-716 8109
Built in 1901; still retains its nostalgic, early 20th-century ambiance and first-class service. Enjoy tea-time on the veranda surrounding a huge banyan tree.

Royal Hawaiian Hotel
2259 Kalakaua Avenue, Honolulu,
HI 96815
Tel: 923-7311
Toll free: 866-716 8109
www.royal-hawaiian.com
The "Pink Palace of the Pacific" is a landmark on Waikiki Beach with its familiar coral-pink stucco and Moorish-Spanish design. "Old Hawaii" ambiance. Home of Waikiki's twice-weekly beachfront *lu'au* (traditional feast), it offers great Diamond Head views and is steps away from Waikiki's shops.

Sheraton Waikiki
2255 Kalakaua Avenue, Honolulu,
HI 96815
Tel: 922-4422
Toll free: 866-716 8109
www.sheraton-waikiki.com
Large hotel with 1,852 rooms, many with perfect Diamond Head views. Take the glass elevator to the Hanohano Room for fine dining and spectacular views of Waikiki. Lovely beachfront location.

W Honolulu-Diamond Head Hotel
2885 Kalakaua Avenue, Honolulu,
HI 96815
Tel: 922 1700
Toll free: 877-945 8357
www.whotels.com
A 50-room hotel situated on the oceanside border of Kapiolani Park. Elegant and in a quiet setting; a short walk from central Waikiki. The service is first rate and personal; the rooms are nicely decorated.

$$$$

Hilton Hawaiian Village
2005 Kalia Road, Honolulu,
HI 96815
Tel: 949-4321
Toll free: 800-hiltons
www.hawaiianvillage.hilton.com
Largest hotel in Hawaii with 3,400 rooms in five towers. Landscaped gardens and ponds are home to exotic birds and fish. There are several pools and a free hula show. Also includes a shopping mall with designer boutiques. Friday night fireworks.

New Otani Kaimana Beach Hotel
2863 Kalakaua Avenue, Honolulu,
HI 96815
Tel: 923-1555
Toll free: 800-356 8264
www.kaimana.com
Oceanfront on Sans Souci Beach, at the foot of Diamond Head in Waikiki. Relatively small with just 125 rooms. Hau Tree Lanai restaurant has stunning ocean and sunset view. Close to Kapi'olani Park, Waikiki Aquarium and Honolulu Zoo.

Outrigger Waikiki On The Beach
2335 Kalakaua Avenue, Honolulu,
HI 96815
Tel: 923-0711
Toll free: 800-688 7444
www.outrigger.com
Located on the beach at Waikiki. This 530-room hotel is the best known of the Outriggers on Oahu. The 600-seat showroom features the Society of Seven, a popular local band. Check out the good food and contemporary Hawaiian music at Duke's Canoe Club.

Pacific Beach Hotel
2490 Kalakaua Avenue, Honolulu,
HI 96815
Tel: 923-4511
Toll free: 800-367 6060
www.pacificbeachhotel.com
Two towers with 831 rooms. Located in Waikiki, across from the beach. The centerpiece is a spectacular 3-story, 280,000-gallon indoor oceanarium tank filled with stingrays, angel fish and other marine life, which is visible from the hotel's three restaurants.

Turtle Bay Resort
57-091 Kamehameha Highway,

PRICE CATEGORIES

$ = below US$50
$$ = US$50–100
$$$ = US$100–150
$$$$ = US$150–200
$$$$$ = US$200 and up
Substantially discounted rates are common, with the best deals often found on websites.

Kahuku, HI 96731
Tel: 293-6000
Toll free: 800-203 3650
www.turtlebayresort.com
Located on the North Shore of Oahu. This relaxing and quiet 485-room hotel with suites and cottages has many activities to choose from including golf, tennis, horseback riding. Great surfing spots nearby.

Waikiki Beach Marriott Resort
2552 Kalakaua Avenue, Honolulu, HI 96815
Tel: 922-6611
Toll free: 800-367 5370
www.marriottwaikiki.com
Across the street from Waikiki Beach. Large complex with 1,346 rooms and a mall of shops.

Waikiki Parc Hotel
2233 Helumoa Road, Honolulu, HI 96815
Tel: 921-7272
Toll free: 800-422 0450
www.waikikiparc.com
Relatively small for a Waikiki hotel with 298 rooms. Affordable sister hotel to Halekulani, which is located across the street on Waikiki Beach.

$$$

Ala Moana Hotel
410 Atkinson Drive, Honolulu, HI 96814
Tel: 955-4811
Toll free: 800-367 6025
www.alamoanahotel.com
Conveniently located next to Ala Moana Center, one

of the largest open-air shopping malls in the world. Approximately a five-minute drive from Waikiki. Ala Moana Beach Park is just one block away.

Ohana Islander Waikiki
270 Lewers Street, Honolulu, Hawaii, HI 96815
Tel: 923-7711
Toll free: 800-688 7444
www.ohanahotels.com
A very convenient and well-priced hotel located within an elevator-ride of shops and restaurants.

Ohana Waikiki Beachcomber Hotel
2300 Kalakaua Avenue, Honolulu, HI 96815
Tel: 922-4646
Toll free: 800-462 6262
www.ohanahotels.com
Great central location. Shopping at International Marketplace and Royal Hawaiian Shopping Center nearby. Home of the legendary Don Ho show.

Park Shore Waikiki
2586 Kalakaua Ave, Honolulu, HI 96815
Tel: 923-0411
Toll free: 866-282 4773
www.parkshorewaikiki.com
Across Kapahulu Avenue from Kapi'olani Park and a half-block from the beach; a quiet setting for this 227-room hotel.

Queen Kapi'olani Hotel
150 Kapahulu Avenue, Honolulu, HI 96815
Tel: 922-1941
Toll free: 800-367 2317
www.queenkapiolani.com

This 315-room hotel is located at the Diamond Head end of Waikiki. Across the street is Kapi'olani Park and the Honolulu Zoo. Within walking distance of Waikiki Beach.

Royal Garden at Waikiki
440 Olohana Street, Honolulu, HI 96815
Tel: 943-0202
Toll free: 800-367 5666
www.royalgardens.com
Located several blocks *mauka* of Waikiki Beach. Elegant surroundings and friendly staff. Mediterranean and Japanese dining available.

$$

Best Western Plaza Airport Hotel
3253 N. Nimitz Highway, Honolulu, HI 96819
Tel: 836-3636
Toll free: 800-800 4683
www.bestwesternhonolulu.com
A 274-room hotel near the Honolulu International Airport. Primarily used by business travelers, and visitors with late-night or early-morning flights.

Manoa Valley Inn
2001 Vancouver Drive, Honolulu, HI 96822
Tel: 947-6019
www.manoavalleyinn.com
Eight-room country-style inn. Located in a residential neighborhood, close to the University of Hawaii at Manoa. Built in 1912 and listed in the National

Register of Historic Places.

Pagoda Hotel & Terrace
1525 Rycroft Street, Honolulu, HI 96814
Tel: 941-6611
Toll free: 800-367 6060
www.pagodahotel.com
A 362-room hotel with affordable rates. Very popular with residents traveling inter-island. A five-minute drive from Ala Moana Center, it is set amidst high-rise apartment buildings and strip malls.

ResortQuest Waikiki Joy Hotel
320 Lewers Street, Honolulu, HI 96815
Tel: 923-2300
Toll free: 877-997 6667
www.resortquesthawaii.com
This 93-room boutique hotel is located on a side street in Waikiki. Karaoke studio; shops, restaurants and movie theater nearby.

CONDOMINIUMS

$$$$$

Castle Waikiki Shore
2161 Kalia Road, Honolulu, HI 96815
Tel: 952-4500
Toll free: 800-367 5004
www.castleresorts.com
The only condominium resort located on Waikiki Beach. Roomy studios fitted with air-conditioning.

ResortQuest Waikiki Beach Tower
2470 Kalakaua Avenue, Honolulu, HI 96815
Tel: 926-6400
Toll free: 877-997 6667
www.resortquesthawaii.com
Luxurious and spacious 140-suite hotel with four suites per floor. Paddle tennis court on property.

$$$

ResortQuest at the Waikiki Banyan
201 'Ohua Avenue, Honolulu, HI 96815
Tel: 922-0555
Toll free: 877-997 6667
www.resortquesthawaii.com
Located on Diamond Head side of Waikiki. Children's playground, tennis courts and barbecue area.

BELOW: Turtle Bay Resort, Kahuku.

MAUI

HOTELS

$$$$$

Fairmont Kea Lani Maui
4100 Wailea Alanui Drive, Wailea,
HI 96753
Tel: 875-4100
Toll free: 800-257 7544
www.fairmont.com/kealani
Oceanside in Wailea. A
450-suite luxury resort with
striking Moorish design.
Beautiful landscaping,
spacious suites and villas.

Four Seasons Wailea
3900 Wailea Alanui, Wailea,
HI 96753
Tel: 874-8000
Toll free: 800-334 6284
www.fourseasons.com/maui
Located in Wailea on one of
the most beautiful beaches
in Maui. Most rooms have
ocean views. Elegant
furnishings. Tranquil
surroundings with gardens,
waterfalls, fountains and
pools.

Grand Wailea Resort
3850 Wailea Alanui Drive, Wailea,
HI 96753
Tel: 875-1234
Toll free: 800-888 6100
www.grandwailea.com
With 737 ocean-view suites
and a 2,000-ft (610-meter)
water feature with slides,
waterfalls, caves and
grottoes. The Spa Grande
at the Grand Wailea is one
of the largest hotel spas in
the nation with water
therapies, *lomi lomi*
massage (traditional
Hawaiian) and various other
beauty and body
treatments.

Hotel Hana-Maui
PO Box 9, Hana, HI 96713
Tel: 248-8211
Toll free: 800-321 4262
www.hotelhanamaui.com
Intimate, casually elegant
and upscale 96-unit hotel
with a magnificent
oceanfront setting and a
hometown-friendly staff.

Hyatt Regency Maui
200 Nohea Kai Drive, Ka'anapali,
HI 96761
Tel: 661-1234
Toll free: 800-554 9258
http://mauihyatt.com
An 815-room oceanfront

resort in Ka'anapali.
Collection of exotic and
tropical birds and penguins.
Spectacular "Drums of the
Pacific" *lu'au* (traditional
feast).

Maui Prince Hotel
5400 Makena Alanui, Makena,
HI 96753
Tel: 874-1111
Toll free: 888-977 4623
www.mauiprince.com
Located near Makena
Beach, south of Wailea. Set
apart from the other
resorts in Kihei. Scenic
views of neighboring
islands.

Napili Kai Beach Resort
5900 Lower Honoapi'ilani Rd,
Napili, HI 96761
Tel: 669-6271
Toll free: 800-367 5030
www.napilikai.com
Old-fashioned family hotel
beside the beach at lovely
Napili Bay, north of
Ka'anapali in West Maui.
While upgraded to a high
standard, it still offers
lower rates and a more
intimate atmosphere than
the giant resorts.

Ritz-Carlton Kapalua
One Ritz-Carlton Drive, Kapalua,
HI 96761
Tel: 669-6200
Toll free: 800-241-3333
www.ritzcarlton.com
This lush 37-acre (15-
hectare) resort on Maui's
northwest shore has
548 rooms with spacious
lanais (balconies). With
a 143-seat amphitheater,
large air-conditioned fitness
center and spa. Hiking
and nature programs
available to guests on
request.

$$$$

Diamond Resort
555 Kaūkahi Street, Wailea,
HI 96753
Tel: 874-0500
Toll free: 800-800 0720
www.diamondresort.com
This resort is nestled on
the slopes of Haleakala
and has panoramic views
of Wailea beaches,
Haleakala and Wailea golf
courses. There are 72 one-
bedroom suites in 18 two-
story buildings, and the

entire area is quiet and
secluded.

Ka'anapali Beach Hotel
2525 Ka'anapali Parkway, Lahaina,
HI 96761
Tel: 661-0011
Toll free: 800-262 8450
www.kbhmaui.com
The least upscale of
Ka'anapali's hotels, it
enjoys a prime beachfront
location and a homey feel
that's a plus. This 423-
room hotel offers com-
fortable rooms with *lanais*
(balconies). Hawaiian arts
and crafts classes and
demonstrations.

**Marriott's Maui Ocean
Club**
100 Nohea Kai Drive, Lahaina,
HI 96761
Tel: 667-1200
Toll free: 800-845 5279
www.marriott.com
720 units with large rooms,
located in Lahaina. Tropical
gardens, *koi* ponds,
fountains and waterfalls.
Tennis courts and beach
activities.

Outrigger Palms at Wailea
3700 Wailea Alanui, Wailea,
HI 96753
Tel: 879-1922
Toll free: 888-294 7731
www.outrigger.com
Located oceanfront at
Wailea. Spacious rooms
with private *lanais*
(balconies). Grounds
contain lush, tropical
foliage.

Renaissance Wailea Beach
3550 Wailea Alanui Drive, Wailea,
HI 96753
Tel: 879-4900
Toll free: 800-992 4532
www.renaissancehotels.com
Luxury hotel on pristine
Mokapu Beach in Wailea
with a tropical, airy feel.
Elegant 347-room resort.
Many recreational
amenities including fitness
center, two fresh-water
swimming pools, basketball
court, shuffle board (point-
scoring Hawaiian game),
ping pong and beach
activity center. There are
tennis and golf facilities
located nearby.

Sheraton Maui Resort
2605 Ka'anapali Parkway, Lahaina,
HI 96761
Tel: 661-0031

Toll free: 866-716-8109
www.sheraton-maui.com
Opened in 1963 as
Ka'anapali's first resort,
and entirely rebuilt in
1996. Low-rise buildings
with 492 guest rooms in an
expansive garden setting.
There's a large pool area
and a torchlighting and cliff
diving ceremony. It's within
walking distance of Whalers
Village Shopping Center.

Westin Maui
2365 Ka'anapali Parkway, Lahaina,
HI 96761
Tel: 667-2525
Toll free: 866-716 8112
www.westinmaui.com
Located along the
Ka'anapali coast, this
761-unit hotel has Asian
influences and artwork
throughout. Beautiful
landscape with many
waterfalls and lagoons.

$$$

Lahaina Inn
127 Lahainaluna Road, Lahaina,
HI 96761
Tel: 661-0577
Toll free: 800-669 3444
www.lahainainn.com
In the heart of Lahaina.
Restored 1860s boutique
hotel located off Front
Street in Lahaina. Twelve-
room property with
sumptuous antique
furnishings. No children
under 15 years.

Royal Lahaina Resort
2780 Keka'a Drive, Lahaina,
HI 96761
Tel: 661-3611
Toll free: 800-280 8155
www.2maui.com
On the beach at
Ka'anapali, a 592-room
resort adjacent to Ka'anapali's North and South golf
courses. Quaint wedding
gazebo in courtyard.

PRICE CATEGORIES

$ = below US$50
$$ = US$50–100
$$$ = US$100–150
$$$$ = US$150–200
$$$$$ = US$200 and up
Substantially discounted
rates are common, with the
best deals often found on
websites.

$$

Aston Maui Lu
575 S. Kihei Road, Kihei, HI 96753
Tel: 879-5881
Toll free: 877-997 6667
www.resortquesthawaii.com
Affordable units situated on
28 lush oceanfront acres
(11 hectares) with private
beach coves.
Best Western Pioneer Inn
658 Wharf St, Lahaina, HI 96761
Tel: 661-3636
Toll free: 800-457 5457
www.pioneerinnmaui.com
Historic hotel in the heart
of old-town Lahaina,
overlooking the port, with a
décor to match its century-
old roots but a good
standard of comfort. If you
need quiet, ask for a room
facing the courtyard.
Kula Lodge (cottages)
RR 1, Box 475, Kula, HI 96790
Tel: 878-1535
Toll free: 800-233 1535
www.kulalodge.com
Located in lush, rural
upcountry Maui. Five units
in two cozy wooden cabins
surrounded by forest. No
phones or televisions in
rooms.

The Mauian
5441 Lower Honoapi'ilani Rd,
Napili, HI 96761
Tel: 669-6205
Toll free: 800-367 5034
www.mauian.com
This charming, small-scale
hotel is set right on one of
West Maui's finest
beaches.
Old Wailuku Inn at Ulupono
2199 Kaho'okele St, Wailuku,
HI 96793
Tel: 244-5897
Toll free: 800-305 4899
www.mauiinn.com
This charming plantation-
style home, set in pleasant
gardens, holds 10 guest
rooms at assorted prices.

CONDOMINIUMS

$$$$$

Kapalua Villas
500 Office Road, Kapalua, HI 96761
Tel: 669-8088
Toll free: 800-545-0018
www.kapaluavillas.com
Three condominiums with
fairway settings. Spacious,
elegantly furnished.

$$$$

Ka'anapali Ali'i
50 Nohea Kai Drive, Ka'anapali,
HI 96761
Tel: 661-3339
Toll free: 800-642 6284
www.kaanapaliAlii.com
With 264 units in four
buildings, 209 of which are
for rental. A beautifully
landscaped condo resort in
the middle of Ka'anapali's
resort hotels.

$$$

**The Whaler on Ka'anapali
Beach**
2481 Ka'anapali Parkway, Lahaina,
HI 96761
Tel: 661-4861
Toll free: 888-211 7710
www.the-whaler.com
Well-situated on Ka'anapali
Beach just north of
Whalers Village Shopping
Center and 36-hole
Ka'anapali Golf Courses.
There are 360 spacious
units with panoramic ocean
and garden views, on-site
tennis, sauna and work-out
room, small beachside
pool.

$$

Kamaole Sands
2695 S. Kihei Road, Kihei,
HI 96753
Tel: 874-8700
Toll free: 800-822 4409
www.kamaolesands.com
Located at the foot of
Haleakala, across the
street from Kihei Beach,
with 315 condominium
units. Tennis and pool on
property. Golf nearby.
Mana Kai Maui Resort
2960 S. Kihei Road, Kihei,
HI 96753
Tel: 879-2278
Toll free: 800-367 5242
www.crhmaui.com
Located on the beach in
Kihei. Modest 126-unit
accommodation with great
ocean views.
**ResortQuest Ka'anapali
Shores**
3445 Honoapi'ilani Highway,
Lahaina, HI 96761
Tel: 667-2211
Toll free: 877-997 6667
www.resortquesthawaii.com
Oceanfront, 463-room
condominium resort on the
north end of Ka'anapali
Beach.

MOLOKAI AND LANAI

HOTELS

$$$$$

**Four Seasons Resort
Lanai, at Manele Bay**
PO Box 630310, Lanai City,
HI 96763
Tel: 565-2000
Toll free: 800-919 5053
www.fourseasons.com
Set on a cliff overlooking
the beach at pristine
Hulopo'e Bay. Views of the
ocean and the island of
Maui. Amenities include
health club, tennis courts
and a pool. The luxury spa
offers Hawaiian
treatments.
**Four Seasons Resort
Lanai, The Lodge at Ko'ele**
PO Box 630310, Lanai City,
HI 96763
Tel: 565-4000
Toll free: 800-919 5053
www.fourseasons.com

Cool mountain retreat in
the uplands of Lanai. This
102-room country estate-
like hotel is in an attractive
rural setting surrounded by
pine trees. The hotel's
Formal Dining Room is
superb. The varied activities
include horseback riding,
tennis, golf and Lanai Pine
Sporting Clays.

$$$$

**Molokai Ranch Lodge and
Beach Village**
PO Box 259, Maunaloa, HI 96770
Tel: 660-2824
Toll free: 888-627 8082
www.molokairanch.com
This 54,000-acre (21,850-
hectare) working cattle
ranch has a luxurious 22-
room lodge. Great for both
adventure holidays with a
difference and romantic
getaways; the ranch also
operates luxury beachside
campsites.

$$$

Ke Nani Kai
PO Box 289, Maunaloa, HI 96770
Tel: 679-2016
Toll free: 800-490 9042
www.kenanikai.com
Property surrounded by
Kaluakoi golf course. A few
minutes away from
secluded beach. Of the
120 units, 35 are available
to rent. Numerous facilities
include parking, TV,
swimming pool, tennis
court, golf, jacuzzi; there's
a minimum stay of 2 nights.

$$

Hotel Lanai
PO Box 520, Lanai City, HI 96763
Tel: 565-7211
Toll free: 877-665 2624
www.hotellanai.com
A charming 11-room inn
situated in Lanai City, the
island's only town. This is
the affordable way to visit

Lanai, which otherwise can
be pretty pricey.
Hotel Molokai
Kamehameha V Hwy, Kaunakakai,
HI 96748
Tel: 553-5347
Toll free: 800-535 0085
www.hotelmolokai.com
Good-value hotel, right on
the waterfront. Spacious
rooms arranged around
central lawns. So long as
you can accept slightly
slapdash standards and
service, it's a great place
to get a feel for Molokai's
homely charms.

PRICE CATEGORIES

$ = below US$100
$$ = US$100–150
$$$ = US$150–200
$$$$ = US$200–250
$$$$$ = US$250 and up
Substantially discounted
rates are common, with the
best deals often found on
websites.

HAWAII (BIG ISLAND)

HOTELS

$$$$$

The Fairmont Orchid at Mauna Lani
One North Kaniku Drive, Kohala Coast, HI 96743
Tel: 885-2000
Toll free: 800-845 9905
www.fairmont.com
A wonderfully elegant 537-unit hotel with a great beach and spacious rooms that reveal a Ritz-Carlton pedigree. The Hawaiian program is a definite plus.

Four Seasons Resort at Hualalai
PO Box 1269, Kailua-Kona, HI 96745
Tel: 325-8000
Toll free: 888-340 5662
www.fourseasons.com
Located on 625 acres (253 hectares) on the Kohala Coast, just a seven-minute drive from Keahole-Kona Airport. Thirty-six low-rise ocean-view bungalows house 243 rooms and suites. Serene, intimate atmosphere. Informative exhibits are on view at the resort's Hawaiian Interpretive Center. Natural anchialine ponds and oceanfront pools, plus a championship golf course carved out of lava rock.

Hapuna Beach Prince Hotel
62-100 Kauna'oa Drive, Kohala, HI 96743
Tel: 880-1111
Toll free: 888-977 4623
www.hapunabeachprincehotel.com
With 350 units, this oceanfront resort is a half-hour's drive from the Keahole-Kona Airport. Full-service resort with upscale amenities and fine service. Great golf course nearby.

Hilton Waikoloa Village
425 Waikoloa Beach Drive, Waikoloa, HI 96743
Tel: 886-1234
Toll free: 800-445 8667
www.hiltonwaikoloavillage.com
This 1,238-room resort (a 30-minute drive from the airport) is an expansive Hawaiian playground with championship golf, fabulous frolicking dolphins and wall-to-wall extravagance.

Kona Village Resort
PO Box 1299, Kailua-Kona, HI 96745
Tel: 325-5555
Toll free: 800-367 5290
www.konavillage.com
On the beach at Ka'upulehu, just 5 miles (8 km) north of Kona airport. Unique resort with 125 individual thatched *hale* (huts or bungalows). Oceanfront units are the ultimate in romance. Pure bliss for visitors seeking a total escape from reality (there's no in-room TV, radio or telephone).

Mauna Lani Bay Hotel & Bungalows
68-1400 Mauna Lani Drive, Kohala Coast, HI 96743
Tel: 885-6622
Toll free: 800-327 2323
www.maunalani.com
This 350-unit, beachfront full-service resort scores highly for its elegant-yet-comfortable ambiance and is located near a golf course. Hosts the annual "Cuisines of the Sun," a food symposium spotlighting cuisines from sunny climates.

$$$$

Holualoa Inn
76-5932 Mamalahoa Highway, Holualoa, HI 96725
Tel: 324-1121
Toll free: 800-392 1812
www.holualoainn.com
Quaint, 6-unit country inn located just a few minutes from Kailua-Kona. Tranquil atmosphere. Great for rest and relaxation.

Kona by the Sea
75-6106 Ali'i Drive, Kailua-Kona, HI 96740
Tel: 327-2300
Toll free: 877-997 6667
www.resortquesthawaii.com
Intimate oceanfront resort, just south of Kailua-Kona town. Comfortable rooms, each with a private *lanai* (roofed balcony).

Shipman House B&B Inn
131 Kai'ulani St, Hilo, HI 96720
Tel: 934-8002
Toll free: 800-627 8447
www.hilo-hawaii.com
Lavish B&B in a superb old Victorian mansion, in a quiet rainforest setting but very close to the heart of Hilo.

Waikoloa Beach Marriott
69-275 Waikoloa Beach Drive, Waikoloa, HI 96738
Tel: 886-6789
Toll free: 888-236 2427
www.marriotthawaii.com
Just a 20-minute drive from Kona Airport. Most rooms have delightful ocean views. The hotel is bordered by royal fishpond and beach. Frequent Hawaiian arts and crafts demonstrations add yet more colour.

$$$

Kilauea Lodge
PO Box 116, Volcano, HI 96785
Tel: 967-7366
www.kilauealodge.com
A cozy 17-unit lodge set in Volcano, near the southeast portion of the Island. Relaxing hot tub available for guests.

King Kamehameha's Kona Beach Hotel
75-5660 Palani Road, Kailua-Kona, HI 96740
Tel: 329-2911
Toll free: 800-367 2111
www.konabeachhotel.com
Full-service, 460-unit hotel. Slightly dated but on an historic site and conveniently situated by Kona's beach and pier.

Outrigger Keauhou Beach Resort
78-6740 Ali'i Drive, Kailua-Kona, HI 96740
Tel: 322-3441
Toll free: 800-688 7444
www.outrigger.com
Oceanfront hotel with 310 units on Kailua-Kona's main artery. Features nightly buffets with pleasant, friendly service.

Royal Kona Resort
75-5852 Ali'i Drive, Kailua-Kona, HI 96740
Tel: 329-3111
Toll free: 800-222 5642
www.royalkona.com
Formerly the Kona Hilton, this newly-renovated 452-room hotel is within easy walking distance of Kailua-Kona town. It overlooks Kailua Bay.

$$

Hale Ohia
PO Box 758, Volcano, HI 96785
Tel: 967-7986
Toll free: 800-455 3803
www.haleohia.com
Upscale B&B accommodations set in the gorgeous grounds of a lush tropical home just outside Volcanoes National Park. Tastefully furnished.

Hilo Hawaiian Hotel
71 Banyan Drive, Hilo, HI 96720
Tel: 935-9361
Toll free: 800-367 5004
www.castleresorts.com
Bayside 290-unit upmarket hotel. Spectacular views, facing Coconut Island, and friendly kama'aina service. Home of Hilo's best buffet.

Kamuela Inn
65-1300 Kawaihae Road, Kamuela, HI 96743
Tel: 885-4243
Toll free: 800-555 8968
www.hawaii-bnb.com/kamuela.html
Unassuming 31-unit inn set in the rolling paniolo countryside of Kamuela (also known as Waimea).

Naniloa Volcanoes Resort
93 Banyan Drive, Hilo, HI 96720
Tel: 969-3333
www.naniloaresort.com
Located at Hilo Bay, just a few minutes from Hilo Airport and adjacent to a popular nine-hole golf course; 325 units with a pleasant atmosphere and great bay views.

Uncle Billy's Hilo Bay Hotel
87 Banyan Drive, Hilo, HI 96720
Tel: 961-5818
Toll free: 800-367 5102
www.unclebilly.com
On the waterfront at Hilo Bay. Gracious hospitality. Run by Uncle Billy and his family. Free hula show and Hawaiian music nightly.

Uncle Billy's Kona Bay Hotel
75-5739 Ali'i Drive, Kailua-Kona, HI 96740
Tel: 329-6488
Toll free: 800-367 5102
www.unclebilly.com
Situated in the heart of Kailua-Kona, across from Kailua Bay. Friendly, casual atmosphere and homely service.

Volcano House
PO Box 53, Hawaii Volcanoes
National Park, HI 96718
Tel: 967-7321
www.volcanohousehotel.com
Valued for its location
inside the Hawaii
Volcanoes National Park
overlooking Halemaumau
crater. Small and cozy
place to stay. Has 42
rooms.

$

Kohala Village Inn
55-514 Hawi Rd, Hawi, HI 96719

Tel: 889-0404
www.kohalavillageinn.com
Rudimentary but very
pleasant little hotel, dating
from Hawaii's plantation
era, tucked away in
beautiful, little-visited North
Kohala.
Manago Hotel
PO Box 145, Captain Cook-Kona,
HI 96704
Tel: 323-2642
www.managohotel.com
Family-run hotel located in
the center of Captain Cook.
Small hotel with 64 rooms.
Overlooks Kealakekua Bay.

CONDOMINIUMS

$$$$$

**ResortQuest Shores at
Waikoloa**
69-1035 Keana Place, Waikoloa,
HI 96743
Tel: 886-5001
Toll free: 877-997 6667
www.resortquesthawaii.com
Luxury condominium resort
on Kohala Coast. Next to
Waikoloa Golf Club's famed
Beach Course. Well-

appointed suites with
gourmet kitchens.

$$$$

Kanaloa at Kona
78-261 Manukai Street, Kailua-
Kona, HI 96740
Tel: 322-9625
Toll free: 800-959 5662
www.outrigger.com
Oceanfront condominium
bordered by a champion-
ship golf course and Heeia
Bay. Elegantly furnished
suites with garden or ocean
views.

KAUAI

HOTELS

$$$$$

**Grand Hyatt Kauai Resort
and Spa**
1571 Po'ipu Road, Koloa, HI 96756
Tel: 742-1234
Toll free: 800-554 9288
www.kauai-hyatt.com
Large, 600-room hotel
located on the oceanfront
in sunny Po'ipu. Water-
slides cascade through the
landscaped gardens to
reach an artificial lagoon
beach.
Hanalei Bay Resort
5380 Honoiki Rd, Princeville,
HI 96722
Tel: 826-6522
Toll free: 800-827 4427
www.hanaleibayresort.com
Beautifully landscaped
North-Shore resort,

overlooking Hanalei Bay,
with a lovely pool and
restaurant.
Hilton Kauai Beach Resort
4331 Kauai Beach Drive, Lihu'e,
HI 96766
Tel: 245-1955
Toll free: 800-445 8667
www.kauaibeachresort.hilton.com
A 341-room beachfront
hotel near Wailua River, 4
miles (6 km) from Lihue
Airport. Secluded beach.
Kauai Marriott Resort
Kalapaki Beach, Lihu'e, HI 96766
Tel: 245-5050
Toll free: 800-220 2925
www.marriott.com
Set along Kalapaki Beach,
fronting Nawiliwili Bay. One
mile (1.5km) from Lihue
Airport. Elegant property
within Kauai Lagoons
Resort.
Princeville Resort
5520 Ka Huku Road, Princeville,
HI 96722

Tel: 826-9644
Toll free: 866-716 8110
www.princevillehotelhawaii.com
Attractive and luxurious
252-room property set on a
cliff overlooking Hanalei
Bay. Excellent food,
wonderful views, great
ambiance.
Sheraton Kauai Resort
2440 Hoonani Rd, Koloa, HI 96756
Tel: 742-1661
Toll free: 866-716 8109
www.sheraton-kauai.com
Beachfront and garden
wings at the heart of
Po'ipu. Crescent sands and
sunsets are the rewards.
**Waimea Plantation
Cottages**
9400 Kaumuali'i Highway, Waimea,
HI 96796
Tel: 338-1625
Toll free: 877-997 6667
www.resortquest.com
Seaside cottages set
amidst a 27-acre (11-
hectare) coconut grove just
outside Waimea.
Renovated and updated
former homes of sugar
plantation workers.

$$$$

**ResortQuest Kauai Beach
at Makaiwa**
PO Box 830, Kapa'a, HI 96746
Tel: 822-3455
Toll free: 866-774 2924
www.resortquest.com
Great central location in
Kapa'a. Reasonably priced
hotel offering a full range of
resort services including a
nightly *lu'au* (traditional
feast) and an after-dark
torchlighting ceremony.

$$$

**Kauai Coast Beachboy
Resort**
4-484 Kuhio Highway, Kapa'a,
HI 96746
Tel: 822-3441
www.kauaicoastresort.com
On Waipouli Beach,
adjacent to Coconut
Marketplace, a popular
open-air shopping mall.
With 243-rooms in three
low-rise buildings.
Koloa Landing Cottages
2704B Ho'onani Road, Koloa,
HI 96756
Tel: 742-1470
Toll free: 800-779 8773
www.koloa-landing.com
Four comfy cottages
including a studio. Lovely
friendly and relaxed
atmosphere.

$$

Garden Island Inn
3445 Wilcox Rd, Lihu'e, HI 96766
Tel: 245-7227
Toll free: 800-648 0154
www.gardenislandinn.com
Small, modern hotel in
Kauai's main town, with
three levels of reasonable
rooms of varying sizes.

PRICE CATEGORIES

$ = below US$100
$$ = US$100–150
$$$ = US$150–200
$$$$ = US$200–250
$$$$$ = US$250 and up
Substantially discounted
rates are common, with the
best deals often found on
websites.

BELOW: Waimea Plantation Cottages, Kauai.

E ATING OUT

RECOMMENDED RESTAURANTS, CAFES & BARS

How to Choose

There are many good Hawaiian restaurants on the islands, so don't pass up the chance of eating well.

In addition, there are numerous ethnic cuisines to be enjoyed, with Thai, Vietnamese, Korean, Chinese and Japanese all noteworthy. The chefs here enjoy experimenting, adding a little Asian to Continental, or Italian to Pacific. The results are excellent, including the popular "Pacific Rim" cuisine that has gained international respect.

The Lu'au

A unique form of Hawaiian celebration that generally begins at sundown is the *lu'au*, traditionally a feast, a celebration of life. There is a wide range of *lu'au* offerings and styles, from the Hollywood-tinsel "Polynesian" revue with the requisite drums, fire dancers, and shimmering hula dancers, to some quite authentic presentations, mostly on the neighbor islands. Whatever type you choose, it's usually worth the $60 or so per person, which includes copious amounts of food and a

satisfying show of varying authenticity. Check with your hotel for the nearest *lu'au* options. Several hotels also hold *lu'au* themselves.

The listing below is anything but comprehensive. Exclusion from this list indicates nothing about an establishment's quality; there are simply too many restaurants to list. For a more comprehensive listing, get a copy of the Hawaii Visitors and Convention Bureau Entertainment and Dining Guide *(see page 344)*.

Abbreviations: B = Breakfast; L = lunch; D = dinner.

(see page 344)

RESTAURANT LISTINGS

OAHU

$$$

Alan Wong's Restaurant
1857 S. King Street (3rd flr), Honolulu
Tel: 949-2526
A Honolulu hot spot for Hawaiian Regional Cuisine. D

Chef Mavro
1969 S. King Street, Honolulu
Tel: 944-4714
Contemporary elegance and the masterful French-Hawaiian culinary artistry

PRICE CATEGORIES

Price categories are for a meal for one, not including alcohol:
$ = less than US$25
$$ = US$25–50
$$$ = more than US$50

of chef George Mavrotha-lassitis make this one of Hawaii's best restaurants. LD

Hoku's, Kahala Hotel & Resort
5000 Kahala Avenue, Honolulu
Tel: 739-8888
Quiet setting with an appealing contemporary elegance. The fusion cuisine is deliciously prepared and beautifully presented. D

Sam Choy's Diamond Head
449 Kapahulu Avenue, Kapahulu
Tel: 732-8645
Hawaii Regional Cuisine in generous portions from the renowned chef. D

Bali by the Sea
Hilton Hawaiian Village, 2005 Kalia Road, Waikiki
Tel: 941-2254
Continental. Open-air,

upscale restaurant with touches of both the Pacific and Asia on menu. BLD

Hanohano Room
Sheraton Waikiki, 2255 Kalakaua Avenue, Waikiki
Tel: 922-4422

Elegant and classy establishment. BD

La Mer
Halekulani Hotel, 2199 Kalia Road, Waikiki
Tel: 923-2311
French. Very upscale, with

BELOW: shrimps for sale, any way you want them.

ABOVE: Cholo's Mexican-style restaurant.

touches of the Pacific on the menu. Jacket required. D

Roy's Waikiki Beach
226 Lewers St, Waikiki
Tel: 923-7697
Inventive Pacific Rim dishes from Hawaii's most popular chef, in the new BeachWalk development. D

$$

Chai's Island Bistro
Aloha Tower Marketplace, Honolulu
Tel: 585-0011
Lovely flowery setting with great fusion foods and a Thai twist plus top-class Hawaiian music nightly. LD

Cholo's
62-250 Kamehameha Highway, Haleiwa
Tel: 637 3059
Homestyle Mexican restaurant located in the North Shore Marketplace. Great fish tacos. Authentic, colorful artwork from Mexico (most for sale) adorns the walls. LD

Crouching Lion
51-666 Kamehameha Highway
Tel: 237-8511
Notable North Shore fixture that makes a good dining break. LD

Indigo
21 Nu'uanu Avenue, Honolulu
Tel: 521-2900
Downtown favorite offering Eurasian cuisine. LD

Jameson's by the Sea
Kamehameha Highway, Hale'iwa
Tel: 637-4336
American. Good seafood, even better sunset views. BLD

Legend Seafood
100 N. Beretania Street, Honolulu
Tel: 532-1868
Bustling Chinese eatery. LD

Roy's Restaurant
6600 Kalaniana'ole Highway, Hawaii Kai
Tel: 396-7697
Nouvelle cuisine with global flourishes. LD

3660 On The Rise
3660 Wai'alae Avenue, Kahala
Tel: 737-1177
Eurasian Pacific Rim. Popular, trendy eatery with pleasant ambiance. D

Ciao Mein
Hyatt Regency Waikiki, 2424 Kalakaua Avenue, Waikiki
Tel: 923-2426
Chinese/Italian. An upscale blend of East and West. D

Duke's Canoe Club
Outrigger Waikiki Hotel, 2335 Kalakaua Avenue

Tel: 922-2268
American. Casual and trendy steak-and-seafood place. BLD

Golden Dragon
Hilton Hawaiian Village, 2005 Kalia Road, Waikiki
Tel: 946-5336
Award-winning upscale Cantonese cuisine. D

Hau Tree Lanai
New Otani Kaimana Beach Hotel, 2863 Kalakaua Avenue, Waikiki
Tel: 921-7066
American. On the beach, outside the site where poet Robert Louis Stevenson once sat. Fabulous sunset views. BLD

House Without A Key
Halekulani Hotel, 2199 Kalia Road, Waikiki
Tel: 923-2311
Order delicious *pupus* (hors d'oeuvres) and catch the sunset with the hula, an Hawaiian quartet and Diamond Head to set off the stunning views. LD

Keo's in Waikiki
2028 Kuhio Avenue, Waikiki
Tel: 951-9355
Thai food in a lively setting. Popular with locals and celebrities. Another branch at Ward Centre. D

Nobu
Waikiki Parc Hotel
2233 Helumoa Road, Waikiki
Tel: 921-7272
Japanese, Pacific Rim. Cutting-edge fusion cuisine from international super-chef Nobu Matsuhisa. D

Prince Court
Hawaii Prince Hotel, 100 Holomoana Street, Waikiki
Tel: 944-4494
Regional. Emphasis on local ingredients, blending East and West. BLD

Sansei Seafood Restaurant and Sushi Bar
Waikiki Beach Marriott, 2552 Kalakaua Ave, Waikiki
Tel: 931-6286
Superb sushi and Japanese seafood. D

$

A Little Bit of Saigon
1160 Maunakea Street, Honolulu
Tel: 528-3663
Vietnamese. A Chinatown favorite with a solid following. LD

Auntie Pasto's
1099 S Beretania St

Tel: 523-8855
Italian cuisine. Popular local eatery; no reservations so expect a wait. LD

Garden Café
Honolulu Academy of Arts, 900 S. Beretania Street, Honolulu
Tel: 532-8734
Island cuisine. Pleasant, open-air spot for lunch. L

Genki Sushi
885 Kapahulu Avenue, Honolulu
Tel: 735-7700
Reservations at the door for this very popular restaurant, where quality sushi is well priced and selected from a counter-side conveyor belt. LD

Makai Market
Ala Moana Shopping Center, Honolulu
Tel: 955-9517
A lively, crowded food court offering a wide variety of ethnic foods. LD

Maunakea Market Place
1120 Maunakea Street, Honolulu
Tel: 524-3409
Chinatown marketplace lined with ethnic foods of all types. D

Ono Hawaiian Food
726 Kapahulu Avenue
Tel: 737-2275
Tasty Hawaiian cuisine, reasonable prices. Very popular, so expect to wait in line. LD

Sweet Basil
1152A Maunakea St, Honolulu
Tel: 545-5800
Simple Chinatown restaurant serving cheap but very tasty Thai food. LD

Wai'oli Tea Room
2950 Manoa Rd, Honolulu
Tel: 988-5800
Light snacks and old-fashioned "high tea" in a lovely garden setting. BL

XO
1718 Kapi'olani Blvd, Honolulu
Tel: 942-2020
Top-quality Chinese food a short walk from Waikiki. LD

Arancino
255 Beach Walk, Waikiki
Tel: 923-5557
Small hole-in-the-wall eatery. There may be lines but the Italian specialties are worth the wait. LD

Eggs N Things
1911-B Kalakaua Avenue, Waikiki
Tel: 949-0820
Super-sized breakfasts make this restaurant popular. BLD

MAUI

$$$

David Paul's Lahaina Grill
Lahaina Inn, 127 Lahainaluna Road, Lahaina
Tel: 667-5117
Pacific Rim. Part of restored historic Lahaina Hotel. Casual ambiance, sophisticated food. For an appetizer try the Kona lobster crab cake with mustard cream. D

The Feast at Lele
505 Front St, Lahaina
Tel: 667-5353
An expensive but irresistible all-you-can-eat feast of Hawaiian and other Polynesian delicacies, enjoyed at beachfront tables and accompanied by live hula. D

Gerard's
Plantation Inn, 174 Lahainaluna Road, Lahaina
Tel: 661-8939
French. Sit outdoors or inside a restored plantation home. D

Hakone
Maui Prince Hotel, 5400 Makena Alanui, Makena/Wailea
Tel: 875-5888
Japanese elegance with authentic food and ambiance. D

Pacific Grill
Four Seasons Resort, 3900 Wailea Alanui, Wailea
Tel: 874-8000
Pacific Rim with Asian influences. BD

Spago
Four Seasons Resort, 3900 Wailea Alanui, Wailea
Tel: 879-2999

Pacific Rim courtesy of Wolfgang Puck. D

$$

Flames of Avalon Restaurant & Bar
844 Front Street, Lahaina
Tel: 667-5559
Inventive Asian and Pacific cuisine. Outdoors in busy courtyard. LD

Hali'imaile General Store
900 Hali'imaile Road, Hali'imaile
Tel: 572-2666
Eclectic American food with Asian overtones. LD

Hula Moons
Outrigger Palms at Wailea
Tel: 879-1922
Good food served in colorful Hawaiian-style atmosphere. LD

Mama's Fish House
799 Poho Pl, on highway near Pa'ia
Tel: 579-8488
Maui's best seafood in an oceanfront setting. LD

The Plantation House
2000 Plantation Club Drive, Kapalua
Tel: 669-6299
Specializing in seafood. Elegant atmosphere; excellent views. BLD

Roy's Kahana Bar & Grill
4405 Honoapi'ilani Highway, Kahana
Tel: 669-6999
Euro-Asian cuisine. D

Sansei Seafood Restaurant
1881 S Kihei Rd, Kihei
Tel: 669-6286
Busy, dynamic Japanese restaurant, renowned for its creative sushi. Excellent-quality dishes at

surprisingly reasonable prices. D

$

Casanova Italian Restaurant and Deli
1188 Makawao Avenue, Makawao
Tel: 572-0220
Italian. Popular local hangout; good for people-watching. LD

Cheeseburger in Paradise
811 Front Street, Lahaina
Tel: 661-4855

BELOW: refreshing cocktails for two.

On the water, with live music. LD

Cilantro Fresh Mexican Grill
170 Papalaua Ave, Lahaina
Tel: 667-5444
Inexpensive but high-quality Mexican food, to eat in or take back to your condo. LD

Saeng's Thai Cuisine
2119 Vineyard Street, Wailuku
Tel: 244-1567
Thai. Pleasant and friendly garden setting. LD

MOLOKAI AND LANAI

$$$

Dining Room
The Lodge at Ko'ele, Lanai City
Tel: 565-4580
Chef Andrew Manion-Copley uses local produce to create a delicious and unusual menu. D

$$

Ko'ele Terrace
The Lodge at Ko'ele, Lanai City
Tel: 565-4580

Outstanding Hawaiian cuisine with tranquil garden views. Lunch is the best value. Contemporary American cuisine with Hawaiian overtones. BLD

Maunaloa Room
Molokai Ranch Lodge, 100 Maunaloa Hwy, Maunaloa
Tel: 660-2725
Molokai's elegant gourmet restaurant serves most major world cuisines, with a good Asian buffet on Sundays. Catch of the day

served in a choice of styles (Chinese, Mediterranean, Hawaiian). BLD

$

Molokai Pizza Café
Wharf Road, Kaunakakai
Tel: 553-3288
Lively, friendly family restaurant with Molokai's best pizza and pasta as well as excellent fish or chicken plate dinner specials. LD

Pele's Other Graden
811 Houston Street, Lanai City
Tel: 565-9628
Excellent New York-style deli fare, fresh and organic. LD

PRICE CATEGORIES

Price categories are for a meal for one, not including alcohol:
$ = less than US$25
$$ = US$25–50
$$$ = more than US$50

HAWAII (BIG ISLAND)

$$$

CanoeHouse
Mauna Lani Bay Hotel and
Bungalows, South Kohala
Tel: 885-6622
Pacific Rim. Beautiful open-
air views of the Pacific and
Kohala sunset. D
Merriman's
Opelo Plaza, Highway 19, Waimea
Tel: 885-6822

BELOW: Huggo's On The Rocks.

Regional. Renowned chef
Peter Merriman's Hawaiian-
and-Pacific menu. LD

$$

**Bamboo Restaurant and
Bar**
Hwy-270, Hawi
Tel: 889-5555
Atmospheric village bistro
in North Kohala. LD

Café Pesto
308 Kamehameha Avenue, Hilo
Tel: 969-6640
Popular Italian café. Superb
pizzas use local
ingredients, from blackened
ahi to lobsters. Traditional
and nouveau establish-
ment. Other branches in
Kohala and Kawaihae, tel:
882-1071. LD
Huggo's On the Rocks
75-5828 Kahakai Road,
Kailua-Kona
Tel: 329-1493
Ocean-front setting. Light
meals. LD
Jameson's by the Sea
77-6452 Ali'i Drive, Kailua-Kona
Tel: 329-3195
American. On the
waterfront, with fresh local
fish and salmon. LD
Kilauea Lodge
Old Volcano Road, Volcano Village
Tel: 967-7366
Continental. Spacious
country dining, casual but
upscale. D
Roy's Waikoloa
Kings Shops at Waikoloa
Tel: 886-4321
The same great Pacific Rim
food as the original. LD

$

Aloha Angel Café
Highway 11, Kainaliu
Tel: 322-3383
Diverse menu with terrace
seating dotted around an
old theater building. BLD
The Coffee Shack
Hwy-11, Captain Cook
Tel: 328-9555
Filling snacks and fresh-
picked coffee. BL
Holuakoa Café
76-5901 Mamalahoa Highway
Holualoa (above Kailua-Kona)
Tel: 322-2233
Easy-going espresso bar
offering light, simple meals
and the best coffee
around. BL
Manago Hotel
82-6155 Mamalahoa Highway,
Captain Cook, Kona
Tel: 323-2642
American. Casual
fundamentals in family-run
hotel. BLD
The Seaside Restaurant
1790 Kalaniana'ole Ave, Hilo
Tel: 935-8825
Very local fish specialists,
overlooking their own fish
farm. D

KAUAI

$$$

Beach House
5022 Lawai Rd, Po'ipu
Tel: 742-1424
Many say this is Kauai's
best seafood restaurant.
Stunning sunset views of
the ocean. D

$$

Bar Acuda
5-5161 Kuhio Hwy, Hanalei
Tel: 826-7081
Spanish, Mediterranean.
Exquisite dinners or tapas
in the heart of Hanalei. LD
Brennecke's Beach Broiler
2100 Ho'one Road, Po'ipu
Tel: 742-7588
American food and
atmosphere. Seriously
casual, steak and seafood
on the beach. LD
Café Hanalei
Princeville Hotel, Princeville,
North Shore

Tel: 826-9644
Contemporary establish-
ment overlooking Hanalei
Bay. BLD
Caffe Coco
4369 Kulio Highway, Kapaa
Tel: 822-7990
An unexpected find, with a
charming, relaxing
atmosphere amidst
Kapaa's shopping malls.
Nightly entertainment. BLD
Casa di Amici
2360 Nalo Road, Poipu
Tel: 742-1555
A real gem serving
excellent Italian cuisine. LD
Gaylord's at Kilohana
3-2087 Kaumuali'i Highway, Puhi,
near Lihu'e
Tel: 245-9593
Continental eatery.
Situated in a restored
1935 plantation estate.
Outside seating. LD
Keoki's Paradise
Po'ipu Shopping Village, Po'ipu
Tel: 742-7534

Polynesian-style setting.
Particularly notable for its
seafood dishes. LD
Postcards Café
Kuhio Highway, Hanalei
Tel: 826-1191
Memorably good food in a
charming plantation-era
setting. A must. BD
Roy's Po'ipu Bar & Grill
Po'ipu Shopping Village, Po'ipu
Tel: 742-5000
Yet more creative morsels
from chef extraordinaire,
Roy Yamaguchi. D

$

Hamura Saimin
2956 Kress St, Lihu'e
Tel: 245-3271
This very simple diner is
renowned for preparing
Hawaii's definitive *saimin*
(noodle soup). LD
**Hanama'ulu Restaurant
and Tea House**
3-4253 Kuhio Hwy, Hanama'ulu

Tel: 245-2511
Authentic Asian tearooms
with fishponds, serving
good Chinese and
Japanese food. Sushi is
served in the evening only.
LD
Mermaids Café
1384 Kuhio Hwy, Kapa'a
Tel: 821-2026
Healthy, good-value meals
and snacks in downtown
Kapa'a. LD
Ono Char-Burger
Kuhio Highway, Anahola
Tel: 822-9181
Roadside in Anahola,
burgers at their Kauai
best. LD

PRICE CATEGORIES

Price categories are for a
meal for one, not including
alcohol:
$ = less than US$25
$$ = US$25–50
$$$ = more than US$50

A CTIVITIES

ATTRACTIONS, FESTIVALS, CHILDREN'S ACTIVITIES, SHOPPING AND WATERSPORTS

ATTRACTIONS

Options

Beyond peeking out at paradise from behind tinted tour bus windows, you can dip in and out of fantasy settings of your choice, choosing between glider, helicopter and small-propeller plane tours; off-shore dinner and sunset "booze" cruises; catamaran and glass-bottom boat rides.

For more information about these tours and other places of interest, consult the numerous free visitors' publications available in Waikiki, the daily newspapers' entertainment and community calendar sections, or call the **Hawaii Visitors Bureau**, tel: 923-1811, or visit the website: www.gohawaii.com.

Oahu, Honolulu and Environs

Aloha Tower, Pier 9 at Honolulu Harbor. Tenth-floor observation deck open daily 9am–5pm; www.alohatower.com.
Battleship USS *Missouri*. Tel: 973 2494; www.ussmissouri.org. Historic WWII battleship at Pearl Harbor. Shuttle from USS *Bowfin*. Open daily 8.30am–5pm. Admission fee.
Bishop Museum & Planetarium, 1525 Bernice Street, Kalihi. Tel: (museum) 847-3511; www.bishopmuseum.org. Open 9am–5pm daily except Christmas. Admission fee. Planetarium Show at 11am and 2pm daily; Fri and Sat also at 7pm. Admission fee.
Contemporary Museum, 2411 Makiki Heights Drive. Tel: 526-1322; www.tcmhi.org. Open Tues–Sat

10am–4pm, Sun noon–4pm. Admission fee.
Foster Botanic Garden, 180 N. Vineyard Boulevard (entrance on Vineyard Boulevard at Nu'uanu Stream). Tel: 522-7065. Open daily 9am–4.30pm. Admission fee.
Hawaii Maritime Center, Pier 7 downtown Honolulu, adjacent to Aloha Tower. Tel: 536-6373; www.bishopmuseum.org. Open daily 8.30am–5pm. Admission fee.
Honolulu Academy of Arts, 900 S. Beretania Street, *mauka* of Thomas Square. Tel: 532-8701; www.honoluluacademy.org. Open Tues–Sat 10am–4.30pm and Sun 1–5pm, closed on Mon. Admission fee.
'Iolani Palace, S. King Street, across from the Kamehameha statue. Tel: 522-0832; www.iolanipalace.org. This beautifully restored palace was completed

by King Kalakaua in 1882. Open Tues–Sat 9am–3pm, the 90-minute tour includes a visit to the palace and its exhibits such as Hawaii's crown jewels. Under 5s not admitted. Admission fee.
Mission Houses Museum, 553 S. King Street. Tel: 531-0481; www.missionhouses.org. Open Tues–Sat 10am–4pm. Tours: Tues, Wed, Fri, Sat 11am and 2.45pm. Admission fee. Guided tours last about 45 minutes.
National Memorial Cemetery of the Pacific, in Punchbowl Crater, top of Puowaina Drive. Tel: 532-3720. Open Sept 30–Mar 1 daily 8am–5.30pm, Mar 2–Sept 29 daily 8am–6.30pm, Memorial Day 7am–7pm. Free.
Queen Emma's Summer Palace, 2913 Pali Highway, Nu'uanu Valley. Tel: 595-3167; www.daughtersofhawaii.com.

BELOW: drummers performing at the Polynesian Cultural Center, Oahu.

Open daily 9am–4pm. Admission fee.

Royal Mausoleum, 2261 Nu'uanu Avenue, Nu'uanu Valley. Tel: 536-7602. Open Mon–Fri 8am–4pm, closed holidays. Advance reservations for groups. Free.

USS *Arizona* Memorial, at Pearl Harbor, conducted by the National Park Service via US Navy-operated shuttle boats. Tel: 422-0561; www.nps.gov/usar. Open daily 7.30am–5pm. Free.

USS *Bowfin* Submarine Museum & Park, at Pearl Harbor, near USS *Arizona* Memorial. Tel: 423-1341; www.bowfin.org. Open 8am–5pm daily. Admission fee.

In Waikiki

Honolulu Zoo, Diamond Head end of Kalakaua Avenue in the Kapi'olani Park complex. Tel: 971-7171; www.honoluluzoo.org. Open daily 9am–5.30pm. Admission fee.

Kapi'olani Park, at the foot of Diamond Head across from Queen's Surf Beach. The range of features includes a 1.8-mile (3-km) jogging course, soccer field, tennis courts, picnic tables, aquarium, amphitheater, zoo and bandstand. Free.

Kuhio Beach Hula Show. An hour-long crowd-pleaser on a beachside hula mound nightly at dusk. Free.

US Army Museum, Kalia Road, Fort DeRussy, near Diamond Head end of the Hilton Hawaiian Village. Tel: 438-2821. Open Tues–Sun 10am–4.15pm. Free.

Elsewhere on Oahu

Byodo-In Temple, 47-200 Kahekili Highway, Windward Oahu. Tel: 239-8811. Open daily 8.30am–4.30pm. Admission fee.

Hawaiian Waters Adventure Park, 400 Farrington Highway, Kapolei. Tel: 674-9283; www.hawaiianwaters.com. Acres of slides and pools. A big hit with kids. Opening hours vary, call for details. Admission fee.

Polynesian Cultural Center, at La'ie on Oahu's North Shore. Tel: 293-3333; www.polynesia.com. Open Mon–Sat noon–9pm. Admission fee.

Senator Fong's Plantation & Gardens, 47-285 Pulama Road, north of Kane'ohe on the Windward Side. Tel: 239-6775; www.fonggarden.com. Open daily 10am–2pm. Admission fee. Tours are also available.

Waimea Valley Audubon Center, 59-864 Kamehameha Highway, at Waimea on Oahu's North Shore. Tel: 638-9199; www.audubon.org. Open daily 9.30am–5pm. Admission fee.

Maui

Alexander & Baldwin Sugar Museum, 3957 Hanson Road, Pu'unene, near Kahului Airport. Tel: 871-8058; www.sugarmuseum.com. Open daily 9.30am–4.30pm. Admission fee. An underrated museum that not only displays the history and processing of sugar, but also the cultural and ethnic lifestyles of Hawaii's early plantation workers.

Hale Ho'ike'ike (Bailey House), 2375-A Main Street, Wailuku. Tel: 244-3326; www.mauimuseum.org. Open Mon–Sat 10am–4pm. Admission fee. Missionary home featuring a collection of Hawaiian artifacts, as well as clothes and furniture of the times.

Baldwin Home, 120 Dickenson Street, Lahaina. Tel: 661-3262. Open 10am–4pm daily. Admission fee. Learn all about missionary life in the 19th century at this 150-year-old clapboard private residence of the Rev. Dwight Baldwin.

Lahaina-Ka'anapali Pacific Railroad, 957 Limahana Place, Suite 203, Lahaina. Tel: 667-6851, toll free: 800-499 2307; www.sugarcanetrain.com. Call for times. Admission fee. This 1890s locomotive, which is also known as the Sugar Cane Train, transports sightseers between Lahaina and Ka'anapali with an additional stop at Pu'ukoli'i.

Whalers Village Museum, Whalers Village, 2435 Ka'anapali Parkway, Ka'anapali Resort. Tel: 661-5992. Open 9am–10pm daily. Free. A very well-presented exhibit on whaling and its impact on Hawaii.

Hawaii (Big Island)

Hawaii Volcanoes National Park, PO Box 52, Big Island. Tel:967-7311; www.nps.gov/havo. Visitors Center open 7.45am–5pm daily. Admission fee. The Visitors Center features displays and films about the volcanoes on the Big Isle. Information on current volcanic activity is posted.

Kaloko Honokahau National Historic Park, 73-4786 Kanalani St. #14, Kailua-Kona 96740. Tel: 329-6681; www.nps.gov/kaho. A beachfront historic park with *heiau* (temple) platforms, sled runs (*holua*) and fishponds. Located north of Kailua-Kona.

Lapakahi State Historical Park, Hwy-270, North Kohala. Tel: 889-5566. Open daily 8am–4pm except holidays. Free. This 600-year-old Hawaiian fishing village has been restored to illustrate the harsh realities of the ancient Hawaiian way of life, and includes small shrines and even play areas.

Lyman House Memorial Museum, 276 Haili Street, Hilo. Tel: 935-5021. Open 9.30am–4.30pm Mon–Sat. Admission fee. A restored 1800s missionary house.

Parker Ranch Visitor Center & Historic Homes, Mamalahoa Highway, Waimea 96743. Tel: 885-7655; www.parkerranch.com. Open daily 9am–5pm; historic homes daily 10am–5pm. Admission fee. Museum of the Big Island's Parker family, owners of the largest ranch in Hawaii.

Pu'u Kohola Heiau, Kawaihae 96743. Tel: 882-7218. Open daily 7.30am–4pm. Impressive and historically significant, this was the last major *heiau* (temple) built in Hawaii, completed by Kamehameha in 1791.

Pu'uhonua O Honaunau National Historical Park, PO Box 129, Honaunau. Tel: 328-2288; www.nps.gov/puho. Visitors Center open daily 8am–5.30pm. Admission fee. Historic site featuring ancient artifacts, and the Hale O Keawe Heiau.

Kauai

Guava Kai Plantation, PO Box 80, Kilauea. Located on Kauai's north shore, 25 minutes from Lihu'e. Tel: 828-6121. Open daily 9am–5pm. Free. Self-guided tours of this 480-acre (194-hectare) guava orchard; learn about the production and processing of guava products.

Kauai Museum, 4428 Rice Street, Lihu'e. Tel: 245-6931. Open Mon–Fri 9am–4pm, Sat 10am–4pm. Admission fee. This former library contains a wealth of geological and ethnic displays in a compact space.

Koke'e Natural History Museum, PO Box 100, Kekaha. Tel: 335-9975. Open daily 10am–4pm . Donations are appreciated. This is a small museum featuring exhibits on the natural history of the area.

National Tropical Botanical Gardens, with three sections on Kauai – the main island's gardens at Lawai, the adjacent Allerton Estate in the south, near Po'ipu, and the Limahuli Gardens on the North Shore where native species thrive; www.ntbg.org.

Wai'oli Mission House Museum, Hanalei. Tel: 245-3202. Open 9am–3pm Tues, Thur, Sat. Admission fee.

FESTIVALS

Here are the main festivals to look out for throughout the year. An up-to-date calendar of events can be accessed at www.gohawaii.com.

January

Hula Bowl: Annual college all-star football game spotlighting the top senior players in the nation. Held on Oahu for 51 years, the game relocated to Maui in 1998 and is played (usually the second or third Saturday) at the 24,500-seat War Memorial Stadium. Tel: 871-4141.
Lunar New Year: A 15-day celebration starting on the day of the second new moon after the winter solstice (around mid- to late January). Drums, firecrackers and traditional lion dances chase bad spirits out of homes and shops in Chinatown, downtown Honolulu, clearing the way for a *kung hee fat choi* (Prosperous New Year). Tel: 533-3181.
Narcissus Festival: Five weeks of various Chinese shows, exhibits and events coinciding with Chinese New Year; topped with the coronation of the Chinese Narcissus Queen. Event continues into February. Tel: 533-3181.
Champions Skins Game: Annual golf event hosted by the Grand Wailea Resort on Maui. This two-day event, held during Super Bowl weekend, features four golf legends – Jack Nicklaus, Arnold Palmer, Lee Trevino and Tom Watson are among past participants. Tel: 875-7450; www.championsskinswailca.com.
State Legislature Opening: Annual Legislative session is initiated in style at the State Capitol in Honolulu on the third Wednesday of January with a colorful ceremony, *lei* presentations, Hawaiian entertainment and speeches.

February

Great Aloha Run: Annual 8.2-mile (13.2-km) fun run on Oahu benefiting local charities. Held every President's Day; begins at Aloha Tower and finishes at Aloha Stadium. Tel: 528-7388; www.greataloha.com.
Pro Bowl: Annual all-star football game featuring the top players from the National Football League. Held on Oahu at Aloha Stadium on the Sunday following the Super Bowl. Tel: 486-9300.
Punahou Carnival: Largest and most popular school carnival in the state, taking place in early February. Fruit jams, jellies and other homemade local foods on sale; white elephant tent; art sale; games; rides. Manoa Valley, Honolulu. Tel: 944-5711.

March

Girls' Day (Hinamatsuri) Dolls Festival: Japanese customarily honor young girls on March 3 with a gift of a doll for their heirloom collections. Several department stores feature intricate doll displays.
Hawaii International Sport Kite Championships: Kite-flying demonstrations and competitions featuring expert kite-flyers from around the world. Held in early March at Kapi'olani Park, Waikiki.
Honolulu Festival: A Waikiki parade is the highlight of this series of events that highlight links between Hawaii and Japan. Tel: 926-2424; www.honolulufestival.com.
Kamehameha Schools Song Festival: On the Friday before spring break, a Hawaiian choral singing competition between classes for Hawaiian and part-Hawaiian youths is staged at the Neal Blaisdell Center, Honolulu. Tel: 842-8495.
Kuhio Day: March 26 is a state holiday honoring the birthday of Prince Jonah Kuhio Kalaniana'ole. Celebrations include parades, memorial services at the Nu'uanu Royal Mausoleum and ceremonies at Kawaiaha'o Church in downtown Honolulu. A Prince Kuhio Festival takes place on the weekend closest to his birthday on the island of his birth, Kauai. Tel: (808) 245-3971.

April

Celebration of the Arts: Annual festival featuring hula and chant performances, art workshops and demonstrations. Held early April at the Ritz-Carlton, Kapalua on Maui. Tel: 669-6200.
Easter: Sunrise services held at the former leprosy colony of Kalaupapa, Molokai; and at the National Memorial Cemetery of the Pacific, Punchbowl Crater, Honolulu.
Merrie Monarch Festival: A *ho'olaule'a*, arts and crafts fair, and a parade highlight the week-long hula festival, which honors King David Kalakaua. The Merrie Monarch hula competition is considered Hawaii's finest and most prestigious. Hilo, island of Hawaii. Tel: 935-9168; www.merriemonarchfestival.org.

May

Boys' Day: Long, colorful paper or cloth carp are strung up on May 5 outside Island homes to honor boys in the family – so that they may pursue their goals like the strong-spirited carp that fights upstream currents. Imported from Japan.
Honoka'a Western Weekend and Rodeo: Annual Big Island festival with a rodeo, parade, ethnic foods, arts

BELOW: garlands galore at the Lei Day festivities in Kapi'olani Park.

TRANSPORTATION

ACCOMMODATIONS

EATING OUT

ACTIVITIES

A – Z

LANGUAGE

and crafts, entertainment and country dance.

International Festival of Canoes: a fascinating glimpse of an art form and craft as exhibited by islanders from around the Pacific. In Lahaina, Maui, two weeks. Tel: 667-9175.

Lei Day: Every May 1, people celebrate May Day island-style – dressed in cheerful, printed *mu'umu'u* and aloha shirts, lots of *leis* (garlands) and smiles. Students throughout the islands – notably at elementary school level – perform multi-ethnic dances and songs in full costume.

Molokai Ka Hula Piko: Annual festival celebrating the birth of the hula on Molokai. Held the third Saturday of May, the event includes a sunrise ceremonial, hula and music performances, arts and crafts, and food booths. Papohaku Beach Park, Molokai. Tel: 800-800 6367; www.molokaievents.com.

World Fire Knife Dancing Championships: Hosted by the Polynesian Cultural Center in La'ie on Oahu, this annual competition features top fire knife dancers from around the world performing amazing feats with the traditional Samoan fire knife. Tel: 293-3333; www.polynesia.com.

June

50th State Fair: Hawaiian quilt-making contests, local musicians and a rainbow of ethnic dances, produce and livestock shows, food booths, carnival rides and commercial booth displays and specially scheduled entertainment; usually at Honolulu's Aloha Stadium. Tel: 486-9300.

Hawaii State Farm Fair: Midway rides, carnival games, food booths, agricultural exhibits and entertainment are featured at this annual fair – held late June or early July – at the Aloha Stadium on Oahu. Tel: 848-2074.

King Kamehameha Celebration: June 11 is King Kamehameha Day, honoring Hawaii's great king who united all the Hawaiian islands under single rule. Festivities are held throughout the month. Oahu events include a *lei*-draping ceremony at the King Kamehameha Statue in downtown Honolulu. Tel: 586-0333.

Pan-Pacific Festival: Also known as the Matsuri in Hawaii Festival, this event celebrates the cultures of Hawaii, Japan and the Pacific. Cultural demonstrations and entertainment take place at various sites in Honolulu, Oahu. Tel: 926-8177.

Pu'uhonua O Honaunau Festival: Week-long Hawaiian celebration at Pu'uhonua O Honaunau in Kailua-Kona on the Big Island, featuring traditional Hawaiian games, entertainment, food and cultural demonstrations. Held end of June. Tel: 328-2288.

July

Bon Odori Dance Festival: Japanese Buddhists honor deceased ancestors at this lively dance (in July or August) under paper lanterns and around a tower supporting a drum beater and vocalists. Temples throughout the islands hold these dances (around 7.30pm to midnight) throughout July and August, and visitors are invited to join. The season ends with the Floating Lanterns Festival at the Jodo Mission in Hale'iwa. Tel: 637-4382.

Fourth of July: America's Independence Day is celebrated with special activities throughout the state. Check local newspaper listings. The most popular – and most crowded – event is a glorious fireworks show off Magic Island at Ala Moana Beach Park in Honolulu.

Hawaii All-Collectors Show: Collectors of things Hawaiian (and even non-Hawaiian) should not miss this annual end-of-July production at the Neal Blaisdell Exhibition Hall in Honolulu. Antique coins, postcards, dolls, toys, records, aloha shirts and more are available for sale. Tel: 941-9754.

Hawaii International Jazz Festival: Top international jazz musicians and vocalists gather on Oahu each July for a four-day jazz celebration. Various sites across Honolulu and Waikiki. Tel: 941-9974.

Kapalua Wine & Food Festival: Three-day event which gathers winemakers and chefs from around the globe and includes seminars, demonstrations, tastings and spectacular evening galas. Kapalua Resort, Maui. Toll free: 800-KAPALUA. www.kapaluamaui.com

Koloa Plantation Days: Week-long

Kona Coffee

Hawaii's own homegrown and roasted coffee beans are produced in Kona on the only commercial coffee plantations in the United States. This Big Island product is accorded a gourmet status in international coffee-drinking circles. Stay away from the blends, which require only 10 percent Kona beans. And there's more beyond Kona: gourmet coffee is being grown on Molokai, Kauai and Maui as well.

Kauai festival in July pays tribute to Hawaii's once-thriving sugar plantations. Entertainment includes sporting events, rodeo, cooking demonstrations and a parade. Tel: 742-6096.

August

Hawaiian International Billfish Tournament: Held in early August; giant marlin are caught during this popular tournament at Kailua-Kona on the Big Island. Tel: 329-6155.

Maui Onion Festival: Food demonstrations (featuring the famous Maui onion), entertainment and a Maui onion cook-off highlight this festival at Whalers Village in Ka'anapali, Maui. Don't forget your breath mints. Tel: 661-3271.

Pu'ukohola Heiau Cultural Festival: Annual Hawaiian festival at Pu'ukohola Heiau National Historic Site on the Big Island. Highlights include cultural demonstrations, food tastings, arts and crafts workshops, and hula performances. Tel: 882-7218.

Queen Lili'uokalani Keiki Hula Competition: Statewide hula competition featuring Hawaii's top young hula students. Neal Blaisdell Center, Honolulu. Tel: 521-6905.

September

Aloha Festival: Hawaii's biggest festival, with statewide, month-long celebrations encompassing beautiful floral parades, street parties, special ceremonies and community events to celebrate the spirit of aloha. Try not to miss it. Tel: 589-1771.

A Day at Queen Emma Summer Palace: Hawaiian arts and crafts, entertainment plus food highlight this annual September 21 tribute to Hawaii's Queen Emma. Honolulu, Oahu. Tel: 595-6291.

Honolulu International Bed Race: Fund-raising craziness with teams pushing decorated beds down Kalakaua Avenue at Kapi'olani Park in Waikiki. Also featured are entertainment events, food booths and displays. Tel: 239-5546.

Honolulu Symphony: The symphony season generally runs from September to May with performances at the Blaisdell Concert Hall and Hawaii Theatre in Honolulu. Check newspaper listings. Tel: 524-0815.

LifeFest Maui: Empowering health and healthy lifestyles, this three-day event at the Wailea Resort features well-known names in the field. Tel: 242-6717.

The Maui Marathon: Popular with runners from around the world, the

26-mile run starts at Kahului and ends at Ka'anapali. Tel: 661-3271; www.mauimarathon.com.

Okinawan Festival: Kapi'olani Park, Oahu. Labor Day weekend cultural event featuring Okinawan food demonstrations, dance and entertainment. Tel: 676-5400.

October

Halloween in Lahaina: Hawaii's biggest Halloween party takes place on Halloween night in Lahaina, Maui, with costumed parades and plenty of raucous entertainment. Tel: 667-9175.
Ironman World Triathlon: A 2.4-mile (4-km) open-ocean swim, followed by a 112-mile (180-km) bike ride and a full 26-mile (42-km) marathon is the order of the Kailua-Kona day on the Big Island. Tel: 329-0063; www.ironman.com.
Molokai Hoe: International Molokai-to-Oahu canoe race. Event starts at Hale o Lono Harbor on Molokai and ends at Fort DeRussy Beach in Waikiki; first finishers are expected around noon–12.30pm.
Tel: 526-1969; www.ohora.com

November

Grand Slam of Golf: The winners of golf's four main championships — the Masters, US Open, British Open and PGA Championship – compete for a $1-million purse. Po'ipu, Kauai. Tel: 800-4742-8258; 800-PGATCKT.
Hawaii International Film Festival: Acclaimed two-week festival features international films and celebrates an "East meets West" theme. Generally held on Oahu during the second week of November, followed by a week-long stint on the neighbor islands. Tel: 528-3456; www.hiff.org.
Kona Coffee Festival: Week-long festivities in early November; includes judging of coffee recipes, Kona coffee-farm tours, and local parade and pageantry. Kailua, Big Island. Tel: 326-7820; www.konacoffeefest.org.
Mission Houses Museum Christmas Fair: Handcrafters' fair in late November features more than 50 of Hawaii's finest craftspeople, a special display in Honolulu's 1831 Chamberlain House and much free entertainment. Tel: 531-0481.
Surfing Contests: November through February are the Big Surf months on Oahu's North Shore. World championship contests are scheduled each year, dates determined by the condition of the surf. The surf here at this time is regarded as the world's best. Check local newspapers for day-by-day announcements. Tel: (361) 727-9900/524-0722.

ABOVE: face to face with marine life at the Waikiki Aquarium.

December

Festival of Art & Flowers: From floral displays of Maui-grown protea and other tropical flora to arts and crafts. There are workshops and Hawaiian music. Held in Lahaina's Banyan park. Toll free: 888-310 1117.
Honolulu City Lights: During the holiday season, downtown Honolulu dresses itself at night with bright lights and festive Christmas displays.In the daytime, check out Honolulu Hale (City Hall), which displays colorful, decorated Christmas trees and wreaths. Tel: 523-4834.
Honolulu Marathon: At the crack of dawn one morning every December, thousands of dedicated runners set off from the Aloha Tower on a 26-mile, 385-yard (42.2-km) AAU-certified (American Athletic Union) marathon course along Oahu's south shore. The Honolulu marathon ends at Kapiolani Park Bandstand. Tel: 734-7200; www.honolulumarathon.org.
Kamehameha Schools Christmas Song Festival: Comprises songs performed in both Hawaiian and English by the Kamehameha Schools' Glee Club Orchestra. Held early December at the Neal Blaisdell Concert Hall in Honolulu. Tel: 842-8495.
Na Mele O Maui Festival: Several Ka'anapali hotels participate in a celebration of Hawaiian music and dance. Maui. Tel: 661-3271.
Pearl Harbor Day: In memory of those who were killed during the Japanese bombing of Oahu on December 7, 1941, a memorial service is held every year at the USS *Arizona* Memorial. Tel: 422-2771.

CHILDREN'S ACTIVITIES

By far the biggest attraction for kids in Hawaii is the ocean. All beaches offer free access to all visitors all the time. However, few have lifeguards, so it's important to be aware that the waves and currents can be very dangerous. Surfing and windsurfing lessons are widely available in all the major tourist areas, and snorkeling and whale-watching cruises and kayaking excursions are offered everywhere.

Other activities suitable for older kids include downhill bike rides, on Maui and Kauai; horse riding on every island; ATV expeditions; and commercial "jungle hikes".

There are many water-themed attractions. Oahu has **Sea Life Park**, 41-202 Kalaniana'ole Highway, at Makapu'u Point. Tel: 259-7933; www.sealifeparkhawaii.com. Open daily 9.30am–5pm. Admission fee. Along the Kapi'olani waterfront is the **Waikiki Aquarium**, 2777 Kalakaua Avenue; tel: 923-9741; www.waquarium.org. Open 9am–5pm daily. Admission fee. **Hawaiian Waters Adventure Park**, 400 Farrington Hwy, Kapolei; tel: 674-9283; www.hawaiianwaters.com. Open daily 10am–dusk.

Maui boasts the **Maui Ocean Center**, 193 Maalaea Rd, Wailuku; tel: 270-7000; www.mauioceancenter.com. Open daily 9am–5pm, July and August until 6pm. Admission fee. Visit the Hammerhead Harbor, Turtle Lagoon and Marine Mammal Discovery Center.

TRANSPORTATION ACCOMMODATIONS EATING OUT ACTIVITIES A – Z LANGUAGE

SHOPPING

What to Buy

Cosmopolitan residents and visitors shop for a variety of international goods and domestic creations in shops throughout the islands, but Hawaii has its own distinct goods. Items range from Polynesian kitsch *tiki* gods with olivine stone eyes to fine Ni'ihau shell *lei* that may cost as much as $2,500 for four strands.

Aloha wear

Hawaii has its own fashions, the *mu'umu'u* and aloha shirt. The first *mu'umu'u*, designed and introduced by the early missionaries, was a loose, lengthy, high-necked, long-sleeved shroud. Because of variations in its style, *mu'umu'u* has come to refer to just about any casual smock, long or short, made of Hawaiian print fabric. The aloha shirt was first marketed in the 1930s by a Chinese tailor in Honolulu. *Mu'umu'u* and aloha shirts are sold and worn everywhere. Some island occasions, such as wedding receptions and dinner parties, specify "aloha attire" as the preferred mode of dress.

Art/collectibles

Hawaii is awash with galleries offering all types of fine arts, with names like Picasso, Erte, Chagall, and the like featured. In addition, local artists flourish in painting, watercolor, ceramics, glasswork, woodwork, and multi-media arts.

Chinese preserves

Introduced by the Chinese, these preserves have become a favorite snack treat in Hawaii. Plums, cherries, mangos, guavas, apricots, lemons and limes are salted and preserved in the form of sweet-sour pickles known as "crack seed." Shops specializing in these pickled seeds can be found downtown and in major suburban shopping areas.

Dried gourds

Called *ipu* in Hawaiian, the tan bottle gourd is hollowed-out and dried and used as a food and water receptacle, a drum or a hula instrument.

Feather leis and hat bands

Feathers of birds such as the pheasant and peacock are made into attractive *leis* (garlands) and hat bands. In ancient Hawaii, items made of feathers were reserved for royalty and high-ranking *ali'i*.

Hawaiian instruments

Popular Hawaiian hula instruments include the *ipu*, *pu'ili* (slashed percussive bamboo sticks), *'uli'uli* (a feather-topped gourd rattle filled with seeds) and *'ili'ili* (small smooth stones used like castanets in a set of four). There are also the *hano* (nose flute) and *'ukulele*. All are available at island hula supply shops and some music stores.

Jellies, jams and preserves

Tropical fruits such as guava, *poha*, mango, passion fruit, papaya and coconut are made into unique, luscious spreads.

Kukui nut and seed lei

The tradition of stringing and wearing the brown and black-and-white *kukui* nuts, commonly called candlenuts, is still very popular. *Koa* seed *lei* are also appealing, but most of these are strung in the Philippines.

Macadamia nuts

Delicious roasted and eaten plain or chocolate-covered, this rich nut is true gourmet fare. Macadamia nut products are grown and packaged in Hawaii.

Ni'ihau shell lei

Small, rare shells are washed up onto the beaches of the privately owned island of Ni'ihau, where some of the 200-plus residents will gather and string them into *lei* or necklaces. There is a beautiful range of delicate, subtle colors. The *lei* are very expensive, and found only in upscale shops, especially on Kauai.

Photographs of old Hawaii

Peer into Hawaii's past. Leaf through the photo albums at the Hawaii State Archives (tel: 586-0329), downtown off S. King Street in the 'Iolani Palace grounds. The archives are open Mon–Fri 9am–4pm. Copies are available but generally take up to two weeks for delivery (by mail). Or visit the archives at the Bishop Museum (tel: 848-4182), by far the largest in the state with more than 500,000 images. Here, copies are more expensive, but the choice is greater.

Plants

Exotic hibiscus, anthurium, bamboo, orchid, *ti* and bird of paradise plants (and their seeds) are potted in sterile peat moss and agriculturally inspected. (Warning: be sure they were inspected by the Agricultural Inspection Board before attempting to take them on to the mainland.) Some sellers will ship these pre-fumigated.

Scrimshaw

This Pacific art came into its own in the 1800s when bored sailors on whaling vessels scratched pictures on whale teeth. Nowadays, a number of non-endangered materials are used, such as fossilized walrus tusk. Predictably, Maui is a good place to look at and purchase scrimshaw, particularly in West Maui.

Sea shells

Forget these. A souvenir whose time has passed. Shells taken locally deprive sea life of shelter. Also, many of the shells found in souvenir shops come from places like the Philippines.

Surfboards

Custom-made fiberglass surfboards can be adapted to your height, weight and personal taste in design by some of the finest board shapers in the world.

Tapa

Tapa (bark cloth), properly called *kapa*, is made into popular items – place mats, wall-hangings, bags and hats. However, the *tapa* for sale may not be Hawaiian *kapa*, but a related fabric made in Samoa and Tonga. The art of making real Hawaiian *kapa* was lost during the 19th century, but is now enjoying a revival with a new generation of artisans.

Wood

Monkeypod, *koa* and *milo* are three popular island woods used in the making of furniture, *calabashes* (large ceremonial bowls) and other fine wood creations. *Koa* and rosewood are also used to make quality guitars and *'ukuleles*.

Woven goods

Lauhala (pandanus), coconut fronds, makaloa sedge and the rootlets of the *'ie'ie* forest vine are used to weave mats, baskets, bowls, hats and more.

Shopping Areas

All the Hawaiian islands, with the exception of less-developed Molokai and Lanai, offer endless retail possibilities, from shopping centers to surf shops to small-town treasures or chic resort boutiques.

Oahu

Ala Moana Center, the largest mall in the state and one of the largest open-air malls in the world, housing about 200 stores (including more than two dozen eateries) and covering 50 acres (20 hectares)

across from Ala Moana Park. Free island entertainment regularly takes place on the mall's centerstage. Open Mon–Thur 9.30am–9pm, Fri 9.30am–10pm, Sat 8am–10pm, Sun 10am–7pm. Tel: 955-9517; www.alamoana.com.
Aloha Tower Marketplace, located at Pier 9 near the downtown business district. This harbor-side complex features an interesting array of shops and restaurants. The adjacent Hawaii Maritime Center celebrates Hawaii's maritime heritage. Open Mon–Sat 9am–9pm, Sun 9am–6pm; restaurants and bars close later. Tel: 566-2337; www.alohatower.com.
Chinatown, an integral part of downtown Honolulu and by far the most interesting shopping area in the islands. Watch noodles being made, take your ailments to an acupuncturist's or herbal shop, choose from more than 30 restaurants, or visit the shops and galleries on side streets from Hotel Street. At night, a section of Hotel Street retains its sailors-on-liberty flavor, with strip joints and bars that should not be entered alone.
Downtown Honolulu, on Bishop Street, which was named after the islands' first banker and is today the financial center of Hawaii. All the major banks are here, along with airlines, restaurants and shops. Every Friday there are entertaining free concerts at Tamarind Park, which spotlight the best Hawaiian, contemporary and jazz musicians. Business hours are 8am–5pm.

BELOW: colorful Hawaiian prints for sale.

Kahala Mall, in the Kahala residential district just east of Diamond Head and Waikiki, home of the designer pizza and a movie complex. Openings are staggered, beginning at 8.30am. Most shops close at 9pm, although the supermarkets are open 24 hours. Tel: 732-7736; www.kahalamallcenter.com.
Kapahulu Avenue, which ends in Waikiki, offers an interesting selection of shops that feature collectible Hawaiiana approximately 1 mile (1.5 km) from the beach.
Pearlridge Center, 1005 Moanalua Road, in 'Aiea. A massive mall in two "phases," divided by a watercress farm whose owner refused to sell his land to the developer. (A nice reminder that Hawaii's motto says the land is perpetuated in "righteousness.") Open Mon–Sat 10am–9pm, Sun 10am–6pm. Tel: 488-0981; www.pearlridgeonline.com.
Waikele Center, 94–790 Lumiaina Street, Exit 7 off H-1, about 15 minutes west of Honolulu. Home to 50 outlets including Calvin Klein, Ralph Lauren and the like – discounts abound at the factory outlet shops. Open Mon–Sat 9am–9pm, Sun 10am–6pm. Tel: 676-5656; www.waikelecenter.com.
The Ward Centers, on Auahi Street in Kakaako. With Hawaii's largest multiplex (16 screens) and trendy shops and restaurants like Dave & Buster's (games and dining), the complex is slated for further expansion and redevelopment in 2008. Open Fri & Sat 10am–10pm,

Sun 10am–7pm. Tel: 591-8411; www.wardcenters.com.

Waikiki
DFS Galleria, 330 Royal Hawaiian Avenue, at the corner of Kalakaua Avenue. The nautically themed complex, complete with a multi-level aquarium, features resort-wear, cosmetics and souvenirs. Open daily 9am–11pm; tel 931-2655; www.dfsgalleria.com.
Hyatt Regency Shopping Center, on the first three floors of the Hyatt Regency Waikiki, 2424 Kalakaua Avenue. Visit the café on the first level, next to a three-story waterfall.
International Market Place, 2330 Kalakaua Avenue, across from the Sheraton Moana Surfrider, in the heart of Waikiki. Open daily 9am–11pm. Shops and stalls with what sometimes appears to be little more than an endless array of "genuine" gold jewelry and tourist souvenirs. There are better places elsewhere.
King's Village, 131 Ka'iulani Avenue, behind the Hyatt Regency Waikiki. Open daily 9am–11pm. This rambling, split-level commercial complex takes its theme from the 19th century, right down to a changing of the King's Guard every night at 6.15pm.
Rainbow Bazaar, 2005 Kalia Road, on the grounds of the Hilton Hawaiian Village. Shops and restaurants scattered over several acres. Open 8am–11pm daily; www.kingsvillage.com.
Royal Hawaiian Shopping Center, along Kalakaua Avenue, offering a wide variety of shops and cafés on three levels. Daily entertainment at its central courtyard. Open daily 9.30am–10.30pm; tel: 922-0588; www.shopwaikiki.com.

Maui
Kahului is the focus of Maui's urban commerce, but don't overlook the street shopping of historic Wailuku, just above Kahului, and of Makawao and Pa'ia, toward Upcountry. As nearly everybody visiting Maui stays in either the Wailea or Ka'anapali resorts, those are rich with shopping opportunities, mostly within the resorts. Lahaina lives off both shopping and eating; ramble its streets to find an abundance of cash and credit card possibilities.
Kapalua Shops, Kapalua Bay Hotel and Villas, Kapalua, West Maui. The resort is currently undergoing extensive renovation and expansion and expects to reopen in 2008. Tel: 669-3754.
Lahaina Cannery Mall, 1221 Honoapiilani Highway. West Maui's most comprehensive indoor shopping

mall, north end of Lahaina. Open daily 9.30am–9pm; tel: 661-5304; www.lahainacannerymall.com.

Queen Ka'ahumanu Center, 275 Ka'ahumanu Avenue, Kahului. Maui's largest mall with over 75 shops and eateries. Open Mon–Sat 9.30am–9pm, Sun 10am–5pm; tel: 877-3369; www.queenkaahumanu center.com.

The Shops at Wailea, 3750 Wailea Alanui. An elegant upgrade of the old shopping village, with dozens of shops and restaurants in a multi-level mall. Open daily until 9pm; tel: 891-6770; www.shopsatwailea.com.

Whalers Village, Ka'anapali Resort, West Maui. Includes more than 50 shops, a whaling museum and a 40-ft (12-meter) sperm whale skeleton. Several popular restaurants on the beach. Outdoors. Open daily 9.30am–10pm; tel: 661-4567.

Hawaii (Big Island)

The commercial centers of Hilo and Kona are the obvious choices here. Historic downtown Hilo is small, compact and undergoing a revival, and is good for quiet walking and browsing. Kona's waterfront thrives on tourism, and the offerings range – with the stress on low-end souvenirs – from T-shirts and postcards to at times dubious art. The resort hotels of Kohala – Mauna Lani, Waikoloa, Mauna Kea – have what those with gold cards are looking for.

Holualoa, Honoka'a, Volcano, Waimea Small town Hawaii, Big Island style, home to artists and artisans whose works are exhibited in shops and galleries.

Kings' Shops, Waikoloa Beach Resort. Hawaiiana exhibits throughout this shopping complex complement the nearly 40 shops and restaurants. Open 9.30am–9.30pm; tel: 885-8811.

Prince Kuhio Plaza, 111 East Puainako Street, Hilo. Largest enclosed mall on the Big Island. Open Mon–Thur 10am–8pm, Fri 10am–10pm, Sat 9.30am–10pm and Sun 10am–6pm; tel: 959-3555; www.princekuhioplaza.com.

Kauai

In keeping with its personality, Kauai's shopping is lower-key than other islands, but pleasurable and often unique. Shopping centers are found in Lihu'e, Po'ipu, Koloa, Kapa'a, Princeville and Hanalei on the North Shore. Shopping tends to be decentralized, with small, quality pockets of stores.

Coconut Marketplace, on main highway, near Kapa'a. Open-air shopping mall with 70 assorted shops, a good selection of casual restaurants and a movie theater. Open daily 9am–9pm; tel: 822-3641; www.coconutmarketplace.com.

Kapa'a is defined by a series of strip malls that serve both visitors and residents.

Kilohana, Route 50, 1½ mile (2 km) north of Lihu'e. Plantation estate with high-quality retail shops, galleries. Open daily 9.30am–9.30pm; tel: 245-5608; www.kilohanakauai.com.

Koloa/Hanapepe/Hanalei/Waimea, Small town Hawaii with a mix of enjoyable shops.

Kukui Grove, Highway 50, near Lihu'e. Kauai's largest mall. Open Mon–Sat 9.30am–7pm, Fri until 9pm; tel: 245-7784; www.kukuigrovecenter.com.

Poipu Shopping Village, 2360 Kiahuna Plantation Drive. Pleasant outdoor mall with shops and restaurants. Open Mon–Sat 9am–9pm, Sun 10am–7pm; tel: 742-2831.

WATERSPORTS

Not surprisingly, Hawaii offers a sizable menu of watersports, including surfing, windsurfing, parasailing, jet skiing, snorkeling, scuba diving, fishing, kayaking, yachting, and, newest of all, kiteboarding.

Hotels and activity desks can arrange any of these wet 'n' wild adventures for you, including lessons. One of the advantages of booking arrangements through a hotel is that the hotel has a stake in your satisfaction. If concerned about quality, go to one of the high-end luxury hotels and make arrangements through their activities desk. The price may well be 5–10 percent higher, but those hotels have international reputations to maintain, so they won't refer guests to questionable activity operators.

Windsurfing

Hawaii has world-class windsurfing, especially at Kailua Beach on Oahu and Ho'okipa Beach on Maui. In fact, both locations are the sites of major international competitions. Most of the activities desks at resort hotels offer lessons to both guests and non-guests. Check around for prices, and for an instructor who you're comfortable with – you'll be out there with him or her in full view of everyone on the beach, probably falling in the water a great deal, and the less stress the better.

Scuba Diving

While the diving in Hawaii is not equal to that in Fiji or Palau, it is quite good and often unique, especially around the Big Island, which is too young for a decent coral reef but which has lots of interesting underwater lava formations. The waters are usually warm, although in winter a full wetsuit is recommended, and the experience of swimming with the fish is like nothing else on earth.

There are scores of dive shops and operators in Hawaii. Standards are high, with experienced staff providing a quality experience. Shops cater to everyone, from novices to experts. Make sure that you sign on for the dive suited to your skills.

The activities desks of the larger hotels usually have a long-term working relationship with a single dive operator with a good track record.

If you're looking for diving lessons leading to certification, make sure the dive instructor is *PADI* (Professional Association of Diving Instructors) or *NAUI* certified. Depending on the schedule used for instruction, it can take two to five days to complete the lessons, and you usually begin in a swimming pool. Again, hotel activity desks can set you up with lessons.

Kiteboarding

The newest sport to hit Hawaii, kiteboarding (or kitesurfing) is self-explanatory; stand on a surfboard with a kite attached, and fly above the water. The first ever kiteboarding school is in Maui, five minutes from the Kahului International Airport at 22 Hana Highway.

Sailing and Kayaking

Oddly enough, few people think of taking a yacht trip through the islands. It is pricey, perhaps, but the experience is unmatched. There are several yachts available for charters, complete with meals and captain. They can be customized for big-game fishing, scuba diving or just a leisurely holiday jaunt. The majority of them are based on the Big Island.

Kayaking is gaining popularity in the islands. River kayaking is limited mostly to Kauai, particularly on the Hanalei River. Ocean kayaking is found everywhere. Popular excursions include multi-day paddles along the Na Pali Coast of Kauai and the north coast of Molokai.

Fishing

Hawaii is world-famous for big game of fishing, especially for catches taken off the Kona Coast of the Big Island. World-class fishing tournaments held there each summer draw competitive game fishermen from across the globe.

It's all done by charter boats, most of which are located at Kona Harbor or at another harbor up near the Kona airport. Fishing charters also depart from Lahaina and Ma'alaea on Maui, and Kewalo Basin on Oahu.

ABOVE: the only way to travel.

WATERSPORTS OPERATORS

Boat Tours

Oahu

Ali'i Kai Catamaran tel: 954-8652
www.robertshawaii.com
Atlantis Submarines tel: 973-9811
www.atlantisadventures.com
Navatek I tel: 973-1311
www.atlantisadventures.com
Star of Honolulu tel: 983-7827
www.starofhonolulu.com

Maui

Atlantis Submarines tel: 667-2224
www.atlantisadventures.com
Hokua tel: 249-2583
www.alohabluecharters.com
Maui Princess tel: 661-8397
www.mauiprincess.com
Pacific Whale Foundation
tel: 249-8811
www.pacificwhale.org
Pride of Maui tel: 242-0955
www.prideofmaui.com
Quicksilver tel: 661-3333
www.bossfrog.com

Hawaii (Big Island)

Atlantis Submarines tel: 800-548
6262 www.atlantisadventures.com
Body Glove tel: 800-551 8911
www.bodyglovehawaii.com
Captain Zodiac tel: 329-3199
www.captainzodiac.com
Fair Wind tel: 345-0268
www.fair-wind.com
Sea Paradise tel: 322-2500
www.seaparadise.com

Kauai

Captain Andy tel: 335-6833
www.napali.com
Captain Sundown tel: 826-5585
www.captainsundown.com
Holoholo Charters tel: 335-0815
www.holoholocharters.com
Kauai Sea Tours tel: 826-7254
www.kauaiseatours.com
Na Pali Catamaran tel: 255-6853
www.napalicatamaran.com

Na Pali Explorer tel: 338-9999
www.napali-explorer.com

Diving

Oahu

Aloha Dive Shop tel: 395-5922
www.alohadiveshop.com
Ocean Concepts tel: 677-7975
www.oceanconcepts.com
Surf'n'Sea tel: 637-3337
www.surfnsea.com

Maui

Maui Dive Shop tel: 879-1775
www.mauidiveshop.com
Maui Dreams tel: 874-5332
www.mauidreamdiveco.com
Pacific Dive tel: 667-5331
www.pacificdive.com
Prodiver tel: 875-4004
www.prodivermaui.com

Hawaii (Big Island)

Big Island Divers tel: 329-6068
www.bigislanddivers.com
Aloha Dive Company tel: 325-5560
www.alohadive.com
Jack's Diving Locker tel: 329-7585
www.jacksdivinglocker.com
Kohala Divers tel: 882-7774
www.kohaladivers.com
Pacific Rim Divers tel: 334-1750
www.pacificrimdivers.com

Kauai

Bubbles Below tel: 332-7333
www.bubblesbelowkauai.com
Dive Kauai tel: 822-0452
www.divekauai.com
Fathom Five tel: 742-6691
www.fathomfive.com
Mana Divers tel: 335-0881
www.manadivers.com

Surfing and Windsurfing

Oahu

Kailua Sailboards & Kayaks
tel: 262-2555

Maui

Goofy Foot Surf School
tel: 244-9283
www.goofyfootsurfschool.com
Nancy Emerson tel: 244-7873
www.mauisurfclinics.com
Windsurfari tel: 871-7766
www.windsurfari.com

Kauai

Kauai Surf School tel: 651-6032
www.kauaisurfschool.com
Margo Oberg tel: 332-6100
www.surfonkauai.com
Titus Kinimaka tel: 651-1116
www.hawaiianschoolofsurfing.com
Windsurf Kauai tel: 828-6838

Kayaking

Oahu

Hawaiian Watersports
tel: 255-4352
Kailua Sailboards & Kayaks
tel: 262-2555

Maui

Kelii's Kayak Tours tel: 888-874 7652
www.keliiskayak.com
South Pacific Kayaks tel: 875-4848
www.southpacifickayaks.com

Kauai

Kayak Kauai tel: 826-9844
www.kayakkauai.com
Pedal & Paddle tel: 826-9069
www.pedalnpaddle.com
True Blue tel: 246-6333
www.kauaifun.com
Wailua Kayak Adventures
tel: 822-5795
www.kauaiwailuakayak.com

Snorkel Rental

Snorkel equipment is available for rental from numerous outlets, including Snorkel Bob's (www.snorkelbob.com), which has stores on all the major islands.

A – Z

A HANDY SUMMARY OF PRACTICAL INFORMATION, ARRANGED ALPHABETICALLY

A dmission Charges

The typical admission fee to museums or other public buildings in Hawaii, and also to state or county parks, is $4 or $5 per adult, half that for children (though the maximum age for half-price tickets can range from 12 to 17). The two national parks, Haleakala on Maui and Hawaii Volcanoes on the Big Island, charge $10 each, but the fee covers all passengers in a single vehicle. The only charges that will make a serious impact on your budget are likely to be those for commercial tourist attractions, and especially so on Oahu, where the very cheapest adult admission to the Polynesian Cultural Center costs $55, and an adult entrance to Sea Life Park is $29.

B udgeting for Your Trip

Broadly speaking, Hawaii ranks at the expensive end of American vacation destinations. Prices are generally high, as so much of what is consumed in the islands has to be shipped there from across the Pacific or beyond. In addition, many tourists are happy to pay premium rates for a once-in-a-lifetime holiday in paradise.

However, it is possible to keep your costs down. The finest hotels tend to charge at least $250 per room per night, and often double that, but for pretty good accommodation close to the sea it's perfectly possible to pay $125–150 in a hotel, or perhaps $100 for a rented condo. All the islands hold significantly cheaper options too, well worth considering if you expect to spend most of your time exploring.

Only on Oahu is it realistic to think you won't need a car; typical rental rates would be $150–200 per week for a compact vehicle. Gas isn't cheap, but you won't use all that much, because you can't drive very far on such small islands.

The average visitor spends about $30 per day on food and drink; even if you buy and prepare your own meals, it's hard to go much lower than say $20 per day, while at the other end of the spectrum there are plenty of fine-dining restaurants charging $50 or more for a single meal.

You'll never have to pay to go on the beach, but prices for any kind of commercial activity – a snorkel or whale-watching cruise, a bus tour, a submarine ride, a guided hike or bike ride – also tend to be high.

Business Hours

Typical opening hours for offices and small businesses in Hawaii are 9am or 10am in the morning until 5pm or 6pm in the evening. Shops, especially in malls and tourist areas, usually stay open later, until 10pm.

C limate

There are seasons in sub-tropic Hawaii, it just takes time to recognize them. Most of Hawaii experiences balmy 73–88°F (23–31°C) weather from April through October, and cooler, wetter 65–83°F (18–28°C) weather from November through March. Rarely does the mercury drop below 60°F (15°C), nor go higher than about 90°F (32°C).

While sunbathing is a common activity here, don't overdo it. Slowly create a tolerance for Hawaii's strong sunlight by taking no more than 30 minutes of direct sun exposure the first day, 40 minutes the second day, 50 minutes the third day and so on. To prevent sunburn, be sure to wear sunscreen and keep applying it – you will find instructions on use on the container.

The surrounding sea and

CLIMATE CHART

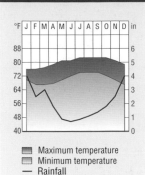

°F J F M A M J J A S O N D in

88 ──────────── 6
80 ──────────── 5
72 ──────────── 4
64 ──────────── 3
56 ──────────── 2
48 ──────────── 1
40 ──────────── 0

▨ Maximum temperature
▢ Minimum temperature
— Rainfall

northeasterly trade winds are a natural air-conditioning system. However, when the trade winds stop, and less frequent southerly winds take over, the result is often sticky and humid.

Certain areas on each island – usually on the windward side of mountains – receive more rainfall than others. One of the wettest spots on Earth is Mount Wai'ale'ale on Kauai, which has been drenched by as much as 486 inches (1,234 cm) of rain in a year.

In higher places such as Upcountry and Haleakala on Maui, and Koke'e on Kauai, temperatures range from 48°F to 72°F (9–22°C), and in mountainous parts of the Big

Island the average temperature drops to 31°F–58°F (-1–14°C) during the winter and at night. Snow falls on Mauna Kea (and sometimes Haleakala on Maui) in the winter, so bring warm clothing if you intend to tour these areas.

Sometimes during volcanic eruptions on the Big Island, a smoky pall lingers over the islands for several days, especially in the Kona area. Islanders call this volcanic haze "vog," or volcanic smog. People suffering from asthma or other respiratory problems may wish to take extra precautions during "voggy" weather.

Flash Floods

In the mountain areas, intense rain can cause flash floods. If you are hiking, take care during heavy rains as flash floods can occur without warning. If a flash flood watch has been issued by the National Weather Service, be alert: flooding is possible. A warning means that flooding is imminent or already occurring. If you are in a flood-prone area, get to higher ground immediately.

Hurricanes

Hurricanes are infrequent in Hawaii, but when they do touch the islands, they generally hit hard. Take all warnings seriously. Phone directories contain detailed information, including flood and tidal wave zones for each island, and public shelter locations.

Consulates

American Samoa, tel: 847-1998.
Australia, tel: 524-5050.
Japan, tel: 543-3111.
Korea, tel: 595-6109.
Philippines, tel: 595-6316.
Taiwan, tel: 595-6347.
Thailand, tel: 845-7332.
Tonga, tel: 953-2449.

The hurricane season is from June through November. In general, Pacific storms do more damage when coming from the south than from other directions. There are several classifications of storms, up to hurricane status.
• Tropical depressions are low-pressure systems with sustained winds of less than 40 miles (60 km) per hour.
• Tropical storms are cyclones with winds of 40–75 mph (60–120 kph).
• A hurricane is declared when a tropical cyclone has winds greater than 75 miles (120 km) per hour.

When a tropical depression forms, the National Weather Service issues a series of advisories, based on the position and strength of the approaching storm. If a hurricane watch has been issued, a hurricane is expected within 36 hours. A hurricane warning means a hurricane is expected within 24 hours.

When the civil defense sirens

BELOW: the perfect climate for sunbathing – in moderation.

Electricity

Standard US 110–120 volts, 60 cycles AC. Large hotels are usually able to provide voltage and plug converters.

sound, tune to local radio or television stations for emergency disaster instructions. Stay indoors during high winds, and evacuate areas that may flood. Evacuation orders by authorities must be followed at all times.

Tsunami (Tidal Waves)

Earthquakes, particularly on the Big Island, sometimes forebode a *tsunami*, the correct term for a seismic or tidal wave. Earthquakes elsewhere, including Alaska, can send a *tsunami* to Hawaii. They can occur with little warning or time for preparation. When a *tsunami* warning is issued, leave coastal areas immediately. Use the *tsunami* evacuation maps published in island telephone directories. Should civil defense sirens sound, tune in to a radio or TV for instructions. If outside of the danger zones indicated in the telephone directory maps, remain there. If you are in a flood-prone area, head for higher ground.

Crime and Safety

Hawaii has earned a reputation for hospitality and all the good cheer that the word *aloha* implies. However, travelers should be warned that all types of crime – including burglaries, robberies, assaults and rapes – do occur on the islands. On the whole, however, Honolulu is one of the

Emergencies

Fire, Police, Ambulance
Tel: 911
Coast Guard Search and Rescue
Tel: (800) 552-6458
American Red Cross
Tel: 734-2101
Dental emergency service
Tel: 944-8863
FBI
Tel: 566-4300
Lifeguard Service
Tel: 922-3888
Poison Center
Tel: 941-4411
Sex Abuse Treatment Center
Tel: 524-7273
Suicide and Crisis Center
Tel: 832-3100
US Secret Service
Tel: 541-1912

safest cities in North America.
Follow the usual precautions as when traveling anywhere else. Use common sense. Don't carry jewelry, large amounts of cash or other valuables. In areas far from population centers, car break-ins and beach thefts of unattended personal property are becoming common, even at popular tourist sites.

Civil Defense

The Emergency Alert System, which warns of natural disasters or a nuclear holocaust, is tested at 11.45am on the first business day of every month. In the event of an actual emergency, civil defense instructions are broadcast on all radio, TV and cable TV systems.

State Civil Defense, tel: 733-4300.
Oahu, tel: 523-4121.
Big Island, tel: 935-0031.
Maui County, tel: 270-7285.
Kauai, tel: 241-1800.

D isabled Travelers

Hawaii is very well geared towards meeting the needs of disabled travelers. Download detailed reports on facilities from the website of the State of Hawaii Disability and Communication Access Board (tel: 586-8121; www.state.hi.us/health/dcab/). Specific information on Hawaiian hotels is also available from Access–Able (www.access–able.com). Vehicles on Oahu's excellent TheBus transportation network are adapted for travelers with disabilities.

E ntry Requirements

Visas and Passports

Details of the visa waiver scheme, under which travelers carrying passports issued by Britain, Ireland, and most European countries, as well as Australia and New Zealand, do not need visas for trips to the United States lasting less than 90 days, can be obtained from your travel agent or via http://travel.state.gov.

Animals and Agriculture

Hawaii is free of rabies, snakes and poison ivy, and state officials work hard to keep it that way. Incoming animals are placed in quarantine for 120 days at the owner's expense, although recent legislation now permits dogs and cats that meet certain pre- and post-arrival requirements to be quarantined for only 30 days.
Baggage is inspected coming and going through the airport. Papayas,

avocados and bananas must be treated before being exported. Coconuts and pineapples do not need treatment.
US Dept of Agriculture, tel: 861-8490.
State Dept of Agriculture, tel: 973-9560.
Animal Quarantine Station, tel: 483-7171.
Plant Quarantine Station, tel: 832-0566.

G ay and Lesbian Travelers

For information on the gay scene throughout Hawaii, access the www.gayhawaii.com website. That's run by Pacific Ocean Holidays (tel: 944-4700, http://gayhawaiivacations.com), which also arranges vacation packages for gay and lesbian travelers. Among specific gay-friendly accommodation options are the Cabana at Waikiki on Oahu (www.cabana-waikiki.com), the Sunseeker Resort on Maui (www.mauisunseeker.com), and the Mahina Kai B&B on Kauai (www.mahinakai.com).

H ealth and Medical Care

Most of the larger hotels have a physician on call. Other medical services can be obtained at several main Honolulu hospitals:
Kaiser-Permanente
(clinics throughout Hawaii), 1010 Pensacola Street
Tel: 593-2950
Kaiser's Urgent Care Clinic
2155 Kalakaua Avenue
Tel: 597-2860
Kapi'olani Medical Center for Women and Children
1319 Punahou Street
Tel: 983-6000
Queen's Medical Center
1301 Punchbowl Street
Tel: 538-9011
Straub Clinic and Hospital
888 S. King Street
Tel: 522-4000

Hawaiian Time

Time in the islands is not noticeably defined by the four seasons, and Hawaii's balmy climate tends to warp any rigid schedule. Islanders can be lax about time, especially when going on dates and to meetings outside of strictly commercial business circles. This habit of being "fashionably late" by around 10 minutes is generally known as being on "Hawaiian time."

Internet

Internet access is widely available throughout Hawaii. Upscale hotels invariably offer high-speed access from guest rooms (though usually for a fee of around $10 per day), while all the resort areas hold internet cafés. In addition, all state libraries and most university libraries provide free access.

Maps

By far the best maps of the Hawaiian islands are published by the University of Hawaii, for around $4 each and are available at island bookstores. If you are doing any serious exploring or adventuring, don't rely on the free maps distributed by hotels or rental-car agencies. If you need detailed hiking maps, then make a visit to the state parks office in Honolulu.

Media

Hawaii has a handful of island daily and weekly newspapers – most notably the liberal-leaning *Honolulu Weekly* and the mainstream *Midweek*, both free – and numerous magazines. There are two statewide circulated major dailies, *The Honolulu Advertiser* and *The Honolulu Star-Bulletin*. Both newspapers publish morning and afternoon editions.

Neighbor islands also have their own daily newspapers, with circulation restricted to that specific island. A variety of other newspapers are

BELOW: celebrating Kamehameha Day.

published by ethnic groups, the military, religious organizations, and by the tourism and business industries. The Associated Press maintains a bureau in Honolulu to cover both Hawaii and the areas around the Pacific.

Radio

Honolulu's listeners tune in to some 30 radio stations, with programs ranging from Top 40 hits, jazz, classic rock and Hawaiian music to news, talk and sports. Foreign-language programs are available on certain stations. Check listings in the local newspapers *(see above)* for the relevant frequencies.

Television

There are more than 10 broadcast television channels that originate in the state of Hawaii. These include channels 2 (KHON-FOX); 4 (KITV-ABC); 5 (KFVE); 9 (KGMB-CBS); 11 (KHET-PBS); and 13 (KHNL-NBC). For broadcasts originating in Honolulu, relay transmitters serve the neighbor islands, while private companies provide cable TV programming by subscription only.

Public Holidays

Hawaii observes all the US national holidays, plus three state holidays – Prince Kuhio Day, Kamehameha Day and Admission Day.

On national holidays, all government offices, banks, post offices and most businesses, except shops, close. On state holidays, local government offices and banks close, but federal offices and post offices remain open.

- **New Year's Day** January 1
- **Martin Luther King Day** third Monday in January
- **Presidents' Day** third Monday in February
- **Prince Kuhio Day** March 26
- **Good Friday** Friday preceding Easter Sunday
- **Memorial Day** last Monday in May
- **Kamehameha Day** June 11
- **Independence Day** July 4
- **Admission Day** third Friday in August
- **Labor Day** first Monday in September
- **Columbus Day** October 12
- **Veterans Day** November 11
- **Thanksgiving Day** fourth Thursday in November
- **Christmas Day** December 25

The majority of moderate-to-good hotels offer cable viewing to guests, showing a vast array of channels and, in a separate facility, first-run movies.

Money

Hawaii uses standard US currency and coins in all denominations. $1 = 100 cents. All major credit cards are accepted, including American Express, Visa, MasterCard, Discover, JCB and, to a lesser degree, Diners Club. Most car rental companies require a credit card. Cash machines (ATMs) are everywhere, especially at banks and shopping centers; ATMs accept bank cards from the mainland and are accessible 24 hours a day.

Currency Exchange

Currency conversion is readily available at Honolulu International Airport, in the customs area and at most major banks in Hawaii. Currency exchange is also available at most hotels, although the rate tends to be a little less favorable than at a bank.

Normal banking hours are Monday to Thursday 8am–4pm, and Friday 8am–6pm. Many banks are open on Saturday until noon. Note that there are no street money changers in Hawaii.

Postal Services

Normal American postal rates apply. From Honolulu, it costs the same price to mail a letter to Maui as it does to New York City. **Honolulu District Office** (at the airport), 3600 Aolele Street, tel: 800-275 8777; Window service: Mon–Fri 7.30am–8.30pm. **Waikiki**, 330 Saratoga Road, tel: 800-275 8777. There are also sub-stations at several locations in Waikiki. Customer information: Tel: 800-275 8777.

Religious Services

Bethany Assembly of God (Assembly of God), 98-1125 Moanalua Road, 'Aiea. Tel: 488-3231. **Cathedral of Our Lady of Peace** (Roman Catholic), Fort Street Mall at Beretania Street, downtown Honolulu. Tel: 536-7036. **Central Union Church** (United Church of Christ), 1660 S. Beretania at Punahou Street, Honolulu. Tel: 941-0957.

Time Zones

Hawaii is GMT -10 hours.
Pacific Standard Time -2
Central Standard Time -4
Eastern Standard Time -5
As Hawaii does not adjust to
daylight savings time, add 1 hour
to the time difference from April
through October, when in effect.

Chabad of Hawaii (Jewish),
419 Atkinson Drive, Honolulu.
Tel: 988-1004.
**Church of Jesus Christ of the
Latter Day Saints** (Mormon),
1500 Beretania Street, Honolulu.
Tel: 942-0050.
Daijingu Temple of Hawaii (Shinto),
61 Pu'iwa Road, Honolulu.
Tel: 595-3102.
**First Church of Christ Scientist
Honolulu** (Christian Scientist),
1508 Punahou Street, Honolulu.
Tel: 949-8403.
**First Presbyterian Church of
Honolulu**, 1822 Ke'eaumoku
at Nehoa Street, Honolulu.
Tel: 532-1111.
**Greek Orthodox Church of
Sts Constantine and Helen**,
930 Lunalilo Street, Honolulu.
Tel: 521-7220.
Hare Krishna Temple,
51 Coelho Way, Nu'uanu.
Tel: 595-4913.
Honpa Hongwanji Mission
(Buddhist), 1727 Pali Highway,
Nu'uanu. Tel: 522-9200.
Services in both English and
Japanese.
Jehovah's Witness Central Kingdom,
1228 Pensacola Street, Honolulu.
Tel: 521-7372.
Kawaiaha'o Church (Congregational),
957 Punchbowl at King Street,
downtown. Tel: 522-1333.
Services in Hawaiian and English.
**Korean Buddhist Dae Won
Sa Temple of Hawaii**,
2420 Halela'au Place, Honolulu.
Tel: 735-7858.
Nichiren Shoshu Honseiji (Buddhist),
44-668 Kane'ohe Bay Drive,
Kane'ohe.
Tel: 235-8486.
Prince of Peace Church (Lutheran),
Princess Kaiulani Hotel, Waikiki.
Tel: 922-6011.
Religious Society of Friends
(Quakers), 2426 Oahu Avenue,
Manoa Valley. Tel: 988-2714.
St Andrew's Cathedral
(Episcopalian), Corner of Queen
Emma and Beretania Streets,
Downtown. Tel: 524-2822.
St Augustine's Church (Catholic),
130 'Ohua Avenue, Waikiki.
Tel: 923-7024.

Seventh Day Adventist Church,
2313 Nu'uanu Avenue, Honolulu.
Tel: 524-1352.
Temple Emanuel (Jewish),
2550 Pali Highway, Nu'uanu.
Tel: 595-7521.
Todaiji Hawaii Bekkaku Honzan
(Buddhist), 426 Luakini Street,
Nu'uanu. Tel: 595-2083.
United Methodist Church,
20 S. Vineyard, Honolulu.
Tel: 536-1864.
Waikiki Baptist Church,
424 Kuamo'o Street, Waikiki.
Tel: 955-3525.

T elecommunications

From the middle of the Pacific, you
can dial directly to almost anywhere
in the world. Because of underwater
fiber-optic cables, the quality of
phone calls to both Asia and North
America is excellent.

Both inter-island and mainland/
international calls are usually
discounted in the evening and at
night. Check about weekends. Many
hotels charge $0.75–$1 for local
calls. Public telephones cost $0.35
for local calls.

Telephone Area Code

The telephone area code for all the
Hawaiian islands is **808**.

Dialing Codes

Same-island calls:
dial number.
Inter-island (direct):
1 + 808 + number.
Inter-island (operator assisted):
0 + 808 + number.
Mainland (direct dial):
1 + area code + number.
Mainland (operator assisted):
0 + area code + number.
International (direct dial):
011 + country + city + number.
International (operator assist):
01 + country + city + number.
Home-country direct: Operators in
some countries can be called
directly from Hawaii by special toll-
free 800 numbers. Call 643-1000
for a list of numbers and foreign
countries where this particular
service is available.

Directory Assistance

Operator assistance: dial 0.
Same-island: 1 + 411.
Inter-island: 1 + 808 + 555-1212.
Mainland: 1 + area code + 555-1212.
Verizon consumer line: 643-3456.

Access Codes

AT&T: 1-800 CALL ATT
Sprint: 1-800 877 8000
MCI: 1-888 757 6655

Tipping

Tipping for service is expected in
Hawaii, as tips are considered part
of a service worker's overall salary.
In general, airport porters' baggage-
handling fees run at roughly $1 per
bag, and taxi drivers are usually
tipped 15 percent in addition to
about 25¢ per bag. A 15–20 percent
tip at a fine restaurant is the norm,
and at other eating establishments
you should tip whatever you feel is
fair, typically 15 percent.

Tourist Information

In Hawaii

There are no longer visitor-focused
tourist offices for Hawaiian tourism –
rather, they concentrate on develop-
ing corporate tourism. But you can
contact the office below, who will
field questions. For brochures, call
0800 60 HAWAII toll-free.
● **Hawaii Visitors and Conventions
Bureau**, 1801 Kalakaua Avenue,
Honolulu 96815.
Tel: 973-2255; fax: 973-2253.
Hilo, tel: 961-5797.
Kona, tel: 886-1655.
Kauai, tel: 245-3971.
Maui, tel: 244-3530.
www.go.hawaii.com

Other Tourist Information

**Hawaii Visitors and Convention
Bureau**, tel: 923-1811.
Brochures, etc,
tel: 800-GO-HAWAII (464-2944).
Hawaii Tourism Authority,
tel: 973-2255.
Airport visitor information,
tel: 836-6413.

Tour Operators

Many US-based tour operators offer
tours in Hawaii that are available to
customers from anywhere in the
world; the most useful include
Backroads (tel: 527-1555,
www.backroads.com), **Globus and
Cosmos** (tel: 800-221 0090,
www.globusandcosmos.com), **Pleasant
Hawaiian Holidays** (tel: 800-742
9244, www.pleasantholidays.com), the
Sierra Club (tel: 415-977 5522,
www.sierraclub.org), and **Tauck Tours**
(tel: 203-226-6911, www.tauck.com).

U seful Numbers
Cultural

Neal S. Blaisdell Center
(ticket office), tel: 591-2211
Honolulu Symphony
(ticket office), tel: 538-8863
Aloha Stadium
(ticket office), tel: 486-9300

Waikiki Shell
(ticket office), tel: 591-2211

Reference
University of Hawaii
Tel: 956-8111
UH Information Center
Tel: 956-7235
UH Bookstore
Tel: 956-6884
Library recorded information
Tel: 956-7204
Hamilton Library reference desk
Tel: 956-7214
Hawaii State Library
Tel: 586-3500

Miscellaneous
Time of Day
Tel: 983-3211
Governor's Office
Tel: 586-0034
Honolulu Mayor's Office
Tel: 523-4141
Office of Consumer Protection
Tel: 586-2630
Police (Honolulu) lost and found
Tel: 529-3283

W ebsites

General
www.planet-hawaii.com
www.gohawaii.com
www.bestofhawaii.com
www.hawaiiguide.com
www.search-hawaii.com
www.discoveringhawaii.com
www.gohawaiianvacations.com
www.travel-kauai.com
www.bestplaceshawaii.com

Hotels and Restaurants
www.hi-inns.com
www.hotel-in-hawaii.com
www.hawaiihotelsontheweb.com
www.hawaiihotels.com

Links and Indexes
www.hawaii.com or www.hawaii.net

Bishop Museum
www.bishop.hawaii.org

What to Bring

Although Hawaii is a sub-tropical destination, characterized at sea level by consistently comfortable temperatures, you're likely to encounter rain at some point during your stay, so you'll be glad of light waterproof clothing. If you plan to venture at all higher, to areas like Maui's Upcountry, Waimea on the Big Island, or Koke'e on Kauai, you'll need something warmer too. And if you head towards the summits of the volcanoes, most notably for the dawn at Haleakala on Maui, you should be

prepared for literally freezing temperatures. All the islands hold rough volcanic terrain, so good walking shoes or hiking boots are very useful, and in many places the ocean floor can be rocky and abrasive, so reef shoes are a good idea too. Some sort of sun protection is essential as well. That said, you'll be able to buy any sports and water-related equipment you may need, and for that matter Hawaii is very much part of the modern US, so if you forget to bring something, you'll be able to buy it there. Camera equipment and accessories are widely available in tourist areas, but there are surprisingly few bookstores or map outlets in the resorts.

What to Wear

Dress is cool and casual in Honolulu and even more so beyond the city proper. Light, loose garments are suitable for the summer months. Hawaiian-print *mu'umu'u* and aloha shirts are practical all-round garments. Thongs, flip-flops, slippers, *zoris* – all different names for the same thing – are ideal for pacing the pavement or at the beach.

A few exclusive restaurants and nightclubs require a coat, maybe a tie, and definitely shoes, but they are

Weights and Measures

Hawaii uses the Imperial system of weights and measures. Metric weights and measures are rarely used.

the exceptions. Leather sandals and shoes are appropriate for night life. In most island homes, shoes are removed at the entrance.

For the cooler, wetter months, pack a sweater and an umbrella. A parka and heavy jacket are advised to keep you warm when hiking in mountainous areas on Maui, Kauai and, particularly, on the Big Island.

Aloha Friday

Friday is usually greeted in the islands with aloha wear, where even businessmen don aloha shirts of bright and cheerful Hawaiian prints instead of formal suits and ties. Ladies often tuck a fragrant plumeria behind their ear, or drape a *kukui* nut or flower *lei* on their shoulders. These are appropriate accessories for their *mu'umu'u*. This is a Friday custom that has become *de rigueur* here, even in state, federal and business offices and at public schools. And in most businesses, it is no longer limited to Friday only.

BELOW: making flower adornments for Aloha Friday.

L ANGUAGE

UNDERSTANDING THE LANGUAGE

Words and Phrases

In its development, the Hawaiian language has acquired several interesting grammatical complications, as well as a pronunciation system known for its complex vowel combinations and small number of consonants. The Hawaiian alphabet has eight consonants, each roughly similar in pronunciation to their equivalent letter symbols in English, with the exception of w and the glottal stop: '.

h	hula	(Hawaiian dance)
k	kai	(sea)
l	lani	(heaven)
m	manu	(bird)
n	niho	(tooth)
p	pua	(flower)
w	wa'a	(canoe)
'	'ala	(fragrance)

In Hawaiian, the letter w varies in pronunciation between a w and v sound. To English speakers, w often sounds like a v after a stressed vowel, as in the place name Hale'iwa. At the beginning of a word or after an unstressed vowel, w sounds like an English w as in the place names Waikiki and Wahiawa.

Meanwhile, the consonant symbol ' – called the 'okina in Hawaiian – represents a glottal stop, which indicates a stop-start pronunciation. Common to Hawaii, it is also found in several dialects of English such as in the Cockney pronunciation of "a little bottle of beer" (which comes out as "a li'l bo 'l a beer").

The five Hawaiian vowels come in both short and long duration forms. Long duration vowels are marked by a bar (called a macron in English) and sometimes differ from short vowels in quality as well as duration.

Pronunciation of vowels is similar to Spanish or Japanese: no sloppy or lazy sounds as found in English.

a as in father	nana	(look)
e as in hay	nene	(goose)
i as in beet	wiwi	(skinny)
o as in boat	lolo	(feeble mind)
u as in boot	pupu	(snack)

If you would like more kokua (help) with Hawaiian language, refer to three excellent books on the subject: *Spoken Hawaiian*, by Samuel Elbert; *Let's Speak Hawaiian*, by Dorothy Kahananui and A. Anthony; and *The Hawaiian Dictionary*, by Samuel Elbert and Mary Kawena Pukui.

Word List

ali'i **ancient Hawaiian royalty, nobility**
aloha **love, greeting, farewell**
'Ewa **toward 'Ewa**
hana hou **one more time, encore**
haole **technically all foreigners, now refers mainly to people of Caucasian ancestry**
hapa **half, part**
hapa-haole **part-Caucasian**
heiau **traditional Hawaiian place of worship, a temple**
ho'olaule'a **celebration, party**
imu **underground cooking oven**
kama'aina **island-born or longtime resident of Hawaii**
kanaka **man, person, especially a native Hawaiian**
kane **man**
keiki **child, children**
kokua **help, assistance**
lanai **porch, balcony, veranda**
lauhala **pandanus leaf, for weaving**
lu'au **traditional feast**

mahalo **thank you**
makai **toward the ocean**
malihini **newcomer or visitor to the islands**
mana **spiritual power**
mauka **toward the mountains**
mauna **mountain**
Mele Kalikimaka **Merry Christmas**
'ohana **family**
'okole **rear end, buttocks**
'ono **delicious, tasty**
pakalolo **marijuana**
pali **cliff, precipice**
paniolo **cowboy**
pau **finished, completed**
pau hana **end of work**
poi **food paste made from taro roots**
puka **hole, opening**
pupu **hors d'oeuvre**
shaka **slang for an island hand greeting**
wahine **woman**

Feedback

We do our best to ensure the information in our books is as accurate as possible. The books are updated on a regular basis, however, some mistakes and omissions are inevitable and we are ultimately reliant on our readers to put us in the picture. We would welcome your feedback on any details related to your experiences using the book "on the road". We will acknowledge all contributions, and we'll offer an Insight Guide to the best letters received. Please write to us at:
Insight Guides
PO Box 7910
London SE1 1WE
United Kingdom
Or send e-mail to:
insight@apaguide.co.uk

FURTHER READING

History and General

The Art of the Hula by Allan Seiden. Honolulu: Island Heritage, 1999. Richly illustrated history of Hawaii's nature dance.

Atlas of Hawaii University of Hawaii Press, 1983. 2nd edition. The definitive reference for diverse information about the islands.

The Betrayal of Lili'uokalani by Helena G. Allen. Glendale: Clark, 1982. All-important biography of Hawaii's last queen.

The Death of William Gooch by Greg Dening. University of Hawaii Press, 1995. Focusing on the murder of three British seamen on Oahu in 1792.

Diamond Head, Hawaii's Icon by Allan Seiden. A comprehensive look at Hawaii's renowned landmark.

Discovery by Bishop Museum Press. Honolulu: 1993. A superb collection of essays and photographs addressing ancient, contemporary and future Hawaii.

Exalted Sits The Chief by Ross Cordy. Mutual Publishing, 2000. An archeologist's view of Hawaiian history.

From Fishponds to Warships – An Illustrated History of Pearl Harbor by Allan Seiden. Mutual Publishing, 2002. The full story, from geology and natural history to the war and the present day.

Hawaii 1959–89 by Gavan Daws. Publishers Group Hawaii, 1989. A thorough history of Hawaii's first 30 years of statehood.

Hawaii: The Royal Legacy by Allan Seiden. Honolulu: Mutual Publishing, 1993. The illustrated story of Hawaii's chiefs and Kings.

Hawaii's Birds by Hawaii Audubon Society. Honolulu, 1981. A local birdwatcher's bible.

Hawaii's Story by Hawaii's Queen by Queen Lili'uokalani. Boston: Lothrop, Lee & Shepard Co., 1898; and Ruthland, Vermont & Tokyo: Charles E. Tuttle, 1990. Queen Lili'uokalani's memoirs.

Hawaiian Dictionary by Mary Kawena Pukui and Samuel H. Elbert. University of Hawaii Press, 1965. The definitive reference on Hawaiian vocabulary.

Hawaiian Hiking Trails by Craig Chisholm. The Touchstone Press, 1977. A must for backpackers and nature-seekers.

The Hawaiian Kingdom by Ralph Simpson Kuykendall. 3 vol. University Press of Hawaii, 1938–67. A key work on Hawaii in the 19th century.

Hawaiian Legends by William Hyde Rice. Bishop Museum Press, 1977. Attractive reprint of a 1923 classic, with new photos by Boone Morrison.

Hawaiian Music and Musicians by George S. Kanahele. University Press of Hawaii, 1979. Hawaii's musical heritage.

Hawaiian Mythology by Martha Warren Beckwith. New Haven: Yale University Press, 1940; and University Press of Hawaii, 1970. Definitive and comprehensive.

Hawaiian Son: The Life and Music of Eddie Kamae by James Houston with Eddie Kamae. 'Ai Pohaku Press, 2006. The illuminating biography of the ukulele-playing co-founder of the Sons of Hawaii makes a great introduction to Hawaiian music.

Hawaiian Yesterdays by Ray Jerome Baker. Honolulu: Mutual Publishing, 1982. Edited by Robert E. Van Dyke with text by Ronn Ronck. A wonderful collection of historic photos by Hawaii's pioneer cameraman.

Honor Killing by David Stannard. Penguin 2006. The gripping real-life story of a crime that exposed Hawaii's underlying racial tensions in the 1930s.

History Makers of Hawaii by A. Grove Day. Mutual Publishing, 1984. A biographical dictionary of the people who shaped Hawaii from ancient times to the present.

I Can Never Forget by Thelma Chang. Sigi Productions, 1991. A poignant documenting the heroic World War II exploits of the 100th/442nd Regimental Combat Team, which was composed mainly of Japanese-Americans from Hawaii.

Kaho'olawe: Na Leo O Kanaloa, 'Ai Pohaku Press, 1995. Images of the Forbidden Island of Kaho'olawe.

Ka Poe'e Kahiko, the People of Old by Samuel Manaiakalani Kamakau. Bishop Museum, 1964; and **Ruling Chiefs of Hawaii**. Honolulu: Kamehameha Schools, 1961.

Important memoirs by a 19th-century Hawaiian historian.

Mark Twain's Letters from Hawaii by Mark Twain. New York: Appleton-Century, 1966. Twain's look at Hawaii in the 1860s.

Na Leo I Ka Makani: Voices on the Wind by Palani Vaughan. Mutual Publishing, 1987. A pictorial look at early Hawaii.

Na Mele o Hawaii Nei by Samuel Elbert. University of Hawaii Press, 1970. Hawaiian folk songs reviewed.

Oceanwatcher, An Above-Water Guide to Hawaii's Marine Animals by Susan Scott. Honolulu: Green Turtle Press, 1988.

Pau Hana by Ronald Takaki. Honolulu: University of Hawaii Press, 1983. A history of plantation life.

The Price of Paradise, Volumes 1 and 2, edited by Randall W. Roth. Mutual Publishing, (Vol. 1) 1992 and (Vol. 2) 1993. A collection of essays highlighting important issues in contemporary Hawaii.

Shark Dialogues by Kiana Davenport. Maxwell MacMillan, 1994. An historic novel of 20th-century Hawaii.

Volcanoes in the Sea by Gordon A. MacDonald. University of Hawaii Press, Second Ed., 1983. A historical and scientific look at Hawaii's spectacular volcanoes.

A Voyage to the Pacific Ocean, 1776–1780 by Captain James Cook and James King. London: 1784, 3 vols. Official account of Cook's discovery of Hawaii.

Voyagers by Herb Kawainui Kane. WhaleSong Incorporated, 1991. A collection of words and paintings by the famed local artist.

Waikiki Beachboy by Grady Timmons. Editions Limited, 1989. A colorful history of Waikiki's famed beachboy era.

Insight Guides

Pocket Guide: Hawaii
Carefully planned itineraries and recommendations for those with little time to spare.

Compact Guides: Hawaii, Oahu, Maui
Handy, pocket-sized quick reference guides, intended for independent-minded travelers. Comprehensive, portable, readable and reliable.

ART & PHOTO CREDITS

4 Corners 21R
Alamy 6BR/BL, 7, 8, 75R, 147R, 145, 164, 168, 179, 181, 183, 197, 120L, 216, 224/225, 241L, 250/251, 318, 326, 327, 329, 330, 331, 333
Arago, Jacques 99
Baker, Ray Jerome 19, 87
Bernice Pauahi Bishop Museum 28, 43
Choris, Louis 37, 38
Corbis 3, 6, 48, 96/97, 165, 173T, 215, 221, 234/235, 242, 274R, 343
Dahlquist, Ron 60, 61, 67, 75L, 96, 122, 178, 200, 202/203, 204, 211, 219R, 220L, 222, 223, 229, 232, 236, 240, 248, 266, 272L/R, 274L, 277, 279L/R, 300R, 304, 306, 310, 312
Emmert, Paul 101
Fullard-Leo, Betty 113, 136, 308
Rowell, Galen 58/59, 261, 269, 270
Getty 9TL, 64, 89, 111, 154
Haas, Jim 14, 140L, 299L
Höfer, Hans 163, 281, 309, 311
Herter, Eric 54, 55, 56, 57, 90, 171
Istockphoto 6
Karnow, Catherine 112, 135T, 139, 150T, 176/177, 182, 189, 271
Krist, Bob 104, 254, 301
Laif 9TR
Lueras, Leonard 88, 103, 169, 307
Morrison, Boone 69R, 70/71
Newbert, Chris 212
Panini Productions Collection 102
Mark Read 7BR, 8BR, 9B
Roll, Warren 201
Riou, E 25, 27
Robert Van Dyke Collection 33, 36, 40, 41L/R, 42, 44, 49, 50, 52, 84, 100
Rutherford, Scott 72, 73, 78, 105,

109, 110 L/R, 124, 174T, 186T, 187, 192, 194/195, 198, 208, 209, 214, 217, 218, 226, 228, 230, 231, 233, 258, 262L, 263, 264, 267, 268, 275, 278, 282, 284, 285, 286, 287, 290/291, 292, 296, 298, 300L, 302, 303L/R, 305L
Don Severson Collection 34/35, 45, 69L, 77, 93, 95
Perrottet, Tony 53, 114/115
Sakamoto, Ken 144, 280
Salmoiraghi, Franco 66, 86, 91, 112, 196, 237, 244, 245, 247, 249, 276
State of Hawaii Archives 38
Stone, Sarah 32
Sloan, James 272R
Terence Barrow Collection 30
Tim Thomson 7BL, 8TL, 8BR 16, 46/47, 79, 82, 83, 85, 116/117, 118/119, 130, 131, 132T, 132, 133134R/L, 136T, 137, 138, 141, 142, 143, 146/147, 148, 149, 150B, 152L/R, 153, 155, 156R/L, 157T, 157, 158, 159, 162, 166, 167R/L, 170T, 170, 172T, 172, 173, 175, 180, 184, 185, 186, 188, 190, 191T, 191, 192T, 193, 317, 320, 322, 328, 335, 337, 339, 341, 345
Topfoto 10/11, 51
Webber, John 20/21, 22, 26, 29, 31
Wilkings, Steve 174, 199
Yanagi, Eric 137T, 219L

PICTURE SPREADS

Pages 68/69: *Top row from left to right:* Monte Costa/Photo Resource Hawaii, Jack Jeffrey/Photo Resource Hawaii, Jack Jeffrey/Photo Resource Hawaii, G. Brad Lewis/Photo Resource Hawaii. *Center row:* Marc

Schechter/Photo Resource Hawaii. *Bottom row from left to right:* Jack Jeffrey/Photo Resource Hawaii, Jack Jeffrey/Photo Resource Hawaii, G. Brad Lewis/Photo Resource Hawaii, Monte Costa/ Photo Resource Hawaii.

Pages 80/81: *Top row from left to right:* Mark Read, James Davis Travel Photography, Chris Coe/ Axiom, Scott Rutherford. *Center row:* Jim Cazel/Photo Resource Hawaii, Franco Salmoiraghi/Photo Resource Hawaii. *Bottom row from left to right:* Stephen Trimble, Franco Salmoiraghi/ Photo Resource Hawaii.

Pages 106/107: *Top row from left to right:* James Davis Travel Photography, Stephen Trimble, Stephen Trimble. *Center row:* Chris Sattlberger/Panos Pictured. *Bottom row from left to right:* Tami Dawson/ Photo Resource Hawaii, Marc Schechter/Photo Resource Hawaii, Chris Coe/Axiom, Stephen Trimble.

Pages 288/289: *Top row from left to right:* Franco Salmoiraghi/Photo Resource Hawaii, G. Brad Lewis/ Photo Resource Hawaii, Stephen Trimble. *Bottom row from left to right:* Ka Maile/Photo Resource Hawaii, G. Brad Lewis/Photo Resource Hawaii, G. Brad Lewis/ Photo Resource Hawaii, James Davis Travel Photography, G. Brad Lewis/Photo Resource Hawaii.

Map Production: Apa Publications

© 2008 Apa Publications GmbH & Co. Verlag KG (Singapore branch)

✕ INSIGHT GUIDE

HAWAII

Cartographic Editor **Zoë Goodwin**
Production **Linton Donaldson**
Design Consultants **Klaus Geisler, Graham Mitchener**
Picture Research **Hilary Genin**

INDEX

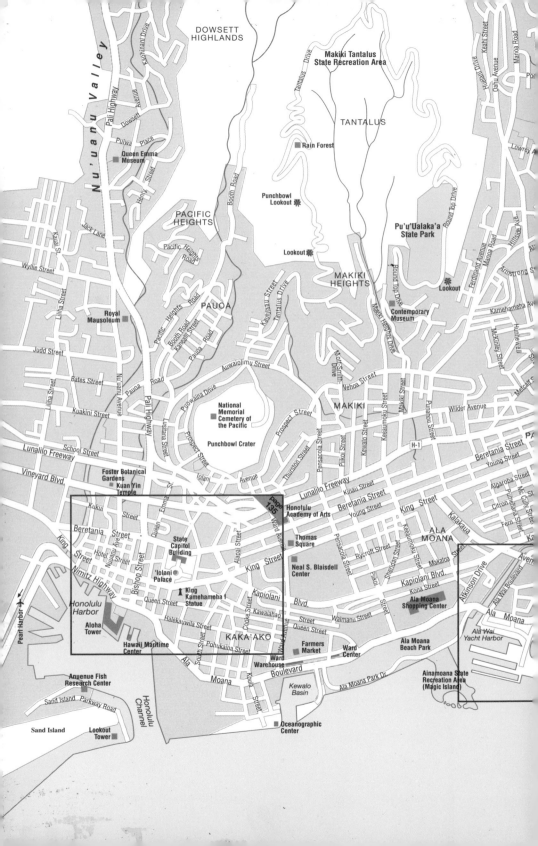